RELIGION
AND
THE MAKING OF
NIGERIA

RELIGIOUS CULTURES OF AFRICAN AND AFRICAN DIASPORA PEOPLE

SERIES EDITORS. Jacob K. Olupona, Harvard University
Dianne M. Stewart, Emory University and Terrence L. Johnson, Haverford College

The book series examines the religious, cultural, and political expressions of African, African American, and African Caribbean traditions. Through transnational, cross-cultural, and multidisciplinary approaches to the study of religion, the series investigates the epistemic boundaries of continental and diasporic religious practices and thought and explores the diverse and distinct ways African-derived religions inform culture and politics. The series aims to establish a forum for imagining the centrality of black religions in the formation of the "New World."

RELIGION AND THE MAKING OF NIGERIA

OLUFEMI VAUGHAN

Duke University Press   Durham and London   2016

© 2016 Duke University Press
All rights reserved

Designed by Courtney Leigh Baker
Typeset in Garamond Premier Pro by Westchester Publishing Services

Library of Congress Cataloging-in-Publication Data
Names: Vaughan, Olufemi, [date] author.
Title: Religion and the making of Nigeria / Olufemi Vaughan.
Other titles: Religious cultures of African and African diaspora people.
Description: Durham : Duke University Press, 2016. | Series: Religious cultures of African and African diaspora people | Includes bibliographical references and index.
Identifiers: LCCN 2016021449 (print)
LCCN 2016023797 (ebook)
ISBN 9780822362067 (hardcover)
ISBN 9780822362272 (pbk.)
ISBN 9780822373872 (ebook)
Subjects: LCSH: Religion and state—Nigeria. | Church and state—Nigeria—History. | Islam and state—Nigeria—History. | Political culture—Nigeria—Religious aspects.
Classification: LCC BL65.S8 V38 2016 (print) | LCC BL65.S8 (ebook) | DDC 322/.109669—dc23
LC record available at https://lccn.loc.gov/2016021449

COVER ART: Stephen Folaranmi, *Tolerance*, 2016. This work depicts a cross, a crescent and star, and an Opon Ifa (Yoruba Ifa divination plate).

Duke University Press gratefully acknowledges the support of Bowdoin College, Office of the Dean, which provided funds toward the publication of this book.

IN MEMORIAM: Gladys Aduke Vaughan
(Otun-Iyalode, Ibadan), 1920–2014

CONTENTS

Acknowledgments
ix

Introduction
1

ONE. Islam and Christianity in the Making of Modern Nigeria
13

TWO. Islam and Colonial Rule in Northern Nigeria
39

THREE. Christianity and the Transformation of Colonial Southern and Northern Nigeria
69

FOUR. The Politics of Religion in Northern Nigeria during Decolonization
89

FIVE. Religion and the Postcolonial State
112

SIX. Religious Revival and the State: The Rise of Pentecostalism
139

SEVEN. Expanded Sharia: The Northern Ummah and the Fourth Republic
158

EIGHT. Expanded Sharia:
Resistance, Violence, and Reconciliation
181

NINE. Sharia Politics, Obasanjo's PDP
Federal Government, and the 1999 Constitution
199

Conclusion
223

Notes
233

Bibliography
273

Index
295

ACKNOWLEDGMENTS

I have accumulated considerable debt to many friends and colleagues during the years this book was in the making. I am grateful to these wonderful people for their support and kindness. Zach Warner and I had many interactions on conceptual and contextual questions that undergird the entangled histories of Christianity, Islam, indigenous religious beliefs, and the Nigerian state. A generous and excellent scholar, Zach provided insightful critiques and ideas that enhanced the overall quality of the book. I am grateful to Zach for his unflinching commitment to the objectives of this book. During the initial stages of the book's research, I benefited from the support of several young friends who worked as my research assistants. Rory Brinkman, Suraiya Zubair Banu, Tony Perry, Tyler Silver, Renee Velkoff, and Sarah Watts worked with me to analyze extensive archival materials, many documents of religious institutions, and piles of newspaper reports. I am grateful to Rory, Tony, Tyler, Renee, Suraiya, and Sarah for their assistance and support. Discussions with many friends in several humanistic social science disciplines informed an essential cross-disciplinary perspective that, I believe, gave this book greater scope and depth. Some of these friends read the finished work and offered insightful critiques: my special thanks to Wale Adebanwi, Niyi Afolabi, Okon Akiba, A. B. Assensoh, Peniel Joseph, Insa Nolte, Ebenezer Obadare, Deji Ogunnike, Funke Okome, Joel Rosenthal, Samuel Zalanga, and Nimi Wariboko. I am grateful to Patty McCarthy for providing excellent editorial assistance. Patty is a patient and thoughtful editor who reminded me that a book of this nature must not only speak to scholars in the field, but must also be accessible to students, policy makers, and intelligent lay learners who are willing to wade through the muddled waters of religion and state making in Nigeria. And to Eileen Johnson, I express my gratitude for the excellent maps contained in this book.

The scholarship on religion and society in Nigeria is authoritative in African studies. As a student of Nigerian history and politics, I benefited enormously from the stellar works of many scholars in this important field. While my citation will show the extent of my intellectual debts, I would like to acknowledge the important contribution of the following scholars whose works shaped my thoughts on a wide range of complex issues analyzed in this book: Rowland Abiodun, Afe Adogame, Laolu Akande, Pade Badru, Toyin Falola, T. G. O. Gbadamosi, Rosalind Hackett, Johannes Harnischfeger, Robin Horton, John Hunwick, Julius Ihonvbere, Simeon Ilesanmi, Kelechi Kalu, Ogbu Kalu, Matthew Kukah, Ricardo Rene Larémont, Murray Last, Paul Lubeck, Ruth Marshall, Moses Ochuno, Mathews Ojo, Jacob Olupona, John Paden, John Peel, Frank Salamone, and Nimi Wariboko.

The intellectual perspective for this book was refined while I was a fellow at the Woodrow Wilson International Center for Scholars in 2006–2007. In spring 2013, I returned to the Wilson Center as a public policy scholar to complete the book manuscript. In both of my residencies at the Wilson Center, I had the good fortune of developing lasting friendships with some remarkable people in the center's Fellowship Program and Africa Program: Arlyn Charles, Lindsey Collins, Kim Conner, Lucy Jilka, Bob Litwak, Steve McDonald, Monde Muyangwa, Andrew Selee, and Mike Van Dusen. I am grateful to these special friends for their kindness and generosity over the years. Seun Ajayi is a blessing and a joy—thank you, Seun, for your kind hospitality during my second residency at the Wilson Center. The research for this book project required extensive archival work, and I would like to thank the archivists and librarians who provided assistance during the early stages of my research. I am particularly grateful to the archivists and librarians of the Wilson Center Library; the Library of Congress; Rhodes House Library, Oxford; Center for Mission Studies, Oxford; and the University of Ibadan Library. I would also like to thank my colleagues at Bowdoin College's Africana Studies Program and History Department for their collegiality and friendship. Bowdoin College's Committee for Faculty Development provided supplementary funding to support a critical sabbatical leave in 2012–2013. I am grateful to the college for this generous support.

Jacob Olupona, the editor of the series in which this book is published, along with his colleagues, Dianne Stewart and Terrence Johnson, believed that this work can make an important contribution to Africanist scholarship and at the same time encourage a serious dialogue on religious reconciliation in a post-9/11 world. I am indebted to them for their steadfast support for this work. The remarkable professional expertise of Miriam Angress, associate editor at Duke University Press, is second to none. Miriam diligently marshaled the manuscript through various stages in the publication process with exceptional professionalism. I am grateful to Miriam for her kindness and support. I should also thank two anonymous reviewers for their insightful comments and critiques of the manuscript.

Many relatives and friends in Nigeria, the United States, and the United Kingdom opened the doors of their homes to me while I was conducting field and archival research for this book. My expression of thanks does not adequately capture the extent of my gratitude to these special people. I am particularly grateful to Segun and Desi Abegunrin, Kolade and Yinka Adebayo-Oke, Gbenro and Funso Adegbola, Soji and Fran Adelaja, Jide and Ama Eniola, Bassey and Consola Ewa-Henshaw, Dawari and Data Longjohn, Fidelis and Priscilla Oditah, Bode and Emelda Oladeji, Tony and Diana Oyekan, and Charles Small for their love and support over the years.

Finally, my loving gratitude to my wife, Rosemary, our children, Moni, Ayo, and Olu—and to our extended family in Ibadan (particularly Ronke Adefope, Biola and Funso Osideinde, Biodun Pomary, Shubu Vaughan, Wole Vaughan, and Iyabo Yerima). In addition to her steadfast devotion to our children, Rosemary's love and support for my work is boundless. If I have attained any professional success, it is in large measure because of Rosemary's resolute support and encouragement. Thank you, Makamba, for engaging my endless discussions on African studies and African diaspora studies—and for all your love over these wonderful years.

In April 2014, right around the time I finished the final draft of this manuscript, my mother, a granddaughter of early CMS (Church Missionary Society) converts in Ibadan in the second half of the nineteenth century, passed on (the role of the CMS in Ibadan is covered in chapter 3 of this book). She was already in her late eighties when I began working on the book, and I discussed various aspects of it with her during our many telephone conversations and my brief summer visits to Ibadan. In retrospect, I can now see how her life and work—along with other forebears—might have inspired my commitment to the excavation of the crucial role of religion in Nigerian history and politics. It is something of a cliché to underscore the bond between mothers and sons, but in this one case, I hope this tie will live on in the legacy she left behind. I am grateful for her remarkable life and cherish her amazing work in Ibadan. As a token of my gratitude for her life and work, I dedicate this book to her memory. It is certainly not my place to recite her *oríkì* (lineage praise verses), but I know she will allow me to evoke this first line for this special purpose: Àdùké Òpó Omo Eegunjénmí—È báà tà'kìtì k'ée f'orí so'lè baba ni baba njé!

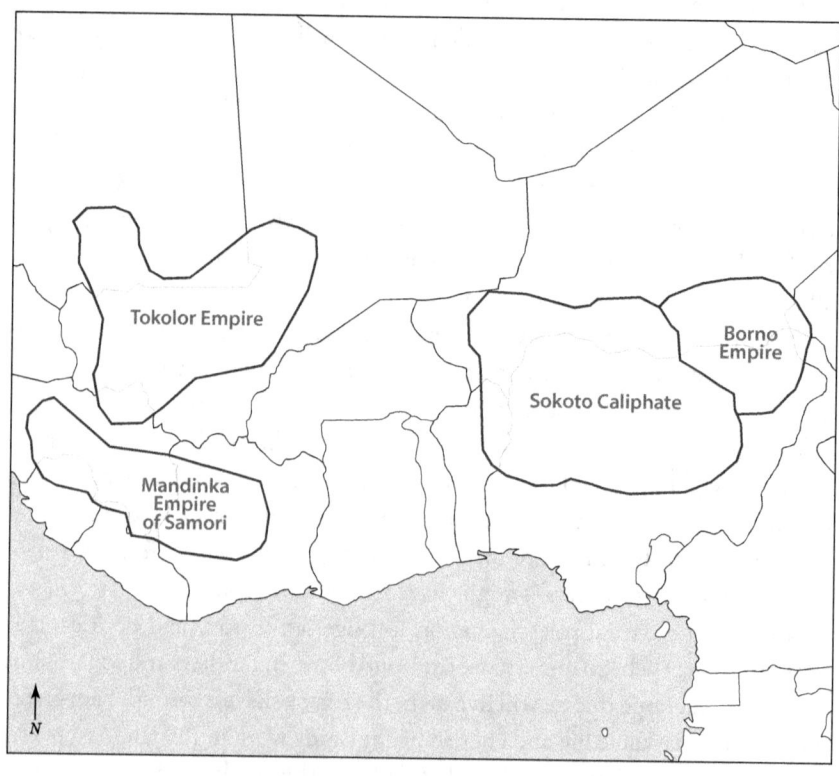

MAP 1. Political Units: Muslim Empires in Eighteenth- and Nineteenth-century West Africa

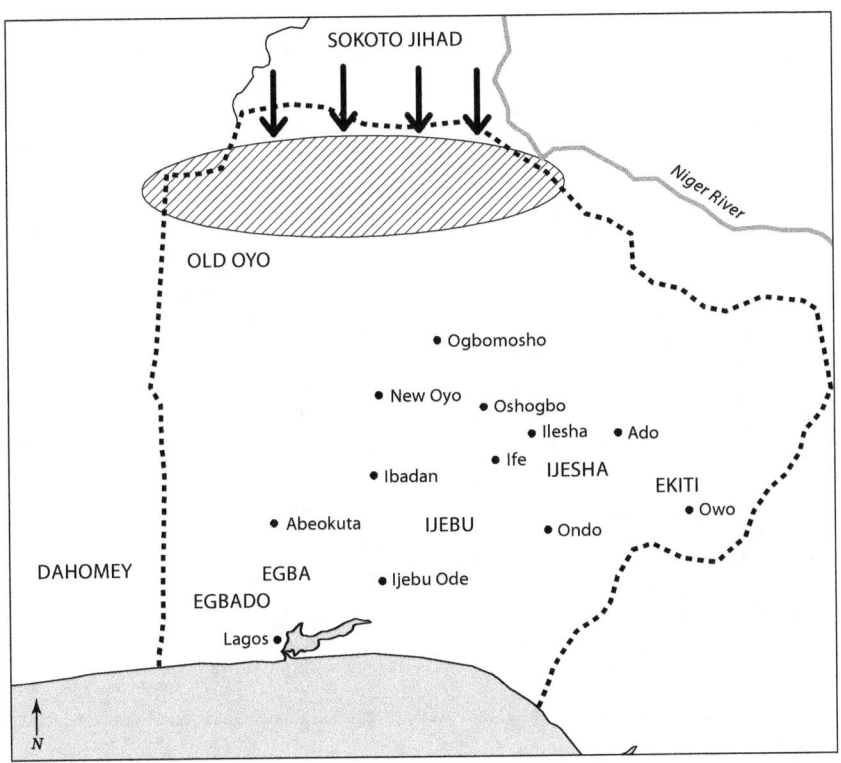

MAP 2. Yoruba Towns (Sokoto Jihad)

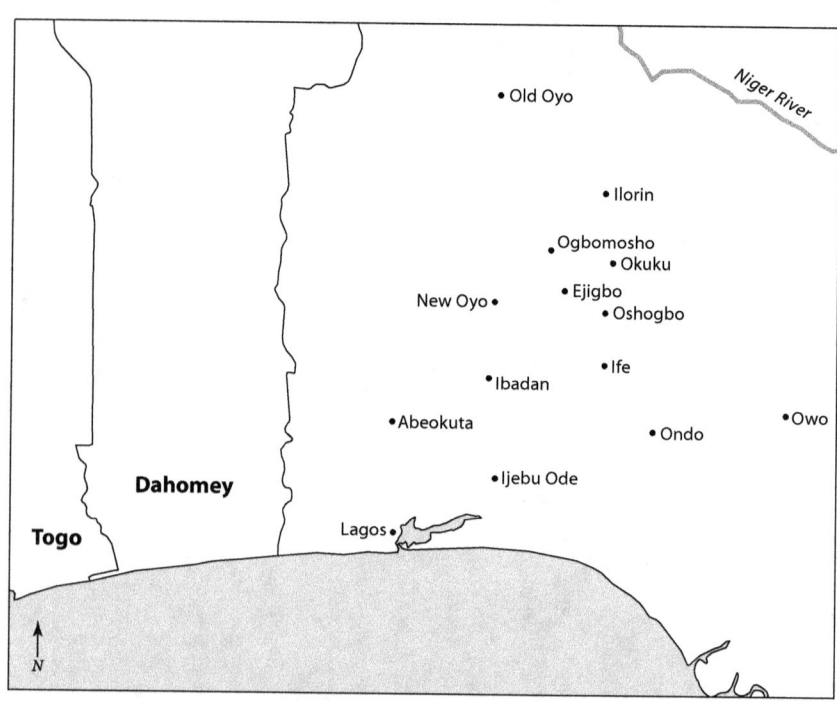

MAP 3. Yorubaland and Neighbors

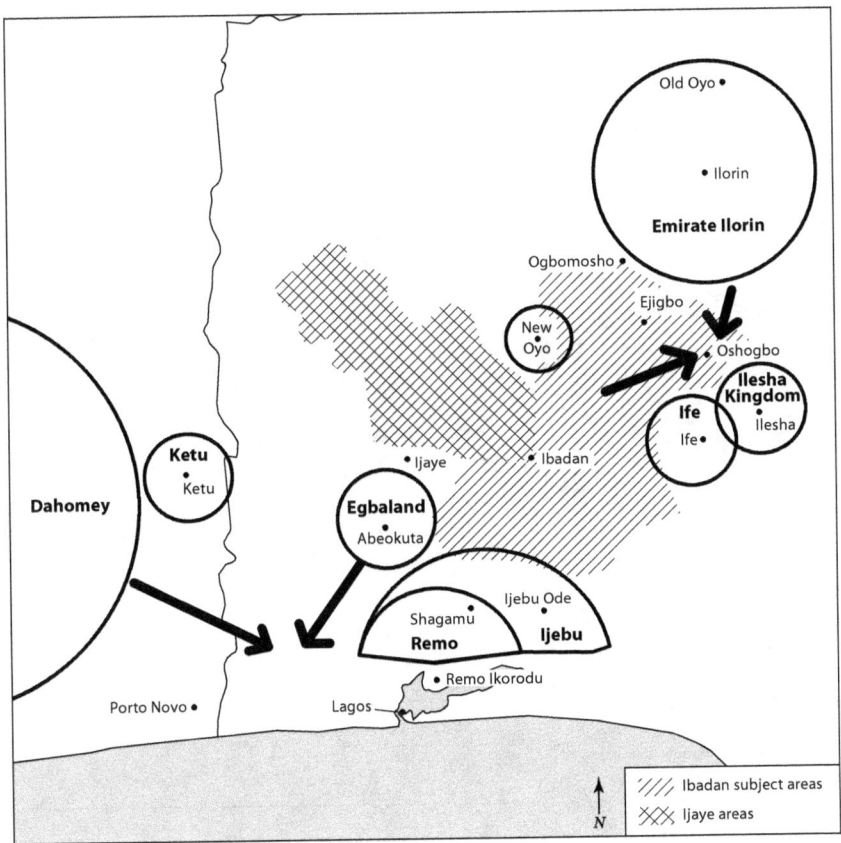

MAP 4. Yorubaland, 1840–1870

MAP 5. Islam and Indigenous Religions in the Northern Nigerian Protectorate, 1900–1940

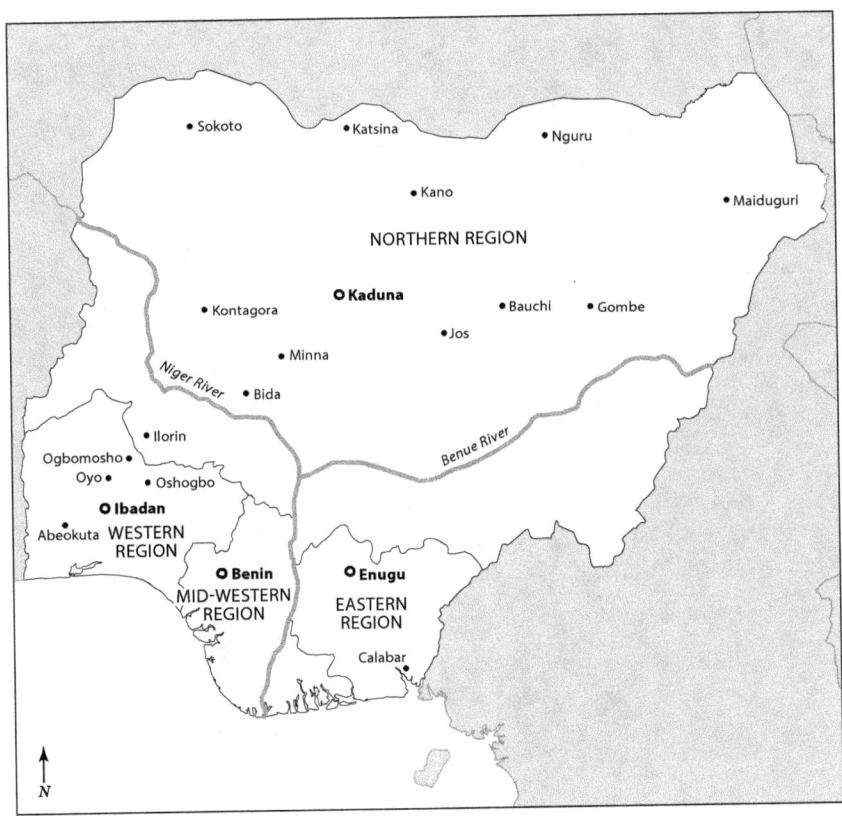

MAP 6. Nigerian Regional Governments, 1960–1966

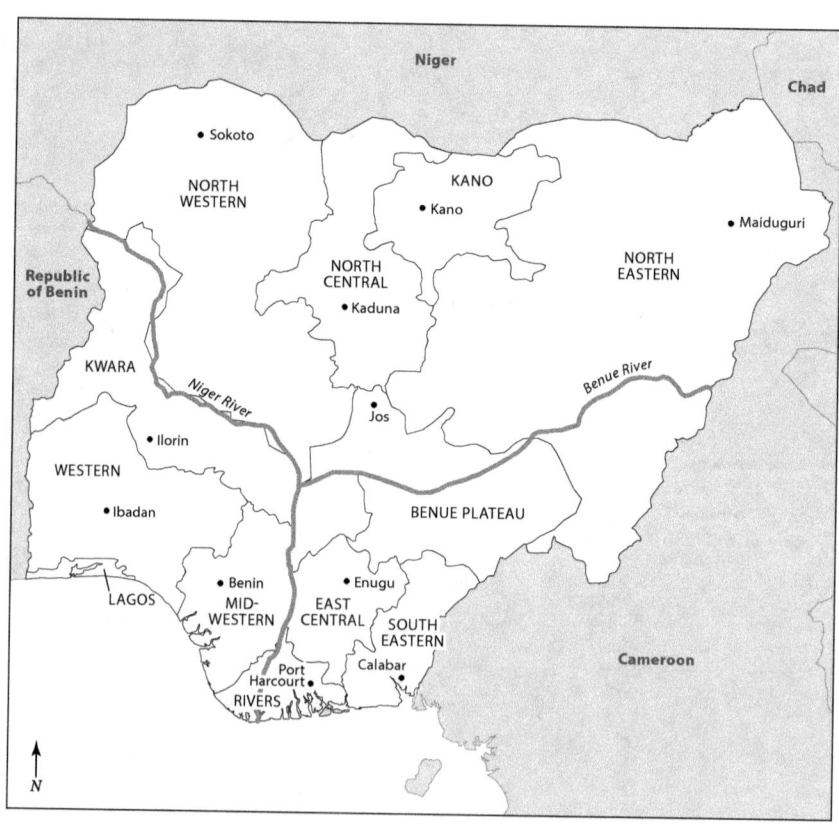

MAP 7. The Twelve States of the Federal Republic of Nigeria, 1967–1975

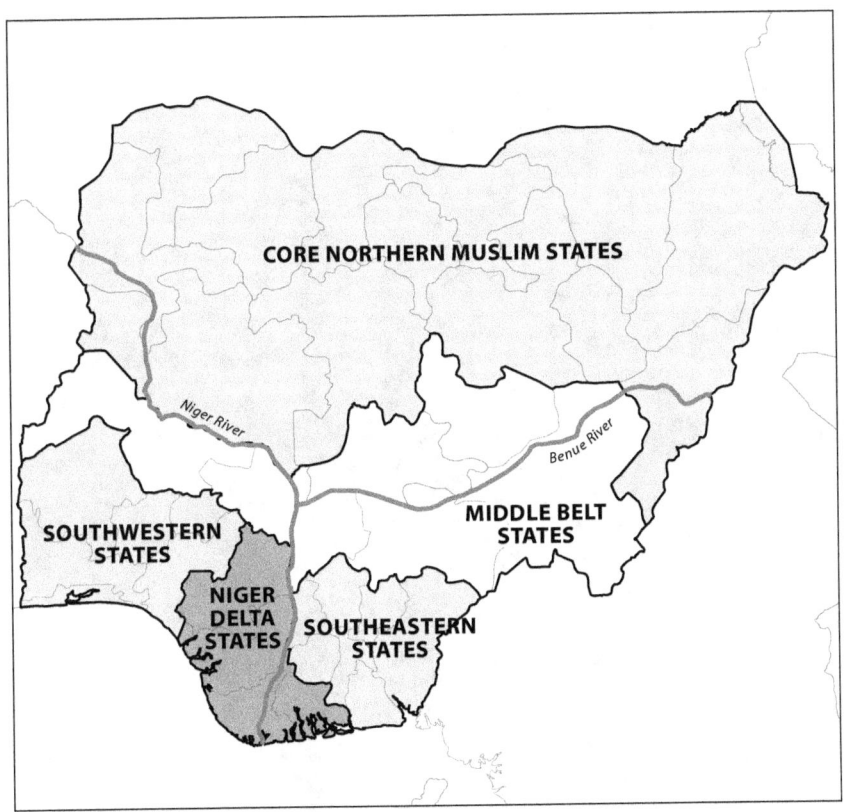

MAP 8. Nigeria's Geopolitical Zones and the Thirty-Six States, 2000s

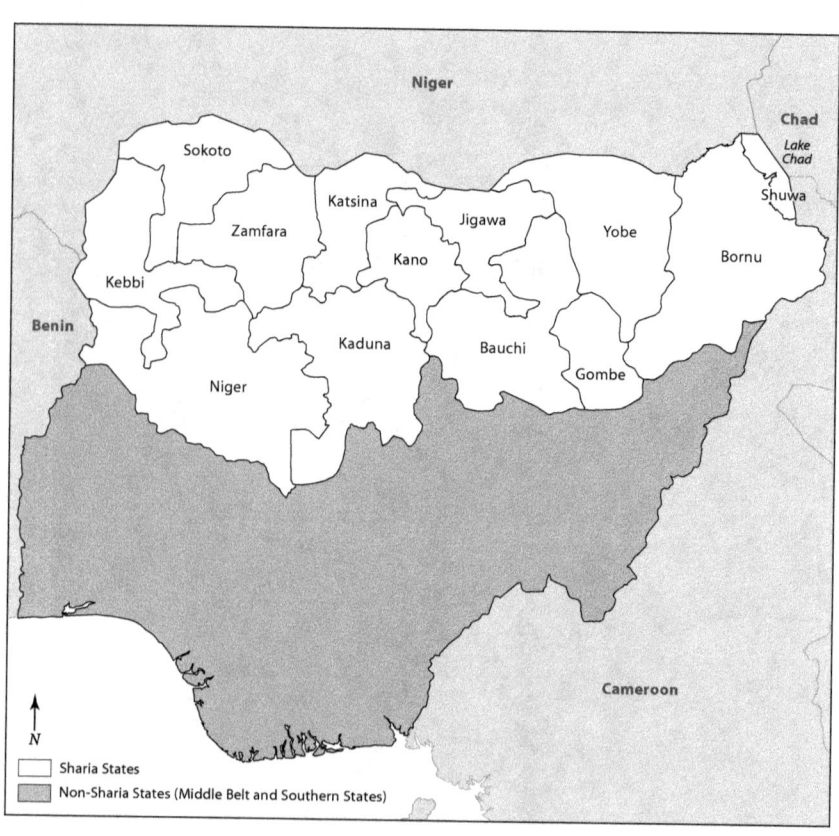

MAP 9. Northern Nigeria's Sharia States, 2000s

INTRODUCTION

Nigeria holds political and economic prominence in Africa. A major oil producer with a population of 180 million (in 2015) and more than 250 ethnic groups, Nigeria is home to millions of Christians, Muslims, and adherents of indigenous religions. With complicated relations between Christians and Muslims in the Northern and central regions of the country, Nigeria is one of the world's major laboratories for the study of religious-based conflict and reconciliation. While many scholars have focused on recurring Christian-Muslim confrontations as an aspect of endemic sectarian conflict in Nigeria—showing how an obdurate political class exploits ethno-religious divisions to mobilize collective political action[1]—I contend that Christian, Muslim, and indigenous religious structures are integral to the formation of the modern Nigerian state and society. Specifically, I will analyze how the underpinnings of religious doctrines, the nature of social structures, and the proclivities of the political class have shaped the evolution of modern Nigeria since the turbulent nineteenth century. I am persuaded that the intersections of these competing religious traditions—Islam, Christianity, and indigenous religions—are decisive in the making of modern Nigeria.

Starting with a major Muslim reformist movement—the Sokoto Jihad—in contemporary Nigeria's vast Northern Region, and a Christian evangelical movement, propelled by the influential English missionary organization called the Church Missionary Society (CMS), in Atlantic Yoruba communities in southwestern Nigeria during the nineteenth century, I argue that Muslim and Christian structures made up the foundation on which the Nigerian colonial state was grafted in the early twentieth century. In what later became the Northern Nigerian Protectorate, the Sokoto Jihad of 1804–1808 transformed not only the Hausa city-states, but also shaped the geopolitics of their neighbors to the south, especially the diverse communities in contemporary central and northeastern Nigeria (modern Nigeria's Middle Belt region) as well as the Yoruba region in the southwest. As the Sokoto Jihad consolidated a theocratic confederacy (the Sokoto Caliphate) under the control of Fulani Muslim reformers in the northern Hausa region by the mid-nineteenth century, Christian evangelical movements, fueled by the activities of Yoruba CMS returnees from Sierra Leone, penetrated Nigeria's Southwest, steadily transforming the social structure of Southern and central Nigerian communities by the late nineteenth century. These two world religious currents, along with their entangled social and political histories, set the stage on which Muslim and Christian structures would shape the processes of state-society formation in colonial Nigeria since the imposition of British rule at the turn of the twentieth century. Consequently, Islam and Christianity fundamentally shaped—and have been shaped by—local religious, social, and political structures since the transformative nineteenth century.

Drawing from an interdisciplinary Africanist scholarship, I contend that the impact of these Muslim and Christian movements on Nigerian communities did not simply serve as a precursor to British colonial rule, but provided essential structural and ideological frameworks for the rationalization of colonial society throughout the first half of the twentieth century. My analyses emphasize how these two major religions shaped collective political and social action and complicated Nigeria's tapestry of identities, especially ethnic and regional forms of identifications. Given the transformative impact of these world religious movements on structures of society, I will analyze their manifestations in their broad historical, political, and sociological contexts,[2] emphasizing the dialectical tensions between local and global forces. This perspective underscores how the persistence of Muslim and Christian structures has consistently produced contending—and competing—doctrines, practices, and ideologies to transform Nigeria's complicated social and political landscape.

The history of the communities in this West African region is characterized by interwoven religious, social, and political strands that reflect entrenched hierarchies of power integrated into communal, kinship, gender, and class identities[3] and conditioned by spatial and demographic factors. In this dynamic process, Nigeria's formidable Muslim and Christian structures are at the center of the country's history, expanding Nigeria's chronology to fully incorporate the critical religious, social, and political developments of the turbulent nineteenth century into the processes of Nigerian state formation. Simply put, Muslim and Christian movements have flourished in modern Nigeria because their institutions and doctrines are consistently embedded in the structures of society, shaping social relations and the configuration of power.

Given the decisive impact of these two world religious currents on the diverse communities in the Nigerian region, it is useful to draw on landmark theoretical analyses that explain the conversion of local communities in the region from indigenous religions to Christianity and Islam.[4] For more than four decades, anthropologists Robin Horton and John Peel's intellectualist paradigm has shaped the theoretical debate on this conversion process.[5] Focusing on the cosmological rationale for traditional West African religions to "explain, predict and control" the challenges that confront local people, Horton argues that the processes of conversion from indigenous religions to Christianity must be articulated in a specific nineteenth-century context of rapid social and political change.[6] Preoccupied with parochial conditions in isolated communities before the complex transformation of the nineteenth century, Horton contends that local deities that underscore *microcosmic* cosmologies essentially dominated the everyday world of local people in small-scale locales. As West African communities took on the more complicated social, political, and economic conditions at the intersection of local, regional, and global forces in a tumultuous nineteenth century, prevailing local cosmologies shifted from their small-scale (microcosmic) preoccupation to large-scale, *macrocosmic* framework that could explain the rapidly changing conditions of the time. In short, Horton stresses that age-old West African cosmologies expanded their scope to accommodate the more complicated regional and global forces unfolding in the region in the nineteenth century. Accordingly, this shift in focus encouraged the macrocosmic worship of the "cult of the Supreme Being,"[7] opening the door to the monotheistic Christian faith evangelical missionaries introduced along with other far-reaching Western social, economic, and political transformations starting in the early 1800s. While these shifts in religious practice were often characterized as conversion from indigenous religions to Christianity by the turn of the twentieth century, Horton contends that this phenomenon reflected trends that were already in motion in much of the nineteenth century.[8]

In the case of the Yoruba people of southwestern Nigeria, Peel argues that the new emphasis on the "cult of the Supreme Being" was crucial in the conversion experience of Yoruba communities from their indigenous religion to Christianity starting in the second half of the nineteenth century. This complicated process of conversion provided a new narrative that shaped the way the Yoruba embraced the promise of a better future following the cataclysmic upheavals from prolonged regional warfare in much of the nineteenth century. This dialogue that integrated indigenous cosmology to Christianity ultimately explains the remarkable success of the Yoruba Christian church movement, Aladura, during the period of colonial rule in the first half of the twentieth century.[9]

Drawing from Southern African case studies to complicate Horton and Peel's intellectualist theory, historian Terence Ranger argued that the macrocosmic framework already was prevalent in indigenous cosmologies by the time they came into contact with mission Christianity in the mid-1800s, and that the concept of a Supreme Being subsequently reified in world religions was, in many instances, reflected in microcosmic conditions.[10] For Ranger, indigenous religious systems had long possessed adaptive cosmological qualities to explain larger-scale regional transformations. Consequently, the Christian missionary impact that accompanied Western-induced social, political, and economic conditions should not be seen as the only radical development that expanded the scope of indigenous African cosmologies. While Ranger agrees that the nineteenth century was a critical turning point in African history, he asserts that the radical shifts from a microcosmic to macrocosmic framework starting in the nineteenth century cannot fully explain the conversion of Africans from indigenous religions to Christianity. Ranger concludes that "much of the continuing history of religion in Southern Africa, whether of Christianity or of African religion, lies in the working out of this dialectic between the local and the central."[11] Thus the new Christian doctrines that were embedded in indigenous cosmologies to articulate the rapidly changing social conditions in the early years of colonial rule were following trends that had been established in earlier moments of major transformations in the region. Despite this revision of a paradigm that underscores the integration of mission Christianity to African cosmologies in the context of the rapid social transformation at the turn of the twentieth century, Ranger's analysis still falls within the framework of Horton and Peel's intellectualist imperative in the conversion of Africans from indigenous religions to world religions.

In this context, with the imposition of colonial rule in Southern Nigeria, mission Christianity and its trappings of modern education provided appealing religious explanations in an increasingly novel world. The appeal of Christianity, from this perspective, was not simply in its emphasis on the transcendent "macrocosm," but rather in its relation to and ability to "explain, control, and predict" the dynamic conditions of the time. Indigenous religions, as Jack Goody reminds us, have serious limitations in the modern world because of their inability to generate requisite modern institutions, professional skills and technical expertise essential to navigate the major social, economic, and political developments of the twentieth century—attributes that world religions, especially mission Christianity, possess in abundance because of their long history of transregional networks, scientific engagement, professionalization, and extensive traditions in literacy.[12] Incorporated into indigenous cosmologies, Christianity and Islam provided frameworks for large-scale modes of identity as well as instruments for an "intellectualist paradigm" that reflects the rapidly changing conditions that were becoming prevalent starting in the second half of the nineteenth century.[13] "The changing social environment in which conversion so often unfolds is not simply a product of material forces," Robert Hefner perceptively notes; it also reflects a "sense of self-worth and community.... [The] problem of dignity and self-identity in a pluralized and politically imbalanced world lies at the heart of many conversion histories."[14] This was the dynamic social, political, and economic context in which the world religions—especially Christianity—flourished in various Nigerian communities immediately after the imposition of colonial rule.

Given this dynamic process in the transformation of Nigerian communities since the nineteenth century, my methodological emphasis is at the intersection of historical, political, and sociological analyses. Focusing on the enduring structures of precolonial Nigerian communities, I will emphasize the *longue durée* of Muslim and Christian movements[15] in the making of Nigeria, analyzing how the historical evolution of three major Nigerian geocultural regions—notably the Hausa-Fulani Muslim North, the non-Muslim Middle Belt, and the Yoruba Muslim-Christian crossroads of the southwest—have consistently intersected since the nineteenth century to complicate the formation of the Nigerian state and society.

Following Peel's contention that precolonial West African political and social relations are shaped by hierarchies of communities,[16] I contend that the Islamic reformism of the Sokoto Jihad established a precolonial state-society system that presided over the allocation of resources such as tributes, taxes, and slaves, and controlled trade routes and markets in a vast and heterogeneous region that included Hausa-Fulani Muslims and adherents of indigenous religions (the so-called pagan tribes of Northern Nigeria). Starting in the second half of the nineteenth century, the dominant power of Hausa-Fulani Muslim rulers was complicated by the advent of mission Christianity in the southern fringe of the Sokoto Caliphate along the confluence of the Rivers Niger and Benue. With the growing influence of mission Christianity by the turn of the twentieth century, non-Muslim communities some of whom had been brought under the suzerainty of the Sokoto Caliphate—especially new converts to Christianity—made use of Christianity's universal doctrines to challenge the dominance of Hausa-Fulani Muslim rulers and assert their autonomy under colonial rule. In this intense political environment, conversion from indigenous religions to Christianity by missionary societies was far from a simple religious act; Christian conversion became a crucial medium of collective action against Hausa-Fulani Muslim rulers. Nevertheless, since the Sokoto Caliphate provided the framework on which the British colonial system of indirect rule was constructed, Hausa-Fulani Muslim rulers consolidated their power base under British rule during the first half of the twentieth century.

This process in which Muslim and Christian structures were integral to state-society formation encouraged the development of ethno-national identities in Nigeria's emergent geocultural regions. In the Hausa region that served as the epicenter for Britain's Northern Nigerian Protectorate, Fulani Muslim reformism of the Sokoto Caliphate effectively appropriated the dominant Hausa culture and language as the essential structural framework for Hausa-Fulani ethno-religious identity. This large-scale ethno-national identity was instrumental in the mobilization of Hausa-Fulani Muslim consciousness in colonial Nigeria after the conquest of the Sokoto Caliphate by the British in 1903. As this process of modern Nigerian state-making unfolded under British colonial rule, Hausa-Fulani Muslim rulers consolidated their control over their non-Muslim neighbors as the "pagan"—and consequently the Christian—other throughout the region. While British colonial authorities traced Hausa-Fulani Muslim hegemony to its precolonial status as natural ruler of "backward pagan" vassals, especially those in the southern boundaries of the Sokoto Caliphate, British colonial policy inadvertently encouraged the formation of a new regional sociopolitical identity—Middle Belt regional identity—by the late colonial period.[17] Drawing on highly subjective local and regional narratives and mythologies[18] that sought to legitimate this emergent Middle Belt regional identity in contradistinction to Hausa-Fulani Muslim identity, mission Christianity's modern institutions and doctrines emerged as a formidable medium of "infrapolitics" for non-Muslim communities to resist Hausa-Fulani Muslim hegemony throughout the region.[19] However, since the British colonial system of indirect rule was grafted on the prevailing Hausa-Fulani emirate system, British rule inevitably intensified the structural imbalance between Hausa-Fulani emirates and the non-Muslim communities of the region. This dynamic system that continues to shape Nigeria's geopolitics even to this day is deeply rooted in the enduring structures of Northern Nigeria's fragmented society going back to precolonial times. This political arrangement was predicated on a problematic tributary system that depended on slave raiding and other forms of primitive extraction in the precolonial caliphate era. As Moses Ochonu deftly analyzed, this colonial arrangement was, in part, sustained by highly subjective British ethnographic studies that affirmed the claims of Hausa-Fulani Muslims as natural rulers of their "pagan" neighbors. These British imperial studies were replete with imagined social, habitual, and physical attributes that rationalized the natural order of things under a superior Hausa-Fulani Muslim "race."[20]

In the Yoruba region, Peel has written convincingly about the transformative role of Yoruba CMS missionaries and early converts—to articulate a pan-Yoruba ethno-national consciousness following the protracted social upheaval from the Yoruba wars of the nineteenth century.[21] This emergent ethno-national identity, shaped profoundly by mission Christianity by the end of the nineteenth century, was a critical precursor for Yoruba sociocultural and political renewal under colonial rule in southwestern Nigeria. As this pan-Yoruba consciousness emerged, the first generation of Yoruba-educated Christians embarked on a discourse of modern Christian civilization as a counternarrative to the prolonged turbulence that consumed much of the Yoruba region in the nineteenth century.[22] Derived from contested histories and mythologies,[23] this complicated precolonial and colonial process profoundly shaped the meaning of power and identity for Yoruba communities within the wider context of modern Nigerian state-society formation.

Following decolonization after World War II and the attainment of Nigerian independence in 1960, these religious structures were essential to the mobilization of collective action by ethno-regional political elites in a rapidly shifting context. With a weak nation-state derived from the imposition of colonial rule, neopatrimonial regimes embraced patronage-clientage networks structured on communal relations as the framework for the distribution of scarce resources.[24] Again, this encouraged the recasting of ethno-religious identity—along with other critical modes of communal identity. Amid political uncertainty, insecurity, and instability, Muslim and Christian structures consistently retained prominence from decolonization in the 1950s to the country's civil-democratic government at the turn of the twenty-first century.

Focusing on more than two centuries of detailed historical analysis, I will show how religious forces—especially the dominant force of Islam and Christianity—profoundly shaped the formation of the modern Nigerian state and society since the turbulent nineteenth century. The extensive social science scholarship on Nigeria surprisingly has ignored a methodological approach that focuses on the entangled histories of Islam and Christianity as a pathway for analyzing the making of Nigeria. In this book, I seek to deeply analyze the significant impact of the history of Islam and Christianity on the formation of the modern Nigerian state and society.

The book is divided into two sections. The first section analyzes the impact of Islam and Christianity on three major Nigerian regions where the two world religions consistently intersect to shape the evolution of modern Nigeria from the nineteenth century to the twenty-first century; these three intersecting regions are the Hausa-Fulani and Kanuri Muslim North (the region dominated by the Sokoto Caliphate), the traditionally non-Muslim Middle Belt region (a religious and culturally distinct section of Britain's Northern Nigerian Protectorate in contemporary central and northeastern Nigeria), and the Yoruba Muslim-Christian crossroads in the southwest region of Britain's Southern Provinces. The second section provides detailed analyses of how the recurring crisis of sharia (Islamic law) in postcolonial Nigeria essentially reflects the structural imbalance between emirate Northern Nigeria on the one hand, and Nigeria's Middle Belt and Southern Regions on the other, going back to the amalgamation of Britain's Northern and Southern colonial provinces in 1914. The fierce contestation between Northern Muslim rulers and Christian elites from other parts of the country over the imposition of expanded sharia in predominantly Northern Muslim states were far from straightforward disagreements between Muslims and Christians on matters of religious beliefs; rather, they were emblematic of deep structural imbalance that evolved with the formation of the modern Nigerian state under colonial rule. The persistent call for expanded sharia by the Northern Muslim political class has consistently intensified this structural imbalance along ethno-religious and ethno-regional lines between the Muslim north and the rest of the country during the postcolonial period.

Specifically, the book explores four major issues of importance to the critical roles of Muslim and Christian movements in the formation of the modern Nigerian state and society: the role of Islamic reformism and mission Christianity in the transformation of precolonial Nigerian communities in a turbulent nineteenth century; Islam, Christianity, and colonial rule in Nigeria's Northern and Southern Provinces; Islam, Christianity, and the political transformation of the Northern and Middle Belt regions during Nigeria's decolonization process; and Islam, Christianity, and the crisis of the postcolonial Nigerian nation-state.

Chapter 1 proceeds on the understanding that the Sokoto Jihad in the Hausa region and the emergence of mission Christianity from Atlantic Yoruba communities in the nineteenth century were pivotal in the transformation of the Nigerian region before the imposition of colonial rule at the turn of the twentieth century. Specifically, the chapter analyzes the institutional and theological basis on which the Sokoto Caliphate was constructed in the nineteenth century. In a similar vein, starting in Nigeria's coastal southwest region, this chapter discusses how mission Christianity set the stage for the social and political transformation of Southern and non-Muslim Northern Nigeria, providing a framework for social change in these regions during the colonial period. This chapter is not a prelude to modern Nigerian history. It deeply examines how

Islam and Christianity were essential in framing social and political relations among Nigeria's diverse communities in the critical decades before the imposition of British colonial rule.

Chapter 2 analyzes the complex interactions between Hausa-Fulani Muslim rulers and British colonial rulers from 1903, when the Sokoto Caliphate and Kanem-Bornu Empire came under British rule, to the 1950s, when British authorities started the decolonization process in Nigeria. Using the case-study analytical approach, this chapter examines Hausa-Fulani emirate structures' broad influence on colonial state formation in the Northern Nigerian Protectorate, and how the structures of this Northern Muslim confederacy were woven into the colonial system of indirect rule. The political implications of the interactions among Hausa-Fulani Muslim rulers, non-Muslim communities, and British colonial policies are analyzed against the backdrop of evolving power configurations in the Northern Nigerian Protectorate—as these were expressed by Hausa-Fulani Muslim rulers and their Muslim subjects, Hausa-Fulani Muslim potentates and their non-Muslim "subordinates," and Hausa-Fulani Muslim "metropolitan" centers and "tributary" communities.

The outcomes of the interactions between mission Christianity and colonialism in diverse communities in Southern and Northern Nigeria are dissected in chapter 3. Although Christianity, unlike Islam in the Northern emirates, did not play a formal political role in colonial administration, the objectives of Christian missionary groups nevertheless advanced British interests, while paradoxically, challenging the hegemony of Hausa-Fulani emirate rulers in non-Muslim areas of the Northern Provinces, especially in the Middle Belt region. Christian missionaries and colonial administrators worked creatively to deploy complementary doctrines of Western training and enlightenment to advance colonial imperatives. While local structures of society remained resilient—revealing the depth of indigenous cosmologies in various communities—Christian missionary impact was far-reaching. Paradoxical relationships consistently were revealed in the everyday life of local people: they were played out in the objectives of colonial authorities and Christian missionaries, reflecting contending and competing forces between the temporal and the spiritual, between colonial state power and the power of Christianity.[25]

The main focus of chapter 4 is the importance of Muslim and Christian structures in Nigeria's decolonization process. Analyzing that process in the context of rapid political change after World War II, I explore the critical role of Hausa-Fulani emirate structures in the regionalization of state power in the Northern Nigerian Protectorate. The prevailing Hausa-Fulani Muslim structures were incorporated into hierarchies of power that sustained an emergent modern political system during decolonization in the 1950s. The social transformations of Southern Nigerian Provinces—and the Middle Belt region—by Christian missions intensified the imbalance between Muslim Northern Nigeria and the rest of the country during this time. Mission Christianity was a decisive factor in the Yoruba Muslim-Christian crossroads of the Southwest, transforming Yoruba ethno-national consciousness during the late colonial period, and it provided ideological and structural frameworks for a Christian identity in non-Muslim communities in the Northern Provinces. In the Middle Belt region and among non-Muslim minorities in Northern emirate society, overarching institutions and ideologies derived from emerging mission Christianity—and subsequently independent African church movements and Pentecostal movements—provided a way for disparate ethnic groups to resist Hausa-Fulani Muslim domination in local, regional, and national politics, from decolonization on.

Chapter 5 is concerned with the nature of Nigeria's Muslim and Christian movements during the struggles by ethno-regional and ethno-religious elites for control of state power in the postcolonial period. The configurations of power at regional and national levels are analyzed in the context of the evolution of Nigeria's ethno-regional, neopatrimonial political system through the policies of various civilian and military governments—from the attainment of independence in 1960 to the outbreak of the sharia crisis that overwhelmed Nigeria during the Fourth Republic at the turn of the twenty-first century. The chapter highlights several features of the relations between Nigeria's problematic nation-state and its deeply divided society, emphasizing how dynamic Muslim and Christian movements repeatedly were reconstructed, reimagined, and redeployed to complicate the contestation for state power by ethno-regional political classes, while seeking to respond to the day-to-day concerns of local communities in an environment of endemic political crisis. The major politico-religious conflicts of the postcolonial period, notably the Nigerian Civil War (1967–1970), the 1978 sharia debate, the controversy over Nigeria's membership in the Organization of Islamic Conference, and the 'Yan tatsine riots in the 1980s, are analyzed in detail in this chapter.

A wave of new Pentecostal movements starting in the 1960s transformed the inner core of Christianity in Nigeria, and the resulting changes are analyzed comprehensively in chapter 6. The significance of this huge religious movement in Nigerian society is examined in the context of the deepening crisis of the postcolonial state, viewed through the prism of growing statism, neopatrimonialism, and neoliberalism in the age of globalization. Consequently, this Pentecostal revolution is analyzed in the context of the complex political, social, and economic transformations that have engulfed Nigerian society throughout the postcolonial period.

Chapter 7 maps out the history of sharia since the colonial period, including Hausa-Fulani Muslim advocates' imposition of expanded Islamic law in twelve predominantly Northern Muslim states at the turn of the twenty-first century. I do not pretend to present an objective analysis of the major constitutional and political issues unleashed during the highly contentious struggle over expanded sharia during Nigeria's fourth attempt at democratic government (the Fourth Republic); instead, my analysis suggests that Northern Muslim protagonists of expanded Islamic law were, in some ways, effective at starting a discourse around sharia that reflected multiple religious and regional identities, even as the crisis of the state deepened and the structural fault lines between the Muslim North and the rest of the country widened. Conversely, the limitations of expanded sharia during this period of political turbulence reveal the complicated process of the configuration of power in postcolonial Nigerian politics. Overall, this chapter underscores the paradoxical and contradictory role of expanded sharia in Nigeria's religious and ethnically diverse society.

Chapter 8 analyzes the constitutional and political arguments that were advanced and strategies deployed by religious and regional opponents of expanded sharia (Southern, Middle Belt, and Northern-minority Christians). All told, religious, regional, and ethnic structures were critical in shaping alliances to sustain the politics of sharia in the Fourth Republic; and this intense resistance to expanded sharia, especially from the intelligentsia of the predominantly Christian Southern and Middle Belt states, as well as from Northern Christian minorities, further deepened the structural imbalance between Hausa-Fulani Muslim society and other regions of Nigeria.

Chapter 9 underscores the severity of the constitutional and political crisis that consumed Nigeria during the critical years of democratic transition at the beginning of the twenty-first century, further exposing structural divisions between the Northern Muslim hierarchy and the dominant Southern, Middle Belt, and Northern minority Christian elite. Diverse problems that profoundly affected religious and regional relations are evaluated, such as factors that led to widespread support for expanded sharia in the Northern Muslim states; bitter conflicts surrounding sharia in Nigerian politics since decolonization in the 1950s; and the extent to which the political crisis precipitated by the sharia crisis is embedded in Nigeria's religious, regional, and ethnic configurations. Political, social, and economic factors that ultimately undermined the sharia policies of the twelve Northern Muslim states are also examined in this chapter.

These critical issues with important public policy implications prompt pertinent questions that are analyzed throughout this book. To what extent did the expanded sharia policies of the twelve Northern Muslim states pose serious constitutional challenges to the authority of the Nigerian federal government? What are the causes and consequences of religious alliances between Nigeria's ethno-regional political classes and their local constituencies? How might we assess the political roles of Muslim and Christian movements in Nigeria's deeply divided society? What are the implications of enduring political and social roles of these formidable religious movements for the legitimacy of the Nigerian nation-state? How have the complicated relations between Christian and Muslim groups shaped governance and development in contemporary Nigerian society? What are the strengths and weaknesses of the local and national conflict-resolution mechanisms used to address Nigeria's recurring religious crises? In addition to their scholarly objectives, I hope that the analyses in this book will provide some thoughtful reflection for those interested in the important public policy dimensions of the critical role of Christian-Muslim relations in the governance of Nigeria. Overall, this book attempts to address these critical questions through a comprehensive analysis of relations between state and society, and the political struggles between Hausa-Fulani Muslim society and other regions in the country.

The conclusion brings the issues analyzed in the book together. The persistence of religion-based conflicts in Nigeria underscores an urgent need to devise viable constitutional and political mechanisms to mitigate recurring religious violence in Nigeria's Northern and Middle Belt communities. Finally, whether through the dominance of Islam and Christianity in local communities or in the resilience of indigenous religious beliefs, it is clear that religious structures have not only been remarkably adaptive to rapidly shifting social and political conditions in Nigerian society since the turbulent nineteenth century but also, more importantly, have been central to the making of modern Nigeria.

CHAPTER ONE

ISLAM AND
CHRISTIANITY IN
THE MAKING OF
MODERN NIGERIA

The critical foundation in the making of modern Nigeria was constructed on the convergence of two monumental world religious movements that transformed the Nigerian region, starting in the nineteenth century. These were the celebrated Islamic reformist movement that established the Sokoto Caliphate in the Hausa region of Northern Nigeria and a Christian evangelical missionary movement that gave impetus to the social transformation of coastal southwest Nigeria, beginning in the second half of the nineteenth century. Although shaped by regional and global forces, these religious movements had enduring consequences for the diverse peoples of the Nigerian region because they were also products of the internal dynamics among the local communities that would later constitute the modern Nigerian state and society. While these religious developments emerged from two distinct geocultural areas in the Nigerian region during the nineteenth century, I contend that the processes of their convergence after the imposition of British colonial rule at the turn of the twentieth century was essential in the making of modern Nigeria. Starting with a comprehensive analysis of the ideologies and structures of the Sokoto Jihad, which transformed the Northern Nigerian region, and the Christian evangelical movement, which precipitated the social transformation of Southern Nigeria, I argue that the scope and depth of these historic movements provided the social and political platform on which modern Nigeria was constructed after the imposition of colonial rule at the beginning of the twentieth century. In terms of chronology, this process began with the profound impact of the Muslim reformism of the Sokoto Jihad in the Hausa city-states of contemporary Northern Nigeria, culminating in the establishment of the historic Sokoto Caliphate at the beginning of the nineteenth century.

The Rise of the Sokoto Caliphate

Many of the major city centers in today's Hausa region of Northern Nigeria were derived from the traditional Hausa city-states that had evolved as political entities as early as 1000 AD: Kano, Katsina, Zaria, Gobir, Biram, Rano, and the principal city, Daura. These major Hausa city-states were linked to outlying towns of Zamfara, Kebbi, Yauri, Gwari, Nupe, Kororofa, and Yoruba through complex social, political, and economic networks.[1] Drawing on a common language and social interactions over the centuries, "the term 'Hausa,' 'Hausawa' and 'Kasar Hausa,' that defines contemporary Hausa ethno-religious consciousness in modern Nigerian society," Moses Ochonu notes, "is a concept that gained momentum with the monumental political and social transformations unleashed since the Sokoto Jihad" of the early nineteenth century. Ochonu further asserts that prior to the Sokoto Jihad "the peoples of the [Hausa] states, and ordinary Fulani migrants who lived among them, were likely to refer to the Hausa state citizens by their state of origin: 'Katsinawa' for those from Katsina, 'Kanawa' for those from Kano, 'Gobirawa' for those from Gobir and so on."[2] This strong identification with the city-state defines the essence of a formidable politico-social system in the Hausa region before the imposition of the Sokoto Jihad in the early nineteenth century.

At the apex of the political-social system in each Hausa city-state was the office of *sarki*, the sovereign authority on which the political, judicial, and military powers of the Hausa states were invested. The sarki was expected to be a shrewd ruler adept at manipulating the strings of politics to satisfy competing interest in upper Hausa society. Under the sovereign authority of the sarki was a class of aristocratic titleholders, known as the *sarauta*, who advised the sarki on a wide range of political and social matters. Relations of state and society were sustained largely through entrenched patron-client ties: consequently, in traditional Hausa society, the privileged class retained its legitimacy through patronage-clientage networks that were based on personal control of public office and management of economic resources.³ Hausa society was thus rigidly divided between the aristocratic class, the sarauta, and the masses of commoners, known as the *talakawa*.

Starting in the fourteenth century, Islamic influence steadily encroached on Hausa city-states through complex networks of commercial and social interactions across the Sahel and the Maghreb. First came the Sudanese Muslim diasporas that migrated southwestward to the Hausa region; over time, the clerics of these Muslim populations converted local Hausa rulers to Islam through their teaching, preaching, and commercial activities.⁴ However, indigenous Hausa religious beliefs proved resilient to the transformative impact of Islam, especially among the talakawa. Nevertheless, Muslim administrative and judicial institutions steadily became prominent in many Hausa city-states. An important indicator of the prominence of Islam in Hausa society was the rise by the early eighteenth century of the *ulama* (predominantly Fulani Muslim clerics) in the courts of the Hausa sarki as advisers in local administration. As Islam gained greater prominence in Hausa society, ulamas became more influential in local communities; on the growing significance of ulamas in Hausa society, Mohammed Umar contends that these Muslim clerics generally exhibited two distinct qualities: ulamas who were active in state affairs served as judges, ministers, and scribes to Hausa rulers, reflecting the Maghilian tradition; conversely, many other ulamas, inspired by the Suwarian tradition, limited their activities to their clerical work and avoided direct involvement in state affairs.⁵ Significantly, the origins of the religious trends of the former, the Maghilian, was inspired by the singular contribution of the notable North African cleric Muhammad al-Maghili in the late fifteenth century.⁶

As the exponent of the famous Maghili School, Muhammad al-Maghili arrived in Kano, the Hausa region's most dominant city, in 1493 from the Kingdom of Tlemcen in modern-day Algeria, where he had fled the Reconquista. He preached against the syncretism that he found among Kano Muslims and campaigned for Islamic reform and the establishment of sharia. Through his works, al-Maghili established the Kano School, which dominates Islamic thought in Northern Nigeria even to this day.⁷ Al-Maghili is credited with writing the first Muslim constitution for Kano, which was officially received by Mohammed Rumfa, Kano's sarki (1463–1499), and thereafter consecrated as the famous manual on Islamic government in the Hausa region. In content and specification, al-Maghili's manual was precise in the definition of the role of Islam in local administration:⁸ in accordance with Islamic doctrine, he recommended a nine-member council of rulers; a treasury with professional accountants; a system of sharia courts run by a *qadi* and scribes; and provisions for public appeal to the sarki's court.⁹ Consequently, through al-Maghili's influence, sharia was established as state law in Kano during the reign of Rumfa in the late fifteenth century.¹⁰

With the growing influence of ulamas in state affairs, the relationship between sarkis and ulamas deteriorated by the late eighteenth century as the influence of Islamic reformism grew in the Sahel and Maghreb regions. With this growing influence of Islam, ulamas increasingly based Islamic thought on the sovereignty of Allah, contending that Hausa sarkis can only exercise legitimate political authority when they comply with strict dictates of Islamic law. In this context, Umar argues, "Islam limits political power by requiring its exercise in accordance with sharia rule of law. This limit gives the ulama, as experts of sharia law, considerable political clout to challenge the authority of a ruler by arguing that he loses his legitimacy if he fails to uphold the law of God."¹¹ With their growing politico-religious influence, derived from scriptural texts and religious injunctions, ulamas asserted their authority in Hausa society during this moment of regional Islamic reformation. Significantly, the Islamic reformist teaching of Usman dan Fodio, which led to the historic Sokoto Jihad in the early nineteenth century, proved to be the most important manifestation of this growing trend by the late 1700s.¹² In addition to the critical theological role of the ulamas to the transformation of Hausa society, the huge success of the Sokoto Jihad can also be attributed to the rapidly shifting demographic conditions that were transforming the social and religious environment in the Sahel by the eighteenth century. Indeed, just as the Sokoto Jihad was inspired by earlier Fulani-led West African jihads—notably Futa Bundu, Futa Toro, and Futa Jallon—between 1650 and 1750, it, in turn, would inspire several jihads in this vast region, including Masina, Seku Ahmadu, and Tukulor later in the nineteenth century. As the most far-reaching example of Fulani-led Muslim reformist movements, the Sokoto Jihad reflected a global trend of Islamic reformism that was pervasive in the Muslim world in the eighteenth and nineteenth centuries.¹³

USMAN DAN FODIO AND THE SOKOTO JIHAD

Much has been written about the family lineage of Usman dan Fodio, the Fulani ulama who spearheaded the Sokoto Jihad in the Hausa region from 1804 to 1808. Fodio was born in Maratta in the Hausa city-state of Gobir in 1754, and like many from his Toronkawa Fulani clan,¹⁴ Fodio's forebears had migrated to Gobir from Futa Toro in modern-day Senegal. Young Fodio learned Islamic theology, philosophy, science, and Arabic, as well as the reformist doctrines that were widespread in the Muslim world of the time from renowned

North African cleric Sheikh Jibril Ibn Umar. By age twenty, he started preaching in Gobir and neighboring communities, drawing large crowds during his travels. During his teaching, Fodio challenged the religious syncretism that was widespread in Hausa society and denounced the abuse of power in the court of the sarki of Gobir, Yunfa Nafate. When tensions between Fodio and Yunfa reached their climax, Fodio and his followers retreated to Gudu, performing the *hijra*, the ritual flight that preceded the formal declaration of a jihad, on February 12, 1804. In Gudu, with the support of his able lieutenants, his brother Abdullahi and son Mohammed Bello, Usman dan Fodio launched a successful military assault against Yunfa's army at Tabkin Kwaith. This victory announced the Sokoto Jihad, which transformed what became Northern Nigeria in the nineteenth century.[15] Michael Crowder notes that Fodio and his followers "justified their jihad against Yunfa and other Habe [Hausa] kings on the grounds that though they professed Islam, in mixing traditional practices with their observance of the true faith they were juridically pagans against whom it was legitimate to rebel."[16] Beyond authorizing jihads against Hausa rulers—and eventually the Muslim rulers of Kanem-Bornu Empire to the northeast—Usman dan Fodio sanctioned military campaigns against the non-Muslim communities that were scattered throughout the region, especially contemporary Northern Nigeria's Middle Belt region. Thus Usman dan Fodio notes: "The waging of Holy war (al-jihad) is obligatory by assent ... and to make war upon the heathen king who will not say 'There is no God but Allah' is obligatory by assent and to take the government from him is obligatory by assent."[17] Consequently, in keeping with its injunction for Muslim piety,[18] Usman dan Fodio established his Islamic reformist teaching as the foundation for the Sokoto Jihad in the early 1800s.

Usman dan Fodio was educated in the well-known Islamic system passed down to the Hausa region from Timbuktu. He wrote many books, mostly religious texts and poems, in Arabic, Hausa, and Fufulde. His extensive written works also covered themes as varied as Islamic law and statecraft. Fodio's impressive scholarly and religious works—along with those of his brother, Abdullahi, and son, Mohammed Bello—provide critical insight into the ideological and institutional framework for the Sokoto Jihad as it swept through the Hausa region in the early nineteenth century. In his *Kitab al-Farq*, written immediately after the declaration of the jihad in 1804, Fodio contrasts the conditions in the Hausa sarauta system to the righteous Muslim theocracy he envisioned. In his book *Tanbih al-ikhwan 'al ahwal al-Sudan* (*Concerning the Government of Our Country and the Neighboring Sudan*), Fodio observes: "The government of this country is the government of its king without question. If the king is a Muslim his land is Muslim; if he is an unbeliever, his land is of an unbeliever. In this circumstance, it is obligatory for anyone to leave it for another country." In his indictment of Hausa sarkis, Fodio underscores the scriptural injunctions that insist that legitimate Muslim rulers must submit to the dictates of Allah: "As for the sultans, they are undoubtedly unbelievers, even though they may profess Islam, because they practice polytheistic rituals and turn the people away from the path of God and raise the flag of world kingdom above the banner of Islam. All this is unbelief according to the consensus of opinion."[19]

Usman dan Fodio thus insisted on the imposition of Muslim theocracies in the Hausa city-states to eradicate "un-Islamic" practices common in the courts of Hausa sarkis, notably, the lack of consultation with ulamas in state affairs, the prevalence of exploitative taxes, and oppressive laws on talakawa commoners by officials of Hausa sarkis.[20] Fodio identified five major foundations of his new Muslim polity: political authority shall be given only to those who are willing to govern according to Islamic law; political rulers must govern with the consent of local communities; rulers must abandon harsh punishments; justice in accordance with Islamic law is sacrosanct; and members of the ummah are called upon to do good deeds. On the structure of the Muslim state, Fodio identified specific functions for occupants of four principal offices in the ummah: the trustworthy vizier should be steadfast and compassionate toward the people; the judge must submit to Allah; the chief of police shall obtain justice for the weak; the tax collector shall discharge his duties in accordance to sharia. In the declaration of his jihad, Fodio, imploring Allah's name, called on "every scholar and righteous man . . . in these countries to assist me in building up the characteristics of the Muslims in their governments."[21]

During the formative years of the Sokoto Caliphate, the three men who established the foundation of the new theocratic confederacy were Usman dan Fodio; his brother, Abdullahi; and his son and successor as leader of the Muslim faithful, Mohammed Bello. They articulated the moral authority of their politico-religious project in accordance with a clearly defined vision of the ummah as espoused in the Qur'an and the hadith.[22] According to Robert Hefner, in classical and modern times "movements of Islamic reform [such as the Sokoto Jihad] often involve the attempts of pious preachers to link their religious ambitions to some disadvantaged or aggrieved social class. Where such a linkage is created, movements of Islamic reform may extend their horizons beyond the aim of heightening piety toward the goal of social and political transformation."[23] In this context, Fodio's insistence on an ummah premised on justice for all resonated with Hausa talakawa commoners and disaffected

Fulani masses, who by the eighteenth century had become a major demographic group in the region.[24]

The subject of Islamic law was central to the works of Usman dan Fodio and featured prominently in the discourse of the Sokoto Jihad (*Shifa' al-Ghalil fi ma ashkala min Kalam Shakh Shuykhina*). Consequently, Fodio drew enormous inspiration from texts of the *Bayan Wujub al-Hijra ala Ibad* to filter his prescriptions for the governance of the ummah. He insisted that the just Muslim ruler must be qualified to render independent judgments and execute his decisions; must provide guidance on all state affairs; and must draw a clear demarcation of authority among public officials, especially between the *waziri* (chief judge) and local judges. Rules regarding the handling of war booty, the use of lands acquired through conquest, and the levying of taxes also were stipulated in the works of Usman dan Fodio.[25]

Abdullahi dan Fodio and Mohammed Bello also contributed immensely to the growth of Islamic thought, details of which are elaborated in the works of Islamic scholar Ibraheem Sulaiman.[26] In *Diya al-Imam*, Abdullahi stresses personal integrity and Islamic piety as pivotal qualities for political leadership: the imam (emir) must perform his functions as the ruler for the sake of Allah; treat the common people with compassion and leniency; and ensure that all state functions are clearly defined. Emphasis is placed on accountability; as such, all public officers must declare their assets, and if someone is found to have wealth above what he earns from his work, the ruler shall confiscate and restore it to the treasury.[27] Indeed, Islam not only provided a widely respected legal system, "it also provided a defense against encroachment by the Muslim Fulani. . . . Thus, public observance of the five daily prayers became common. Total abstinence from alcoholic beverages, especially from those associated with traditional religious practices were enforced. Prestige within the emirate was clearly and closely associated with Islam."[28]

The constitutional treatment of public office and division of powers received elaborate treatment in Abdullahi's *Diya al-Tawil*. There, as Sulaiman explains, the Shura was vested in three interrelated powers of the consultative assembly, the ulama, and the community. The consultative body was a formal constitutional group responsible for the efficient operation of the state. It comprised mujtahids, scholars, military generals, and community leaders.[29] Usman dan Fodio's pillar of state sovereignty was the *hisba*, the police system charged with the responsibility of "commanding the good and prohibiting the bad." In Abdullahi's *Diya ahl al-Ihtisab* and *Diya al-Iman*, the institution of hisba, like the sharia from which it derives its authority, rests on the notion that local people must be properly educated about their responsibilities in a just Muslim society. In short, the hisba deals with the regulation of the market, the promotion of justice, and the preservation of public morality.[30]

In the *Usul al-Siyasa*, Mohammed Bello, the first caliph of Sokoto, focused on issues of integrity and modesty in leadership. Thus the first principle of government excludes anyone who covets a political position; indeed, the imam (emir) must strive to select men of conscience, piety, and probity as advisers. Given the emphasis on accountability, it is logical that Bello would condemn sycophancy among political leaders; he warned specifically against gains achieved through double-dealing and trickery. Basic premises of the rule of law are set forth in *al-Gayth al-Wabl*. The application of sharia rests on three interrelated principles: all people must be treated equally before the law; the law must follow its natural course without interference from the political elite; and the imam must not alter the law to suit narrow political interest.[31] Significantly, Sulaiman's analysis of the works of the founders of the Sokoto Caliphate focuses exclusively on the pathways to good governance in a righteous Muslim state, suggesting a moral contrast between Usman dan Fodio's Sokoto Caliphate and the modern Nigerian state.

After only a few years of Fulani assault on the armies of Hausa rulers and non-Hausa communities in the region,[32] Usman dan Fodio became the leader of the most populous geopolitical territory in nineteenth-century West Africa. He was succeeded on death (1817) by his son, Mohammed Bello, as the *amir al mu 'minin* (commander of the Muslim faithful) and sultan (caliph) of the Sokoto Caliphate. The empire that succeeded the Sokoto Jihad was consolidated during Bello's reign from 1815 to 1837. Bello was charged with the control of the eastern emirates in the caliphate. His uncle Abdullahi, emir of Gwandu, took charge of the western emirates of Nupe and Ilorin. Sections of Bauchi and Adamawa also later came under the control of the Sokoto Caliphate while Sokoto Jihadists unsuccessfully attempted to incorporate the Muslim-ruled Kanem-Bornu Empire into the caliphate. Caliph Bello had to repel opposition from other potentates, including his brother Atiku, who later succeeded him as sultan, and rebellion from dissidents such as Dan Tunku of Kano, an old ally of his father. Thereafter, Bello emerged as a pragmatic empire builder. He consolidated the gains of the caliphate through a careful balance of religious doctrine and strategic political calculation, conceding authority to the emirs over the administration of their emirates and overlooking many precaliphate Hausa religious and social practices that his father had decried.

Mohammed Bello was an astute ruler who possessed a keen eye for statecraft: he presided over a theocratic confederacy that unified the previously autonomous

Hausa city-states under the politico-religious authority of the Sokoto Caliphate. This endeavor included integrating Islamic and sarauta institutions, incorporating Fulani pastoralists into agrarian life within Hausa communities, establishing mosques, and encouraging the education of talakawa commoners and women.[33] The intellectual perspectives of his leadership included original discourses (*Infakul Maisuri*) on the theological and political visions on which the caliphate was built, including detailed narratives about the history of the jihad. Ochonu tells us that Bello's *Infakul Maisuri* contains critical discussions on "epistolary efforts to place the Caliphate above Bornu in the hierarchy of Islamic piety."[34] The writing is the first treatise to articulate a Sokoto imperial hegemony over the non-Hausa Muslim areas of central and northeastern Nigeria (contemporary Nigeria's Middle Belt region). Indeed, the Sokoto Caliphate was not only defined as the custodian of Muslim values, but was delineated as the locus of regional power.[35]

The early era of caliphate rule saw the establishment of Maliki law;[36] in addition, the new rulers monopolized judicial, religious, and political leadership.[37] Alkali courts, emirs' courts, and courts of appeals established during Usman dan Fodio's time were updated and incorporated.[38] The sheer volume of Sokoto leaders' writings on sharia indicates the prominence of Islamic law throughout the caliphate;[39] and Murray Last has pointed out that "any complainant could expect to see the Emir (or his local headman) personally any day after the dawn prayer; [and] people's complaints served to feed into governmental intelligence."[40]

How effective was the new political and legal system in dispensing justice in the emirates that constituted the Sokoto Caliphate in its formative years? The dominant scholarship suggests that sharia was not firmly established in many of the communities that would constitute the Northern Nigerian Protectorate after the British conquest of the Sokoto Caliphate and Kanem Bornu Empire in the early twentieth century.[41] Indeed, arbitrary rule did much more than erode the integrity of the political system; it also rendered the Sokoto Caliphate insecure.[42] Similar to their Hausa predecessors, many of the Fulani Muslim rulers ignored Usman dan Fodio's injunctions against hereditary leadership and the discredited Hausa system of taxation.[43] Equally important, with the many wars of conquest from the jihad, slavery was pervasive in the new emirates.[44] Not surprisingly, Fulani misrule created pockets of local resistance, military brigandage, and Mahdist agitations.[45] But opposition among the disaffected sectors of Hausa society was weak,[46] and protests were easily contained and brutally suppressed. In effect, therefore, Fulani Muslim rulers under the new political and religious dispensation were largely despotic, failing to guarantee for local communities the just ummah promised by Usman dan Fodio's jihad. In the military execution of the jihad, Crowder insists, "the ranks of his [Usman dan Fodio's] army were swollen by the faithful as well as the usual band of adventurers that followed any Soudanese army. This curious admixture of religious fanaticism and opportunism accounts for the charges of slaughter and plunder that accompanied most Fulani victories. The Shehu [Usman dan Fodio] was quick to condemn such actions on the part of his followers."[47]

Additional features of local administration under the Sokoto Caliphate that indicated misrule were reflected in arbitrary taxation that Usman dan Fodio had denounced: for example, Fulani Muslim rulers reinstituted the arbitrary *jangali* taxes that Hausa rulers had imposed on the nomadic Fulani during the preexisting political order. Among diverse communal groups, the word *jangali* inscribed the ethnic meaning of the tax, for the word is derived from the expressions *yan jangare* and *galla*, which imply the transient existence of Fulani nomads. Before the Sokoto Caliphate, the jangali tax affirmed the distinction between nomadic Fulani and non-nomadic Hausa groups. Under the Sokoto Caliphate, the jangali tax system was retained, but its utility was revised to reflect new interests and power dispositions. Instead of abolishing it, the new Fulani Muslim rulers reversed the concept of jangali to collect tax from non-Muslim (pagan) Fulani. Origins of the practice are associated with Emir Umoru Dellaji, the first Fulani emir of Katsina, who differentiated between Muslim Fulani and Fulani *rehazawa* or *kitiju* (pagans) by levying a tax called *zakka* (heretofore a Hausa tax) on Muslim Fulani. The jangali tax, then, took on the dual function of marking the religious and ethnic identity of non-Muslim Fulani outside the political echelon, while the zakka tax expanded its significance to include Islamic and ethnic connotations.[48] Sokoto Jihadists had charged that jangali was an arbitrary tax imposed on the Fulani under Hausa rulers. When Fulani Muslim rulers rose to power in the early nineteenth century, they continued the exercise of this arbitrary power by imposing the tax on "pagan" Fulani herders.[49] Thus, although the Sokoto Jihadists argued that the Hausa taxation system was oppressive toward the Fulani and they swore to ensure a thorough reform of all extractive policies to humanize society, in fact the new Fulani Muslim rulers ignored the rallying call for Islamic justice articulated in the Jihad of Usman dan Fodio. Needless to say, taxes, tributes, and other forms of extraction were symbols of official power and dictated the character of social relations.[50] Indeed, under the Sokoto Caliphate, the new Fulani Muslim rulers deployed preexisting modes of coercion to enforce new political and social relations: for example, Fulani Muslim rulers used the old Hausa *jakada* system (feudal army) to dominate tributary communities, especially outside the confines of the new

Hausa-Fulani emirates. Ochonu notes the ideological framework on which this vast and diverse territory was constructed:

> The Fulani Islamic reform jihad of 1804–08 superimposed a central political and religious authority on the fragmented Hausa states of present-day Northwestern Nigeria and, through conquest and discourse, disciplined them into one politico-linguistic unit. More importantly, the jihad inscribed Islamic piety as one of the most important markers of Hausa identity.... [Thus] what the jihad did was to initiate the process of homogenization and the construction of a politically useful narrative of Hausa identity, a narrative which was underwritten by religious and cultural associations.[51]

Nigeria's first prime minister, Sir Abubakar Tafawa Balewa, wrote the novel *Shaihu Umar* (1966), in which the political and social effects of the Sokoto Caliphate system are creatively narrated. Specifically, it sought to reimagine a proper Muslim man, family, and society under Fulani Muslim rule. Set in late nineteenth-century emirate society, it portrays "the *fin de siècle*; the last days of a century of turbulence, bloodshed, and slavery," amid caliphate breakdown.[52] The plot revolves around three Hausa institutions: the Islamic court, slavery, and the tradition of itinerant Muslim preachers. Balewa portrays the court as corrupt and riddled with intrigue among Muslim clerics; societal ambivalence is revealed in how Muslim clerics condone slavery; although slavery is sometimes condemned as evil by puritanical Muslim clerics, powerful notables who actively engage in the practice are hardly denounced by ulamas; the system of itinerant preachers and Qur'anic education can embody Islamic piety. In short, Balewa's novel depicts an emirate society at the turn of the twentieth century that was far from the pious ummah Usman dan Fodio had envisioned in the early 1800s.

Whatever the deficiencies of the Sokoto Caliphate, Fulani Muslim rulers brought the Hausa city-states under their control, effectively asserting their dominance under the compromise of Fulani and Hausa Muslim rulers. Defined and inspired by Usman dan Fodio's Islamic reform, the Sokoto Jihad imposed a Muslim theocracy on the Hausa city-states. Fulani Muslim influence spread beyond the Hausa region, and as far away as Northern Yoruba communities.[53] By 1900, when the British declared their colonial control over the Sokoto Caliphate, the consequence of Usman dan Fodio's Jihad was glaring: Islamic rule was entrenched in northwestern Nigeria; many contemporary northeastern Nigerian communities were under Hausa-Fulani Muslim rulers; Fulani Muslim rule had been projected into contemporary central Nigerian communities; Muslim influence had grown significantly in the Yoruba hinterland of Oyo and Oshun, as well as among Southern Yoruba subgroups around the Atlantic coast, especially Ijebu, Egba, and Lagos.[54]

The Yoruba Region: The Coming of Christianity

At the time when Hausa-Fulani Muslim rule was transforming the communities that soon would constitute Britain's Northern Nigerian Protectorate, mission Christianity began to make inroads into the diverse communities that would become colonial Southern Nigeria by the late nineteenth century.[55] This process had started in the early 1800s when several prominent western Christian evangelical societies began to explore opportunities for the establishment of missions in West Africa.[56] These missionary societies received an enormous morale boost from the convergence of favorable internal and external forces by the 1820s.[57] From the beginning, the remarkable work of the preeminent missionary society in West Africa, the Church Missionary Society (CMS), was sustained by notable Englishmen such as William Wilberforce, the celebrated abolitionist; Charles Grant of the East India Company; Thomas Clarkson and Zachary Macaulay of the Sierra Leone Company; and Lord Teignmouth, a former governor-general of India. These men had a mix of humanitarian and economic interests in Africa and India; they were strongly united by the antislavery campaign and mounted strong opposition against the human calamity. They found a common missionary platform in the establishment of the Society for Mission to Africa and the East, soon to be known as the Church Missionary Society.[58] More importantly, CMS missionary efforts in West Africa benefited significantly from the enthusiasm of Thomas Fowell Buxton, a British Parliamentarian who was also the vice president of the CMS. In his landmark book *The African Slave Trade and Its Remedy*, Buxton harbored boundless hope for the positive transformation of the African continent through the promotion of "legitimate" commerce and the abolition of the Atlantic slave trade. To achieve these important objectives, Buxton called on British authorities to encourage the exploration of the Niger River and establish treaties with West African rulers.[59]

Much of the Christian missionary work that set the foundation of the transformation of the Nigerian region is thus inextricably linked to the history of the CMS mission in West Africa. Henry Venn, son of the Reverend John Venn, a founder of the CMS and its secretary-general from 1841 to 1872, contributed significantly to the policies that shaped the objectives of this great missionary society in the Nigerian region. Venn's long service as secretary-general encouraged local leadership of the new CMS mission stations in West Africa.[60] He insisted on a mission that would be self-supporting and self-governing. Following Venn's vision, significant resources were invested in grooming Christian educated West Africans from British colonial Sierra Leone to lead local CMS missions in the Nigerian region, starting in the mid-nineteenth century.[61] Consequently, the CMS began its missionary work in earnest in the West African Atlantic coast of the Nigerian region in 1841 under the leadership of a German missionary, the Reverend Jacob Friederich Schon, and the Reverend Samuel Ajayi Crowther, a Yoruba repatriate from Freetown, Sierra Leone, who as a young boy had been liberated by British squadrons from a Portuguese slave ship off the coast of West Africa in 1821. From the onset, the mission forged a strong relationship with British colonial authorities in Lagos. This relationship was bolstered when the CMS arranged a meeting for Reverend Crowther with the prime minister, the colonial secretary, Queen Victoria, and Prince Albert in London in 1850.[62] Crowther subsequently was consecrated Anglican Bishop of the Diocese of the Niger Territories in 1864. He would serve as bishop until 1890, when the territory and other CMS areas in the region were consolidated into the Diocese of Western Equatorial Africa.

Initially, CMS missionaries operating in the second half of the nineteenth century could not directly draw on British power to support their efforts in the Nigerian region.[63] Rather, these pioneering missionaries worked with European merchants to secure the support of local rulers to establish mission stations in Yoruba and other Nigerian communities.[64] As J. F. Ade Ajayi noted: "Traders and missionaries were interdependent. The Christian missions made a considerable impact on the trading situation. In turn, the expansion of European trade and political influence greatly facilitated the work of missionaries."[65] Thus CMS missionaries collaborated with European merchants to open up the Yoruba hinterland, the Niger-Benue confluence, and the Niger Delta region to Christian evangelism and European trade.[66] However, by the 1850s CMS missionaries established an effective partnership with colonial authorities stationed in Lagos. For example, the British government in Lagos supported three CMS Niger expeditions from the 1840s to the 1850s.[67] Indeed, with the support of Yoruba Sierra Leonean returnees, the CMS Niger Mission opened the area around the River Niger to trade, leading George Taubman Goldie, leader of the Royal Niger Company, to amalgamate British companies and seek a royal charter for monopoly in 1886.

The convergence of these regional and global developments in the second half of the nineteenth century,[68] shaped so profoundly by CMS missionary work and British imperial interests, were carried out against the backdrop of the intense military conflict among the rulers of Yoruba city-states for control over resources and trade routes throughout much of the nineteenth century. Indeed, the consequences of this protracted conflict among Yoruba city-states would have far-reaching implications for CMS missionary work, ultimately shaping the direction and dimension of the social transformation of Yoruba communities since the turbulent nineteenth century. It is to this military conflict with such important implications for the work of the emergent Christian missions that we turn in the next session.

About the Yoruba Wars: A Detour

With the collapse of the dominant Yoruba city-state of Old Oyo in the early nineteenth century, regional wars disrupted political relations in the Yoruba region for much of the century.[69] The historical literature is clear that the collapse of the Old Oyo Kingdom, for several centuries the hegemon in the region, and the southern expansion of the Fulani Jihad into the Oyo-Yoruba city-state of Ilorin in the early nineteenth century unleashed protracted conflict among Yoruba city-states that was only brought to an end with the imposition of British rule in the last decade of the century. The human costs of the Yoruba wars are often measured in terms of the destruction of many Yoruba communities—indeed, Old Oyo Kingdom itself was destroyed and abandoned in the 1820s; large-scale human displacement led to the mass migration of many Oyo-Yoruba communities pushing southward; adding to the trauma was the inevitable competition for space among the mix of people pouring in waves southward, pushing other Yoruba subgroups, especially the Owu and Egba peoples, farther south at the expense of the Egbado.[70]

These major demographic shifts had several significant social and political consequences. First, there was the epochal shift in the hierarchy of power among Yoruba states: the age-old Yoruba monarchical principle continued to be observed in theory, but in practice it was the age of warrior entrepreneurs who mobilized hundreds of fighting men and utilized slave labor to produce palm oil for the European export trade in return for firearms. Second, instability became the order of the day: the new centers of power, now dominated by warriors, continually rained fear among populations by challenging existing monarchies for the exercise of power.[71] Third, these disruptions produced new political experiments and alliances: for example, the displaced Egba and sections of the Owu regrouped in a new town, Abeokuta, about forty miles from the port city of Lagos. They welcomed missionaries hoping to use their influence with British colonial authorities and European merchants to build commercial and political power and outshine their closest rivals, the Ijebu; the most successful of these political experiments were carried out by displaced Oyo warriors who established a new garrison town of Ibadan. They defeated the Ijaye, the only Oyo power to rival them, and built a novel chieftaincy system that consolidated the extensive power of Ibadan's new military rulers. Ibadan rulers emerged to control much of Southern Oyo, Ife, Ijesha, Ekiti, and Akoko, where they competed with regional powers—Benin, Nupe, and Ilorin—for hegemony.[72] Eventually, responding to Ibadan's growing military threat, several Yoruba subgroups, the Ijesha, and Ekiti war chiefs formed a grand alliance (the Ekitiparapo) with the Ife, Ijebu, and Egba to control a route in Eastern Yorubaland to the coast in Lagos for the supply of breech-loading rifles.[73]

Thus as military conflicts consumed many Yoruba communities, warlords displaced elders as leaders of local communities, and wealth derived from war booty gained importance, destabilizing traditional modes of social hierarchy. With warfare among Yoruba city-states intensifying over control of economic resources and trade routes, captives from armed conflicts, displaced refugee populations, domestic slaves, and other forms of unfree labor disrupted preexisting demographic arrangements in many Yoruba communities. These cataclysmic disruptions in one of West Africa's major geocultural regions fueled the Atlantic slave trade through the port cities of Lagos and Porto Novo, even as the slave trade declined in the Americas in the first half of the nineteenth century. Significantly, this coincided with the efforts of the British government, once the engine for the Atlantic slave trade in the previous century, to undermine the trade at this new West African source. A direct outcome of the Yoruba wars, Yoruba returnees who had been liberated by the British Royal Navy off the West African coast and settled in Freetown, Sierra Leone, emerged as the most ironic story in this tragic saga. Several decades after their departure from their homelands, these Yoruba returnees would play a critical role in the transformation of the Yoruba region from the mid-1800s to the early 1900s, when Britain consolidated its colonial control in the region.[74]

REBIRTH AND EVANGELISM

As these Yoruba disruptions converged with global forces derived from British antislavery efforts against the slave trade, evangelizing efforts by the CMS, Wesleyan Methodists, and Baptists expanded in the coastal city of Lagos and in Abeokuta to its immediate north. New opportunities opened for Christian missions and European commercial interests in the Yoruba hinterland. In addition to their religious and moral claims, Christian missionaries also had explicitly secular ideas about the virtues of commerce, ideas of vocational training, and economic development, contending that "civilization" was contingent on the formation of a Western-oriented Christian elite that would spearhead the progressive transformation of Yoruba society. Alongside the turbulence of the Yoruba wars, Yoruba returnees socialized in a pan-Yoruba consciousness in Sierra Leone emerged as agents of this modernization process in their homelands. As Christian missionary impact gained momentum by the late nineteenth century in many Yoruba communities, Yoruba religious practices revealed a mix of indigenous and global religions, consisting of Yoruba adherence to a supreme god; cults dedicated to *orisas* (lesser deities); Islam; and Christianity. However, Yoruba Sierra Leonean (Saro) Christian missionaries constructed the concept of a monotheistic Christian faith in contrast to the Muslim and "pagan" other, separating Christian religious practice from other aspects of life and positioning Christianity as the religion of peace. This message would resonate among war-weary Yoruba communities.[75]

In the Yoruba region, the first major group of Christian missionaries charged with the responsibility of evangelizing the hinterland arrived through the auspices of the CMS in Badagry in 1842, preceded there by small groups of Yoruba returnees from Sierra Leone. Finding little success in this unwelcoming coastal town, they moved to the new and vibrant city of Abeokuta, where local chiefs led by Sodeke welcomed them, hoping they would serve as intermediaries on behalf of Abeokuta rulers with British authorities in Lagos to forestall the growing threat of the Dahomey Kingdom farther to the west. The success of these pioneering CMS missionaries—and successive missions, including the Wesleyan Methodist and the Baptist—led to the establishment of mission stations in Lagos, where Yoruba returnees from Sierra Leone, Brazil, and Cuba were settling in large numbers by the 1850s.[76]

From this vibrant beginning, Christian missions expanded rapidly throughout the Yoruba region. From bases in Abeokuta and Lagos, missionaries pushed inland, opening stations in major Yoruba towns such as Ibadan and Ijaye in 1853, and subsequently in Ikorodu, Sagamu, and Igbesa. By the late nineteenth century, missionaries, mostly Yoruba repatriates, became a regular feature in the Oyo-Yoruba towns of Oyo (New Oyo), Iseyin, Saki, Ogbomosho, and Awaye and in the western Yoruba towns of Ilaro, Ketu, Ibara, and Isaga. While political conditions limited their success in Ijebu-Ode, Ife, and Modakeke, a strong CMS mission was established in Ode-Ondo. This mission eventually served as the headquarters for CMS missionary work northward and eastward in Ife, Ijesha, and Ekiti, ultimately leading to the establishment of mission stations in Ife, Modakeke, Ado-Ekiti, Ijero, Aiyede, Akure, Ise, Owo, and Akoko, from the 1870s to the end of the century. In the eastern Yoruba hinterland of Ondo and

Ekiti, the arrival of Christian missionaries, most of them Yoruba Sierra Leonean (Saro) returnees, meant a reprieve from decades of Yoruba wars.[77] Lamin Sanneh notes the social and economic impact of Saro returnees in the transformation of Yoruba communities in the second half of the nineteenth century:

> In the intervening years when government and mission were still wary of any reckless scheme of territorial overreach, the re-captives [Saro] bought ships and traveled up and down the coast, demonstrating that expansion beyond Sierra Leone was viable and logical development of the antislavery cause.... Such advances in the personal circumstances of the settlers and re-captives produced the educated and successful individuals who could plan and direct the antislavery outreach to Nigeria and elsewhere. Preachers, pastors, schoolteachers, traders, and clerical personnel composed the ranks of this buoyant cadre of modernizing agents, with their skills supporting their mobile lifestyle.[78]

Saro returnees represented a significant component of the Yoruba cities of Lagos and Abeokuta in the second half of the nineteenth century. E. A. Ayandele estimates that in Lagos they numbered over five thousand, and about ten thousand in Abeokuta by the end of the century.[79] Indeed, Saro returnees had turned Abeokuta into a vibrant republic with modern administrative and infrastructural systems by the time the British consolidated their colonial rule in the early twentieth century.[80]

MISSIONARY MOMENTUM: EDUCATION AND HUMAN DEVELOPMENT

Concomitantly, CMS mission stations grew in strides in Yoruba communities, reflecting the significance of elementary, secondary, and vocational education as a critical expression of progressive social transformation. By 1846, four years after their arrival in Abeokuta, Reverends Crowther and Schon had founded a church and several schools. With the growing influence of the British authorities in Lagos, the work of missionaries intensified, leading to a significant increase in the number of schools in the city.[81] As early as 1856, the CMS alone had 256 elementary-level pupils in Lagos and 549 students in nine schools throughout the Yoruba region. And with the opening of the CMS Grammar School in Lagos in 1859, the CMS began instruction at the secondary school level. A decade later, the mission opened a girls' secondary school, and in 1896, the CMS had opened a teacher-training college, St. Andrews College, in Oyo. By 1930, three decades after the imposition of British colonial rule in Nigeria and only four decades after the devastating Yoruba wars, the CMS alone had a total of 567 elementary, secondary, and vocational schools with a total of 34,140 students in Southern Nigeria.[82]

In Abeokuta, under the leadership of Yoruba Sierra Leonean returnees, the Egba United Kingdom collaborated with the local government to establish elementary and secondary schools in the late nineteenth and early twentieth centuries. These efforts resulted in the enrollment of about two thousand pupils in Egba schools by 1904, and the establishment of Nigeria's first community secondary school, the Abeokuta Grammar School, five years later. After the conquest of the Ijebu by the British in 1892, the CMS made quick inroads into the Ijebu region's primary city, Ijebu-Ode, leading to the establishment of a vibrant Anglican Church movement by the early twentieth century. This effort led to the establishment of a local secondary school, the Ijebu-Ode Grammar School, in 1913. Similarly, in Ibadan, following the establishment of a CMS mission by David Hinderer and Daniel Olubi in 1857, local Ibadan CMS leaders encouraged the mission to found a local community secondary school for boys, the Ibadan Grammar School, in 1913. After several years of hard work, the local Ondo CMS established a community secondary school, Ondo Boys High School, in 1919. A second secondary school in Ondo Province, Christ School, was created through the agitation of local CMS church leaders in Ado-Ekiti in 1933.[83] Moreover, in the eastern district of Lagos in the early years of colonial rule, Yoruba CMS missionary Thomas Ayegumbiyi describes the extent of local commitment to education:

> Monday July 13 accompanied by Mr. Olubi, I attended a meeting of the parochial committee as a visitor. The chief topic for the discussion was the schoolmaster's salary; it seems the fund was exhausted and there was a difficulty to raise what was wanted even for the current quarter; the Bale [head chief] of the town, a Mohammedan was invited into the room to have a say in the discussion and out of the interest he has in the education of the young of the town, readily promised to do all he could to get his co-religionists to lend a helping hand. I understand that he has since got them to promise 6 pounds annually towards the fund.[84]

Several other Christian missions, notably the Southern Baptist Convention (USA), Wesleyan Methodist, and Catholic Missions, followed the lead of the CMS, not only in the Yoruba region, but also in other Southern Nigerian regions, especially the Niger Delta and the southeast area of the Igbo people. Inspired by evangelical movements from Western Europe and missionary work in India, the American Baptist Convention began to send missionaries abroad in the early nineteenth century. However, with growing divisions between contingents from Northern U.S. states, who opposed slavery, and their Southern counterparts, who condoned it, an intractable conflict led to the formation of the Southern (USA) Baptist Convention. This splinter group—the Southern Baptist Convention—ultimately emerged as pioneering white American Baptist missionaries to southwestern Nigeria, starting in the mid-nineteenth century. Thomas Jefferson Bowen pioneered the missionary efforts of the Southern Baptist Convention to the Yoruba region, initially settling in Ijaye in 1853 and ultimately encouraging the building of mission stations from Lagos on the coast through the Yoruba hinterland and on to the River Niger. His successors carried the work forward, establishing mission stations that eventually became prominent centers of Southern Baptist Convention missionary work among Oyo and Oshun Yoruba subgroups, establishing pioneering Christian missions in major towns at the turn of the twentieth century.[85] The triumph of the Baptist mission in the Yoruba region by the early twentieth century, despite the hard work of American missionaries, ultimately required the commitment of Yoruba pastors and church leaders. Through the work of Yoruba pastors such as Reverends Moses Ladejo Stone, Mojola Agbebi, and Lajide Tubi in the First Baptist Church of Lagos, Ebenezer Baptist Church, and Araromi Baptist Church in Lagos in the late nineteenth century, early Baptist missionary work led to the establishment of several schools in Lagos and Abeokuta.

Similarly, in many other Oyo and Oshun-Yoruba communities—and later in Ekiti towns—the Southern Baptist Convention was particularly successful because of strong collaboration between American missionaries and local Baptist leaders from the late nineteenth century to the end of colonial rule in the mid-twentieth century.[86] As challenging economic conditions forced new Oyo-Yoruba educated Baptists—especially Ogbomosho natives—to seek their fortune outside their hometown, they migrated not only to the major Yoruba cities of Lagos and Ibadan, but also settled far afield in Northern Nigeria, the Gold Coast, Dahomey, and Togoland. As they migrated to these alien regions, they established Yoruba diaspora churches wherever they went.[87] In Northern Nigerian cities such as Kaduna, Zaria, Kafanchan, Funtua, Minna, Bida, Katcha, and others, Ogbomosho Baptist immigrants, taking advantage of new economic opportunities in the early decades of colonial rule, became pastors, lay leaders, and active members of Baptist churches throughout the region. Indeed, Thomas Birch Freeman, a British-African Wesleyan missionary with experience among the Asante in the Gold Coast, accompanied by his wife and another West African missionary, William DeGraft, had added to this momentum of rapid social transformation of Yoruba communities by the early 1840s. Freeman and his associates had established a mission in Badagry and Abeokuta in 1842. Their work led to the establishment of some of the first elementary and secondary schools in Nigeria, including Methodist Boys' High School, Lagos, founded in 1878, and a girls' secondary school, Methodist Girls' High School, Lagos, founded in 1879. These churches and schools would serve as pioneering institutions for vibrant Methodist religious and educational institutions not only in the Yoruba hinterland, but throughout Southern and central Nigeria by the mid-twentieth century.[88]

Under the strong leadership of a French priest, Father Pierre Bouche, the Catholic Society of African Missions, following the lead of Protestant missions, established its educational work in Lagos, as well as the Igbo towns of Onitsha and Ibuzo, with secondary school instruction at St. Gregory College in Lagos, and Christ the King College in Onitsha, as well as teacher-training colleges in Onitsha and Ibuzo, by the turn of the twentieth century. In the specific case of Nigeria's southeastern region, Magnus Bassey notes how the Holy Ghost Fathers of the Catholic mission challenged the educational work of CMS missionaries from the late nineteenth century to the mid-twentieth century:

> The period between 1885 and 1932 witnessed intense missionary rivalry in southern Nigeria, occasioned by the entry of the Holy Ghost Fathers of the Roman Catholic Mission into the missionary field in eastern Nigeria. In 1885 with the arrival of Father Lutz as the Catholic Superior of the mission, the Holy Ghost Fathers, who were put in charge of the Lower Niger, started work. That same year Father Lutz opened a mission at Onitsha on a piece of land donated by the Obi of Onitsha through the instrumentality of the Anglican Bishop Crowther. In 1900 Father Lejeune succeeded Father Lutz as the Catholic Superior. Lejeune was one of the greatest advocates of the policy of evangelization through the schools.... Lejeune further believed that good education would enable African students to earn a good living as well as exert their influence in society to the favor of the Roman Catholic Church.... When Father Shanahan took over from Father Lejeune he expressed a similar concern. Under Father (later Bishop) Shanahan, the RCM spread its variety of religion and education to most parts of the Igbo, Ibibio, and Ogoja provinces east of the Niger.[89]

Starting with CMS missions as early as the 1840s, '50s, and '60s, Christian missionaries of all denominations embraced the idea that missionary work required some investment in basic medical services to address the needs of their mission stations and, whenever possible, to meet the basic health needs of the local community. Following the works of Bishop Crowther and other pioneering missionaries, Christian missionaries provided vaccination against smallpox and established medical dispensaries from the 1840s. Indeed, the genealogy of the modern Nigerian medical profession can be traced to the training of a handful of gifted Saro CMS men who pioneered modern medicine in Nigeria.[90] Naturally, with the slow growth of the medical profession, CMS missions established health clinics to meet enormous health problems of local communities. Following the establishment of health clinics in the Yoruba hinterland, where Saro returnees had led mission stations by the late nineteenth century, the CMS expanded modest health care facilities to their new Southern and central Nigerian missions by the early twentieth century. For example, several decades after Saro returnees pioneered the CMS mission, Sybil K. Batley, a CMS missionary, notes the enormous need for modern health care in Iyi-Enu Medical Mission: "The maternity department has increased markedly. Growing numbers of women are attending for ante-natal advice, over 5,000 of these attendees having been made through the Government Department."[91] Nevertheless, the daunting challenges confronting the CMS missions' health care initiatives—as well as other missionary health care programs—would persist late into the colonial period.

The most significant impact of Christian missionary work in Southern Nigeria, however, would lie in the cultural implications of Western literary traditions, vigorously pushed by Saro missionaries in Yoruba communities, beginning with the arrival of the CMS missions in the 1840s. Ajayi's vivid analysis of the significance of the translation of the Bible to the Yoruba language by Crowther and his CMS associates underscores this important development not only in Yoruba society, but in various Southern and central Nigerian communities by the turn of the twentieth century. In this context, the translation of the Bible from English to Yoruba was not only essential to the propagation of Christianity; it was also critical for the flowering of a literary tradition in Yoruba communities. Noting the significance of Crowther's critical role in the translation of the Bible to the Yoruba language, Ajayi observes:

> He published a few extracts in 1848; the Epistle to the Romans in 1850; Luke, Acts, James, and I and II Peter in 1851; Genesis and Matthew in 1853; Exodus and the Psalms in 1854; Proverbs and Ecclesiastes in 1856 and revisions of earlier text. After 1857, he had to work with others. Thomas King had collaborated with him on Matthew in 1853. In 1857–62, they worked on the Epistles—Philippians, I and II Colossians, I and II Thessalonians, I and II Timothy, Titus, Philemon, Hebrews, John,

Islam and Christianity 33

Jude, Revelations, thus completing the New Testament in 1861....
When people remark casually on the literary quality of the Yoruba Bible
and the foundation it has laid for developing the Yoruba language as a
vehicle for education and communication, let us remember that it took
hard work, scholarly study, and high literary skills. Wherever Crowther
went, he collected vocabularies, probed histories, concepts and ideas.[92]

The literary pursuits necessitated by the translation of the Bible and other
Christian theological documents to Yoruba—along with the establishment of
schools—soon opened the door to a vibrant Nigerian printing industry by the
early twentieth century. Starting with the establishment of the headquarters
of the CMS Press in Lagos in 1913, the CMS established bookshops in many
Yoruba cities, notably Ibadan, Ijebu-Ode, Ile-Ife, Ilesha, Akure, Ondo, Owo,
Ado-Ekiti, and Ikare. With Yoruba CMS laymen as managers, these bookstores encouraged the growth of literacy throughout Nigeria.[93] And with
the growth of literacy in these Yoruba cities, print culture became a crucial
medium of collective social action, shaping the meaning of identity in an
increasingly diverse society. Adebanji Akintoye notes the implications of this
print medium not just for literacy, but for the articulation of a Yoruba ethnonational identity:

The men of Yoruba origin employed in the Christian missions, and the
growing number of literate people in various parts of the country were
attracted to the fascinating traditions of the past preserved in every Yoruba community, and began to write about them, as well as about current
happenings in Yorubaland. John Augustus Otunba Payne of Lagos became the leading person among the early writers, with his *Lagos and West
African Almanac* published annually from 1874.... Writing on Yoruba history and institutions was to grow very richly during the last decade of the
nineteenth century and to become even richer in the twentieth century. The
reduction of the language into writing during the nineteenth century, and
the emergence of a common Yoruba orthography, enabled some of the writers to produce their works in Yoruba language—and this was to become a
very significant cultural development during the twentieth century.[94]

Christian missionaries also facilitated the growth of modern apprenticeship
in Nigeria. Yoruba returnee Christians from Sierra Leone, Brazil, and Cuba,
with the support of missionary groups, brought to Nigeria their artisanal skills
in bricklaying, masonry, carpentry, tailoring, watch repair, painting, and basic
architecture.[95] Indeed, with the establishment of the Yoruba CMS mission in

the 1840s, CMS secretary-general Henry Venn, critical of the orientation of Saro elite toward literary education, stressed the importance of industrial training in the new mission: "In 1853, for example, he sent Mr. R. Paley, a young Cambridge graduate, to go and turn the Abeokuta Training Institution into a model self-supporting institution where learning will be combined with industrial labor in the manner of the Basle missionaries in the Gold Coast.... The institution organized a system of apprenticeship, and trained a few carpenters, tailors, printers, brick-makers, and masons."[96] The growth of artisans enabled the further development of apprenticeships through missionary schools. Within a short period of time, the products of missionary apprenticeship became a small but influential middle class in Yoruba cities around the Atlantic coast, such as Lagos and Abeokuta. Many in this upwardly mobile class went into other businesses and had become successful by the time the Yoruba region came under British colonial rule at the end of the century.[97]

By the early twentieth century, the strong partnership between Nigerian and European missionaries had shaped the rapid growth of the Niger Diocese of the CMS in southeastern Nigeria. In Nsukka, an important CMS stronghold in Igboland, for instance, there were about sixty established churches for local clergymen to manage. Clergymen and other church officials traveled great distance to consolidate the successes of the CMS mission stations in many Southern and central Nigerian communities.[98]

In this overview, I have underscored how the activities of local missionaries—especially Yoruba CMS missionaries and Christian converts—gave impetus to the rapid process of social change: Christian missionaries consistently shaped social, political, and economic factors to create the peculiar environment on which emergent Southern Nigerian communities were built from the beginning of the twentieth century. British imperial interests also played critical roles in this transformative process, creating local administrative institutions that coordinated the social transformation of Southern Nigeria. These emerging Southern Nigerian communities were fundamentally different from patterns that were being consolidated in the Hausa-Fulani Muslim confederacy north of the River Niger,[99] analyzed above. The Nigerian colonial state—at least in Southern Nigeria, especially the Yoruba region—had started with the colonization of Lagos between 1851 and 1861 and the incorporation of Nigerian producers into global markets through the activities of the Royal Niger Company. But it was the ingenuity of Yoruba missionaries and new Christian converts that provided the essential social framework for the growth of these political and economic developments by the early decades of colonial rule.

CHRISTIAN, ETHNO-NATIONAL, AND DIASPORAN IDENTITIES

It is essential to underscore the peculiarities of social change at this juncture and the characteristics of the purveyors of these complex processes of social transformation. In addition to the Saro returnees discussed above, the process of mission Christianity and migration was complicated by the arrival of another important returnee population, the Afro-Brazilians, during this era of Yoruba social transformation. Having been a casualty of the many disruptions among West African city-states, especially the Yoruba wars, Afro-Brazilian returnees began to arrive in Lagos in the second half of the nineteenth century. Popularly known as the Aguda because of their distinctive Catholic identity, Afro-Brazilians demonstrated strong connections to Luso-Brazilian culture and were connected to the religious universe of the Yoruba Diaspora that dominated the Bahian world they left behind in Brazil.[100] While elite Saros, through the educational institutions of the CMS, dominated the modern professions—especially clergy, education, medicine, law, and civil service—by the beginning of the twentieth century,[101] Afro-Brazilians emerged as exceptional craftsmen and traders who took advantage of the dynamic conditions taking place in Lagos by the late 1800s.[102] While some Afro-Brazilians became wealth merchants, engaging in trade between Lagos and the Lusophone world, many became successful as masons and carpenters.[103]

I have already highlighted the consequences of the collapse of the Old Oyo Empire that heralded the seven-decade-long "age of confusion" during the Yoruba wars. Mission Christianity provided a new lens for looking at this turbulent Yoruba world. I have also discussed the emergence of new cultural identities: Saro missionaries combined evangelical Christianity with Yoruba ethnic identity, and the intersection of historical space-time and evangelism produced new interpretations of Christian theology. The Catholicism of Afro-Brazilians enriched the throbbing social and cultural space, especially in the rapidly growing cities of Lagos and Abeokuta. Christian notions of sin and salvation dominated debates among local clergies and their congregations. Debates on culture and religion reverberated throughout the Yoruba region's emerging colonial society. The transformative impact of Christian missions in these Yoruba communities reflects David Chidester's observation that "although Christian missionaries from Europe insisted that they were bringing light into a region of darkness, their gospel of sin and salvation was experienced by Africans as a local problem of translation.... African Christian communities engaged [the issues] in an ongoing process of intercultural translation, moving back and forth between indigenous religious knowledge and the terms of Christian doctrine, practice, and authority."[104]

In many ways Christian missions adapted to local social and political conditions in southwestern Nigeria.[105] In most Yoruba communities early Christian converts were typically the poor, former slaves, or those cut off from mainstream local communities. The so-called age of confusion had produced these marginal groups in large numbers, seeking empowerment under the growing hegemony of British imperial power sustained by the new ideas of mission Christianity and British commercial interests. To win converts, missionaries abandoned preaching for dialogue, connected the realms of heaven and earth, and emphasized Christ's sacrifice to link Christianity with indigenous cosmology. This contrasts with Muslim conversion efforts, which had been making inroads into the Yoruba region since the early nineteenth century.[106] Muslim preachers from the Sokoto Caliphate had refused to translate the Qur'an or abandon Arabic terms. While Islam in the Yoruba region focused on its foreign origins, mission Christianity was shaped by the ideas of Yoruba Christian missionaries. These missionaries articulated a Yoruba national consciousness,[107] propelled by modern science and rationality. While they professed Western ideas of civilization derived from the missions, Yoruba returnee missionaries found creative ways to reconcile their Christian beliefs with local Yoruba traditions. Thus, as Femi Kolapo reflects, the Yoruba experience reveals that returnee missionaries

> were sojourning neighbors, fellow countrymen, traders in new imported manufactures, and friends to white men with powerful gunboats. In addition, they had plenty of money to spend in the local economy and could redeem or buy off obstreperous or aging slaves. They were equally involved in political situations that, willy-nilly, positioned them as friends or as foes in respect of other settler groups. They constituted an economic and political group with corresponding obligations to the communities in which they were established.[108]

Consequently, conversion to Christianity gained momentum in Yoruba cities and towns by the late nineteenth century. The end of the Yoruba wars and the imposition of the colonial state led to waves of conversion to Christianity by the early twentieth century. A sizable Christian population emerged, taking on mainline Catholic and Protestant denominations: Anglicans, Methodists, Baptists, and, later, African independent and Pentecostal churches, which emphasized the spiritual force of prayer, individual connection to Christ, and vocal expression of Christian piety.

Yoruba missionaries were engaged in the tasks of reimagining an ethnonational identity, and it is said that the turn to Christianity brought with it the birth of Yoruba nationalism starting in the early twentieth century.[109] Yoruba subgroups possess strong understanding of intersecting historical experiences as a people, articulated in the emergent modernist project of Yoruba mission Christianity. An ethno-national discourse of shared Yoruba culture predicated on the powerful myths of common origin were incubated during this transformative moment of Yoruba history: the influential traditions centered on Ile-Ife as the cradle of Yoruba civilization and Oduduwa as the progenitor of the Yoruba people; a common pantheon of Yoruba gods and spirits; interconnected political experiences; and universal belief in the common ancestry of Yoruba dynastic traditions. It is true that the Yorubas lived in their many city-states and villages as subethnic groups; notwithstanding, I concur with Akintoye that the enduring structures that sustained this modern ethnonational consciousness were not simply contingent on the social realities of the times but, significantly, drew from the Yoruba peoples' tradition, religion, and customary ways. Precisely for this reason, Akintoye concludes: "Common consciousness of the larger ethnic group ran through their lives, their politics, their rituals, and worship, their economic institutions and practices, and their total worldview."[110] The Yoruba wars of the nineteenth century were traumatic, though the experience also expanded Yoruba ethno-national consciousness. And Christianity, the new religion that supplanted the "age of confusion," did not erode Yoruba consciousness; it simply built on it.

This Yoruba encounter with mission Christianity from the mid-nineteenth century to the advent of colonial rule at the turn of the twentieth century—along with other Southern Nigerian experiences—contrast sharply with the social and political consequences of the Muslim reformism of the Sokoto Jihad, imposed on the Hausa city-states and other groups in what soon became Britain's Northern Nigerian Protectorate. The political and social destiny of these vastly different regions, shaped so profoundly by the Muslim reformism of the Sokoto Jihad and the Christian evangelization of the second half of the nineteenth century, were ultimately enclosed in Britain's colonial territories of Northern and Southern Nigerian Protectorates in the first half of the twentieth century.

CHAPTER TWO

ISLAM AND COLONIAL RULE
IN NORTHERN NIGERIA

In the vast Northern Nigerian emirates, where the Sokoto Jihad had profoundly altered relations of state and society in the nineteenth century, Islam proved critical to the British colonial enterprise in local communities starting in the twentieth century. As crucial structural and ideological frameworks on which colonial society was ultimately rationalized, Islamic structures were decisive in the administration of the heterogeneous communities that were incorporated into Britain's newly established Northern Nigerian Protectorate.

The presence of the British in the Sokoto Caliphate, the epicenter of what would become colonial Northern Nigeria, began with the visits to Sokoto by Captain Hugh Clapperton, a Scottish explorer, who met Sultan Mohammed Bello in 1822 and 1825. This was followed by visits by two Cornish explorers, Richard Lander and his brother John, in 1830 and by German explorer and scholar Heinrich Barth in 1852.[1] The initial visits by these European explorers were followed by the establishment in 1860 of a British consul in Lokoja, at the confluence of River Niger and River Benue. With the rapid growth of the Royal Niger Company, which was chartered in 1882, British authorities established a foothold in two southern emirates of the Sokoto Caliphate, Ilorin and Bida, before the conquest of the caliphate in 1903. Following the extension of constabularies from Ilorin and Bida emirates to some of their northern neigbors in 1897, the West African Frontier Force, under the command of Colonel Frederick Lugard, formally proclaimed all communities within the Sokoto Caliphate and the old Kanem-Bornu Empire as the British Protectorate of Northern Nigeria on January 1, 1900. This culminated in the fall of Sokoto in 1903. With the exception of Satiru and Hadejia uprisings in 1906, British rule encountered little serious resistance from dissidents in emirate society in the early years of colonial rule.[2] In the Sokoto Caliphate, as well as in most of Nigeria's Southern Provinces, the administration of local communities was sustained by the now-famous system of indirect rule, imposed by Lugard, governor of Northern Nigerian Protectorate and later governor-general of Nigeria, after the amalgamation of the Northern and Southern Provinces in 1914.[3]

Many scholars of British rule in Northern Nigeria agree that prevailing Hausa-Fulani emirate structures were transformed into a more centralized administrative system under the British system of indirect rule. This colonial system established the Northern Nigerian Protectorate as a distinct political unit in which Muslim and non-Muslim communities were brought under the control of Hausa-Fulani Muslim rulers within clearly defined administrative jurisdictions. Mohammad Umar notes the political implications of this administrative system for Hausa-Fulani Muslim rulers and the diverse communities that constituted the Northern Nigerian Protectorate following the imposition of colonial rule:

> One reason for the seemingly smooth running of colonial rule in Northern Nigeria was the British appropriation of the ancient sarauta-emirate political institutions to form the basis of British indirect rule. Between the imposition of colonialism in 1903 and the beginning of decolonization in 1945, the British transformed the sarauta-emirate system in various ways. Beginning with territorial reorganization that got rid of absentee district heads in the 1900s, subsequent development of territorial administration turned sarauta-emirates into colonial machinery of local government administration, while the introduction of technical departments (agriculture, health, works, etc.) made sarauta-emirate institutions part of British colonial bureaucracy. Loyalty to the British took precedence over all the sarauta-emirate political values, including Islamic values. But the British found much to admire in sarauta political institutions and values, preserving, strengthening, and modernizing them. An important aspect of the colonial transformation of the sarauta-

emirate was its extension over ethnic minorities who had resisted Sokoto imposition of the system in the nineteenth century.[4]

For these expedient reasons, British authorities coopted Hausa-Fulani Muslim rulers, largely influenced by the *qadiriyya* order,[5] which dominated the politico-religious hierarchy in the region when the Sokoto Caliphate came under British rule.[6] Additionally, it was colonial rule that formalized Islamic law as a legal system throughout the Northern Protectorate, and only with the colonial rulers' arrival was Maliki inheritance law first enforced and slavery and concubinage banned in the region.[7] Importantly, colonial administrators paid attention to contending interpretations of Islamic practices and then entrenched the power base of the dominant politico-religious ruling class. The response of British administrators to religion at this juncture was made difficult by the protean nature of Islam in a culturally heterogeneous region. In many cases, interpretations of Islam were far from discrete ideas and categories; rather, prevailing political, religious, and social conditions encouraged varied interpretations of Islam, even among those who claimed to share the same Muslim belief. Contested interpretations of Muslim authority required British administrators to invest considerable imagination in constructing doctrines to legitimate Islamic political authority.

Consequently, in order to control the diverse people of the newly established Northern Protectorate, British authorities did not simply embrace the existing political structures under the leadership of the rulers of the Sokoto Caliphate; British administrators strengthened Fulani conquerors and imposed their political hegemony on the "subject" peoples of the region.[8] However, this expedient system of local administration was incongruous with the diverse religious, social, and political realities of the vast region. Moreover, by embracing caliphate rulers as junior partners, British colonial administrators consolidated the powers of the dominant Muslim rulers as legitimate traditional rulers, while marginalizing their competitors in local politics. Naturally, this policy strengthened the authority of the dominant qadiriyya order, while simultaneously jettisoning the leaders of other Sufi orders.

Jonathan Reynolds's conceptualization of "good" and "bad" Muslims provides a useful framework to explore how British authorities navigated this complicated power structure among Hausa-Fulani Muslim rulers. Reynolds holds that colonial construction of political authority in Northern Nigeria was shaped by British preference for the dominant Muslim aristocracy in this region, especially in the early decades of colonial rule. While British administrators claimed neutrality on local religious matters, colonial officials embraced leaders of the major Sufi order they deemed "good" Muslims because they legitimated the colonial order. The beneficiaries of this colonial policy were leaders of the qadiriyya order that dominated the *masu sarauta,* the Hausa-Fulani emirate structure. As the qadiriyya consolidated their power base, competing Sufi orders, such as the *tijaniyya, sanusiyya,* and *mahdiyya,* were officially castigated as "bad" Muslims because of their tendency to question colonial policies.[9] In the case of the relationship between the qadiriyya and their main competitor, the tijaniyya,[10] tensions would grow between the two groups in Kano, where the tijaniyya became more powerful in the 1930s and 1940s.[11] Nevertheless, colonial authorities identified the qadiriyya as "good" Muslim rulers because of their willingness to embrace new colonial rules and reject religious doctrines British administrators considered "fanatical."[12] Captain G. Callow, the district officer in Adamawa, captures the affinity of British administrators for the qadiriyya:

> The majority of the Muslims here [Adamawa] follow the Khadariya [Qadiriyya] form of worship. It appears to be by far the most lenitive [soothing] sect . . . and perfectly harmless to the state; I think it would be quite impossible to arouse followers of this sect to any fanaticism; they take their religion much too easily, rather in fact like the average Englishman of today [1926], who reserves his devotional exercises for Sundays—if it is too wet to play golf.[13]

Consequently, British authorities embraced the rulers of the emirates and the qadiriyya order to which most of them belonged, while gathering intelligence and employing repressive measures against leaders of movements they deemed subversive, especially Mahdism.[14]

Mahdism and Colonial Surveillance

It is understandable that British authorities, given the emphasis on local administrative control, were obsessed with the maintenance of order, and this comes through clearly in the intelligence reports and memoranda of G. J. Lethem, an astute British administrator in the Northern Nigerian colonial service. British authorities claimed that the Mahdist movement harbored "bad" Muslims who perpetuate anticolonial propaganda, and they devised strategies to monitor Mahdist activities throughout the Northern Nigerian Protectorate. Lethem's detailed records of Mahdist and other "fringe" Muslim movements also shed light on how various Islamic doctrines shaped the social and political landscape of the Northern Provinces in the early decades of colonial rule.[15]

Colonial authorities had good reasons to place Mahdists on their watch list, because the movement's ideology contained doctrines of impending anarchy that threatened colonial order. Mahdist clerics prophesied a period of political tumult that will eventually lead to the end of all political hierarchies; with the arrival of the Mahdi (the Direct One), this process was predicted to lead to the end of the world in 1980 (1400). More importantly for British colonial rule, some Mahdist leaders insisted that the disruptions precipitated by European colonial rule would ultimately trigger this millenarian process. Thus British administrators contended that neo-Mahdism harbors seeds of violence, since many followers of the Mahdi had fiercely resisted foreign rule in the Sudan in the late nineteenth century.[16]

In the specific case of Bornu Province, the revival of this new trend of Mahdism among the Fulani was partly due to colonial administrative policy that transformed the preexisting political order. Some threatened local Muslim rulers capitalized on the political uncertainties of the earlier years of colonial rule to incite disaffected Muslim clerics against British colonial authorities and their local interlocutors. While some colonial administrators thought the Mahdist threats were exaggerated, Lethem's intelligence reports emphasized that some new colonial policies made Mahdist doctrine attractive to the masses of poor Muslims, especially marginalized Fulanis. In truth, the rise of Mahdist doctrine among the Fulani coincided with harsh colonial policies, especially the imposition of jangali taxes and other levies. Indeed, local Fulani clerics tailored Mahdist doctrine to the prevailing political context, even going so far as to appropriate the legacy of Usman dan Fodio as a manifestation of Mahdism.[17]

Mahdism had evolved into a movement of international significance when Muhammad Ahmad adapted its basic principles to form a radically enhanced religious strand, with the capacity for fierce military resistance against foreign incursion. Its main purpose was to fight imperial rule in his native Sudan in the late nineteenth century; later the movement would confront "enemies of Islam" in Ethiopia and Egypt.[18] Thus the Mahdiyya state was created in the 1880s to serve as the political base of the Mahdi movement; the entity never gained sovereign standing in international law, though it provided an organizational platform for its adherents to confront British and Egyptian forces.[19] Ahmad's success in creating a political community that challenged colonial rule, at least in the short term, meant that Mahdism was capable of providing an alternative vision for those who saw British rule as anathema.[20] Mahdism's popularity across various religious and social groups meant that it extended beyond the purview of localized political issues. When Ahmad proclaimed a jihad against the Egyptian and British governments following their attempt to arrest him, he gained a large number of recruits among the Baqqara and notable leaders of the Rizeigat and Ta'aisha "tribes."[21] In addition to establishing itself in the Sahel, according to Lethem, Ahmad's Mahdism gained influence in some areas that would constitute Northern Nigeria. After Ahmad's death, Abdullahi ibn Muhammad emerged as the new leader of the Mahdist state, and the struggle continued unabated. He refused to cooperate with religious movements in neighboring countries, such as Ethiopia, which offered to join with the Mahdists against European powers.[22] Instead, Muhammad led attacks on Ethiopia, Egypt, and Eritrea.

In the early twentieth century, Abd Al Rahman emerged as the leader of the Mahdist movement, drawing on the broad support of his predecessors.[23] British administrators traced the rise and fall of neo-Mahdism (or Abd Al Rahman's Mahdism) in the second and third decades of the twentieth century to Northern Nigeria, keeping track of the movement's prominence in the region. To do this, British intelligence officers in Northern Nigeria communicated with their counterparts in Sudan and Egypt, creating an expansive intelligence apparatus. Lethem's memoranda connected the influence of Mahdism with the improvement of overland communication between East and West and the subsequent circulation of newspapers, letters, and messengers. Lethem seemed to suggest that although the British and French both clamped down on Mahdism in their colonial territories, a lack of coordination of effort undermined the effectiveness of their policies.[24]

Lethem considered Abd Al Rahman an opportunistic rabble-rouser who manipulated information about colonial activities in order to rally local support and to enhance his political power. British administrators nevertheless enlisted his support during World War I to suppress movements sponsored by the Ottoman Empire for a jihad against British occupation. Abd Al Rahman traveled through the Nile Valley to spread a message of strategic support for the British through a more restrained interpretation of Islam, and as he did so, he also expanded his power, wealth, and popularity. His messengers, who were meant to drum up support for Britain, collected *zakat* taxes for Abd Al Rahman and encouraged adherents to use the Mahdist prayer book. In the years following World War I, Abd Al Rahman made similar calculated decisions, offering official interpretation of Islam that enabled him to promote his power under British colonial rule.[25]

Lethem's papers reveal how religious interpretations shaped political dynamics in the Northern Provinces in the early decades of colonial rule. By the second decade of colonial rule, Lugard, through the mechanisms of indirect rule, had embraced Fulani Muslim interpretations that drew on the religious vision of Usman dan Fodio, squashing opposing religious movements in the region. Lugard had defeated various Islamic potentates, such as the sultan of Sokoto, Muhammadu Attahira I, in the Battle of Burmi in 1903. Remnants of radical opposition to British rule within the caliphate were also suppressed: in 1905–1906, Mahdist uprisings were brutally crushed in Satiru by the combined forces of the British and the Sokoto Caliphate; indeed, the whole town was destroyed, and two thousand Mahdist rebels and fugitive slaves were killed.[26] Satiru was a Mahdist stronghold, and Satiruwa, the people of Satiru, had to pay the bitter price of rebellion because their Mahdist ideology threatened the new order. British authorities and the Sokoto Caliphate found common ground to collaborate against Satiru because both felt a deep sense of political insecurity. The British felt threatened because its hold on power was tenuous, and Sokoto was rattled because "revolutionary" Mahdism was a Hausa-based movement of "peasants, fugitive slaves, and radical clerics who were hostile both to the indigenous authorities and the colonial regime."[27] Fear of a common enemy therefore cemented the partnership between British authorities and caliphate rulers,[28] though pockets of resistance continued to pose minor security threats to British rule until the amalgamation of the Northern and Southern Nigerian Protectorates in 1914.[29]

Frontal attack by the colonial authorities on fringe "Islamic radical" elements was mostly effective by the 1920s. For example, in 1924, the *shehu* of Bornu, under the prompting of British administrators, identified sources of potential anti-British revolts, encouraged moderate interpretations of Islam, and arrested "carriers of seditious propaganda." Furthermore, to combat what authorities considered "Islamic fanaticism," British colonial rulers prohibited pilgrimage to the Mahdi holy site in Aba in Sudan in 1923.[30]

Lethem's work is relevant to this study not just because his intelligence reports and memoranda underscored the relations between Islamic doctrine and British colonial rule, but more importantly because he identified conflict triggers that presumably could threaten the colonial order. For example, Lethem focused on the social and political interactions among "fringe" Muslim orders such as the Nazaru and warned that the strict way in which the Nazaru *tariqa* structured the lives of its followers suggested a proclivity for religious intolerance. The Nazaru, Lethem observes, "despise other Muslims, refusing to eat, intermarry, drink, shake hands, or pray with them.... They also would not eat meat prepared by other Muslims and they had to convert" their prospective partners before marriage. Lethem's account of religious "propaganda" in Bornu and other Northern Nigerian communities illustrates that religious interpretations could become freighted with political intent. He wanted colonial administrators and missionaries to work together to stem the strong opposition of some "fanatical" Islamic movements to Western institutions such as Christian schools and hospitals. He advised British colleagues to allay the fears of Muslim clerics about the dangers of Western cultural intrusion. A vast knowledge about local cultures and of their precolonial relations in their setting was evident in Lethem's memoranda, indicating that specific tariqas had differing attitudes toward colonial powers. He noted that Fulani peasants preferred the British to other colonial powers, especially the French and Germans, who had been hostile to the Ouddai regime. The Sanussiyya fought against the British in World War I, but eventually embraced colonial rule by the 1920s. The tijaniyya placed enormous emphasis on loyalty and fairness; they thought the British colonial regime in the region could be trusted.[31]

Lethem's proclivity for details seems self-evident: his memoranda are replete with detailed accounts of many personalities and activities that most colonial administrators in his position would have considered too marginal to the central purpose of colonial intelligence. But Lethem deployed extensive analytical fervor to capture, for example, a religious leader in Bornu (1924) who was preaching the inevitability of an impending millenarian event—a condition that was supposedly linked to colonial domination. The imam was said to have attracted a large crowd and drew significant ovation when he chastised the colonial government and called local Muslim supporters of the colonial administration *kufar*, or unbelievers.

In similar fashion, Lethem's memoranda reveals that political and religious crises in Sudan and Egypt had significant effects on political developments in Northern Nigeria. For example, in the notable case of Bornu he writes about various messengers from the East who predicted the imminent arrival of Isa—the chosen one—who will precipitate the millenarian event. His findings about the crisis in Egypt drew from systematic analyses of political and religious events and included clear narratives of their consequences. His repeated attempts to decipher the causes of religious riots in the Sudan in September 1924 are striking: he investigated a popular imam in Khartoum and his alleged role in inciting riots; commented extensively on the leadership qualities of Ali Abd al Latif (the founder of the White Flag League); and examined the crisis in Gordon Memorial College, Sudan's elite institution of higher learning. Importantly, Lethem reports that the Sudanese crisis might have influenced unrest in Northern Nigeria, especially Bornu. In all of this we can see that Lethem was acutely concerned about the underpinnings of religion-based conflict and defined strategies to mitigate its worst consequences.[32] He demonstrated how the main contours of religious interpretations could fuse with ethnic differences to explode violent crises. In this regard, Lethem insists that the new wave of Mahdism was linked to Fulani aspirations about the future.[33]

With improvement in regional communication and infrastructure in the early twentieth century, religious doctrines steadily spread throughout Northern Nigerian communities. Lethem was exasperated that better means of communication and travel were facilitating the spread of Mahdism into parts of Northern Nigeria. He warned as follows: religion is a major instrument for mobilizing the "masses" in Northern Nigeria across cultural divisions; and Mahdism's message is effective in arousing the "ignorant and credulous African Mohammedan to fanaticism and unrest." But what seemed to disturb him most was that Mahdism had been used to unify some Fulani communities across the Sahel against colonialism.[34]

Native Administration and the Imposition of Islamic Law

Once the Sokoto Caliphate fell in 1903 to the military onslaught of Colonel Lugard,[35] what followed was the imposition of indirect rule on the diverse communities that constituted Britain's Northern Nigerian Protectorate, a region in 1906 that had three hundred thousand square miles and 7 million people, under the control of just seventy-five British military officers.[36] Lugard specifically picked Northern Nigeria for the implementation of his indirect rule system because it was considered an ideal environment to test a decentralized administration, already practiced on a smaller scale in India and Uganda.[37] Taxation was reformed within the bounds of Islamic doctrine, resulting in rapidly increasing revenues. In a 1903 treaty, Lugard guaranteed Fulani rulers that British authorities would not interfere with the practice of Islam; he soon would renege on this promise.[38] As Murray Last writes, the experience of subordination of emirate rulers to a Western (Christian) power must have been a disjuncture of enormous dimensions:

> Here the reader needs to go back briefly to mid-March 1903 and imagine the full shock of having Christian colonial rule suddenly imposed upon you, with the vast, century-old Sokoto Caliphate defeated within the space of a few months. Dar al-Islam was no more; the legacy of Shaikh Uthman dan Fodio [Usman dan Fodio] and his son the Amir almu'minin Muhammad Bello come to naught. And it was Muslim Hausa troops

recruited in Kano, under a few white Christian officers, using bigger and faster-firing guns more professionally than the Sokoto or Kano armies could muster, that did the damage.[39]

Doubtlessly, the region's legal systems were modified to comply with British conception of law and justice.[40] The Native Courts Proclamation Numbers 4 and 5 gave British authorities broad powers of review over Islamic courts, which in principle subjugated sharia to colonial law; and special provisions deriving from it offered non-Muslims protection against the application of some aspects of sharia, and eliminated harsh punishment following convictions for murder, theft, and adultery.[41] Proclamation Number 6 of 1900 (amended in 1901) further regulated Islamic law and transformed alkali courts into formal native courts for indigenes while also establishing common-law courts for British subjects.[42] Most controversial, however, was the establishment of what would become known as the Repugnancy Test,[43] which dictated that punishment found to be "repugnant to natural justice, equity, and good conscience"[44] would be instantly overturned—a sort of *deus ex machina* clause that ensured no British territory would enforce "unconscionable" legal sentences.[45] This included punishments such as cutting off limbs, stoning, and crucifixion.[46] All crimes punishable by death in sharia that were treated as lesser crimes under English common law were reclassified to conform with common-law standards.[47] Moreover, sharia was subject to the authority of British administrators,[48] which ensured that local application of laws did not conflict with written law promulgated by British administrators. The British conception of justice was also infused into Islamic law and practices.[49] For example, alkali courts were compelled to accept police and medical reports as evidence, as well as the testimony of non-Muslims, despite strong objections from Muslim clerics based on Maliki law.[50] Some scholars have noted that British authorities gave Muslim jurists some authority in civil litigation and reviewed only a small percentage of criminal cases for compatibility with repugnancy standards.[51] Be that as it may, the main thrust of reform in the caliphate's legal system was definitive and deliberate.

The Native Courts Proclamation of 1906 further weakened sharia by broadening English common-law courts and streamlining native courts from a four-tier system into a two-tier system.[52] The Judicial Council was created to serve essentially as an Islamic court of appeal. In addition, Islamic law was denied recognition as a system deserving separate jurisdiction unto itself when it was merged with customary law during the unification of Nigeria's Northern and Southern Provinces in 1914.[53] The unification ordinance also dictated that customary judicial sentencing could not break from the requirements of common-law courts, particularly in criminal cases.[54] Most importantly, it extended the Northern court system to the south, violating long-standing principles of separation of jurisdiction between these two very different regions.[55] Reform continued with the 1922 Constitution,[56] as further changes to the criminal and penal codes and the structure of the judicial system eroded the authority of Islamic law. Furthermore, the colonial government took a major step with the Native Courts Ordinance of 1933, which further weakened sharia by expanding the power of common-law courts. High courts were created[57] and given jurisdiction over appeals from native courts (including sharia), an arrangement that lasted until independence in 1960.

Despite the influence of common law on sharia, Islam grew steadily with the modernization that accompanied colonialism. This can be attributed to improved communications among local communities, increased security, better political organization of emirate society, more effective administrative control of non-Muslim regions by emirate rulers through the indirect rule system, and access to modern elementary school education.[58] Most researchers say the last factor was most significant because improvements in education served to link diverse peoples together, especially those who relocated to the cities in search of work. Indeed, this rapid process of social change was significantly encouraged by the arrival of the Lagos-Kano railway in 1912, bringing thousands of Southern Christian migrants who stimulated economic growth in the region. This heterogeneous mix of people, consisting of Christian migrants from the south and Hausa-Fulani Muslim settlers in non-Muslim sections of the Northern Nigerian Protectorate, as well as numerous non-Muslim "tribal" groups throughout the region, were effectively brought under the control of caliphate rulers within the indirect rule system. In the specific case of Zaria, Moses Ochonu underscores the subordination of non-Hausa Muslim peoples to Hausa-Fulani Muslim rule under the indirect rule system:

> Through a long, convoluted process, Zazzau [Zaria] emirate, a strategic frontier caliphate state, came to extend a loose political influence on the non-Muslim Southern Kaduna polities. In the early twentieth century, the British accelerated this historical process. They vested authority in Zazzau, its satellite emirates, and its officials and brought the southern Kaduna peoples under their sway. British imposition of Zazzau subcolonial rule on the Southern Kaduna peoples culminated in a complicated and volatile subcolonial administrative system comprised of Hausa-Fulani colonial chiefs, scribes, administrators, tax collectors, and other colonial operatives working for the British.[59]

A 1917 survey on the social diversity of Keffi and Nasarawa emirates by Resident Morgan further illustrates this complex mix of communities under Hausa-Fulani Muslim rule. Christians of any ethnicity were left uncounted, while nearly 20,000 Muslims were tallied, 75 percent of whom were Fulani and Hausa (with 584 Nupe Muslims). The survey found nearly three times as many "pagans," totaling roughly 55,000 persons, split among Bassa, Gwari-Gangan, Yeskwa, Afo, Gwandara, Igbera, Gade, Agatu, Kinkera, Gwari Yamma, Koro Funtu, Koro, Gana, Toni, Kamberi, and Arago peoples. In addition, the report ruminates on demographic shifts in earlier years, particularly the widespread migration by the "hill top villagers of the pagan tribes" from their overcrowded and "unsanitary" sites to new villages in the open, level country, establishing new farms. However, far from chipping away at Hausa-Fulani Muslim power, the report shows that early British administrators consolidated Hausa-Fulani Muslim hegemony "with detached pleasure."[60] Consequently, the ethno-religious tension that dominated Nigeria's Middle Belt and core Northern Muslim areas with significant non-Muslim communities (so-called pagans) by the period of decolonization in the 1950s was already apparent in the early colonial period. An extract from the 1907 annual report by Thomas Alvarez, a CMS missionary to the CMS secretary in London, is instructive:

> Mr. Low appears to have given the idea in England that the Society wished the Gwari work to be conducted through the medium of Hausa, i.e. that the Gwaris were to be instructed in Hausa and that the scriptures were not to be translated into Gwari. I cannot help feeling that Mr. Low is mistaken, or there has been some misunderstanding of the members of the Gwari tribe. The Gwaris are the most numerous and compact pagan tribe in Northern Nigeria and to endeavor to reach them by means of the language of their inveterate enemies the Hausa-speaking raiders is to my mind ridiculous. . . . So I shall be grateful if you assure Mr. Low that CMS mean to take up the Gwari work seriously and encourage him to try and master the language.[61]

The influence of Hausa-Fulani Muslim rulers also was enhanced in native administration and native courts throughout the Northern Protectorate. For example, in 1931, in Kano Province, British administrators established a mixed court to provide legal services to non-Muslims under the authority of the waziri (the Muslim chief judge), who held power of appeal. And in 1940, the Kano *sabon gari*—the areas of non-Hausa-Fulani native settlers—was placed under the emir's control for the first time since 1903.[62]

The Limits of Indirect Rule

What was stipulated in the legal reforms analyzed above was not always easily reflected in colonial administrative practice. Firsthand accounts of the implementation of local government policies by British administrators on the complicated process of colonial administration reveal the complexities of their rule in Northern Nigeria's diverse communities. In this connection, the memoranda of long-serving administrators revealed how British officials attempted to reinforce the bond between religious, social, and political hierarchies of power in a region where such relations were fluid under the Sokoto Caliphate in the preceding precolonial era.

Commander J. H. Carrow (district officer and resident of Kano and Sokoto) provides a vivid illustration of the challenges to the implementation of colonial policy in a region where the balance between religious, social, and political power was far from clearly defined. After British administrators adopted indirect rule in Kano, they convinced the emir of Kano to reorganize the judicial, financial, and political structure under his authority along the lines of what British administrators considered acceptable Islamic rules. In addition to reforms in the native courts and the tax system, British administrators introduced fixed salaries for native administrators, including the emir. Significantly, to implement their reform, British authorities appealed to what they projected as Kano's Muslim traditions.[63]

While the inhabitants of Sokoto Division were loyal to the sultan of Sokoto as the Sarkin Musulumi (commander of the Muslim faithful), those in Kano Division had conflicting allegiances, presumably because of Kano internecine conflicts in earlier decades and the colonial administrators' initial application of direct rule in the region. The deposition of the waziri of Kano in 1909 is an example of the complicated nature of political allegiances in Kano Emirate. In 1908, British officials appointed Dan Rimi, a "slave" from the Warji "tribe," as waziri. Before he was appointed, Rimi was a confidant of the emir and had served as a messenger to the resident. Once appointed waziri, Rimi separated himself from the authority of the emir, claiming that he was the "appointee of the white man." Rimi soon had his own following and was eventually charged by the emir with contravening Kano's "time-honored traditions." Because of growing instability in the division, the governor sacked Rimi in 1909 and replaced him with a Fulani, a loyal of the emir.[64]

The events surrounding this brief colonial saga in Kano illustrate the varied dimensions of power relations in the Fulani emirates in those years. Even though the Sokoto Caliphate had existed for a century, internecine conflict remained a persistent problem between various groups in Kano Emirate, hampering the ability of the emir, district heads, village heads, chiefs, and various Muslim clerics to effectively rule in their communities. In Kano Province, like many other emirates in the Northern Provinces, communal allegiances were tangled with religious associations. Rimi's ability to gather a significant following under the banner of the "white man" suggests that power within the emirate was not a simple, linear chain of command through the emirate structure. The governor's response to the incident illustrates that colonial administrators sought to centralize the Muslim hierarchy under the leadership of the emir. As he tried to stabilize the upper echelons of the caliphate, the governor relied on his understanding of ethnic conflict, appointing a Fulani, imposing ethnic and hierarchical differences that in fact were not firmly in place when the British conquered the caliphate in 1903.

Resident C. L. Temple's 1909 annual report on Kano Province reveals the ambiguity between legitimacy and authority of Kano Emirate officials. Temple notes that a local leader might often fail to follow the orders of superior members in the emirate. The subdistrict head of Damberta refused to collect the *haraji* tax even though he had been ordered to begin collection several months beforehand; he felt that he had the leeway to conduct his administrative responsibility as he pleased. Temple also mentioned that three sarkis (Sarkin Kura, Sarkin Godia, and Sarkin Kabba) had embezzled funds from the jangali tax they had collected from Fulani "pagans." The overt nature of the sarkis' embezzlement of tax funds reveals that Muslim village heads were not always under the firm control of the emir. When British officers called the embezzlement to the emir's attention, he failed to see the seriousness of the charges, revealing the tendency of some Muslim rulers to ignore British policy.[65]

Despite these underlying conditions, British policies on recruitment to political leadership positions in the Kano Emirate streamlined a tight-knit clique of potential rulers from the established Fulani hierarchy. Temple's 1909 report further reveals that when leaders were deposed for perceived opposition to British policies, their replacements often were drawn from the emir's court. When Chiroma Hamsa (one of the Madaki's subdistrict head men) was deposed after he "failed to fulfill his duties," the emir, with the support of the resident, divided Hamsa's jurisdiction into two parts. The first part was placed under the leadership of Umaru, a son of Madaki Hassan; the younger brother of Hamsa, Malam Aliu, was appointed as the leader of the second district.[66]

The actions of local community leaders reflected their pliant nature in the Kano emirate's politico-religious hierarchy. Temple's report describes local people applying to several local authorities for the adjudication of Islamic law. In conjunction with a growing distrust in the Islamic courts, local people presented their cases to British district officers, suggesting some lack of confidence in the Muslim order derived from the Sokoto Caliphate.[67]

The persistence of slavery added another important layer to the structures of Muslim rule in local communities. Despite the outlawing of slavery in the Northern Protectorate by the British authorities, Temple revealed that slavery remained widespread in Kano Province. Following the famine of 1907–1908, many slave owners quietly transferred their slaves to more affluent slaveholders, and according to District Officer Dupigny, some Gongola "pagans" voluntarily "sold" themselves to wealthy slave owners. The relationship between slaves and slaveholders provided another layer to the hierarchy of social relations in some of Kano Province's communities, often lying beyond the control of the native authority system.

In the face of dynamic political conditions, British officials, with mixed success, attempted to create an overarching colonial order across the Northern Provinces. They worked feverishly to modify the preexisting sociopolitical structure with a more effective local administrative system premised on what they considered legitimate Muslim traditions. In this vein, they insisted on specific Muslim "rules" that affirmed colonial administrative priorities in the levying of taxes and rents. For example, Temple wrote that rents and taxes, based on "Islamic law," would be collected within fixed time frames. The jangali tax was to be collected between July 1 and October 31, while the zakka and haraji was meant to be collected from November 30 to March 31. Temple also stated that district and subdistrict heads had been informed that they would lose their positions if they did not turn in the requisite amount of taxes and rents by the stipulated dates. His report further revealed that there was evidence of the tightening control that British administrators were placing on local rulers: for example, as noted above, the district officer and the emir replaced Damberta; they deposed Sarkis Kura, Godia, and Kabbo for the embezzlement of jangali tax, and deposed Chiroma Hamsa for administrative irregularities.[68]

The tendency of the British to affirm Hausa-Fulani Muslim rulers' conservatism was best shown in the crucial area of colonial policy on education in the Northern Provinces. Carrow's recollection in the 1960s of what stood for British education policy in Kano Province provides a vivid assessment of colonial policy in the region. Before World War I, British administrators had established a Western-type primary school for the children of emirs, chiefs, and Muslim clerics, but these local rulers instead sent their slaves to school. Further, local ambivalence for Western education also was apparent with the poor enrollment of students in another primary school that colonial authorities established in a "pagan" area of Kano Division before the outbreak of World War II. Carrow recalls that the resistance to Western education persisted until the end of the war. Not surprisingly, when British authorities established a school for girls in 1929, opposition from the Hausa-Fulani Muslim rulers was stiff. These rulers naturally believed that Western education would not give their children the requisite religious and traditional training that emirate society required.[69] In the early decades of colonial rule, Islamic schooling remained the dominant form of education in the region. In 1913 there were only 209 Northerners in British schools, but more than 140,000 students in 19,073 Islamic schools; the next year enrollment figures were 527 (British government schools) and 218,615 (Islamic schools) respectively, with only 1,682 in mission schools in the vast Northern Nigerian Provinces. Nevertheless, the marginalization of Western education before World War II led to the crisis that would consume Northern Nigeria for many decades. In the short term, this crisis was evident in the inability of the colonial authorities to carry out basic administrative functions, including staffing the Kano medical dispensaries and administering native courts in the 1920s and 1930s.[70]

As British administrators sought to close the gap between theory and practice in local administration, Hausa-Fulani Muslim rulers were content to use the evolving native authority system to legitimate their power and authority. Tensions again were apparent in Carrow's account in Sokoto and Kano Provinces. In 1932, the Resident of Sokoto sacked the sultan that was appointed in 1924 after persistent fiscal "irregularities" and charges that he practiced "black magic." The new sultan, with the waziri, regularly used religious practices to affirm colonial authority in the Sokoto Caliphate. Although the sultan's religious practices were not always clear to Carrow—who became Resident of Sokoto in 1933—Carrow did think they advanced British colonial influence in the province. For example, he recalled how the sultan and the waziri would take him to the tomb of Usman dan Fodio to pray for Carrow's safe travel each time before traveling out of the province.[71]

Additionally, British administrators were selective about prevailing interpretations of Islam. They picked their battles, as did their caliphate junior partners, and also disagreed on which battles to pick. Although it was easier to administer Sokoto than Kano, Carrow was able to convince the religiously conservative emir of Kano, Abdullahi Bayero, to ban stoning for adultery. Even though there was not a single account of stoning in Northern Nigeria, Carrow felt a need to alter the law so as to state emphatically that Kano Division was in compliance with the British authorities' repugnancy rule. Emir Bayero promptly agreed with Carrow's request, since such a question was largely irrelevant among the custodians of local state administration in the Kano Emirate. Furthermore, when renowned British colonial researcher Margery Perham attempted to gain access to the main section of the chief alkali court in Kano in 1930 and 1931, British administrators refused to overturn the objection of the chief alkali.[72]

Carrow recounts a moment of frustration while working with Emir Bayero of Kano in the early 1920s that illustrates the challenges experienced by colonial administrators when they attempted to apply abstract theory of indirect rule to Northern Nigeria's strong yet sometimes opaque religious environment. When a series of native administration construction projects began and a British engineer requested Western-trained workers, Carrow appointed two Northern Christians who had grown up in a mission school in Zaria, on the condition that they wear traditional Muslim attires and turbans so as not to offend the sensibility of Muslim rulers. Although Carrow felt he had resolved a sensitive problem, he found to his "horror" that Emir Bayero had figured out that the two men were in fact Northern Christians. In a private conversation, the emir told the Resident that he would rather have "a full-blooded Southerner" than an "apostolic Northerner" working on the project.[73]

Carrow also believed that colonial administrators' failure to create a more self-reliant native administration undermined the implementation of indirect rule. He said that Kano was far from the modernizing city some British administrators tended to project. Carrow thought real progress in the Northern Provinces could be achieved only when the native administration began taking responsibility for its own work instead of looking for direction from the district officer. He recalls returning to Kano as Resident in 1943 from Sokoto only to find the "old nonsense" he had left behind a decade before when he was district officer.

Implicit in the assessments of British administrators are tensions between colonial administrators who insisted on preserving the essence of the caliphate system and officers who believed by the 1920s that Northern Nigeria required a more efficient administrative system. No senior colonial administrator in the 1920s exemplifies the tension between these two critical positions better than Herbert Richmond Palmer, lieutenant governor of the Northern Provinces from 1925 to 1930. To confront this problem, Palmer undercut the autocracy of the Islamic aristocracy, while working hard to prop up the mystique of the emirs and members of their courts. In the case of Kano Province, Palmer attempted to modernize the emirate by limiting the power of the emir and his courts. Thus when the elderly and conservative emir died in 1925, Palmer seized the opportunity to push through substantial reforms that significantly altered the province's political landscape. Along with other leading members of

Kano native authority, Palmer urged the new emir to sign on to several reforms before his inauguration. However, to protect the public image of the new emir, Palmer, during the emir's installation in 1927, directed his assistants to create the impression that the emir was the towering political figure in the province from whom all authority flowed down to his subjects.[74]

In the Katagum Division of Bauchi Province in the 1920s colonial administrators sought to make local administration more efficient by reforming the native authority system, including Islamic law that had proven inefficient since the early twentieth century. A careful reading of Assistant District Officer J. C. Guy's touring diary reveals that the inefficiency British administrators attributed to emirs, district heads, and village heads was not always a simple matter of ineptitude, but was sometimes a result of the novel rules of administration that the British imposed in the district. Despite claims that colonial administrative policies were derived from local Islamic traditions, a careful reading of Guy's file reveals that Hausa-Fulani Muslim rulers were not always knowledgeable about the rules inscribed as Islamic law on taxation. For example, the difficulty in implementing jangali tax (cattle tax) in Katagum communities was a reflection of the imposition of uniform jangali tax practices on the diverse communities in the district. When local district heads and village heads recorded significant jangali tax deficits, Guy reprimanded them, threatened to cut their salaries, and persecuted them for criminal neglect. With regard to the application of Islamic law to the reformed judicial system, Guy notes in his memorandum that it would be "useless to imagine or expect them [district heads and village heads] to be paragons of efficiency in Malinka Law." Indeed, the degree to which Guy went to instruct local leaders on how to administer this colonial interpretation of Islamic law would indicate the extent of the novelty of these rules in Katagum communities.[75]

The dynamics of local administration in the Northern Nigerian Provinces were shaped by power configurations of Hausa-Fulani Muslim rulers and the complicated communal identities in local communities. Again, in Sokoto Province, the implication of this problem was apparent in the contradiction between colonial taxation and prevailing communal conditions in the earlier decades of colonial rule. Although British administrators made some gains in implementing the new colonial policy, the elimination of some precolonial tax practices discouraged effective tax assessment and collection. Old *gaisu* taxes and other taxes between major and tributary communities persisted, complicating the implementation of British policies. In addition, British administrators failed to establish an effective strategy of tax collection among nomadic Fulani herders. And as emirs and their local agents reconciled themselves to

British colonial expectations in tax collection, many of these leaders found their new positions at variance to those of the local communities. This problem was manifested in the changing patterns of the use of jakadas[76] for the collection of taxes. In contrast to their precolonial functions where they served multiple roles as intermediaries between Muslim rulers and local communities, emirs now employed the services of the jakadas largely for tax collection. This reflected the patterns of violent appropriation of resources that occurred prior to colonial rule, exacerbating tension between Hausa-Fulani Muslim rulers and local communities, especially those designated as "traditional" tributary communities.[77]

The nature of local administration meant that local rulers and communities responded to the colonial government depending on their ethnic and religious identities within newly drawn colonial jurisdictions. In the Kuta Division of Niger Province, the way native authority subsumed hierarchical relations among diverse ethnic groups under imposed administrative jurisdiction also complicated social relations that had been fluid during the precolonial period. Kuta Division, like most areas in the Northern Provinces, was religiously and culturally diverse. Some groups were still functioning under the precolonial tributary Kofa system, where local people sought the patronage of the emir through his leading men, usually a member of the emir's council.[78]

The British adoption of Hausa-Fulani Muslim rule also reified the ethnic and religious practices that the Fulani had established after the conquest of the Hausa city-states, especially with regard to tax collection and assessment in the early twentieth century. In Agaie-Lapai Division, British colonial reforms enhanced the status of Hausa-Fulani Muslim rulers as gatekeepers of the indirect rule system, cementing the marginalization of non-Hausa-Fulani local communities. This division—which included Lapai Emirate, an amalgamation of Guara, Gulu, Gupa, Edzu, and Sakka districts; Agaie Emirate; and Baro, a third-class township—contained many so-called pagans (Gana-Gana, Gupachi people, and Hausa and Gwari farmers), while Lapai was inhabited principally by ex-slaves of the ruling families. According to Assistant District Officer Matthews's 1919 notes, emirs, district heads, and village heads only had limited success with this motley collection of religious and "tribal" groups. Many of these groups evaded tax collection and the native administrative structure. But not all non-Hausa-Fulani Muslims resisted the new native authority. In Kuta Division, for example, some Gwari headmen manipulated the new indirect rule system under the domination of the Hausa-Fulani Muslim aristocracy as a source of power and influence.[79] Taxation and legal practices before colonization in Northern Nigeria were immensely complex, and they had strong ethnic, religious, political, and martial significance. Indeed, taxation and

Islam and Colonial Rule 57

Muslim legal practices under the indirect rule system were woven into prevailing but contingent networks of power and status. When British colonial rulers attempted to mold the indirect rule system into such interlocking religious, social, and political networks, they experienced mixed results.

This ambivalence between local leaders and their subjects was most profoundly reflected in the political domination of the Hausa-Fulani Muslim ruler over the so-called pagan tribes in the Northern Provinces. As early as the late 1920s, senior colonial administrators in Kaduna and Lagos, drawing on extensive intelligence reports and memoranda of district officers and residents from the Northern Provinces, were well aware that communal and religious divisions posed major problems to local administration throughout the region. E. P. T. Crampton notes:

> One of the problems that faced Lugard was the administration of the "pagans" of the North. The non-Muslim animistic peoples were usually referred to as "pagans," but the word is less used now [1970s] as most of these people who are in contact with the outside world would claim to be Muslim or Christians. There were "pagans" in every province, but especially in hilly, or thickly forested or remote areas. In some parts the conquest by the Fulani was virtually complete and the "pagans" were subdued and living under the control of their own petty village or hamlet heads under the suzerainty of Fulani District Heads. In other parts the conquest was far from complete and the "pagan" was in continual rebellion. In yet other parts, no real attempt had been made to subdue them and they were independent. What Lugard did in these different cases was to be of great importance in their subsequent social and religious history.... It can hardly be doubted that the practice of placing large number of "pagans" under Fulani [Muslim] District Head and supporting the authority of these by the powers of the Government when and where necessary led to the expansion of Islam.[80]

In Adamawa Province from 1905 to 1921, for example, the imposition of Hausa-Fulani Muslims as "natural" rulers of Yunguru "pagans" would lead to tragic consequences. When Yunguru resistance against Hausa-Fulani tax collectors led to the killing of the British-imposed Hausa ruler, his associate, and Hausa settlers, a British-led punitive force massacred Yunguru villagers.[81] And in Idoma in the lower Benue region of the Northern Protectorate, District Officer T. E. Letchworth recorded strong resistance of local people to the Hausa-Fulani Muslim hierarchy, noting that a stranger to the area was "likely to have his head taken off," especially if he was Hausa.[82]

Sir Hugh Clifford, governor of Nigeria from 1919 to 1925, convinced about the serious problems ethnic and religious tensions posed to local administration, tried to introduce reforms that were sensitive to religious and communal diversity, as well as the changing demographic transformation of the Northern Provinces. Such recognition of the region's complicated demographic character by Clifford was at variance with the orthodoxy of old-guard Lugardians in the Northern Nigerian colonial service whom the governor distrusted. Clifford was clear from the onset that religious and ethnic differences throughout the region had a significant bearing on the legitimacy of the native authority system. On examining the "pagan tribes" of the Bauchi Plain, the governor found that masses of local people had opposed taxation because of their age-old antagonism and animosity. To local "tribes" in the Bauchi Plains, British colonial taxation was seen as an offshoot of the slave raids of Hausa-Fulani Muslim rulers after the Sokoto Jihad of the previous century. Despite British administrators' claims that a significant portion of taxes would be used to provide essential social services in local communities, the leaders of the Plain "tribes" contended that the only difference between the extractive practices of Hausa-Fulani Muslim rulers of the caliphate era and Britain's colonial taxes lay in the irritating regularity with which British administrators insisted on the payment of taxes. To rectify this problem, Clifford called for the creation of new administrative units that would promote the aspirations of non-Hausa-Fulani communities. For Muslim immigrants of the Bauchi Plains, Clifford called for the establishment of a special judicial system composed of alkali courts to only adjudicate Muslim legal matters. With regard to the relation between Hausa-Fulani Muslims and numerous non-Hausa-Fulani Muslim groups in the Bauchi Plains, Clifford concluded:

> The pagan tribes of the Bauchi Plateau succeeded in maintaining their independence and end up having succeeded in repelling successive Mohammedan invasions. The Plateau therefore is not and never has been Mohammedan country, and the Hausa and other Muslim settlers, who have established themselves there since our advent, have no more claim or right to exercise administrative authority over any part of it, or over any of its indigenous inhabitants, than has any other section of the immigrant community. Moreover, experience gained in other parts of the Mohammedan world has made me profoundly distrustful of the use which Muslims are accustomed to make of any power which they may seek here over a primitive, non-Mohammedan peoples.[83]

Clifford's executive order signaled an important break from Lugard's policy of indirect rule, which vested the authority of the colonial administrative system in Hausa-Fulani emirate rulers that emerged from the Sokoto Jihad. In Bauchi Province, the theory of indirect rule that had established its traditional claims on the hierarchy of culturally superior Hausa-Fulani Muslim rulers over inferior "pagans" was flawed even at its conception. Yet it would be incorrect to suggest that Clifford's declaration in the Bauchi Plains amounted to a wholesale repudiation of the indirect rule system.

The implementation of British colonial policy thus varied greatly across the Northern Nigerian Provinces, resulting in protracted debates among colonial officials. For Clifford, local confidence in indirect rule required "order" and "justice," and only after gaining the confidence of local communities would colonial taxation be justified, especially to those who did not fall neatly under the authority of the Sokoto Caliphate. Interestingly, the acting secretary under Clifford, S. M. Grier, had a view that resembled Clifford's, but his perception of "pagan" communities appears to differ. Like Clifford, Grier's memoranda reflected the idea that people in "pagan" communities lived under moral and social conditions that were inferior to those of Hausa-Fulani Muslim rulers. But instead of characterizing the extraction of tax from "pagans" as coercive, Grier claimed that pagan communities did not expect or hope for any better condition. Where Clifford leaves open the possibility that "pagan" communities wanted but could not attain less coercive forms of taxation, Grier claims that "pagans" could not conceive of a different state. For Grier, then, indirect rule had more to do with compelling the "pagan tribes" to embrace a higher moral order and a superior form of life.[84]

The response of G. J. Lethem, as district officer of Dikwa District, to these imperial discussions on the implementation of indirect rule is instructive because it offers a way one British administrator interpreted the complexities of religious and communal identity in local communities under his jurisdiction. The files reveal that although certain practices on taxation were discouraged by Clifford's administration, Lethem felt compelled to allow them to continue in remote areas of Dikwa District. In response to Grier and Clifford, Lethem contended that effective adjudication of legal codes had to take specific local conditions into account. Unlike his superiors in Lagos and Kaduna, Lethem contends that legal rules had significant social functions that continue to mediate social relations. Rather than intervene when he toured so-called pagan communities, Lethem claimed that he used the shehu's name (the name of the Muslim ruler in the district), thereby aligning himself with prevailing networks of power. Lethem's interpretation of colonial rule, then, recognized the role of

British collection of taxes, but also believed that preexisting practices did not need to be unduly altered by British colonial reforms.[85]

Assistant District Officer (and later Resident of Bornu Province) T. E. Letchworth's colonial files in Nasarawa Division further reveal the tension between the theory of indirect rule and the reality of local administration among the diverse religious and ethnic groups that constituted Britain's colonial provinces in Northern Nigeria. Like most junior colonial administrators in the Northern Provinces in the 1920s and '30s, Letchworth was not naive about indirect rule's limitations, although only close engagement with the realities "on the ground" gave him a fuller understanding of the extent of the social, political, and religious complexities in Nasarawa Emirate. In Nasarawa, multiple identities were rooted in extensive religious and communal diversity, under the tenuous rule of the emir, district heads, village heads, and Muslim clerics. Lugardian indirect rule had brought these diverse communal groupings under a simplified system that obscured the intricate workings of the emirate's political, religious, and social life. Moreover, the Lugardian system assumed a hierarchy of communities wherein Hausa-Fulani Muslim aristocrats governed as natural rulers over Hausa and Fulani Muslim talakawa and "pagan" tribes. However, these religious and communal identities were far more mutable than indirect rule's simple social stratification would like to admit. By imposing a simplified binary between Islamic aristocratic rulers and the masses of "pagans" in non-Muslim areas of the Northern Protectorate, British administrators not only consolidated the power of emirate rulers, but also accentuated a major politico-religious fault line between the Muslim emirates and communities that adhered to indigenous religious beliefs, many of whom would gradually come under the influence of mission Christianity by the late colonial period in the 1950s. Letchworth would later recall a jarring incident during one of his tours of rural communities under his jurisdiction:

> I had to do the Gade who were mostly in Guada-Guada District I think it was, where three village areas overlap into the home district of the Nasarawa Emirate, which was under a Fulani district head who subsequently became emir, and very early on it became an obvious fact they would have to be lumped into the new Gade District that was to be created for the Gade.... But one illuminating thing happened one day, I was going to one of these villages and we were sitting on the sample saddle of a range of hills.... And I very distinctly heard him [Letchworth's Hausa attendant] say, as the pagans were trekking up the passing, Ga su shanun mu (translation: there they go our cattle). And I thought to myself, this was rather different from what we were taught.[86]

In the simple utterance of the Hausa attendant, Letchworth was immediately aware that the attendant's words did not reflect a central assumption of indirect rule: that Hausa-Fulani Muslim rulers will treat "pagan" tribes as subjects, not, as the metaphor suggests, a means of profit. It is reasonable to assume from Letchworth's statement that his Hausa Muslim attendant did not regard the "pagans" as subjects, at least not as British administrators would have assumed, but rather as a group that was fundamentally different from Hausa-Fulani Muslims, who were deemed natural rulers of the Nasarawa Emirate. Ochonu's conceptualization of Hausa-Fulani Muslim rule over non-Muslims in the Middle Belt is instructive in the rationalization of the indirect rule among the diverse peoples of the Northern Nigerian Protectorate. He notes: "I traced the imperial activities of the defunct Sokoto Caliphates' Hausa-Fulani Muslim agents [of British colonial rulers] in the Middle Belt as they morphed from conducting slave raids and exacting tributes in the mid-nineteenth century... to enforcing subcolonial preparatory rule under the British in the twentieth century."[87]

While British authorities scaled back the more rigid form of the indirect rule system and installed discrete administrative units that recognized the region's communal and religious diversity, the complicated local administrative system persisted throughout the Northern Protectorate even before the outbreak of World War II. For example, in Tangale District in Gombe Division, District Officer J. A. E. Morley's records of tax collection suggest that antagonistic relationships continued to characterize tax assessment and enforcement. The pace of tax collection varied significantly across the district. In some, tax was collected quickly. But in many others, collection was a drawn-out affair that dragged on for many months. When census lines were drawn, British officers knew the more affluent from the poorer areas and had a fair amount of knowledge about the seasonal variants that would affect communities' abilities to pay, as well as when and where crops had done well or failed. It is unlikely, then, that the delays stemmed mainly from mistaken census lines. Instead, the records suggest that the delays occurred because leaders either were unwilling to vigorously enforce the collection of colonial taxes, were simply unable to collect taxes, or embezzled funds collected from taxes.[88]

The proposed reorganization of Waja Native Authority in Gombe Division, based on a secret intelligence report by Assistant District Officer D. T. M. Birks in September 1945, provides vivid insight into the fluid demography of the people who shaped the social landscape of Northern Nigeria. The appropriation, distortion, and manipulation of this history under British colonial rule would continue to influence the processes of decolonization after World

War II. In this account, the creation of local colonial administrative structures reflected the narratives of the highly contentious communal conditions in the early twentieth century, when British colonial rule was imposed, as well as the uncertainties of the early years of colonial rule that were shaped by indirect rule.

Birks's confidential report suggests that colonial rule intensified the process of politico-religious tensions in the area. In the Waja region of the Gombe emirate, indirect rule in the early twentieth century solidified Fulani Muslim domination by formalizing the local administrative structure. In the Plains Waja area, the hegemony of two Fulani Muslim clans led to a growth in religious and political identity, shaping the framework for colonial local administration. According to Birks's report, immediately after the Fulani Jihad, two Fulani clans (Yola and Kukawa) settled in Kunde, near Gombe, an area adjacent to the Waja region. Under the reign of Baba Yero, the Kunde Fulani raided several Plains Waja "tribes," gained political control over them, and eventually achieved a fiefdom over the area. The Kunde Fulani used harsh tactics to subordinate these Waja tribes, burning the resistant Gelengu tribe's village to the ground. However, the Kunde Fulani were unable to gain control over the Hill Waja because their horsemen, although decisive in their subjugation of Plains Waja "tribes," were not effective on the steep hillside of Dogiri.

What followed from the uneven control of Fulani Muslim was a gradual hybridization of the various groups, even as they retained consciously distinct identities. Fulani Muslim rulers in the Waja area more closely identified with the Waja when Emir Kwoiranga married a Waja girl, who became the mother of a later district head of the Waja, Musa Sarkin Yaki (under British colonial rule). Many of the Plains Waja adopted some notable Fulani religious and cultural practices, such as the Waja Tsafi festival called Giwiyendi (or Doki in Hausa). Although several of these groups began to share cultural, religious, political, and lineage ties, they retained distinct identities that characterized a social hierarchy in the region. Despite these ties, Plains Waja "tribes" still paid tributes and homage to their Fulani Muslim rulers, although Fulani control of the area was only a form of suzerainty.

In the case of the Hill Waja, when the British colonized the area in 1906 under the direction of Resident Howard, Birks's intelligence report noted, Waja communities of Reme and Dogiri (what would become the Hill Waja) mounted strong resistance, but British forces ultimately subdued them. Before Howard's departure from the area, he appointed Tukur Sarkin Yaki, a Fulani Muslim ruler from the Gombe royal court, as district head. Resident Howard's actions effectively extended the power of the local Fulani Muslim rulers over the Hill Waja, as Sarkin Yaki's appointment established the first Fulani headship over the Hill and Plains Waja. In 1908, the Waja District was incorporated into the Tangale-Waja independent districts, leading to the appointment of Musa Sarkin Yaki as district head after the request of the people in the area. Sarkin Musa was deposed by the British for "administrative incompetence" in 1926 and was replaced by his son Kwoiranga II.

After Kwoiranga's death in 1936, the Waja people resisted Fulani Muslim rule. In keeping with the trend to reform indirect rule, British administrators subdivided the district into smaller administrative units with independent leadership structures. In 1945, British colonial officers continued to recognize the autonomy of communities in the Waja region, enabling them to solidify their identities. Following Birks's recommendation, British authorities divided the Waja Village head council into two, reflecting the communal differences between Hill and Plains Waja. Birks accumulated interviews with both colonial administrators and Waja elders so that he could piece together a representative (though still somewhat patchy) description of the various Waja communities' histories. A significant portion of his decision appears to be founded on the oral histories of various Waja "tribes" that emphasized cultural, religious, social, and historical differences as a justification for their autonomy.[89]

The limitations of indirect rule were also evident in many other divisions in the Northern Provinces. In the Katagum Division of Kano Province, many local communities resisted the policies of the native authority. In 1915, for example, in his annual report to Resident Temple, Assistant District Officer H. M. Brice-Smith reported widespread disorder in the division, including strong opposition against the authority of the emir, communal violence among Fulani groups, and charges of duplicity against the emir in the implementation of colonial law. In the Chana Fika District, Sarkin Chana Jaju, a subordinate of the emir of Fika, rebelled against the emir's authority and asserted his own authority by marshaling disparate communities, including the Shadi, Fassakande, and Madigongo, against colonial authorities. Brice-Smith expressed dismay at the inability of the emir of Dambam to compel "Kerikeri pagans," along with their allies, the Ngizimawa and Beddawa, to conform to colonial laws. Instead of confronting indirect rule's serious structural problems, colonial authorities criminalized local resistance to colonial policy. Although Brice-Smith recognized the conflict's historical antecedent, describing "the slave raiding of the Fulani groups as an old habit," the district officer, with the support of District Officer Elder from Bornu and District Officer Carlyle, as well as local rulers, mounted armed police opposition against the uprising.[90]

The Consolidation of Hausa-Fulani Muslim Rule

As we have seen in previous cases, perspectives of the governor as the representative of the British crown and the chief executive in charge of colonial jurisdictions often portend the general trend in administrative priorities throughout Britain's Nigerian Provinces. Consequently, as governors changed with the times, so too did official perspectives on general statements of colonial administration in Lagos and the regional headquarters. We recall that Lugard, as the high commissioner of the Northern Nigerian Protectorate from 1900 to 1906, governor of the Northern Nigerian Protectorate from 1912 to 1913, and governor-general of Nigeria from 1913 to 1918, had firmly entrenched a rigid indirect rule system of local administration. In the intervening years between Lugard's two tenures in Nigeria, when Sir William Wallace served as high commissioner of the Northern Nigerian Protectorate, and Henry Hesketh Bell as governor of the Northern Protectorate from 1909 to 1912, indirect rule was consistently affirmed as the governing principle in colonial Nigeria. Thus, during the critical first two decades of British rule, Lugard's rigid conception of indirect rule dominated the nature and form of local administration in Northern Nigeria and beyond.

Hugh Clifford's tenure as governor marked a slight shift in colonial administrative priorities in Nigeria. During his tenure as governor from 1919 to 1925, Clifford sought to encourage a more efficient method of local administration by exploring new strategies to expand the scope of the native authority system, especially in the Northern Provinces. We will recall how Clifford expanded the concept of indirect rule so that the diverse communal groups, especially adherents of indigenous religious beliefs, would have more control over their local affairs. When Clifford left, Graeme Thompson, governor of Nigeria from 1929 to 1931, gave British officers considerable leeway to innovate as colonial administrators within their various jurisdictions. This gave the lieutenant governor of the Northern Nigerian Provinces, Palmer, the ability to reassert a Northern-centered administrative system that further reified the authority of the Fulani emirs, district heads, village heads, and Muslim clerics in native authority structures. It would be left to Donald Cameron, governor of Nigeria from 1931 to 1935, to implement a far-reaching reform of the indirect rule system of colonial administration.

In 1931, Cameron arrived fresh from service in Tanganyika, becoming the new governor and commander in chief of Nigeria. Raised in the British empire-making tradition, Cameron was enmeshed in the colonial project.[91] Arriving at a time when the native authority system had proven inadequate to address

Nigeria's changing society, Cameron felt compelled to institute comprehensive reforms.[92] He imposed austerity measures as a response to the Great Depression and moved to improve security throughout colonial Nigeria. Cameron called for reform of the native authority system, especially in the Northern Provinces. James Harford, a district officer with many years of service in Northern Nigeria, recalled Cameron's "profound mistrust" of indirect rule, on which the Northern Nigerian native authority system was so firmly based. During this critical era before the outbreak of World War II, two competing visions of colonial rule created a "fundamental divergence" between the reform-minded Cameron and his subordinates in the Northern Nigerian colonial service, who favored a slow pace of political evolution under the leadership of Lieutenant Governor H. R. Palmer.[93] Cameron's strident reforms thus drew the ire of Northern Nigeria's colonial administrators, many of whom turned against Cameron for his perceived "vindictiveness and arrogance."

Commander Carrow, who had served for more than two decades as district officer and resident in Kano and Sokoto Provinces, recalled in the 1960s that because of Cameron's uncompromising style of administration, colonial progress was restricted by infighting between British administrators in the Northern Provinces and British officers in Lagos, who were generally loyal to Cameron. From Carrow's perspective, Cameron and his supporters gave little time to the practical considerations peculiar to this vast region and were only concerned with abstract notions of colonial progress. By contrast, his subordinate with extensive experience in Northern Nigeria—Palmer—believed that ideas of colonial progress should reflect the region's peculiar religious, social, and political context, placing these considerations over theories of colonial reforms.

Carrow cites two examples that illuminate the intense disagreement between Cameron and Palmer. The first open conflict occurred at a conference of chiefs in Kaduna, Northern Nigeria's regional capital, in which Cameron was in a "very critical mood." Carrow contends that Cameron's "violent and rude attacks provoked a stupid and equally exaggerated defense from Palmer." A second moment of open disagreement occurred when the two men argued about whether to unchain native administration prisoners. Cameron was staunchly against the practice, while Palmer felt such matters should be left to the discretion of Northern Nigerian native authorities. As conflict between these two senior officers intensified, Carrow observed that their subordinates often were confused about acceptable colonial policy.[94]

At the national level, Cameron reinstituted the Supreme Court, weakened the native courts, abolished the residents' provincial courts, created magistrate courts as appellate bodies, and established a high court staffed by professional judges. The legal hierarchy was thus reorganized into native courts, magistrate courts, the high court, and the Supreme Court. "The essential importance of the 1933 Cameron legal ordinances," Rene Larémont argues, "was that they restored the authority of Muslim jurists in civil cases while still mitigating their authority in capital cases."[95] Notably, this development curtailed the role of British administrators in the day-to-day governance of the region, as described by Resident Letchworth of Bornu Province. Before Cameron's reforms, the Resident's duties had included providing leadership for school administration, provincial institutions, and the Native Authority Council; administering tax policy, budgets, and public works projects; relaying the details of homicide cases to the Executive Council; and serving as registrar for marriages. As Cameron's reforms consolidated the functions of native authorities, however, powers of British administrators such as those held by the Resident were transferred to a native administrative council.[96] To provide requisite educational institution for local administrators, the government opened the Kano Law School on the model of Gordon College (later the University of Khartoum).[97] With Arabic as the language of instruction and a curriculum designed to train elite Muslim jurists, the colonial administration attempted to reform the Islamic legal system.

Ironically, this crucial period of indirect rule undermined non-Muslim autonomy in the Northern Nigerian Provinces. Overlapping colorations of religious, ethnic, and other communal forms of identities had evolved under the aegis of a reformed indirect rule, starting during the governorship of Hugh Clifford. With Cameron's reform came a formalization of the native administrative structures in the Northern Provinces and further sedimentation of emirate societies. Naturally, the growing influence of Hausa-Fulani Muslim rulers, precipitated by Cameron's policy, was resisted by non-Muslim communities. In response, Muslim rulers attempted to fold such dissent into the political hierarchy, reasserting their hegemony as natural rulers of the region's diverse peoples. While divisions were also evident in intra-Muslim relations in the region, the fault lines between Hausa-Fulani Muslim rulers and groups British authorities considered "pagan tribes" widened following the implementation of Cameron's reform policy. As the gap grew wider, and proselytizing by Christian missions intensified in these non-Muslim communities from the 1930s to the 1950s,[98] the universal language of Christianity steadily served as a powerful medium of politico-religious mobilization against Hausa-Fulani Muslim hegemony by the time of decolonization in the 1950s. This development established the foundation for major fault lines that would dominate the processes of collective political action in the Northern Provinces in the late colonial period, and ultimately in the postcolonial era, with its fissures of entrenched ethno-religious identity.

Institutional contestation was central to elite formation in this rapidly changing environment; these efforts essentially amounted to the first deliberate policy that moved Nigeria toward the regionalization of state power. As outlined above, legal formalization required that colonial administrators devolve their authority to the dominant Hausa-Fulani Muslim rulers, yet it also required them to retain some control over the judicial system. Power thus flowed downward from the colonial authorities in Lagos (the national capital) and Kaduna (the Northern regional capital) to the power brokers of the Sokoto Caliphate; the reforms were not transmitted upward from local communities to a Hausa-Fulani Muslim aristocracy. They also set the stage for the consolidation of an ethno-regional power structure vested in the educationally advanced Southern Nigerian Christian elite and Northern Muslim rulers. By the end of World War II, religious and ethnic identities had been consolidated, reflecting the entrenched Hausa-Fulani identity embedded in the region's long and complicated engagement with Islam and the impact of Christian missions on the non-Muslim areas of the Northern Protectorate. Though this pattern was complicated by mass migrations of Southern Christians to the Northern Provinces and the migration of Hausa-Fulani Muslims to the Middle Belt region, Muslim and Christian identities assumed greater meaning in the region (the Middle Belt), especially during the decolonization process.

CHAPTER THREE

CHRISTIANITY AND THE
TRANSFORMATION OF
COLONIAL SOUTHERN AND
NORTHERN NIGERIA

Once Christian missions entered non-Muslim areas in the Northern Nigerian Protectorate, what resulted was a complicated set of interethnic relations among the diverse communities in the region. These relations developed specifically because mission Christianity successfully implanted a framework for disparate communal groups, erstwhile adherents of indigenous religions, to articulate defensive politico-religious doctrines and build unified resistance against Hausa-Fulani Muslim rule. Indeed, a lasting consequence of the impact of Christian missions on the masses of marginalized people throughout the Northern Provinces would be its capacity to provide a medium of "religious renewal" and "newfound mobility for the political, economic, and social transformations occurring after the colonial takeover of the caliphate and the abolition of slavery."[1] Additionally, the caliphate's grip on power was beginning to erode because of colonial reform. Down in the Southwest, Christianity continued to produce sharply different social and political outcomes among Yoruba communities, with various missions expanding their base in major cities such as Ibadan, Abeokuta, Ijebu-Ode, and Lagos. As Yoruba traditions encountered this alien world religion, Christian doctrines and observances adapted to local cosmology, worldview, and custom. Indeed, this rapid growth of Christian missions would also transform indigenous religions and local traditions in other Southern Provinces in the Southeast and the delta regions as well as the non-Muslim areas of colonial Northern Nigeria.

Christianity, Colonialism, and Social Mobility in Yoruba Society

John Peel argues in his groundbreaking book *Religious Encounter and the Making of the Yoruba* that Yoruba conversion to Christianity took place within the framework of a complicated, sometimes contradictory cultural dialogue between the Yoruba belief system and mission Christianity. The methods by which the missionaries' messages were received brought together religious and social forces that were anchored to essential structures of Yoruba indigenous beliefs. While Western Christian evangelical perspectives drew a distinction between the secular and religious, Yoruba Christian converts reconciled temporal and transcendental forces, connecting the power of Christianity to rapidly changing social conditions within a Yoruba frame of reference.[2]

Yoruba Christian converts understood the moral questions undergirding the rapidly changing world profoundly shaped by British colonialism and mission Christianity. Missionary teachings about personal integrity, the family, and achieving material exactitude were not novel ideas to Yoruba people, since these are well embedded in local traditions and customary ways.[3] Ultimately, Christianity flourished in Yoruba communities during the transformative moment of colonial rule because it provided an important means of navigating the increasingly complex social, political, and economic environment of modern Nigerian society at the turn of the twentieth century.[4] Indeed, in an earlier work Peel had argued that Aladura, the popular independent Yoruba Christian church movement, effectively adapted Yoruba religious beliefs to the modernizing project of mission Christianity.[5]

At another level, some earlier studies on mission Christianity, modernity, and Yoruba traditions have looked at the transformation of Yoruba society by connecting the values of the new world religion to an evolving process of social relations that were expressed through changing marriage norms and family structure. Kristin Mann's important book *Marrying Well: Marriages, Status, and Social Change among the Educated Elite in Lagos* is an exemplar among studies of this social process during the colonial period.[6] Mann explains that though Yoruba and neo-Victorian marriage practices among educated Yoruba Christians were not always mutually exclusive, there were notable distinguishing characteristics between these two religious practices: the Yoruba practice of polygamy ensured access to economic networks, while Christian marriage ensured elite status. In traditional Yoruba society, marriage often merged two lineages to form corporate networks of power and status. But as educated Yoruba Christians adopted Christian marriage, they acquired new social status derived from mission education, Christian civility, and elite networks that complicated the meaning of power in Yoruba society. While elite Christian marriages enhanced the economic power of men, in colonial society elite Christian women became dependent on their husbands. In this complicated social context, neither traditional Yoruba marriage nor neo-Victorian Christian marriage guaranteed success, but both became a route to power and economic opportunity. Educated Yoruba Christians moved toward Christian practices as a means of social advancement in a modernizing colonial system,[7] but they continued to build on traditional Yoruba marriage practices to navigate lineage networks and social ties.

Bound to the layered social change caused by these interactions between Christian and Yoruba marriage practices was the economic transformation that mission Christianity and the colonial economy encouraged during this era. Sara Berry offers insightful examples of these concurrent developments in her innovative book *Cocoa, Custom, and Socio-Economic Change in Rural Western Nigeria*.[8] In it she explains that, beyond the ongoing modernizing-elite versus reactionary-elder conflict, cocoa cultivation was tied to the mobilization of traditional social structures. Though the socially unmoored, such as former slaves and migrant laborers, did take up production, the more important demographic groups were those who had access to European merchants and missionaries who were spreading their knowledge of cocoa-farming techniques, particularly missionaries who connected cocoa cultivation to their Christian message.[9] In fact, breaking with established norms of religion often went hand in hand with quitting prevailing agricultural methods and switching to cocoa cultivation.

Michael Ajasin, the renowned Yoruba nationalist and first civilian governor of the Yoruba state of Ondo in postcolonial Nigeria, illustrates the important intersection of mission Christianity and export-oriented cocoa production at the center of his family's social transformation at the turn of the twentieth century:

> I got married to Comfort Babafunke Tenabe. Many years before we met each other and later got married, providence had brought our fathers into an impersonal contact. Pa Isaac Tenabe, father of my wife, was born in Idoani about the year 1870. In 1892, the legendary Ogedengbe Agbogungboro of Ilesha raided Idoani and took Pa Tenabe to Ilesha as one of his captives. While in captivity he was converted to Christianity, a

> religion he began to introduce to Idoani and its districts when he returned home on 13th November, 1892 after the overthrow of Ogedengbe and the abolition of the slave trade. He also brought with him the cocoa plant which he introduced into the area. With the bible in one hand and cocoa plant in the other, he travelled extensively in the area converting people and introducing cocoa farming to them. At Owo, my father became one of his converts to both Christianity and cocoa farming.... My father was converted to the Church Missionary Society (CMS) otherwise known as the Anglican Church denomination.[10]

However, the influence of modern agricultural systems derived from the British was limited, and the rapid rise in cocoa cultivation was not a simple realization of economic opportunity. In Ilesha and Ibadan, Berry contends that cocoa cultivation initially was a fallback option for the many unemployed soldiers who were left over from the recently ended Yoruba wars. Thus, change within Yoruba society dictated the speed and patterns of the new practice of cocoa cultivation. The production of cocoa required large amounts of land and labor, and cocoa trees took several years to mature, so successful cocoa cultivation relied not only on the landowner's wealth but also on his ability to mobilize labor and venture capital, usually through lineage ties. As many farmers sought to establish themselves in new Yoruba communities, landowners relied on unattached migrants for labor, creating an emerging landowner-tenant class relationship. A system of land rentals emerged, and the cost of acquiring rights to land increased. In some ways, this eroded lineage relationships, as migrants entered the traditional landowning system. In sum, the spread of cocoa farming was embedded in prevailing social relations that was transformed by mission Christianity and colonialism, even as economic relationships were broken and reconfigured in the emerging cultivation system.[11]

Christianity, Colonial Rule, and Modernization: Reflections on Ibadan and Ijebu

The transformation of Yoruba communities that started in the mid-nineteenth century was accelerated through a greater intensity of Christian missions after the imposition of colonial rule in the early twentieth century. Ibadan and Ijebu-Ode are two pivotal Yoruba cities in which this transformation induced by mission Christianity was notable in the earlier decades of colonial rule.[12]

In Ibadan, the first CMS mission was established by a German-Swiss missionary, the Reverend David Hinderer, and his English wife, Anna Martin, who arrived in the city in May 1853. We are told in I. B. Akinyele's rendition of local history, *Iwe Itan Ibadan*,[13] that the relationship between the pioneering Christians and local people was generally amicable. In fact, the mission's first primary school was started in a house given to Reverend Hinderer by the city's ruler, Baale Oyesile Olugbode. Toyin Falola notes the steady growth of the CMS mission in Ibadan during the formative years:

> The mission houses expanded slowly and additional converts were made each year. By 1859, 135 converts had been baptized at Kudeti, and the first church was established in 1854. In 1868, a new church, St. Peter's was opened at Aremo and in the following year, St. James' Church was opened at Ogunpa. In 1879, there were two mission schools, with about 67 registered students. By 1899, the three churches had converts numbering 400 people, who were concentrated in the neighborhoods of Kudeti, Alafara, Labiran, Oke Ofa, and Agodi. Whilst this was a small number, Christianity was nevertheless beginning to make its impact in Ibadan. The few strong converts were exclusive, preferring to interact with one another rather than with "pagans and Mohammedans." The clergy became involved in politics, and their preaching and activities partly paved the way for further European penetration.[14]

By the turn of the century, other Christian missions, led by Methodists, Baptists, and Catholics, had emerged in various sections of the city and neighboring towns, further encouraging the pace of social change.

In Ibadan, like most Yoruba communities, Christian missionary activities led to the advancement of Western education. Several decades after the Yoruba wars, mission elementary schools, along with the Baale School (named for the ruler), provided education for the children of Christian commoners, since chiefs were not inclined to avail themselves of this educational resource. The ambivalence of chiefs about Western education is understandable, because the overt proselytizing that accompanied missionary education undermined the indigenous religious traditions in which their traditional authority was based. Thus, anxiety over the destabilizing effects of Christian values on local traditions prevailed in the earlier decades of Christianity in the city.[15]

The influence of Christianity was further enhanced by the establishment of a CMS community secondary school, the Ibadan Grammar School, in 1913. Education and many civic-oriented projects were sustained by a small but influential Christian-educated elite during those critical early decades of colonial rule. By the 1930s, the expansion of missionary education had increased the influence of Western-educated Christians in local affairs, leading to friction between a younger generation of Christian elites and the old guards, largely consisting of traditional chiefs. Educated Christians used the training they had acquired from mission schools to gain access to new professional opportunities that the colonial system afforded and to advance the interests of their ancestral hometown within the colonial administrative system. Influential leaders of this emergent elite group consistently lobbied colonial administrators to incorporate educated Christians into the local administrative system.[16]

My emphasis so far on the significance of mission Christianity should not be mistaken for an underestimation of the importance of Islam in the transformation of Ibadan and other Yoruba communities.[17] Indeed, Islam was a formidable force for change, though Christianity had seized the initiative in constructing a pathway to modernity by the early twentieth century. Be that as it may, the intersection of religious traditions was inevitable, given that Islam had engaged Yoruba communities since the early 1800s and was integral in transforming Ibadan during its emergence as a garrison town following the fall of the Old Oyo Empire. The incursion of Hausa-Fulani jihadists into Yoruba communities following the southward advance of the Sokoto Jihad is another significant historical factor in this regard. With the conversion of Ibadan's famous ruler, Are Latosisa, in the mid-nineteenth century Islam grew in influence, especially among powerful chiefly lineages and wealthy traders. While Islam was embedded in the social structure of emirate society and deployed by British administrators to shape the colonial order in the Northern Provinces, mission Christianity, because of its impact on local communities in the Southern Provinces, profoundly shaped the direction of Ibadan. As social and political developments transformed spatial relations, and competition for scarce resources of the colonial state intensified, subethnic Yoruba and religious identities deepened in Ibadan under colonial rule.[18]

A brief review of the Ijebu case also reveals the extent to which Yoruba communities adapted the modernizing features of Christianity to prevailing local conditions at the turn of the century in the Yoruba region.[19] Social relations and communal consciousness of Ijebu-Ode, the principal Ijebu city, were dramatically transformed because of the far-reaching social and political developments that accompanied the Imagbo War—the war that led to the conquest of the Ijebu by the British in 1892. Before their defeat, many Ijebu towns had remained largely isolated, insistently resisting direct missionary and European commercial encroachment into their communities in the second half of the nineteenth century.[20] But their isolation was to be shattered. The treaty between the British conquerors and Ijebu-Ode's Oba, the Awujale, opened the door to British rule and to Christian missionary activities in the last decade of the nineteenth century. Indeed, because of the close proximity of Ijebu towns to Lagos on the coast and Abeokuta, about forty miles north, where Christian missionary influence had taken hold by the late 1800s, the social impact of mission Christianity would be much quicker in Ijebu towns than in communities in the Yoruba hinterland that came under British control at the turn of the twentieth century.[21] Mindful of these radically new social and political conditions, the enterprising Ijebu, who had retained control over trade routes between the Yoruba hinterland and the coast during the Yoruba wars, strategically embraced Christian missionaries, who held the key to modern development.[22]

At a crossroads, Ijebu Christian converts who had immigrated to Lagos before the Imagbo War collaborated with Christian missionaries to establish elementary and secondary schools in Ijebu towns. The profile of Christian educated elites, notably teachers, clerks, and clergy, increased because of the growing importance of Western education; as the status of Christian educated elites rose in Ijebu communities, their influence superseded those of the custodians of the traditional order, notably local chiefs and heads of lineages. Indeed, by the early decades of colonial rule, community pressure for Western education and modern development would stretch the resources of missionaries as Anglican and Methodist missions failed to meet the high demand for primary and secondary education in Ijebu communities. The strong desire to advance Western education reached an important milestone in 1913, when prominent Ijebu CMS leaders established the first secondary school in Ijebuland, the Ijebu-Ode Grammar School.[23]

Before the outbreak of World War II, mission schools had significantly produced teachers, catechists, clerical workers, and traders, who in turn supported the objectives of the missions in local communities. Indeed, affiliation with Christian missions did not only guarantee membership in the local intelligentsia, but also ensured social mobility in an emergent Ijebu colonial society. Significantly, by 1940, less than five decades after British conquest, there were 187 mission schools in Ijebu communities; and by the Second World War, the Ijebu had become influential in commerce and in local administration in the Yoruba region.[24]

Although Christianity and Western education spread rapidly in Ijebu communities, they did so unevenly and in some peculiar ways. Notably, CMS schools had little centralized supervision after 1900, giving local CMS lay leaders considerable control over the direction of education in local communities. By contrast, Methodist schools were tightly controlled and meticulously cared for by their missionary overseers. Before the government-backed education committee started its work in the 1920s, denominational competition between

Christian missions were prevalent in the earlier decades of Christian missionary work in Ijebu communities.[25] As time passed, various Christian missions would develop differently, interacting with Islam, Ijebu customary practices, and indigenous religious beliefs.[26]

This prevalence of Protestant Christian missions in Yoruba communities under colonial rule was far from a straightforward embrace of progressive ideas committed to modern training and Western enlightenment. Indeed, some European missionaries continued to harbor misgivings about the pace and direction of change in Nigerian communities. What follows is an analysis of such European missionary ambivalence in the form of a critical discussion of the letters of an English CMS missionary to his mother during his service in colonial Lagos.

Letters of a CMS English Missionary

Many Christian educated Yoruba elites were committed to rapid development, and they pushed aggressively for the modernization of local communities,[27] despite the ambivalence of some European missionaries about the nature of social change in local communities in the earlier decades of colonial rule. The detailed letters of an English CMS missionary, the Rev. Canon R. A. Wright, to his mother provide insight into the ambivalence of one European missionary regarding the political and social conditions of Nigerian colonial society. The letters are also instructive because they reveal the condescension that some Yoruba CMS missionaries had attributed to their European counterparts; for example, by the end of the nineteenth century, Saro missionaries, who generally favored literary education and professionalization, had clashed with European missionaries, who called for a slow pace of modernization and advocated vocational training for CMS converts.[28]

Although Canon Wright's letters were written many decades after the arrival of the CMS in the mid-nineteenth century, they nevertheless provide a personal insight into an important aspect of imperial discourse in colonial Nigeria. Wright's letters are decidedly paternalistic, even by the standards of the time (the late 1920s and early 1930s); they capture themes that were pertinent to the imperial discourses of the times, such as popular religion, colonial administration, racial representation, and modernity. British paternalism came through clearly in these letters, and they vividly reveal the mentality of an imperial burden common among Western missionaries since the nineteenth century. In a letter dated September 16, 1929, Rev. Canon Wright notes:

> A native Canon came in to see me about a wedding, the one I mentioned in my last letter. His name is Cole and he seemed a most intelligent person. He had spent five months in England and knew Bishop Burroughs and had met Canon Storr.... It is curious how even in an educated and good man like him there is a sense of inferiority. He is conscious of being a subject race and clearly knew that he was talking to one of his rulers! It is an odd business living in another's country as the military governors, thoroughly bad for one's soul. But as the Emir of Kano told Mr. Tomlinson if we weren't here he would soon enclose the whole of Nigeria in his empire, cartoon off the heads of those he didn't like and enslave the rest! He apparently was quite friendly about it! A well-known native said the other day that if we left Nigeria he will be on the same boat; so perhaps it is best as is.[29]

In a tour through the Southern and Northern Provinces in 1929, Wright provided interesting insight into the administration of a key region in the Southern Provinces. In a letter describing his travel experience, he shares his impression of the city of Oyo, which at that time was the headquarters of Oyo Province under the "rule" of the legendary Captain William A. Ross, and Alaafin Siyanbola Ladigbolu, Ross's "supreme head" of this important province in the Yoruba hinterland:[30]

> The District Officer is a charming fellow.... He sent me back to the rest house after tea, and on the way I passed his office. Six huge natives sitting on the ground suddenly got up and lay flat on their faces while I went past! This sort of thing is common up there and a little demoralizing. When Ross [Captain Ross, Resident of Oyo Province, 1914–1931] goes out whole towns laid quite flat until he signaled that they get up! After breakfast to see the town of Oyo and the palace of the Alaafin who is a kind of combine Pope and Emperor ruling under British protection. This city was made of mud but the Alaafin's house of concrete. He has a wonderful Daimler car. Then [I went] to see a special school for the sons of chiefs who were cheery little fellows. It's a kind of boarding school and I believe a successful experiment ... not Christian but the native teacher is a Christian.... The views were perfectly wonderful and Ross on his job was most illuminating. I don't suppose, in his Province, that any Roman Emperor was ever so absolute. It is reported that when he was prospecting for a site for his house that he could not get through the Bush to the top. So he just said make a road to the top while I have my lunch. In that

time thousands of natives were set to work and some half mile of passable road produced by the time he had finished his coffee![31]

In summing up his travel experiences, Wright harked back to the old mantra of the sacrifice of the custodian of the British imperial mission in colonial Africa. In his view, British empire making in Nigeria, as with other "inferior races" around the world for centuries, was an inevitable moral burden that ordinary subjects of the British Crown had to shoulder. For Canon Wright, it was a good thing for British subjects to help save humanity; and on many occasions, he felt a sense of self-fulfillment when he encountered representatives of His Majesty's Service,

> the kind of men who are ruling the Empire. They are with all their little idiosyncrasies most amazing people, full of life and often quite definitely religious, and embarrassingly anxious to talk about their particular problem in life. Men with families at home and desperately lonely, or a new child arriving, or thinking of getting married and wondering if they should, or some of the many problems which faced men in the outpost of empire. The cadets are just as good as I expected they would be when I first met them.[32]

From the above, it is evident that Wright is inclined to paint a romantic picture of colonial administrators as guardians of the British Empire's civilizing imperative; and he associates these men on imperial duty with a profound sense of responsibility and dedication to Pax Britannia. Although a missionary himself, Wright was suspicious of European missionaries he considered too close to the natives. European missionaries, in his view, were susceptible to local manipulation, unlike British administrators, who he thought demonstrated a healthy detachment from the everyday life of Africans. His assessments were superficial and condescending, lacked context, and grossly simplified social realities. In contemptuous language, Wright observes:

> I have been learning lately that there is something about us which has "shaken" this land more than I realize which is a cause for both thankfulness and very real awe at the responsibility of it all. . . . I didn't tell you yesterday that on arrival in Ibadan I looked around and noticed a chicken tied to the "bumper" at the back. I was just going to ask the boy why he had put it there thinking he had some theory about keeping it fresh, when it suddenly squawked! I was very angry. These people have no idea at all of kindness to animals.[33]

Rev. Canon Wright believed that Europeans are higher moral beings, and Africans of questionable moral standards. This perspective is evident in his conclusions about the circumstances surrounding a "biracial" schoolboy's parentage. The boy was a family friend who attended the elite King's College in Lagos. Wright recalled that he had invited the boy to tea: "Then tea at which I had two boys, friends of Bullen, who are now at King's College. One is a half-caste, the son of a man, a very senior official who married according to native law and custom in the days when Nigeria was a lonelier place than now. He was apparently a very good and faithful husband but the wife was a bad native woman who ran away leaving him with the boy."[34]

Against the backdrop of the Great Depression, Wright does not shy away from expressing a strong opinion on the Port Harcourt labor riots of 1929. In this November 12, 1929, letter, he is critical of the United African Company (UAC) and poll tax, noting that

> the root trouble is a horrid trading combine called UAC who having got the whole of the trade of West Africa into their hands are depressing prices paid to the natives for such things as palm kernels. This happens to coincide with a poll tax. The result is riots etc. and the traders blame the government for the much damage that has been done.... It is also partly due to the fact that taxes are collected by the natives themselves and their "brothers" don't believe anything like the right amount gets to the government. The African trusts no one but a white man. He knows too much about his brother! It is rather interesting to see the problems of Empire before one. We are here by force of arms and levy taxes to run the country. If we go away the place reverts to barbarism—the Northern tribes will sweep down and enslave everyone. Then would follow the traders who as they did before would flood the place with gin and for a few drinks and gold watches buy up most of the land and either force the peasant or make him work at their price. This is what happened before and made it necessary for the government to defend the native. So we literally have to shoot the native for his own sake![35]

Rev. Canon Wright's disdain for the cultures of the peoples of Nigeria, and even the landscape, were amplified in his travels to the southeastern section of the Southern Provinces and Northern Provinces. In an account reminiscent of information contained in the travelogues of European explorers and adventurers of the previous century, Wright wrote in May 1930 from the Igbo city of Umuahia:

> I am very glad to have done the trip. It has given me quite a new idea of everything but in many ways it has been most disappointing. First the country itself is deadly dull. When it isn't tropical forest it is semi open desert of sand. There is practically no color except in a few trees at this time of year which are sort of glorified red. Some of the people wear pleasant clothes but nothing very startling. Generally they are some shade of blue or else white. I met one tribe who literally wore nothing at all and it doesn't worry them a bit because they come into the town just as their more clothed brethren. They are a pagan race who live on the Plateau near Jos, and in spite of the intense cold and heat manage very well without any civilized covering.[36]

As with most Christian missionaries of the time, the dominant role of Hausa-Fulani Muslim rulers and the marginalization of the growing Christian minority communities in the Northern Provinces did not elude Canon Wright. On this important issue, Wright reflected the general frustration of Christian missionaries about the rigidity of the Lugardian system of indirect rule, claiming that this system was grossly inadequate for the complex sociopolitical challenges confronting the Northern Provinces:

> It struck me that our efforts to keep Northern Nigeria a medieval Mohammedan state is not possible forever and when the break comes there will be a row.... The whole question of missions and general Christian government up there is a problem the magnitude of which simply cannot be understood by people outside.... It will take a generation to bring them up into our ideas. They simply don't understand obvious things like monogamy and truthfulness. Slavery to some extent still exists and no one sees any reason why it shouldn't.[37]

This critical review of Rev. Canon Wright's letter to his mother is not a comprehensive assessment of the attitude of European missionaries toward the peoples of colonial Nigeria. Rather, it exemplifies the condescension often associated with European missionaries within the wider context of the imperial discourse of the European civilizing mission in colonial Africa, Asia, and the Pacific.

The Rise of Charismatic Christianity in the Southern Provinces

Following the social ferment in Nigerian communities in the early decades of colonial rule, mission Christianity witnessed its first major break from Western Enlightenment thought,[38] leading to a rescripting of Christian teachings to local practices and charismatic traditions.[39] Common assumptions about the origins of Nigerian "charismatism"[40] often begin with the North American "fundamentalist" resurgence at the turn of the twentieth century.[41] However, Ogbu Kalu tells us that this perspective erroneously assumes that African Christian consciousness follows developments in the West, generally believed to be the "home" of Christianity. For one, the gospel has strong historical connections to African societies, spreading first through Egypt, North Africa, and Ethiopia within four centuries of Christ's death, and later to coastal ports and along the continent's interior waterways in the age of Iberian conquest.[42] In fact, the African charismatic revival and its North American counterpart emerged simultaneously, only later converging to reflect similar characteristics.[43]

Following the waves of mission Christianity at the turn of the twentieth century, the charismatic movements that proliferated in Southern Nigerian communities by the late colonial period reflected antistructural doctrines common among indigenous African cosmologies and worldviews.[44] Thus, the proliferation of charismatic movements in colonial Southern Nigeria[45] was reflected through the (British) Apostolic Church beginning in the late 1920s, the Assemblies of God in Igbo communities in the late 1930s, the Christian Council of Nigeria in 1930, the influential Scripture Union (SU) in the 1950s,[46] and the first indigenous Nigerian Pentecostal church, the Redeemed Christian Church of God (RCCG), founded in 1952. Sorting through this web of charismatic movements, Kalu identifies five distinct categories of fellowships, meetinghouses, and churches: a priestly figure urging change in patterns of personal religious allegiance; a prophetic figure "endowed with healing powers and evangelistic ardor to quicken the pace of Christianization"; African independent churches (AICs—also known as African-initiated churches) such as Aladura (Those Who Pray); holiness groups representing the backbone of Pentecostal teaching; and, later, youthful puritan charismatism that led to the wave of Christian revivalist movements since the decolonization process in the 1950s.[47]

Of these, the AICs are often characterized as distinctive in their teachings and doctrines, and scholars variously include or exclude them from Nigeria's vibrant charismatic movement.[48] Scholars who include AICs in Nigeria's charismatic movement underscore similar historical origins, discourses, and social conditions between the AICs and Pentecostal groups.[49] However, these claims of unity ignore the strong theological opposition of the leadership of Nigeria's Pentecostal movement to the religious practices of the AICs. Many Pentecostal leaders contend that AICs' religious practices violate tenets of the Christian covenant because they venerate indigenous rituals and sacred objects.[50] While such distinctions are crucial to theological classification,[51] the influence of

AICs on Pentecostal groups in colonial Southern Nigeria is undeniably immense; leaders of Nigeria's early apostolic churches had strong connections to the Aladura movement in Yoruba communities (for a detailed analysis, see chapter 6).[52] These contending theological tensions among Southern Nigeria's emerging charismatic church movements reflect the complexities of the region's rapid social, economic, demographic, and political transformations that had been precipitated by the forces of late colonialism. This wave of religious fervor was not limited to the Southern Provinces; it also had an impact on non-Muslim communities in the Northern Provinces, in the context of the Lugardian policy of indirect rule.

Colonial Policy and Christian Missions in the Northern Provinces

Much of the Christian missionary work in key regions of the Northern Provinces at the turn of the twentieth century was carried out by a new generation of European, North American, and Nigerian missionaries from both established and new missionary societies, such as the CMS, the Sudan Interior Mission (SIM), the Lutherans, the Irish Catholic Brothers, and the French Catholic Brothers.[53] As Christian missionary expansion grew in the Northern Protectorate during the colonial period, CMS missionary activities expanded from the Southern Provinces into the Northern Provinces, especially to the non-Muslim Middle Belt and the non-Muslim areas of emirate society, encapsulating the three geopolitical territories in colonial Nigeria: the North, Southwest, and Southeast.

A new Northern Nigerian CMS Diocese was established in the early colonial years and went straight to work in Makurdi and Laffia, largely among Southern Christian migrants, especially Igbo and Yoruba, who had settled in those areas as traders and lower-level colonial functionaries starting in the early 1900s. More importantly, CMS missionary activities, along with other Christian missions, were rapidly transforming the geopolitical framework in non-Muslim Middle Belt areas of the Northern Provinces, especially among the Tiv, Idoma, and other Benue Plateau peoples. Focusing on the work of the SIM in emirate communities of the Northern Protectorate, Shobana Shankar notes that "after the British Colonial Office began to invest more resources in welfare in the 1920s, missions were allowed to play a greater role in education in many parts of Northern Nigeria. In the emirates, missions moved from urban Kano to suburban areas of Kano and other Muslim cities such as Sokoto and Katsina, where they founded leprosariums and other clinics in the 1930s."[54] Furthermore, Lutheran missionaries, through a modern social orientation derived from mission schools, made important inroads in Adamawa Province by the outbreak of the Second World War, providing an ideological framework against Hausa-Fulani Muslim rule.⁵⁵ Indeed, some Southern Christian settlers in the emirates "developed radical new forms of evangelical culture in Muslim and 'pagan' villages, creating spheres of local autonomy over which mission, colonial, and native authorities had little knowledge or supervision."⁵⁶

With contributions in critical areas of health care and education, colonial authorities initially saw the missions as key partners in the provision of essential social services. But as CMS, SIM, Sudan United Mission (SUM), and the Catholic Brothers' mission work thrived in the region, other missions (such as Methodist, Presbyterian Brethren, and the Christian Council of Nigeria) redoubled their efforts, and by the late 1920s, tensions between the dominant Hausa-Fulani Muslim rulers and Christian missionaries had become apparent. This struggle between Christianity and Islam in Northern communities has featured prominently in the region since the turn of the twentieth century. The contest between the two world religions had deepened when the British introduced indirect rule in Northern Nigeria. In a struggle that favored Hausa-Fulani Muslim rulers, British administrators curtailed the advance of Christianity, especially in emirate communities. Nevertheless, many influential British missionaries called on colonial authorities to align their imperial interests with the objectives of the missions in emirate society.⁵⁷

This perspective on Christian missionary work in predominantly Muslim areas in Africa had long been a problem in European missionary history in Africa, at least by the late nineteenth century. In this context, the perspective of renowned French theologian Charles De Foucauld on the implications of French colonial rule for the propagation of Christianity in the predominantly Muslim societies of the Maghreb is instructive:

> My thought is that if the Muslims of our colonial empire in the north of Africa are not gradually, gently, little by little, converted, there will be a major movement like that in Turkey. An intellectual elite will form itself in the big towns trained in the French fashion, but French neither in mind nor heart, lacking all Muslim faith, but keeping the name of it to be able to influence the masses, who remain ignorant of us, alienated from us by their priests and by our contact with them, too often very unfit to create affection. In the long run the elite will use Islam as a lever to raise the masses against us. The population is now 30 million; thanks to peace it will double in 50 years. It will have railways, all the plants of civilization, and will have been trained by us in the use of our arms. If we have not made Frenchmen of these peoples, they will drive us out. The only way for them to become French is by becoming Christian.⁵⁸

As is now well known, this "gentle," "little by little" conversion called for by De Foucauld from Islam to Christianity did not take place in Africa. Although the call for a steady conversion of North African Muslims advocated by De Foucauld would be considered overly optimistic even by the standards of the early 1900s, De Foucauld's statement is useful for at least one important reason. A selective reading of his insightful intervention would suggest that this influential French missionary's perspective adds foresight to late colonialism's contradictory positions in the colonial world, in this instance, North Africa. In the case of Britain's Northern Nigerian Provinces, European missionaries made similar calls for Christian evangelization in the region. However, Lugardian logic foreclosed Christian proselytizing in Muslim communities, only acceding to missionary requests to evangelize among "pagan tribes." Jeffrey Haynes observed that in the earlier years of colonial rule, there were consistent tensions between European missionaries who desired to proselytize in Muslim communities and British administrators who frustrated their efforts at every turn.[59] Consequently, some missionaries in the Northern Provinces, including the famous English CMS missionary physician and linguist Dr. Walter Samuel Miller, called on colonial authorities to permit Christian missionary work in Nigeria's emirate society.[60] Frank Salamone notes the rationale through which European missionaries challenged this policy premised on indirect rule: "Missionaries had their own opposing view of reality. In that view, the Muslim Fulani were not 'natural rulers.' . . . Fulani were seen as interlopers who had imposed their rule on the people, enslaving them indiscriminately as they conquered. Because they were more likely than political officers to mingle among the talakawa and because their work was restricted to non-Muslims, it is not surprising that missionaries, coming from strong anti-slavery movement oppose the official view of reality."[61] In this context, Muslim rulers clashed with Christian missionaries, especially in non-Muslim communities of emirate society, where Hausa-Fulani Muslim rulers claimed political authority going back to the establishment of the Sokoto Caliphate. Indeed, by the 1940s, Christian missionary activities had grown significantly in the Middle Belt region of the Northern Provinces through the expansion of mission schools, proving more than an irritant to Hausa-Fulani Muslim rulers.[62]

The tension between colonial officials and Christian missionaries was brought into sharp focus by the opposition of British administrators to an anti-Muslim publication by British missionary Ethel Miller, sister of Dr. Miller, in Kano in 1926. In an insightful account, Andrew Barnes explores how British administrators attempted to control Christian missionary rhetoric in emirate society because of fears that missionary action would destabilize the colonial administrative system. As the story goes, British administrators went to great lengths to censor Ethel Miller's controversial treatise *The Truth about Mohammed*, which was in part an attack on Lugard's pro-Islam position as espoused in his landmark book *The Dual Mandate in Tropical Africa*; and she reviewed critically the basis of Lieutenant Governor H. R. Palmer's opposition to Christian missionary activities in the Northern Provinces.[63]

Even though Miller's pamphlet was meant for European consumption, colonial authorities denounced it as inflammatory and banned it, contending that it could arouse popular protest from Northern Muslims. Distribution of Miller's pamphlets provided Palmer with an opportunity to move against growing missionary activism. He charged Miller with "violating Section 58 (2) of the Nigerian Criminal Code [which] made it unlawful to publish seditious writings."[64] However, fearing a backlash from influential British missionaries for what some saw as Palmer's overreaction, Nigeria's governor, Sir Graeme Thompson, overruled Palmer and reprimanded Miller, ordering her to desist from distributing her pamphlets.[65] The rest is history, as they say. The Catholic Brothers, an Irish Catholic missionary society, would emerge to carry out critical Christian missionary work in the Middle Belt region of Nigeria's Northern Provinces during the colonial period.

The Catholic Brothers in the Northern Provinces: A Case Study

Haynes has argued that compared to their Protestant counterparts, Catholic missionaries were more deeply engaged with the social conditions of local communities in colonial and postcolonial African societies.[66] In the Northern Protectorate's Middle Belt region, where Catholic missions had firmly established themselves by the early 1950s, European missionaries evolved a strong partnership with influential local intermediaries. Consistent with Haynes's perspective, colonial and missionary records in many Northern Nigerian communities reveal that Christian missionaries in partnership with local elders played a critical role in developing local communities. In the 1930 annual report for Adamawa Province, Resident G. W. Webster recorded evidence of the crucial work by missionaries:

> Proselytizing at present takes a secondary place in the enhancement of the material welfare and health of the people and it is probably this that has contributed greatly to the popularity and success of the mission among the Bura and Margi tribes.... Their attitude to the administration is one of cordial cooperation and in no case has it been observed that

any adherent of the mission has thereby failed to show proper obedience and loyalty to the District authorities.⁶⁷

These intimate relations between missionaries and local communities are vividly presented in Barnes's oral history project, notably a comprehensive interview with a pioneering leader of the Irish brothers, the Rev. Maguire, before his retirement from missionary work in Nigeria in 1993. Barnes's extensive interview with Father Maguire is instructive for our purpose here because it captures the day-to-day activities of the Irish brothers as missionaries in the Benue Plateau region during the crucial early years of the mission. Having gone through rapid social transformation during the interwar period as a colonial mining district, this Middle Belt region attracted migrant workers from Nigeria's Southern Provinces, including new Igbo Catholic converts, thus further complicating the ethnic and religious mix in the region. Father Maguire's retrospective is instructive, given the complex communal groups that the Catholic brothers confronted:

> When the SMA [Society of African Missions] priests first came, they were from Alsace, they were French as well as Alsatian, and they were experts in languages. They learned the language of the people, which at that time was the Goemai people down in Shendam. As time moved on a few years, they had to face the problem of education. And the non-Catholic mission bodies already have some schools, and it was per force that we had to get involved in schools that meant we had to learn the Hausa language, because it was a type of *lingua franca* of the North at the time. So when we Irish came along the language that we learned was Hausa. Another reason too, was that to get involved in all the languages of the different tribes would be a bit much. For example, I started off in Kwande Parish down in the lowlands that are the Goemai people. Then I was transferred to Tiv country. Then I was transferred to Kwa, Kafanchan, eventually up to Pankshin which would be in the Angas, then into Birom land here in Jos.⁶⁸

In the specific case of Plateau Province, where the Irish Brothers initially worked, Father Maguire recalled that mission work was a participatory process in which the Catholic Diocese actively engaged Kabwir leaders to establish churches and rudimentary infrastructure in their local communities. As to providing and maintaining basic social services, Maguire recalled that during the mission's earlier years, catechists from local communities led the discussion about providing education and health care and other amenities that meant so much to local people. The Irish mission was not simply an institution for the propagation of the Catholic faith; more importantly, Catholicism provided a framework for the delivery of much-needed development. Because of the importance of education, local leaders often saw the arrival of missionaries as the prerequisite for establishing mission schools. Thus, for local people a positive outcome of missionary intrusion into their local communities would be the establishment of mission schools. As the focal point of community development, they invested significant portions of their meager resources to constructing and maintaining these schools.[69]

Because major areas in Plateau Province in the 1940s were removed from direct Hausa-Fulani Muslim control, Catholic missionaries had more space to influence native authorities. Unlike in neighboring provinces, where Hausa-Fulani Muslim rulers held sway, the Irish Brothers' work in Middle Belt communities brought many disparate ethnic groups together to articulate a unified idea of the common good in the region by the 1950s. With regard to the relationship between missionaries, community leaders, and British authorities, Maguire asserts that these interactions were mutually reinforcing:

> Now, with regards to the Colonial Government at the time, the relationship in general was good. We got on all right together with no real difficulties. We had to obey the rules and regulations, the laws of the Government as regards the land, as regards buildings, as regards schools. In the main, the Colonial Government was very helpful. The schools were an important part of our lives, and in order to establish a school, we had to get the approval of the government. I can't recollect any time when we didn't get the approval for a school, and the Government was quite willing and helpful in this matter.[70]

Local communities gained support from the Irish Brothers to build churches, schools, and health clinics, and mission Christianity helped forge a new sense of community among the diverse ethnic groups in the region. Moreover, local converts worked with missionaries to influence colonial policy.[71] In addition, wealthy individuals mobilized essential resources for the overall advancement of their communities. Father Maguire thought progressive leaders formed a healthy component for social change:

> He would be a leader of the people, a natural leader. He might be the one who suggested, look, I have heard from this Reverend father in such a place that the people in that community have a school there. We need a school; what do you all think? He would have talked to his male friends,

but possibly some women would be involved as well. That's how they would build the church. And his compound would be the place they would use for their meetings.... [As the leader] the people would look up to him, the people would come to him with their troubles, their difficulties, their worries... and he brought many, many people into the church because of his leadership and because of his own qualities.[72]

Consequently, during decolonization in the 1950s, primary and secondary school education took root in most non-Muslim communities in the Northern Provinces; the literacy rate was on an upward swing, and self-conscious leaders began to use their new Christian identity to unify non-Hausa-Fulani elements in the Middle Belt region of the Northern Provinces. Specifically, Christianity provided much more than an opportunity to build a spiritual faith; it provided a framework in which various ethnic groups would come together to articulate strategies to resist Hausa-Fulani Muslim hegemony. The United Middle Belt Movement emerged in part from the unifying forces of these Christian missionary activities to articulate in much clearer terms the concept of the Middle Belt as a distinct geopolitical zone. Its major objective was to mobilize collective political action against the Hausa-Fulani emirate structure that had been reinforced by the British indirect rule system as the hegemon in Nigeria's Northern Provinces.

CHAPTER FOUR

THE POLITICS OF RELIGION
IN NORTHERN NIGERIA
DURING DECOLONIZATION

The constitutional conferences that were convened from 1946 to 1959 to prepare Nigeria for self-rule—and subsequently independence—during decolonization focused principally on the structural imbalances between Nigeria's Northern and Southern Provinces. As constitutional deliberations focused on this problem, representatives of the colonial government at the conferences were anxious to build viable political institutions necessary for sustained governance among Nigeria's three emerging regional government authorities (Eastern, Western, and Northern administrative regions). Within the three emergent regions, British colonial authorities also had to tailor these constitutional conferences to confront agitations from ethnic and religious minorities for political autonomy.[1]

As a central question in the governance of the Northern Region, Islamic law also came under close scrutiny. Many emirs and Muslim clerics had consistently expressed misgivings about the subordination of sharia to English common law[2] and questioned the colonial policy that subjected Islamic law to the criminal code of common law.[3] Thus, the 1951 Nigerian Constitution Conference (later named after Governor John Stuart Macpherson) charted new legal grounds to accommodate sharia. But the overall focus was to define the process of self-rule. The Macpherson Constitution ultimately granted greater autonomy to the three regions vis-à-vis a weak federal center and recommended the establishment of a professional civil service. This constitutional reform would set the stage for Nigeria's first experiment with constitutional democracy (1951–1966).[4] Following the 1951 Constitution,[5] two successive constitutions in 1954 and 1960[6] provided for the implementation of regional autonomy, federalism, and revenue allocation. More relevant to our immediate concern, the growing fear among non-Muslims in the Northern Region about marginalization never received adequate constitutional treatment—Hausa-Fulani Muslim rulers' domination of politics in the region continued apace and without mitigation by the federal center on behalf of religious and ethnic minorities.[7]

It was also apparent during the constitutional deliberations that the Northern Region faced stiff developmental challenge because of the lack of indigenous Western-educated personnel to manage the bureaucracy that was needed to anchor a modern regional government. The magnitude of the problem comes through in Governor Macpherson's assessment that the Northern Region had started on the road to Western education at least five decades behind its Southern counterparts. The cause of the problem was straightforward enough: in seeking to contain the spread of Christianity in the Northern Provinces under colonial rule, Hausa-Fulani Muslim rulers, in alliance with British administrators, had stiffly rejected not only Christian proselytizing but also its sociocultural underpinnings of Western education. To address this shortfall in professional manpower, Western-educated Christian Southerners were recruited to serve as civil servants, teachers, health officers, and technical experts in the Northern Region following the amalgamation of the Northern and Southern Protectorates in 1914. But this measure soon generated Northern Muslim resentment. With a growing sense of micronationalism in the form of a northernization strategy, the region's dominant political party, the Northern Peoples Congress (NPC), formulated policies to boost the training of Northerners for professional office in the region.[8] Thus, when the NPC took control of the regional government in 1951, it established a "fighting fund" to train promising Northerners in the modern professions, especially as lawyers, engineers, accountants, health workers, and so on.[9] But as is well known, the wheel of reform grinds slowly: attempts to raise the Northern Region's human resource capabilities would require considerable time and patience.

The scale of the problem regarding shortfalls in trained manpower was magnified when the government of the Northern Region tried to establish a fully functioning modern legal system. First, while the Eastern and Western Regions by the 1950s already possessed a large pool of indigenous lawyers trained in the English common-law tradition, the Northern Region had only a handful to serve a population of more than 20 million people. Indeed, by the early 1950s, all of the Northern magistrate courts were staffed by one English judge stationed in the region's capital city, Kaduna. It was customary to transfer cases to adjacent jurisdictions in the Western and Eastern Regions,[10] and reports suggest that the administrative logistics must have bordered on crisis.[11] In the short term, British judges, magistrates, barristers, and solicitors were appointed to serve in the region's legal institutions, including the ministry of justice, high courts, and magistrate courts.[12]

Political Leadership and Decolonization

It is widely accepted from the onset of the decolonization process that the momentum of political change in the Northern Provinces was profoundly shaped by the towering leadership of the charismatic potentate of the Sokoto Caliphate, Ahmadu Bello, the sardauna of Sokoto, a great-great-grandson of Usman dan Fodio.[13] The sardauna's popular appeal was based not only on his charisma but also on his place in the Sokoto Caliphate aristocracy. As a cousin of the sultan of Sokoto and a direct descendant of Usman dan Fodio, the sardauna drew on his religious legitimacy to stake his claim for political leadership. With the exception of "Middle Belt radicals," as some British administrators labeled the leaders of the less compromising Middle Belt Christians, the sardauna's pedigree in the caliphate ensured his widespread popularity throughout the Northern Region. Consequently, he worked to ameliorate intra-Muslim conflict by paying his respects at the tombs of both qadiri and tijani leaders,[14] and he tried to assure leaders of Christian minority groups that they have an important role to play in the administration of an emergent Northern Region.[15] Calling Abubakar Tafawa Balewa, the NPC deputy leader and soon-to-be–prime minister of Nigeria, his "able lieutenant," the sardauna felt that the rough-and-tumble of national politics in Lagos was below his stature, and left others to carry out what the *Times* of London referred to as work not fit for "a Muslim nobleman out of another century." This sense of his own destiny would only increase when he became premier of the Northern Region in 1954. His ability to draw support from a large spectrum of Northern public opinion lent credibility to any agreement to which he was party. Indeed, it was inconceivable to successfully implement constitutional reforms in the Hausa-Fulani emirates without the active engagement of the caliphate aristocracy under the leadership of someone with the sardauna's stature. With regard to the sardauna, Ahmadu Bello, Governor Macpherson notes:

His great advantage from the beginning until almost the end was that he was not only a leader of the North but he was a leader who could claim the following of probably almost all shades of opinion in the Northern Region, apart from a few urban or Middle Belt revolutionaries. It would have been quite impossible to introduce into the conservative, traditional Muslim North anything approaching the democratic system which we did in 1951 and 1954 unless it had been accepted and fathered and worked by a member of the Fulani ruling caste.... The Premier was a descendant of Usman dan Fodio; he was a cousin of the Sultan; he was a big man in his own right. If any form of change or democratic progress were to be introduced, then he was the man to do it. The chiefs would follow him and the NAs [native authorities] would follow him. So far as the Middle Belt was concerned, the pagans and the Christianized Northerners were probably in awe but at least they accepted him.[16]

The sardauna's influence was projected well beyond the borders of Nigeria, as he began to travel in the late 1950s to predominantly Muslim African states such as Niger, Guinea, Senegal, Gambia, Morocco, Algeria, Libya, and Tunisia. And as his influence grew in these African states, Ahmadu Bello sought diplomatic connections to the wider Muslim world, notably Saudi Arabia, Pakistan, Iran, Lebanon, Yemen, Iraq, Kuwait, the United Arab Emirate, and Jordan. The sardauna built mosques at home and positioned himself as the leader of Nigerian Muslims.[17] While connecting Hausa-Fulani identity to his Islamization strategy, the sardauna also built a working relationship with leaders of Christian minorities in the Northern Region, especially in Middle Belt communities. Though they harbored resentment against the politico-religious doctrine from which he drew his legitimacy, non-Muslims in the region grudgingly accepted his leadership.[18] In his autobiography, Bello notes his historic mission in Nigerian political history:

I have never sought the political limelight or a leading position.... But I could not avoid the obligation of my birth and destiny. My great-great-grandfather built an Empire in the Western Sudan. It has fallen to my lot to play a not inconsiderable part in building a new nation. My ancestor was chosen to lead the Holy War which set up his Empire. I have been chosen by a free electorate to help build a modern State.... This, then, is the story of my life.[19]

Equally significant was the position of the Northern Region's main opposition party, the Northern Elements Peoples Union (NEPU). It consisted of a small group of emirate progressives led by Aminu Kano, who during decolonization argued for a powerful central government, in contrast to the NPC's preference for a federal arrangement based on stronger regions vis-à-vis a weak federal center. Thus, while the NPC was committed to a political project legitimated by the Northern Muslim aristocracy, Aminu Kano's NEPU combined egalitarian doctrines in Islam with socialist thought to advocate for social improvements for the talakawa, the masses of Hausa commoners. Aminu Kano possessed strong Islamic credentials drawn from his training in Islamic law and fluency in Arabic.[20] Having worked on women's rights and the promotion of egalitarian policies, Aminu Kano was keenly aware of Usman dan Fodio's strong legacy on Islamic doctrines of social justice. His NEPU colleague, Isa Wali, blamed Hausa-Fulani Muslim rulers for collusion with British authorities and alleged misrule by the *sarakuna*, the Hausa-Fulani Muslim aristocracy.[21] Drawing its religious patronage from the populist tijaniyya order—in opposition to the qadiriyya order that dominated the NPC's Sokoto Caliphate base—NEPU leaders denounced emirate structures as a feudal system that had betrayed the Islamic piety of Usman dan Fodio's jihad.[22] In the long term, NEPU's impact on political reform was negligible because of its limited constituency in emirate society and the strong opposition of British authorities to its call for radical change.[23]

To be sure, both NPC and NEPU shared cultural ties at the initial stages of their formation to Jam'iyyar Mutanen Arewa, the dominant regional sociopolitical organization that had emerged in the early years of decolonization. But it was the NPC that emerged as the official Northern party because of its deep roots in the Sokoto Caliphate. Using its extensive socioreligious networks in emirate society to leverage British authorities, the NPC consolidated the structure of class dominance derived from the caliphate.[24] This emergent Hausa-Fulani power structure of emirs and politicians embraced both "traditional" and "modern" elements of governance. As C. S. Whitaker notes in his magisterial book *The Politics of Tradition: Continuity and Change in Northern Nigeria, 1946–1966*, political development during decolonization was not a linear process from a "traditional" Islamic aristocracy to a more "modern" pattern of constitutional government. Rather, it came out of a dialectical process combining "traditional" and "modern" attributes and drawing its legitimacy from the traditions of the Sokoto Caliphate.[25]

The contending perspectives of Hausa-Fulani Muslim rulers and their Southern Christian counterparts about Nigeria's political future took center stage during the 1953 London Constitution Conference that ultimately led to the 1954 Constitution. According to British administrator A. E. T. Benson,[26] participants from Southern areas were animated during the constitutional deliberations, while Northern delegates "appeared dour and out of their depths." Led by the deputy NPC leader, Abubakar Tafawa Balewa, who later became Nigeria's prime minister, the Northern delegation argued for a loose federation with a weak federal center and called for a slower pace toward independence so that their region could develop on its own terms. In the spirit of developmental catch-up, Northern delegates supported the colonial government's gradual approach to independence.[27]

The divergent perspectives of the Southern delegates at the conference in part reflected the fundamentally different experience they had obtained in mission schools and Western postsecondary institutions, going back to the turn of the twentieth century. For example, Obafemi Awolowo, a product of Christian mission schools from the Ijebu town of Ikenne and a London-trained lawyer, led the Action Group (AG), the dominant party in the Western Region, to the 1953 London Conference. Western Region delegates at the conference[28] called for Nigeria's independence from Britain and insisted on a strong federal system that would ensure autonomy for Nigeria's ethnic groups. Awolowo had earlier argued that any viable constitution for an emergent Nigerian state must underscore the country's ethnic diversity. He contended that the peoples of Nigeria were naturally divided by the River Niger and River Benue into three main areas—the North, West, and East—and further subdivided into ten ethno-national groups: Hausa, Fulani, Kanuri, Tiv, Nupe, Igbo, Ibibio/Efik, Ijaw, Yoruba, and Edo. The differences between the three major ethno-national groups (Hausa-Fulani, Yoruba, and Igbo), Awolowo insisted, were as great as that between the German, French, and British.[29] Reminiscing on the brief history of constitutional changes since the imposition of colonial rule, Awolowo chastised colonial officials, especially those in the Northern Colonial Service, for promoting the interest of the Hausa-Fulani Muslim aristocracy at the expense of the Christian-educated elite from the Western and Eastern Regions.[30] In all, Awolowo called for a clearer definition of the jurisdiction of regional and federal governments, the withdrawal of British administrators from regional and central governments, and the elimination of a numerical principle that gave greater advantage to the Northern Region in the distribution of resources in Nigeria's evolving federal system.

The National Council of Nigeria Citizens (NCNC), the party that controlled the Eastern Region Government, was dominated by the Igbo elite and led by the renowned nationalist Nnamdi Azikiwe. Like the AG, the NCNC struck a political pose against the NPC's conservatism; NCNC supported the AG's stand on immediate self-rule. Reacting against what it considered the negative impact of the NPC's northernization policy on Southerners, especially Igbo settlers in Northern cities, the NCNC pressured the Supreme Court in Lagos for a legal ruling that would protect Southern immigrants in the Northern Region.[31]

In the end, the Northern, Western, and Eastern Regions got some aspects of their political preferences consolidated in the 1954 Constitution, though it was the Northern Region that had more to celebrate: the 1954 Nigerian Constitution accepted the national bicameral legislature, which satisfied the interests of the political parties in the Eastern and Western Regions, though the Constitution also devolved substantial judicial powers to the regional governments, in accordance with Hausa-Fulani Muslim interests.[32] Ultimately, the Northern political establishment was sustained by the NPC, the party of the Hausa-Fulani Muslim rulers, while NEPU, the United Middle Belt Congress (UMBC—the party of Christian minorities from the Middle Belt), and another newly formed regional party, the Bornu Youth Movement (representing the interest of Kanuri Muslims in the Northeast), mounted opposition against the dominant NPC.[33] In practical terms, Hausa-Fulani Muslim rulers emerged the most successful among the three regional power centers in the constitutional deliberations. Representing the interest of the Sokoto Caliphate, the NPC solidified its control over the Northern Region's social structure; for example, 68 percent of Northern Regional parliamentarians were from the Sokoto Caliphate royalty and nobility, while only a small percentage represented religious and ethnic minority groups.[34]

The NPC Regional Government also reformed its relationship with the native authorities,[35] further reinforcing the powers of the masu sarauta in several important ways: the reformed native authority structures were brought under the firm control of emirs and district heads, who also dominated the Regional Houses of Assembly and Chiefs; new set of local government laws gave the NPC Regional Government even greater control over the appointment of native authority officials, and the Regional Government gave the emirate-dominated native authorities more power over religious and ethnic minorities.[36] Lastly, the NPC regional authorities retained statutory control over the NA system.[37] As the prominent Northern Nigerian Catholic theologian Rev. Dr. Matthew Kukah observed, "Royal blood, the Hausa language, and the Muslim religion" remained the criteria for NPC political leadership during the period of decolonization.[38]

Decolonization and the Resurgence of Religious Identity

The process of decolonization was politically significant, not only because it produced rapid constitutional transformation but also because it encouraged significant changes among both Muslim and Christian groups in Nigeria's

Northern Provinces. This was expressed in the intra-Muslim tensions among the dominant Sufi tariqas, the qadiriyya and the tijaniyya. According to John Paden, the Sufi orders were critical to defining the character of politics in the city of Kano, the region's preeminent city. Although the qadiriyya originally (in the early nineteenth century) was associated with the Sokoto Caliphate, the movement gained significant popularity because of its connection to Nasiru Kabara of Kano in the twentieth century. Kabara linked West African forms of qadiriyya with some North African branches, such as the *shaziliyya* (with its two sub-branches, *arosiyya* and *salamiyya*); over time, local trends in emirate Northern Nigerian society would predominate over North African traditions.[39]

However, from the mid-1900s, the competing Sufi order, the tijaniyya, rapidly grew in prominence in many Northern communities and soon became the dominant tariqa in Kano. This growth was precipitated by the work of Ibrahim Niass, a Wolof sheikh from Kaolack, Senegal, who had arrived in Kano during World War II and introduced a "reformed" version of tijaniyya that emphasized group prayers. Initially, this reformed tijaniyya doctrine appealed to the Hausa section of the city, mainly traders and crafts workers; later, with the installation of Muhammad Sanusi, a tijaniyya devotee, as emir of Kano in 1954, reformed tijaniyya spread throughout the emirate and across many urban centers of Northern Nigeria. Reformed tijaniyya embraced modern methods of communication, effectively using radio, print media, and the Hausa language to propagate its doctrines among its long-distance Hausa adherents, who traded between their homes in Kano through tariqa guest houses (*zawiyas*) throughout West Africa. With this rapid growth of the tijaniyya after World War II, intrareligious tensions developed between the region's two dominant Sufi orders in the 1950s.

Although Qur'anic imperatives discourage conflict between these two dominant Northern Nigerian tariqas, Bryan Sharwood-Smith, governor of Northern Nigeria's secret memorandum to the governor-general in Lagos, vividly explains the factors that led to conflict between the two regional tariqas in the 1950s. According to Sharwood-Smith, lingering tension erupted into a theological conflict by the early 1950s, when some prominent tijanis began praying with their hands crossed over their chests, which previously had been viewed as an expression of Mahdism. As previously discussed, Mahdism was a tariqa that had been associated with militancy against duly constituted authority.[40] In the early years of colonial rule, its millenarian doctrine understandably resonated among the masses of the poor, who were likely to follow the self-proclaimed Mahdi and help usher in a righteous Islamic order.[41]

Clashes between these tariqas came to a head in 1956, as some "radical" tijanis crossed the line by openly questioning the qadiris' commitment to Islam. This claim that qadiris were not true Muslims was an expression of contempt for an established Islamic school of thought, denying the unity of Islam. When violence broke out between the two tariqas, British authorities intervened, striking a balance between the leaders of the two Sufi orders while marginalizing Mahdists, seen as a militant Muslim sect that threatened the stability of emirate society.[42]

Meanwhile, Christian missions were working diligently to advance their common cause in evangelization, especially in the Middle Belt region and among non-Muslim minority groups in emirate society. In particular, the Catholic Church achieved remarkable advance under the leadership of Dr. David Matthew, the auxiliary Catholic bishop of Westminster who had been appointed Apostle Delegate of British East and West Africa territories in 1946, giving him supervisory authority over Catholic churches in Nigeria, Sierra Leone, and the Gold Coast. Matthew used his good relations with British administrators to draw the Catholic Church closer to the colonial state. Although local missionaries were ambivalent about Matthew's style of administration, they appreciated his contribution to the growth of Catholic missionary work in Nigeria and admired his influence among British administrators. Matthew's vigorous leadership led to the establishment of the prefecture in the Northern city of Yola (in Adamawa) in 1950, and ecclesiastical jurisdictions were created throughout the Northern Region. Eventually new prefectures were established in the Northern Muslim heartlands of Sokoto, Katsina, and Bornu provinces. The colonial state was a major beneficiary of this Christian missionary project because the new missions provided critical social services for local communities. The Adamawa Native Authority, for instance, depended mainly on the Franciscan Sisters of the Catholic Church for health care and various other social services. Although colonial administrators sought broadly to control missionary activity, in the main there was interdependence between church and state to promote development in the region.[43]

Intra-Christian relations also improved, particularly in the Eastern Region, where the Catholic Church was most dominant. After several decades of frosty relations over theological and ministerial differences, CMS and Catholic missionaries in the Eastern Region built bridges that would have an established role in the new nation. CMS Anglican bishop Cecil Patterson and Catholic archbishop Charles Heerey met regularly to discuss matters of common interest, especially in the important areas of education and health care. In due course, the CMS strengthened its grip in Tiv, Idoma, and other Middle Belt regions, and other Southern Christian missionary groups began to open missions in the Middle Belt and in the non-Muslim areas inside the emirates. But this development soon would generate a political reaction from the Northern Muslim seat of power: Hausa-Fulani Muslim rulers mounted strong opposition against the northward push by the Catholics, CMS, Methodists, Presbyterian Brethren, and the Christian Council of Nigeria. Eventually, as part of the northernization policy that was taking root, and in the interests of stability, British administrators worked collaboratively with the NPC regional government to curtail missionary work in the North.[44]

Restrictive official policies did not dampen the enthusiasm of these Protestant and Catholic missions. In fact, leading Christian missions worked even harder to spread the word; these missionary efforts encouraged national and international partnerships among educators, theologians, and technical experts to promote education, health care, and agriculture. Support came in the form of personnel and financial investments from England, Canada, Australia, and the United States. Moreover, with a new generation of Nigerians now leading the church, CMS work reflected the changing condition of the times. Many of these new-breed CMS ministers had attended leading Anglican colleges of theology in England, such as St. Aidan's College, Birkenhead, London College of Divinity, and St. Augustine College in Canterbury, in the decade immediately after World War II. Indeed, a new generation of outstanding Nigerian CMS clergymen were sponsored for advanced studies in theology and education in England and Canada and at the recently established Nigerian universities.[45] CMS missionary activities had shifted even more from the earlier emphasis on pastoral work to general human development. In collaboration with Methodist and Presbyterian missions, the CMS established two theological training colleges in Ibadan and Umuahia. This collaborative effort provided the three Protestant missions with a wider pool of talented clergy, better equipped to respond to the demands of a rapidly changing society.[46]

The Northern Muslim hierarchy would not be outdone; the NPC tightened its grip over emirate society, creating greater cooperation among various tariqas by the late 1950s, as decolonization was winding down. In particular, the sardauna raised funds from Arab countries to launch what came to be known as the Muslim "conversion campaign" to expand the influence of Islam. As these dynamic religious forces exposed the tension within the Northern Region—and between the Northern Region and the rest of the country—they also revealed contradictions between Islamic law and English common law in the Northern Region during this period of political transition.

Islamic Law in Northern Nigeria: Contending Issues

British colonial authorities convened three major conferences (1953, 1956, and 1959) to emphasize the necessity of legal reform in Britain's African colonies during decolonization. While the first was held at Makerere College in Uganda—East Africa's leading institution of higher learning—the second was held in Jos, Nigeria's principal Middle Belt city. The 1953 and 1956 conferences confirmed the challenges of reconciling "native" law (including Islamic) and English common law in Britain's increasingly complex colonies. In principle, these two conferences sought to develop a viable legal framework to respond to the pressing demands of Britain's African colonies.

Convened by the secretary of state for the colonies in London in 1959, the final conference on the future of law in Britain's African colonies was chaired by the eminent English jurist Lord Alfred Thompson Denning. Conference participants explored the interactions between customary, Islamic, and English law and discussed ways to reduce tensions among the various legal systems at the eve of independence. Significantly, this historic conference and the previous legal conferences were central to the intense debate over the tension between sharia and English common law, particularly in Northern Nigeria. While Lord Denning and his colleagues were optimistic about the future, the developments of the last several decades reveal the enormous challenges of reconciling Islamic, native, and common law in modern Nigerian state and society. Lord Denning noted:

> One group of pieces is founded on the costumes of the African Peoples, which vary from territory to territory, and from tribe to tribe. Another group of pieces is founded on the law of Islam, with all its many schools and sects. Yet another group is founded on the English common law. Another on the Roman-Dutch law, another on Indian statutes and so forth. If the peoples of Africa are to emerge into a great civilization, then these discordant pieces must all be sorted out and fitted together into a single whole. The result is bound to be a patch work, but we should remember that a patch work quilt of many colors can be just as serviceable as one of a single color, and is often more to be admired because of the effort needed to make it.[47]

The laws that were in force in Britain's African colonial territories north of the Zambezi can be broadly divided into two sections: general law and specific law. Applied in default of other provisions to every person within colonial jurisdictions, general law had been based on English common law. It can be further divided into four parts: the received law of England as it was understood at a particular date (for example, January 1, 1900, the formal date of British rule, in the case of Nigeria); common-law doctrines of equity, the statutes of general application in force in England on that date (January 1, 1900); modifications of the colonial legislature; and modifications by act of the imperial parliament, or by an order in Council. These laws, of course, were expected to go through significant modifications once independence was obtained by the colony.[48]

Specific law, on the other hand, includes the bodies of laws applied as exceptions or additions to the general law in a defined class of cases. These laws include customary (or native) laws within specified jurisdictions, and religious laws (for example, Islamic law in Northern Nigeria). The most important expression of specific law was what was generally known in colonial parlance as "African customary law," which consisted of a variety of laws that address the legal concern of diverse communities. Since the vast majority of local inhabitants were subjected to customary or native law, most cases in colonial courts were governed by specific law. During colonial rule, however, the consequences of rapidly changing social conditions meant that customary law was ultimately a mélange of rules from "indigenous" customary practices, English common law, and Islamic law (where applicable, such as Northern Nigeria).[49]

During decolonization, Northern Nigeria was British colonial Africa's ultimate test case for these discussions at the intersections of customary, Islamic, and English common laws. Despite a decade of constitutional reform in Nigeria, and although Islamic law had been applied more extensively in Northern Nigeria than anywhere in the world except Afghanistan and the Arabian Peninsula, Islamic law was still subsumed under native law in the region.[50] To many British administrators in the Northern Nigerian Colonial Service, the institutional design that had evolved under Lugardian indirect rule was "genius," because it allowed for varied application (the so-called sliding scale) that reflected contending socio-religious conditions. In principle, Islamic law was applied strictly in Muslim areas, non-Islamic customary laws ruled in largely non-Muslim areas, and an amalgam of Islamic and customary law was enforced where the population was a combination of Muslim and non-Muslims. For instance, in the Jarawa Court, a non-Muslim Native Authority court in Bauchi Province, "Muslim members" were allowed to advise on Islamic law in cases involving only Muslims while taking into account local custom within the Native Authority jurisdiction.[51] Moreover, the maintenance of the Repugnancy Clause, reaffirmed in 1956, contributed to this malleability by setting an upper bound on the applicability of Islamic law.[52] Thus, institutional flexibility allowed courts to adjust the law to social conditions and work out decisions often agreeable to most parties.[53]

However, this flexible application of the law also was problematic, especially to Hausa-Fulani Muslim clerics, who found it objectionable to mix Islamic codes developed in the Arabian Peninsula, Europe, and North Africa with local customary practices that were presumably indigenous to "tribal" Nigerian communities.[54] Moreover, as Islamic scholar A. A. Oba would later argue, customary law is (by definition) *determined by* cultural practices, whereas Islamic law is a universal code that *determines* cultural practices.[55] In addition to Muslim objections to this classification, the legal variation within jurisdictions that resulted from such flexibility created disparities in access to justice among communities. Most problematic, this varied application lacked an "established framework for distinguishing customary law from non-legal customary practice."[56]

With rapid social change by the period of decolonization in the 1950s, it had become difficult for both British administrators and native court judges to distinguish between legally enforceable normative rules of behavior, drawn from widespread local usage, and legally unenforceable social, moral, and religious obligations that simply reflected customary practice. This ambiguity became pronounced just as the value of customary practice increased, as local people guarded "tradition" more closely than before. The "sliding scale" instead depended on judges to interpret evolving social conditions outside the legislative context; rather than letting such change work its way up through the administrative system, with the law interpreted according to recognized societal norms, this task was left to individual judges. This made institutional adjustment to societal change an uneven process, as there was little real possibility to enact legal recognition of such evolving conditions. Furthermore, this rebounded back on changing social identities; the fact that the legal system could not apply a uniform code intensified varied identities throughout Nigeria's colonial provinces. Ironically, then, as this legal system reflected ambiguous social relations, it also solidified contending communal identities. In short, social upheaval in the late colonial period moved too quickly for the ad hoc customary law to handle; society and the legal system governing it were transforming at different speeds.[57]

This system was grossly inadequate for pressing social and political conditions in the Northern Region during the critical period of decolonization. Consequently, as the pressure for legal reforms grew, regional authorities introduced the Native Court Law of 1956. This reform separated Islamic law from customary law, institutionalizing sharia courts alongside non-Islamic native courts.[58] Moreover, the new law established the first Muslim Court of Appeal.[59] In reality, though, these changes amounted to half-measures. Islamic courts still fell under the broad category of customary law, considered prima facie applicable to

Africans "in the vast majority of cases." The Muslim Court of Appeal was also circumscribed, with jurisdiction over appeals from native courts on matters pertaining to personal law. It was not a "standing" court; instead judges convened on an ad hoc basis. Far weaker than its English common-law counterpart (the High Court), the Muslim Court of Appeal looked more like a patchwork solution to Northern Nigeria's long-term legal problem.[60] Also, while the dreaded repugnancy clause remained in force,[61] the law allowed non-Muslims in the Northern Region to opt out of Islamic law.[62] In sum, this reform recognized the real distinction between Native and Islamic law, but also reified it along a Muslim/non-Muslim axis, ending the "sliding scale" of judicial interpretation of social context. This essentially froze social change from a juridical perspective,[63] cementing religious division in the Northern Region.

This change created numerous legal challenges in the following important ways. First, the distinction between Islamic courts and native courts, heavily influenced by the interests and perspectives of Hausa-Fulani Muslim rulers, was murky at best. The Islamic courts were less flexible, insisting on doctrinal interpretations of Islamic law, and the native courts also rested on Islamic law as a matter of administrative guidance.[64] According to British officers, within a few years it was evident that the average Northern Muslim drew little distinction between Islamic and customary law. But the Northern Region contrasted sharply with the Western Region (the southwestern region of the Yoruba people), which also had a significant Muslim population: the former was two-thirds Muslim, with predominantly Islamic law, while in the latter, although about half of its population was Muslim, Yoruba native law and customs formed the basis of local legal codes. This disparity resulted from the arrival of Islam in Southern Nigeria during a period of European imperial influence, creating a liberal conception of monotheistic religion, while the Northern Region, as discussed in previous chapters, had experienced centuries of Islamization that was consolidated by the success of the Sokoto Jihad.

Second, customary law policies of previous decades were, by the period of decolonization, largely inadequate because of complex social conditions, especially labor migration, which complicated colonial legal designations such as "Muslims," "indigenes," and "settlers." The labor migration, especially the movement of Southern Christians as migrant workers to the Northern Region, meant that many Nigerians now fell within the problematic jurisdictions of Islamic, customary, or English common law that hardly captured their identities.[65] Furthermore, not only had overlapping identities become increasingly salient along religious and ethnic lines in the Northern Region; the impact of Christian missionary work had also increasingly transformed the meaning of "indigenous custom," especially in the Middle Belt region and among non-Muslim minority groups in the emirates. The crude distinction of common law, customary law, and Islamic law was far removed from the complex reality of intersecting ethno-religious identities most local people encountered in everyday life. This rigid imposition of legal categories on dynamic social conditions in local communities was deleterious to the carriage of justice in the reified Northern Region Native Court Law of 1956. This complexity is best reflected in the way elite Northern Muslims utilized Islamic law and common law: they tended to opt out of Islamic law to facilitate commerce, but personal matters, such as inheritance issues, were exclusively decided by Islamic courts. The courts thus became not only an arena for the interpretation of changing social identities, but also a vehicle for the manipulating of these shifting identities.[66]

This shortcoming was particularly pronounced in civil law issues such as marriage and inheritance, as well as disputes over land tenure. In matters of succession, for instance, customary law held that a plurality of heirs would divide the inheritance, whereas English common law split estates according to a legal document. This difference seemed largely unbridgeable,[67] yet rapid integration of the two categories necessitated a compromise. The result was the same fusion before the reform: a poorly defined trichotomy of areas of customary (including Islamic) law tempered by English common-law influence. De jure fusion, in this sense, became a de facto failure of reform. In land-tenure cases, English common law holds property to the individual citizen, whereas indigenous practice (as formulated under native law) recognized communal ownership. Traditionally, local power brokers could not dispose of such land without the consensus of members of the relevant corporate—often family or kinship—groups. As economic migration picked up, however, English laws of transfer came to bear on customary practice. Across Nigeria, Western standards of individual ownership were borrowed and built into local practice, particularly in coastal areas with long-standing European connections. This fusion is most pronounced in cities that evolved almost exclusively from migrants, such as Jos, Kaduna, and Port Harcourt, lacking strong preexisting local traditions and thus indigenous authorities to adjudicate land-tenure matters on a native-court basis. In some cases, colonial planners removed such urban areas from the jurisdiction of customary land tenure altogether, designating them "extra-customary centers," leaving only personal matters under customary law. Thus, in some of the heterogeneous and highly mobile cities of the Middle Belt, with weak centralized customary practices and growing foreign economic interests, coherent land laws were rarely found.[68]

A third problem was that the Native Court Law of 1956 failed to resolve the tensions of running parallel legal systems—which is what had motivated the reform in the first place. The differences between the courts remained vast from a legal perspective. In capital cases, for instance, the ability to enter evidence to support the defense of provocation can bear heavily on an outcome: Islamic law does not recognize such evidence, but English common law does. As a result, justice was determined by the particular agencies trying the case instead of the circumstances of the crime itself. Norman Anderson offered an example of a man allegedly provoked to murder who was arrested by the emir's officers, tried, convicted, and executed, even though he just as easily could have been apprehended by the Nigerian Police and tried under English common law, potentially with a much different outcome.[69] The 1956 reforms thus failed to resolve such issues, and there appears to be little indication that the new system worked any better. While power was further regionalized, debate simply shifted to the disparity in authorities of the legal systems: instead of lamenting the absence of a sharia appellate court, Northern Muslim clerics now lamented its weakness in comparison to common law. The persistence of these legal contradictions during self-rule in the mid-1950s would require a greater review of sharia in the Northern Region as Nigeria approached independence in 1960.

Constructing Islamic Law in the Northern Region

The legal and constitutional foundations on which governance in the Northern Region would be based during self-rule were further explored in the late 1950s, with independence fast approaching. The pressure for reform was initially precipitated when a judicial committee called on the Northern Regional Government to review the defense of provocation in homicide cases under Islamic law.[70] This was paired with recommendations of the Willink Commission, a high-profile commission of inquiry established by the British authorities to investigate the rights of ethnic and religious minority groups in Nigeria's three regions. Significantly, the Willink Commission recommended that the Northern Regional Government exempt non-Muslims from the jurisdiction of Islamic law under the native authority system.[71] The commission also recommended that the powers of Islamic law and native law should be restricted to personal matters in Northern Nigeria.[72] Predictably, prominent Hausa-Fulani Muslim rulers opposed the recommendation. More importantly, with growing queries on the role of sharia in legal administration, the NPC regional government established a fact-finding committee to investigate this enduring problem in state affairs. Governing about 20 million people, two-thirds of them

Muslim, the NPC government, with the guidance of the outgoing Northern colonial service, sent representatives to explore recent legal reform in Libya, Sudan, and Pakistan, all newly independent Muslim countries with considerable non-Muslim minorities.[73] On their return in 1958, the delegates further deliberated and submitted a report that once again kicked off debate over reforming the legal institutions of Northern Nigeria.

In addition to the challenge of reforming the Northern Region's legal system, there was a growing strain between the colonial administrators and the Northern Muslim leadership because of the rising sense of self-confidence among the NPC hierarchy. Hausa-Fulani Muslim rulers had gained significant exposure from the initial exercise of semi-autonomous regional rule; most had traveled abroad, gained diplomatic experience, implemented public policy, and made decisions that sometimes clashed with British policy. Seeing the British in their natural habitat at Whitehall also gave the Hausa-Fulani elite perspective on how governance was inevitably anchored in social context, a discovery they leveraged to their benefit. More importantly, this development transpired with the sardauna's push to bring emirs to heel, effectively bringing the emirate structure under the authority of the NPC government. Thus, emirs and chiefs had to comply with ministerial decrees in 1957 and 1959 as their judgments became subject to appeal of the regional government.[74] Finally, even those changes that state officials agreed on would require review by the Regional Executive Council, the House of Assembly, and the House of Chiefs, all under the control of the NPC regional government.[75] This assertion in the authority of the NPC regional government provided the context for a far-reaching review of the region's judiciary system.

The NPC regional government judicial review committee was chaired by Syed Abu Rannat, chief justice of Sudan; other members of the committee included the chairman of the Pakistan Law Reform Committee and former justice of the Supreme Court of Pakistan, Mohammed Sharif; the waziri of Bornu, Shettima Kashim; the chief alkali of Bida, Mallam Inusa; a former minister of the Northern Region, Peter Achimugu; and Professor Norman Anderson of London University's School of Oriental and African Studies. The commissioner for native courts in the attorney general's office, S. S. Richardson, was appointed secretary of the Reform Committee.[76] Professor Anderson summed up what was at stake for the Northern Muslim political elite:

> After independence they would need to attract foreign capital, so they must have a legal and judicial system which would give confidence to foreigners. They would wish to be members of the United Nations

Organization, so they must expect awkward questions and put themselves in a position to give satisfactory answers. They must have a legal and judicial system of training which would enable them to administer these systems themselves.[77]

Although the committee's proposal invested more powers in a regional Sharia Court of Appeal, it still subjected native courts (including Islamic courts) to the Penal Code and the Criminal Procedure Code under the authority of common-law courts. However, to accommodate the new powers invested in the Sharia Court of Appeal, the committee recommended substantial reform of the procedure governing the Penal Code.

Not surprisingly, the committee's proposals were announced to immediate criticism. Most strident was the opposition to reform the Penal Code, despite claims of judicial indiscretion and abuse.[78] Some British officials, especially common-law judges and many Hausa-Fulani Muslim clerics, disagreed with the proposals; the former engaged in a drawn-out argument over new procedural provisions and the bureaucratic burden of implementing them.[79] This dissent from British administrators stemmed from the fact that the proposals sought to strike a compromise between common and Islamic codes. In doing so, the committee adopted the Sudanese procedure, itself based on the Pakistani approach, which was, in turn, a derivative of Indian innovations on colonial legal procedure. Unlike the British system, where police take statements, interview witnesses and suspects, charge whom they suspect, bring the accused before the court, and leave him or her to the Crown's prosecution, the Indian system saw the magistrate doing the inquisitorial work. No statements were made before the police, nor did they prepare the charges. Instead, the magistrate took the statements, certified them, directed the police investigation, framed the charges, charged the accused, and then either tried the case or sent it to another magistrate. Such a system appalled British jurists, who revered their procedural code as much as Muslim clerics did their own.[80]

To resolve this objection, a final meeting was called at the Kaduna residence of the chief justice of Northern Nigeria, Sir Algernon Brown. Among the attendees were Regional High Court Judge Henry Skinner, S. S. Richardson, Chief Registrar Smith, Attorney General Hedley Marshall, and Marshall's draftsman, Imanus Nunan. Here, Brown criticized the procedural law as "novel, eccentric, and disagreeable," referring to it as a "reactionary and unwarranted deviation" from the time-tested British system.[81] After the meeting, he broke protocol and sent a missive to the colonial office protesting the change, referring to Richardson and Marshall (both officers in Northern Nigerian colonial service) as "Prussian and unyielding."[82] Thereafter, he continued to solicit support from colonial officers, even contacting the inspector general of police in Lagos. Attorney General Marshall pushed back, reminding Brown that he had been bound by similar procedure during his previous tenure as a high court judge in Singapore. At any rate, the Colonial Office supported the proposed reform. Minor concessions were made to appease Brown and like-minded English common-law jurists, but the reforms moved ahead largely as planned. Marshall later recalled:

> The Muslim countries to which the earlier delegation had been sent had come to terms with their Muslim law in a way which had enabled them to keep pace with the modern world and in which, of course, Northern Nigeria had up to then been unable to do.... What I can say, however, is that the carrying out of the proposals of the Panel of jurists involved a tremendous overhaul in the legal and penal structures of the North and involved a considerable amount of legislation.[83]

Opposition of Hausa-Fulani Muslim rulers, on the other hand, mostly came from a perception that the new Penal Code weakened sharia.[84] Northern Muslim clerics felt that the Penal Code was an intrusion into age-old moral codes of emirate society: "The sharia (a divine law) had become subjugated to what they believed was mere human law."[85] In crippling Islamic law, sharia advocate Auwalu Yadudu later reflected, "the Minorities Commission and the Abu Rannat Panel were in effect used as a smokescreen by the departing colonial administration to give local legislative legitimacy to a decision which had long been officially entertained."[86] Protesting the new Penal Code's specific provisions were more conservative emirs such as emir of Kano, Alhaji Sanusi. For such critics in Northern Muslim royalty and aristocracy, the main sticking point was that sharia in criminal cases was subjected to the appellate authority of English common law.

A second major concern was a specific matter of Islamic legal doctrine expressively championed by the emir of Kano: the provocation defense in a homicide case. An intensely religious man described by Marshall as "medieval with his superstitions," the emir was seen as "almost the Henry VII or Louis XI of the Muslim hierarchy," and thus harbor a deep revulsion to any reform that would weaken sharia.[87] British authorities thought they could convince him by mobilizing authoritative Muslim scholars who could overcome his obstinacy. Marshall thus got the sardauna to persuade the emir of Kano to meet with Chief Justice Rannat and the grand mufti of Sudan, who were in Kaduna for a celebration of Northern Nigerian self-government. The parties met at the

Council Chamber in Nasarawa, with Isa Kaita representing the sardauna and the emir appearing very "sulky." The grand mufti brought out a book of Hanafi law to convince the emir that the proposals were in line with the Islamic practice of punishing homicide according to the circumstances of the case. He and Chief Justice Rannat both had been tutors of the emir, and were thus able to persuade him, as Marshall had hoped. With Emir Sanusi's approval, the Penal Code was all but settled.[88]

The panel's other recommendations for reform were broadly accepted. Widespread support for the proposals in large part stemmed from the fact that they were derived from the (substantially Maliki-based) legal systems of the three consulted countries. Thus, the sultan of Sokoto and other emirate rulers were supportive throughout, only dissenting with the removal of Islamic courts from the native authority jurisdiction, which they argued would undermine the authority of the Hausa-Fulani Muslim hierarchy.[89]

Another recommendation approved by the panel was Richardson's nomination as commissioner of native courts in the attorney general's office. Responsible for supervising courts, preparing its rules, and checking its records, he actively participated in formulating policy and drafting legislation.[90] In his negotiations with cautious Northern Muslim clerics, his "cheery, friendly way, his knowledge of Hausa and Arabic, [and] his personal friendship" with many emirate rulers helped to win their support. Even hardliners were converted to Richardson's side. Finally, the proposals were helped by the fact that eminent foreign Muslim jurists authored them.[91] Rannat and Sudan's grand mufti met with various public opinion leaders in the region, particularly emirs and Muslim jurists, to convince them about the merits of the reform. As with the case of the emir of Kano's opposition to the Penal Code, their influence was decisive.

After such support had been corralled, the legislative package was introduced to the Northern Regional Legislature. It consisted of seven parts: the much-debated Penal Code; the far-reaching Native Court Amendment Law; the High Court Amendment Law, which would constitute a Native Court of Appeal division run by the chief justice, the grand qadi of the Northern Region, and other important Islamic judges; the new Magistrate Courts Law; the District Court Law; the Sharia Court of Appeal Law, which established a venue for appeals from Islamic native courts on civil cases; and the Court of Resolution Law, based on the Sudanese Court of Jurisdiction, which resolved jurisdictional issues arising from conflict among the high court and the sharia courts. Attached to this raft of bills was a Supplementary Evidence Amendment Law, which stipulated that the native courts would be guided—but not bound—by the Codes and Evidence Act.[92] Without such a provision, it is likely that many native-court decisions would have failed the repugnancy test on appeal, as procedural violations were rampant. Despite such leniency, the reform was still a major change, as this was the first time that native courts would be subject to the Penal Code and the Criminal Procedure Code.[93]

The judicial system thus was organized into three parallel ladders: Islamic, native, and common law. The Muslim Court of Appeal had been eliminated only four years after its constitution and replaced with the much stronger Sharia Court of Appeal.[94] Oba writes:

> There are only two major differences between the Moslem Court of Appeal and the Sharia Court of Appeal. The first is that appeals no longer lie to the High Court from the court. The decisions of the Sharia Court of Appeal are final. The second is that the Sharia Court of Appeal now has a standing membership consisting of a Grand Qadi and Qadis specifically appointed to man the court.... The High Court retained jurisdiction over appeals from Native courts in Islamic law matters other than Islamic personal law.[95]

In other words, the Sharia Court of Appeal had no original jurisdiction, but full appellate power over lower and provincial courts. It had four justices and was considered duly constituted when three of them sat.[96] Moreover, when an appeal from a native court relating to Islamic law went to the High Court, common-law judges would be aided by a qadi. The Penal Code was passed in 1959 with the backing of religious leaders, despite minor difficulty in the House of Assembly; after much debate but little opposition, the rest of the bills passed the legislature in 1960. The entire program went into force later that year.

Implementation would prove a predictably daunting task. Despite earlier agreeing to back the reforms, the emir of Kano "did all he could to sabotage the [new] system"[97] when the laws came into force. There also were logistical problems, as seven hundred native (mostly Islamic) courts handled 95 percent of the region's system of justice. Given the Northern Region's social complexity and general illiteracy, translating the law into local languages substantially complicated matters. Similarly, five thousand new staff members had to be hired and all existing jurists retrained. As a result of such difficulties, the regional government set the target for full implementation for the mid-1960s. To help meet this goal, it opened a law school at the Institute of Administration in Zaria with the aim of retraining alkalis, native court presidents, and other senior legal officials, as well as stepping up its program to train jurists abroad.[98] Finally, the reform policy needed support from local communities. To win such support, the regional government began public education campaigns, including an adult literacy program, attempting to popularize the new legal system through print, radio, and later television media. Such efforts were particularly necessary for the legitimacy of the new high and magistrate courts, as local people considered both of those courts "English"—that is, distant, corrupt, and representing foreign interests. As these courts were about to come under the jurisdiction of the Northern Region Government, the panel in charge of implementation undertook a public-relations campaign that included educating the public about its functions. Officials also encouraged English common-law justices to learn the Hausa language, the lingua franca of the Northern Region.[99] Such measures completed the reform project.

This was the status of the legal system in the predominantly Muslim Northern Region when independence arrived in October 1960. In the years immediately after the Second World War, British authorities collaborated with the political elite of the three major regions to address the deep structural imbalance between the Northern Region and the Southern Regions (the Eastern and Western Regions). However, despite their best attempts, British reform policies achieved little to ameliorate the deep division between the North and the South. Indeed, with regard to the legal reforms of the 1950s, British reformers soon recognized the steep challenge ahead. By the time of independence, British officials openly confronted the dearth of trained professional staff to run the Northern Region's courts and government offices; in 1960, there were only four barristers for the entire Northern Region and no new crop of legal minds on the immediate horizon. To resolve this serious shortage, the Institute of Administration, Zaria, partnered with several British legal institutions such as the Council of Legal Education and the Masters of the Benches of Lincoln's Inn and the Middle Temple, to prepare promising Northern Nigerian candidates to take the English bar examination. Initially the program was committed to preparing fifteen candidates annually, anticipating a "steady flow of competent, homegrown lawyers, judges, magistrates," and other jurists to replace expatriates and former colonial officers.[100] Such programs indicate the extent to which British reforms had failed to achieve the "balance" administrators had wished for. Moreover, the British system of indirect rule and reform policies during decolonization solidified ethno-regional identities that exacerbated the structural disparity between the Northern and the Southern Regions. As the regionalization of state power intensified, British administrators—especially those in the Northern Civil Service—further reified the authority of emirate structures, delegitimating indigenous religions and cultural practices while extending the powers of the dominant ethno-religious potentates in the region.

To underscore a central issue in this chapter, Western-oriented Southern elites from the Eastern and Western Regions, dominated by products of Christian missions, insisted on independence and pushed for a powerful central government to challenge the Northern Region's superior population. They attempted to control the legal-bureaucratic agencies of the federal government and called for a developmental agenda to transform the country.[101] To a large extent, Hausa-Fulani Muslim elites were able to stem this tide of change and preserve their formal regional autonomy because of British policy preferences, and the remarkable coherence of the masu sarauta. Emirate leaders consistently drew from their religious legitimacy to gain political and legal authority, dictating the shape, content, and direction of the Northern Region administration and its role in the broader Nigerian state project.

CHAPTER FIVE

RELIGION AND THE
POSTCOLONIAL STATE

The challenges posed by ethno-religious identities to Nigeria's emergent postcolonial state was immediately evident after the 1959 federal election that ushered in independence in October 1960. After the elections, officials of the United Middle Belt Congress (UMBC)[1]—the party that represented Middle Belt ethno-religious interests in the elections—alleged that the dominant Hausa-Fulani Muslim party, the NPC (Northern Peoples Congress), used state power to sanction and intimidate their supporters throughout the region. In Tiv communities, a UMBC stronghold in the Middle Belt, UMBC officials claimed that NPC-controlled native authorities used repressive measures to oppress their supporters. In Laffia, another UMBC stronghold in the region, UMBC officials claimed that NPC-controlled native authorities levied punitive taxes on their supporters, imprisoned them illegally, and deprived them access to employment.[2]

These well-founded charges of fragrant abuse of power[3] reflect tensions between Hausa-Fulani Muslim rulers and increasingly assertive ethno-religious minority groups in the Middle Belt since the onset of decolonization in the early 1950s. These recurring conflicts, in part, can be traced to the rapid conversion of so-called tribal pagans in the Northern Nigerian Protectorate to Christianity and the waves of migration of Southern Christians to the region during the colonial period. As Hausa-Fulani Muslim rulers reasserted control over these communities through the NPC-controlled regional government during decolonization, these ethno-religious groups formed new political organizations to assert their autonomy by the early 1950s. As the tensions between Hausa-Fulani Muslims and non-Muslim minorities intensified in the years immediately after independence, NPC leaders further utilized state patronage to coopt some opposition leaders, and deployed repressive measures to intimidate those they considered recalcitrant.[4] Thus, during Nigeria's first democratic government from 1960 to 1966 (the First Republic) intersecting religious, ethnic, and regional identities intensified to spark communal conflicts in Middle Belt communities.

In other parts of the country, ethno-regional and communal power brokers mobilized collective political action by speaking to narrow sectarian aspirations. Adele Afigbo argues that the prevailing ethno-regional and communal tensions during decolonization—especially ethnic, religious, regional, and subethnic—degenerated into major political confrontations during the First Republic.[5] As competition for state patronage and power dominated political alliances among the dominant regional-based parties, overlapping and intersecting divisions shifted back and forth between entrenched regional and local fault lines, complicating religious, ethnic, and subethnic tensions everywhere. In the Northern Region, these conflicts were not limited to ethno-religious rivalries between Hausa-Fulani Muslims and Christian minorities; they also reflected prevailing intrareligious competition among Sufi orders immediately after independence.

As with earlier intra-Muslim conflicts in the 1950s, the schism grew in the context of the exponential growth of the reformed tijaniyya order in many Northern Muslim communities (see chapter 4). In reaction to the growing influence of Ibrahim Niass's reformed tijaniyya, the sardauna of Sokoto, Ahmadu Bello (the premier of the Northern Region), founded the Usmaniyya movement (named in honor of his great-great-grandfather, Usman dan Fodio) in 1963 to check the erosion to his leadership in the Sokoto Caliphate. To reassert the authority of the caliphate among Hausa-Fulani Muslims at a time when the masu sarauta's legitimacy was questioned by tijaniyya leaders, Bello linked the NPC's mission to the political-religious project of his forebears in Hausa states in the nineteenth century. Abdulkader Tayob notes:

Bello had tried to unite the Muslim of Nigeria under a sufi order, called Uthmaniyyah [Usmaniyya], to recall the jihadist leader of the nineteenth century. This particular order would unite Muslims in a nation-state under the symbol of a historical figure associated with the area. The particular construction of a national Sufi order would be reminiscent of constructing a nation in historical and symbolic terms. At the same time, Uthmaniyyah aimed to diminish the political and social roles of the older Qadiriyyah and Tijaniyyah orders.[6]

Indeed, to consolidate his control over Northern Muslims, Bello flew Usman dan Fodio's war banner at rallies, made frequent visits to the Shehu's tomb and presented himself as the extension of Usman dan Fodio, Abdulahi, his brother, and Muhammad Bello, his son in the Hausa-Fulani Muslim hierarchy. By the early 1960s, posters of Bello were even showing a direct link to the Prophet Muhammad, through his connection to Usman dan Fodio.[7] Starting in 1963, Bello and his supporters embarked on "conversion campaigns" to Islam that was characterized as modern-day extensions of the Sokoto Jihad into the Middle Belt and non-Muslim areas of emirate society.[8] Illustrating the wider geopolitical implications of the sardauna's conversion campaigns, Iheanyi Enwerem observes:

> Bello's specific target for the final unification of the North was to convert the "pagan" enclaves in the region to Islam. He was determined to sway them away from the Christian missionaries. This move was understandable, principally because the enclaves were not only the major sources of Christian growth in the North, but could also become the seedbed of a political threat to Islamic interest in the region if the trend were allowed to continue. Besides, Christian missionaries had erroneously resigned themselves to the belief that these "pagan" enclaves were the reserved domain for their missionary enterprise.[9]

In response, UMBC leaders mounted stiff resistance to the sardauna's Islamization policy, considered an assault on Middle Belt communities.[10]

The sardauna also convened the Council of Mallams, an advisory group of senior Muslim clerics appointed by and accountable to him as regional premier. When Niass, the tijaniyya leader, refused to curtail his "confrontational" teachings, the council instigated a theological debate on whether a contentious reformed tijaniyya practice that entailed the crossing of arms (*kablu*)—as opposed to the "arms at ease" (*sadlu*)—practice was an acceptable (*sunna*) method of prayer.[11] Although the council endorsed Niass's teaching as sunna, a gesture of goodwill to encourage Niass to concede ground to the sardauna, Niass's followers still questioned Bello's authority. As relations between tijaniyya adherents and NPC supporters deteriorated, riots, erroneously believed to be the handiwork of Niass's followers, broke out in Argungu in Sokoto Province. Ultimately, in 1965, the Council of Mallams decided to ban imams from leading prayers with arms crossed. As kablu was a reformed tijani practice, the sudden change of course was a deliberate plan to delegitimate Niass among the masses of Northern Muslims, attempting to cut off his challenge to the NPC and its masu sarauta base. Furthermore, as Niass forged an alliance with the Northern Elements Progressive Union (NEPU), the emirate's main opposition to the NPC, Niass's tijaniyya challenge to the masu sarauta took on a more decidedly political dimension.[12]

Nevertheless, the sardauna reworked *ijma* "to characterize not the agreement of the ulama on a particular legal matter, but rather to symbolize the consensus of the Islamic polity and its legitimated leadership."[13] As the putative modern-day embodiment of the Sokoto Jihad, the sardauna and NPC loyalists dismissed their major opponent in emirate society, NEPU, as *kafir* (infidel) despite the strong Islamic traditions of NEPU leader Aminu Kano.[14] NEPU countered that the NPC had betrayed the vision of Usman dan Fodio by collaborating with corrupt British rulers. With regard to Islamic legitimacy, Abubakar Gumi, the dynamic Muslim cleric, provided a theological reply to NPC opponents. After meeting the sardauna during the 1955 hajj, Gumi became his adviser on Islamic affairs, and was appointed deputy grand qadi, and later grand qadi of the Northern Region. With Gumi's help, the sardauna founded the Jama'atu Nasril Islam (Society for the Victory of Islam, or JNI) in 1964 to promote unity among Northern Nigerian Muslims. Following the JNI's inaugural meeting—chaired by the waziri, Junaidu of Sokoto, and attended by the sultan of Sokoto and representatives from each province of the Northern Region—the organization built its headquarters and Islamiyya school in Kaduna, the regional capital.[15]

Following the assassination of the sardauna in 1966 in a failed military coup, and the dissolution of the Northern Region in 1967, the JNI was coopted by other prominent emirate rulers. After the Nigerian-Biafra Civil War (1967–1970), the organization came under the influence of Ibrahim Dasuki, a powerful Sokoto potentate who became the sultan of Sokoto in 1988.[16] To expand its base, the JNI called for Muslim unity throughout Nigeria and formed alliances with international Muslim groups, especially those related to education and development. For instance, with the help of the Kuwaiti Sabbah family, the JNI established the first Muslim post-secondary school in Northern Nigeria, Sheikh Sabbah College in Kaduna.[17] As Hausa-Fulani Muslim rulers strengthened the connection between Muslim piety and Northern identity, the masu sarauta further projected Northern Muslim power into Nigeria's contentious national politics.

Military Rule, Religion, and National Politics

However, the main threat to the NPC's Hausa-Fulani Muslim hegemony emerged after the January 1966 assassination of the sardauna—and Prime Minister Balewa—in a failed coup carried out by predominantly junior Igbo (Christian) officers from the Southeast. Following the crisis that engulfed Nigeria after the coup, the succeeding regime of Major General Aguiyi-Ironsi (an Igbo Christian) relied on traditional rulers, especially Northern emirs on whom the impact of the coup was most devastating, to help restore stability. During Ironsi's short tenure as head of the national government (January 16, 1966–July 19, 1966), prominent traditional rulers, especially Northern emirs, were called upon to bridge the gulf between competing regional interests and the new military regime. Having dismissed regional politicians, Ironsi embraced the emirs as the embodiment of Northern interests.[18] The failure of his policy reveals the limit of the military regime's neotraditional strategy as a viable response to Nigeria's political crisis—as British administrators had learned several decades previously.

After assuming control of the federal government, Ironsi appointed military governors in the three regions, along with a fourth region, the Mid-West Region, which had been carved out of the Western Region during the AG crisis from 1962 to 1966:[19] Lieutenant Colonel Odumegwu Ojukwu, son of a prominent Igbo businessman, to the Eastern Region; Major Hassan Katsina, son of the emir of Katsina, to the Northern Region; Lieutenant Colonel F. Adekunle Fajuyi to the Western Region; and Major David Ejoor to the Mid-Western Region. Brigadier Babafemi Ogundipe, the highest-ranking Yoruba army officer, became chief of staff of Supreme Headquarters; and a thirty-three-year-old Christian, Lieutenant Colonel Yakubu Gowon, an Angas, from the Middle Belt was appointed chief of army staff.[20]

Initially, the new regime enjoyed the goodwill of most Nigerians. Even Hausa-Fulani Muslim elites, who had lost their two foremost leaders in the January coup, the sardauna and Prime Minister Balewa, cooperated with the regime despite the seemingly sectarian nature of the coup. This endorsement was short-lived, however, as Ironsi failed to assuage Northern Muslim anxiety. As far as Hausa-Fulani Muslim leaders were concerned, Ironsi's first transgression was his failure to bring the leaders of the coup to justice, despite the decision of the Supreme Military Council to proceed with their trial in May 1966. When May rolled around, Ironsi postponed the trial indefinitely. To Hausa-Fulani Muslim elites, this confirmed their suspicion that the January coup was a sectarian Igbo (Southern Christian) conspiracy to dominate the Muslim North. In addition, critics claimed that Ironsi surrounded himself with a clique of Igbo advisers, contending that the Federal Military Government (FMG) was dominated by Igbo allies of the military ruler.

It was Decree No. 34 that proved to be Ironsi's fatal miscalculation.[21] The decree dissolved Nigeria's federal structure and established a unitary system of government. Dissolution of the structure that was established during the constitutional conferences of decolonization forced Northern emirs, as new regional intermediaries, onto the center stage of national politics. This was the first and only time since its inception that Nigeria was governed as a unitary state, and the first time the masu sarauta had no formal political structure to articulate its agenda. In addition, two decades of hard-fought battles to win regional autonomy, which had been the legacy of the beloved and martyred sardauna, was wiped off the map with a stroke of the pen. More immediately, the Hausa-Fulani Muslim political class feared that the abolition of Nigeria's federal structure would expose their region to takeover by the more educationally advanced Southern Region. In a matter of days, the decree sparked waves of violence in several Northern cities.[22] As riots intensified, mutinous Muslim mobs turned their rage against vulnerable Southern Christian settlers, especially Igbos, in the Northern Provinces.[23] Afraid for their lives, many Southern Christian settlers—including many Igbo Christians—fled the North for the Eastern, Western, and Mid-Western Provinces.

Federal military authorities responded to the violence against Igbo settlers by seeking help from Northern emirs. Having denounced regional politicians, Ironsi embraced Hausa-Fulani emirs as communicators of his policies to emirate society. He instructed the four military governors to discuss important state policies with traditional rulers in their respective provinces. The most critical of these dialogues were those held between the military governor of the Northern Provinces, Major Katsina, and Northern emirs.[24] The emirs, in turn, discharged their role as intermediaries with great confidence. For example, in June, after many private deliberations with Katsina, the sultan of Sokoto, Sir Abubakar III, submitted a bold memorandum to Ironsi, demanding the repeal of Decree 34.[25]

With growing Northern discontent, Ironsi convened a national conference of traditional rulers in Ibadan on July 28–29, 1966, to find solutions to the country's political crisis. Twenty-four prominent traditional rulers represented the provinces at the meeting, and were charged with finding viable solutions to

Nigeria's crisis. As fate would have it, Ironsi could only attend the first day of the conference; after a state dinner in his honor, Ironsi and his host, Governor Fajuyi (the Western Region's military governor) were assassinated—just two months after issuing Decree 34. The bloody countercoup, led by Northern officers, also claimed the lives of many other Igbo officers.

The countercoup catapulted Chief of Army Staff Gowon to power, and moved the country in yet another direction. As the national crisis deepened, Gowon abandoned Ironsi's strategy of working through emirs and traditional rulers. More importantly, Gowon, a Middle Belt Christian with strong cultural connection to the Hausa-Fulani Muslim elite emerged as a bridge to Middle Belt minorities who were influential in the Nigerian officer corp.[26] For Gowon, the looming crisis required a more comprehensive approach, integrating the efforts of a broad-based coalition of regional power brokers. The affairs of state now revolved around alliances among military administrators loyal to Gowon, senior federal civil servants, and prominent regional politicians—now recognized as essential spokesmen of major ethno-regional groups. Gowon appointed prominent politicians from the failed First Republic as commissioners in his Federal Executive Council and as heads of federal statutory corporations. He encouraged their participation as regional "leaders of thought" in various federal peace initiatives.[27] Recognizing the central place of regionalism in the crisis, Gowon released Awolowo, the preeminent Yoruba political leader, from Calabar Prison in August 1966. In 1963, Awolowo had been convicted of treasonable felony against the federal government during the AG crisis of the preceding democratic era.[28] After his release from prison, Awolowo was chosen by Yoruba obas and elders to lead the Yoruba regional delegation to the critical "leaders of thought" conferences, created by the FMG to recommend solutions to the crisis that ultimately led to the Nigerian-Biafra Civil War. For strategic reasons, Gowon also appointed Awolowo as federal commissioner for finance and vice chairman of the Federal Executive Council in 1967.

Significantly, Gowon reinstated the preexisting federal structure and divided the Northern, Eastern, Western, and Mid-Western Regions into twelve states. This military decision led to the creation of new states, including some that reflected the long-term agitations of ethnic minorities for autonomy in the Eastern and Northern Regions. From the Eastern Region, where the Igbo people were the dominant ethnic group, the FMG carved out three states: East Central, South Eastern, and Rivers. The Northern Region was divided into North Central, North Eastern, North Western, Kano, Benue-Plateau, and Kwara States. Significantly, the last two of these gave—for the first time since colonial rule—ethnic and religious minorities in the Middle Belt and northern

Yoruba areas their own states.²⁹ This decision prompted emirate elites to re-evaluate their perceived eroding power and unite around a strategy that would establish a new partnership with the political class of these new states. At least from a formal-legal perspective, the dream of Islamization, Northernization, and "Hausanization" suffered serious reversal after the creation of the states.

At a national convention to find solutions to Nigeria's political crisis shortly after Gowon's ascent to power, Hausa-Fulani Muslim leaders initially pushed for secession before switching course and advocating a strong central government with new states, Benue-Plateau (Middle Belt region) and Kwara (northern fringe of the Yoruba region). Mobilizing the support of the Council of Mallams and the JNI, the Northern Muslim elite closed ranks, asserting their position as the defenders of Islam and Northern interests.³⁰ By the time of the outbreak of the civil war in early 1967, old NPC stalwarts had established a good working relationship with leaders of the National Christian Association (NCA) in the Middle Belt and Northern minority communities. The Hausa-Fulani Muslim elite's rapprochement with Middle Belt Christians initially worked because of Gowon's strategy³¹ of building a united front against the Biafra (predominantly Igbo) secessionist agenda and sustaining the federation with the support of the political classes of the core Northern emirate, Middle Belt, Yoruba region, and ethnic minorities in the defunct Eastern Region. However, once the NCA was drawn into the Northern alliance, ethnic fissures soon emerged among these Christian minority groups, effectively undermining a unified Christian coalition. Indeed, Hausa-Fulani Muslim power brokers were able to fend off simultaneous challenges from Southerners and Northern Christians at once, meanwhile quashing internal dissent and unifying their base.³²

As former colonial governor, Macpherson later would recall during the Nigerian-Biafra Civil War, this united front from Northern Muslim rulers in the midst of the Biafran secession also contributed to the regionalization and militarization of Nigeria. Recounting his "friends" killed during the Nigerian crisis in the 1960s, Macpherson agreed with the sentiment of Igbo leaders that Odumegwu Ojukwu, the Biafra leader and former military governor of the Eastern Provinces, embodied the apprehension of core Igbo constituency immediately after the countercoup against the Ironsi regime. Drawing on his correspondence with Igbo leaders during the crisis, Macpherson observed during the civil war that Igbos could only participate in a federation that would ensure their protection, especially after the systematic mob attacks on Igbo settlers in Northern communities.³³

In the long term, the absence of vibrant Igbo settlers in Northern cities would have important implications for religion and society in Northern states for many years to come. With the departure of Igbo settlers, mainline missions, especially Catholic churches, redoubled their missionary work among indigenous non-Muslim communities in Northern and Middle Belt states. In the case of the Catholic Church, the missions embraced a strategy to "northernize" church doctrines, tailored missionary work to the unique demographic conditions of the region, and more effectively engage the social conditions of non-Muslims in Middle Belt and Northern states.[34] Enwerem notes the new trajectory in Catholic missionary work in Northern states immediately after the civil war:

> The Catholic Church in Northern Nigeria announced its growth, so to speak, in 1970 with the ordination of ten priests. Many more soon followed, to the extent that by 1979 the region could boast of about eighty-six indigenous priests, within Tivland alone, the historic center for anti-Muslim resistance in the North, leading with forty priests. Women were not found wanting in responding to the call to a religious vocation. In view of this, it became necessary to found the indigenous religious communities of nuns, like the Congregation of Our Lady of Fatima in Jos, the Sisters of the Nativity in Makurdi, and the Dominican Sisters of Saint Catherine of Siena in Sokoto. With the exception of Maiduguri and Yola, all the ten Dioceses in the former North are headed by indigenous bishops. In 1991, Kano became a mini-diocese—a step towards becoming a diocese.[35]

Conversely, the consequences of the civil war encouraged another moment of Hausa-Fulani Muslim ascendancy. The devastating consequences of the war and the consolidation of military rule centered on a Hausa-speaking officer corps would help cement the political influence of the masu sarauta in the 1970s and 1980s. This resurgence of Northern Muslim elite in national politics generated strong, but divided opposition from the Southern states, the Middle Belt, and Northern minority Christians, with serious implications for sharia as the country embarked on constitutional reforms for a democratic government in the 1970s.

Concomitantly, Northern Muslim assertiveness encouraged Southern and Middle Belt Christians to forge alliances across denominational, ethnic, and regional lines. Indeed, Gowon's postwar policy of reconstruction encouraged mainline Catholic and Protestant denominations to coordinate their response to the devastation in Eastern states. For example, the Christian Council of Nigeria—a group of Protestant churches—collaborated with Catholic churches to establish the first national ecumenical project in 1971. This led to the establishment of two important initiatives: the National Institute of Moral and Religious Education and the Christian Health Association of Nigeria; the latter organization coordinated the distribution of international medical relief to war-torn southeastern communities immediately after the war.[36]

This new ecumenicalism notwithstanding, mainline Christian denominations remained cautious in their newfound relations until the formation of Nigeria's preeminent national Christian organization, the Christian Association of Nigeria (CAN), in 1976. While many factors encouraged its formation, most analysts agree that the consolidation of Northern Muslim interest was the catalyst for its establishment.[37] With a strong focus on the Northern Muslim power structure, the political theater for CAN's activities was in the non-Muslim areas in the old Northern Region, where the Sokoto Caliphate had consolidated its power base under the indirect rule system, and Christian missions had made significant inroads since the colonial period.

Sharia Debate and Transition to Democracy

The years immediately after the civil war were expected to be a time of national reconstruction and reconciliation, but wound up being a period when contending political and religious groups reasserted themselves within the framework of Nigeria's prevailing ethno-regional structure. As the Gowon regime embarked on post–civil war reconstruction, Muslim activists, through various national Muslim organizations, especially the recently formed Nigerian Supreme Council for Islamic Affairs (NSCIA), reasserted Muslim interest in national affairs.[38] These agitations opened up a space for discussions on sharia in the Nigerian legal system. With the overthrow of the Gowon administration in 1975, religion gained greater influence in national politics. Gowon's successor, General Murtala Mohammed, a devout Muslim from Kano, openly embraced a public role for Islam in state affairs during his short period as head of state (July 30, 1975–February 13, 1976). Following Southern Christians' outcry against Mohammed's attempt to establish a federal Sharia Court of Appeal, the FMG backtracked to create a unified Customary Court of Appeal in 1975.[39]

It was in the wider context of agitation for post–civil war political and legal reforms that the FMG in 1975 created a committee to draft a constitution that would herald Nigeria's transition to democracy. This deliberation led to the 1979 Nigerian Constitution, and encouraged an animated debate on the role of sharia in Nigerian political and legal affairs.[40] This debate, which brought Hausa-Fulani Muslim elite into direct conflict with the political class of other regions of the country, once again exposed Nigeria's deep religious and regional fault lines. Consequently, sharia emerged as a critical medium for the articulation of Hausa-Fulani Muslim interests during the transition to a democratic government in the mid-1970s.

As the conflict between pro-sharia (largely Northern Muslims) and anti-sharia (Southern, Middle Belt, and Northern-minority Christians) factions intensified during the constitutional debates, a powerful national Muslim coalition emerged to petition for a Federal Sharia Court of Appeal (FSCA) that would have jurisdiction over both civil and criminal cases. Pro-FSCA Constituent Assembly members insisted that since religious injunctions requires that the conduct of Muslims must be regulated by Islamic law, the new Nigerian constitution must grant sharia courts authority to adjudicate on all legal matters that affect Nigerian Muslims.[41] But when it became apparent that pro-sharia delegates would not achieve their objective in the Constituent Assembly, they elected to boycott assembly deliberations. Eventually, a compromise by the Constitution Drafting Committee's judiciary subcommittee established Sharia and Customary Courts of Appeal in Northern states, with limited authority in civil and criminal cases.[42] Ardent anti-sharia activists contended that the subcommittee's compromise would infringe on the constitutional rights of religious minorities in Northern states and would undermine the secularity of the Nigerian nation-state. Despite this limited constitutional victory by Hausa-Fulani Muslim elites, the Northern pro-sharia alliance was largely a marriage of convenience, bringing together emirate elites of different ideological persuasions and political interests. For example, Islamic reformist clerics, notably Abubakar Gumi, were by the mid-1970s challenging the masu sarauta's legitimacy, claiming that the Hausa-Fulani Muslim aristocracy was a component of a corrupt Nigerian oligarchy.[43]

State Crisis and Religious Violence

Political parties in Nigeria's second democratic government, the Second Republic (1979–1983), had their roots in the political alignments formed during decolonization. Aware of the deep divisions among the major regions, and hoping to undermine alternative centers of power, the Ironsi, Gowon, and Mohammed/Obasanjo[44] military regimes had all curtailed partisan political activities during the period of military rule, from 1966 to 1979. In the Northern states, preexisting political associations provided an organizational node for the construction of parties in 1978, when the Mohammed/Obasanjo regime lifted the ban on party politics. Most prominent of these was the National Movement, precursor to the National Party of Nigeria (NPN), which later won the presidential elections of 1979 and 1983. Although the NPN later embraced a diverse coalition of junior partners, notably Yoruba, Igbo, and Edo politicians, as well as ethnic minorities from the Niger Delta and Cross River areas,[45] the party had its foundation in the Northern Peoples Congress—the former Hausa-Fulani party of the preceding civilian government under the leadership of the late sardauna of Sokoto.[46]

Despite this national alliance, the NPN was firmly anchored to the masu sarauta. Significantly, the party was formed when emirs and other Northern Muslim dignitaries assembled in Sokoto, the headquarters of the caliphate, to celebrate the fortieth anniversary of Sir Abubakar III as the sultan of Sokoto and Sarkin Musulmi (leader of Northern Nigerian Muslim).[47] Furthermore, prominent caliphate titleholders, such as Ibrahim Dasuki, Baraden (later sultan) of Sokoto, and Shehu Malami, Sarkin Sudan of Wurno (a major titleholder in the Sokoto Caliphate) played important roles in the critical months before the 1979 elections. The Makaman Bida, one of the caliphate's most influential traditional chiefs and trusted adviser of the late sardauna served as the grand patron of the party in its formative years.[48] Once in control of state affairs, NPN governors and officials emphasized the emirs' role in the preservation of political stability and the maintenance of law and order.[49]

Similar to the initial era of democratic governance when a progressive populist party, Northern Elements Peoples Union (NEPU), opposed the NPC, the party of the masu sarauta, the People's Redemption Party (PRP) emerged to draw its legitimacy from NEPU's progressive traditions; the PRP campaigned against the entrenched power base of the masu sarauta, now articulated under the political machine of the emergent NPN. Although the PRP was the brainchild of political newcomers, notably Abubakar Rimi, Balarabe Musa, and Bala Usman, former NEPU leader Aminu Kano later was elected party leader.

From the Yoruba states of Lagos, Oyo, Ogun, and Ondo, as well as Kwara State and Bendel State (essentially the old Mid-Western State),[50] prominent Yoruba politicians and obas (traditional monarch of Yoruba city-states) rallied the support of the defunct Action Group (AG) loyalists under the leadership of Awolowo, now elevated to the distinguished title of the Asiwaju of Yorubaland (leader of the Yoruba people) by leading obas. This group became known as the Committee of Friends. This committee led to the formation of a Yoruba-centered party in 1979—in collaboration with old Edo, Itsekiri, Ishan, and other Mid-West allies—the Unity Party of Nigeria.

In the Southwest and Southeast, respectively, the "Progressives" of Lagos and the old Eastern Region formed an alliance that drew its support from the proscribed NCNC coalition of the old Eastern, Western, and Mid-Western Regions. The Lagos and Eastern Progressives merged in May 1978 to form the

Committee for National Unity and Progress. This coalition later became the Southern wing of the Nigerian Peoples Party (NPP).[51] Like the National Movement and the Committee of Friends, these organizations combined the experience of an older generation of party leaders with the aspirations of a new cohort of influential power brokers. Despite the objection of a formidable Northern ally, Kanuri political stalwart Waziri Ibrahim, Nnamdi Azikiwe, the former NCNC leader and renowned nationalist, later became the NPP leader and its presidential candidate in 1979.[52] Ibrahim went on to form a breakaway party, the Great Nigerian Peoples Party, which dominated electoral politics in his Bornu stronghold. Consequently, prevailing ethno-regional (and in the case of the Northern states, ethno-religious) alliances provided the framework on which these major political parties were subsequently based during Nigeria's second democratic government.

Given this context, the election that followed the new constitution saw voting primarily along ethno-regional lines. Dominated by the Northern states, the NPN succeeded in attracting a winning coalition through the support of junior allies in the South, especially in the East, Rivers, and Cross Rivers States. Shehu Shagari, the Turaki of Sokoto, a prominent Hausa-Fulani Muslim titleholder, was elected president of the Federal Republic of Nigeria. In addition, the NPN succeeded in securing control over the federal legislature.

With the ascendancy of the NPN in national and regional politics, Hausa-Fulani Muslim power was anchored to the sardauna's northernization and Islamization vision of the previous democratic era. This incited strong resistance from Christian activists, especially in Southern and Middle Belt states, as well as among Christian minorities in Northern states. As Christians accused the NPN of advancing Northern Muslim interests, ethno-religious and regional divisions grew wider.[53] And as Southern, Middle Belt, and Northern Christians trumpeted their opposition against what many considered the monopoly of state power by a Northern Muslim oligarchy,[54] NPN emirate political elites pushed back, insisting on establishing a Sharia Court of Appeal that would have full legal authority in civil and criminal cases in Northern Muslim society, further amplifying Christian anxiety.

The growing ethno-religious and regional tensions brought violence.[55] Starting in 1980, a wave of religious violence by fringe Islamic movements ravaged several Northern communities. Although the origins of these violent conflicts are not always easy to discern, this enduring religious violence tended to reflect several important factors. First, it reflected the deepening religious and ethnic divisions in Northern and Middle Belt states; second, it showed the growing alienation of the masses of Northern Muslims with the neopatrimonialism of the custodians of the Nigerian state; and finally, it revealed the widening gulf among factions of Hausa-Fulani groups over claims of leadership of Northern Muslims. These factors exacerbated prevailing fissures between Hausa-Fulani Muslim rulers and Northern Christian "indigenes"; Hausa-Fulani Muslim indigenes, and Southern Christian "settlers"; Hausa-Fulani elite and Southern Christian intelligentsia; and Hausa-Fulani Muslim elite and Northern Muslim radical groups.[56] With all of these religious crises going on, the moral authority of the holders of state power was seriously compromised, severely undermining Nigeria's fragile democratic process.[57] Compounded by deepening economic crisis from statism and the declining price of petroleum, the Shagari administration's growing neopatrimonialism exacerbated ethno-regional and ethno-religious tension among Nigeria's diverse groups.[58] In addition, these religious conflicts reflect deeper structural crisis endemic to the Nigerian state and society. The tenuousness of Shagari's NPN government was revealed when a military coup brought the Second Republic to an end on New Year's Eve of 1983.

The first major religious conflict with national implications started in the early 1980s with a radical Muslim sect known as 'Yan tatsine (Hausa for, roughly, "those who damn"). 'Yan tatsine (Maitasine) deployed Islamic doctrine and Hausa traditions of protest to gain popular support among marginalized Hausa talakawa in Northern cities. While many analysts emphasized the fanaticism of 'Yan tatsine, Paul Lubeck perceptively traces the *gardawa*—the Qu'ranic students who were foot soldiers of the sect—back to the era of the Sokoto Caliphate in the 1800s. As Nigerian society experienced rapid social transformation, Lubeck contends, "semi-industrial capitalism" further undermined the gardawa in major Hausa urban areas such as Kano, especially in the dry season. Before the petroleum boom of the 1970s, the gardawa had been steadily integrated into the labor market in Northern cities. Huge growth in oil wealth (from $1 billion in 1970 to almost $23 billion in 1980) intensified social inequality among an emergent commercial-bureaucratic class and the masses of Hausa talakawa, as semi-industrial production stagnated. With this economic transformation, the "laboring poor" was effectively marginalized from the mainstream economy, especially in Northern Nigeria's principal city, Kano.[59]

It was in the context of these tensions in 1980, that 'Yan tatsine's opposition to state authorities exploded into twelve days of violent riots in Kano City that had national reverberations.[60] With inadequate response from state authorities, the riot claimed many lives and destroyed property worth millions of naira. In 1981, another religious protest initiated by 'Yan tatsine discontent in Kano ended in a major confrontation between two Muslim sects that reportedly resulted in the death of several thousands. In Maiduguri in Bornu State, 400 people were killed in 1982. Two years later, in Jimeta in Yola State, 763 people were killed. And in Gombe State, more than 100 people were killed in 1985.[61] When Pope John Paul II visited Nigeria in 1982, growing tensions between Christians and Muslims rose to a boiling point, leading to widespread unrest, including the burning of eight churches in Kano by mobs of Muslim youth.[62]

With Muslim and Christian identities further shaping boundaries of political mobilization by the late 1980s and 1990s, religious conflicts became outright confrontations, complicated by a mix of political, social, and demographic conditions, especially in an environment where the legitimacy of the holders of state power was very much in doubt. The trigger for these violent confrontations tended to be in the perceived encroachment of a religious minority—"non-indigenes"—on the "ancestral" space of a dominant ethno-religious group. In this context, Christianity and Islam had emerged as an important framework for the articulation of local interests connected to the distributive resources of the state. This trend intensified the wave of religious conflicts in the emirate states and the predominantly Christian Middle Belt states.[63] Significantly, this trend has effectively posed a serious threat to peaceful coexistence among Christians and Muslims in Northern and Middle Belt states, especially since the 1980s.[64]

In other Northern cities, religious riots were triggered by several unfortunate incidents in the 1980s and the 1990s, notably, a case of an alleged inflammatory speech by a Christian preacher who had recently converted from Islam in Kaduna State; a Muslim protest in Kano in 1982 over the construction of a church near a mosque, which reportedly led to the death of forty-four Christians; and a visit by German evangelist Richard Bonnke in 1991, dubbed a "crusade," which resulted in two days of mayhem that led to the death of more than two hundred people, most of them Christians. In addition, there were reports of a meeting at the Central Mosque of the Ahmadu Bello University campus that called for the "destruction of Christianity in Zaria" and led to riots in the university that spilled into local communities, resulting in the destruction of churches, mosques, and the homes of many Christians; and in Kano City, in May 1995, a confrontation between two alleged Hausa thieves and Igbo shop owners led to religious attacks by irate Muslim youths in the Sabon Gari (settler) quarters, resulting in the death of many Christians.[65] Significantly, these waves of religious crisis were widespread during the military regimes of three Hausa-speaking Muslims after the demise of Nigeria's Second Republic, namely the military administrations of Generals Buhari, Babangida, and Abacha.

Muslim-Christian Relations: Conflict and Compromise under Military Rule

The brief military regime of Major-General Mohammadu Buhari (January 1984 to August 1985) further firmed up the power base of the Northern Muslim political class. Following the massive corruption of the ousted civil-democratic government, Buhari's regime projected stern and dictatorial policies that restricted civil liberties and confronted many professional and civic organizations (including the Nigerian Bar Association, Nigerian Medical Association, Nigerian Labor Congress, and Nigerian University Students Union). However, the regime embraced Hausa-Fulani emirs to harness local support in Northern states. A Hausa-Fulani "Brahmin" from Katsina, Buhari regularly consulted the sultan of Sokoto, Sir Abubakar III, on critical state affairs. Buhari also instructed his state military governors, especially those in charge of Northern states, to embrace emirs as an "informal second tier of authority."[66] Nevertheless, Buhari's brief rule witnessed prompt military response to sporadic religious violence by Muslim militants in Northern states. For example, the Buhari regime moved against religious riots carried out by 'Yan tatsine militants, allegedly with support from Niger, Chad, and Cameroon nationals in Kano in 1984—and intermittent riots in Yola from 1984 to 1985, killing more than one thousand people. State authorities blamed this wave of religious disturbances on demographic pressure from illegal immigrants. As Nigeria's economic crisis deepened and with growing discontent over the restriction of civil liberties, another Hausa-speaking Muslim general, Ibrahim Babangida, ousted Buhari in a palace coup in August 1985.

Under Babangida's regime, Nigeria's Christian-Muslim conflicts took center stage over the country's controversial membership in the Organization of Islamic Conference (OIC, later Organization of Islamic Cooperation) in 1986.[67] Christian leaders claimed that the regime made the decision to join the OIC without consulting the Nigerian public. Nigeria's powerful Catholic bishops, expressing concern over the nation's unity and the rights of Christian minorities in predominantly Northern Muslim states, noted that the OIC charter undermined the essential tenet of Nigeria's plural and secular state.[68] Earlier in the year, at a national conference on Babangida's OIC policy, a prominent Catholic leader, Monsignor Hypolite Adigwe, had argued in a well-circulated conference paper that Babangida's policy would embolden the Northern pro-sharia movement.[69] As the OIC controversy expanded, Adigwe's paper was published as a pamphlet titled *Nigeria Joins the Organization of Islamic Conference, O.I.C.: The Implications for Nigeria.*[70] Adigwe notes:

> The ratification of our membership of the OIC amounts to amending our constitution automatically. It is at variance with Section 10 of our Constitution which declares Nigeria a secular state. Both are mutually exclusive. The OIC is there to foster Islamic religion in all its dimensions—economic, political, cultural, scientific, etc. and every activity has to be in accordance with Islamic law. Our money will therefore be used in spreading Islam, building Islamic schools, universities, and mosques, and maybe fighting a jihad.[71]

Responding to the strong opposition of Christians throughout the country, General Babangida convened a Consultative Committee of leading Christian and Muslim leaders, including Archbishop A. O. Okogie, Catholic archbishop of Nigeria; Bishop J. A. Adetiloye, Anglican bishop of Nigeria; and Ibrahim Dasuki, secretary-general of the Supreme Council of Islamic Affairs—to explore how Nigeria's national interest might "be affected by the recent change from observer status to full membership within the OIC."[72] Significantly, under the chairmanship of a Northern Christian military officer, Lieutenant Colonel John Shagaya (a regime loyalist), the committee was noticeably different in its makeup from the delegation of Northern Muslim notables that had formally presented Nigeria's application for OIC membership at the organization's annual meeting in Fez, Morocco, earlier in 1986.[73] Not surprisingly, the report of the Consultative Committee was vague and perfunctory:

> We note that the assurance given by the Federal Military Government that our full membership of the OIC does not in any way imply Nigeria has become or will become an Islamic state has addressed the undoubted reservations expressed by sections of the country. We also note that these reservations can only be cleared with time and after further consultation. Furthermore, we agree that the peace and stability of our multi-religious nation and the secular character of Nigeria must be preserved.[74]

The following year, when Muslim mobs attacked churches in several Northern cities, Catholic bishops called on federal and state authorities to carry out a thorough investigation to bring those responsible to justice. At the annual Catholic Bishops' conference in Awka in 1987, the bishops again queried Nigeria's OIC membership.

However, as Christian-Muslim tensions intensified, some Catholic leaders also encouraged peaceful dialogue with their Muslim counterparts, drawing on doctrines from the Second Vatican under Pope Paul IV from 1962 to 1965. Significantly, in a high-profile meeting later in 1987, Catholic bishops, in collaboration with the Association of Episcopal Churches, in a communiqué titled "Christianity and Islam in Dialogue," identified common grounds between the two world religions; they called on Muslim leaders to reject discriminatory practices against Christians, including classifying non-Muslims as infidels and imposing heavy penalties on Christian converts from Islam, and on Muslim women who marry Christians.

No Christian leader exemplified this spirit of peaceful dialogue with Nigeria's Muslim leadership during this period more than Cardinal Francis Arinze, a former archbishop of Onitsha and president of the Pontifical Council for Inter-religious Dialogue. He later became a prominent cardinal bishop in the Vatican. As one of Africa's foremost Catholic priests, Cardinal Arinze, an ethnic Igbo, had gained fame for his humanitarian work in the defunct Republic of Biafra during the civil war. Having arrived at the Vatican only a year before the OIC crisis, Cardinal Arinze had acquired extensive experience with Christian-Muslim conflicts in Nigeria. As Nigeria's religious crisis intensified in the 1980s, Cardinal Arinze called for reconciliation and understanding between Christians and Muslims. For example, in a notable keynote address in 1988, he provided important historical and global contexts to Nigeria's enduring Christian-Muslim conflict. Cardinal Arinze contended that while Christianity has existed for twenty centuries and Islam for fourteen, their relations had been characterized by tension and conflict. However, since the Second Vatican, important theological steps had been taken to establish an environment of reconciliation between Catholics and Muslims. Calling for constructive dialogue, Cardinal Arinze argued that religious conflicts are often related to political and economic factors, compounded by historical memories of wars and violence. Drawing on the Second Vatican's call for peaceful coexistence,[75] he pleaded the imperative of accommodation and reconciliation among Nigerian Christians and Muslims.

Cardinal Arinze was, however, realistic about the limitations of interreligious dialogue in Nigeria's deeply divided society. He felt that Nigerian Catholic leaders should nevertheless find inspiration from the doctrine espoused in Vatican II and the works of Pope Paul IV—and subsequently Pope John Paul II. In the *Declaration on Religious Freedom*, Cardinal Arinze notes that Vatican II speaks of the right of every human being to follow his or her conscience in religious matters. It sought to underscore shared beliefs among various religions and the need for understanding and collaboration. Cardinal Arinze noted that Pope Paul received the ulema of Saudi Arabia in 1974. For his part, Pope John Paul II engaged people of various religions, especially Muslims, receiving Muslim representatives and giving addresses on interreligious dialogue around the world. Cardinal Arinze called on Nigeria's Catholic leaders to draw on the inspirational leadership of Paul IV and John Paul II.[76]

In keeping with Cardinal Arinze's passionate call for interreligious dialogue, some Nigerian Catholic priests encouraged constructive dialogue between Catholics and Muslims. In this regard, the work of a renowned Igbo Catholic theologian, the Rev. Dr. Stan Anih, is worthy of note. In his popular pamphlet *The Cathedral and the Mosque Can Co-exist in Nigeria,* Reverend Anih contends: "We believe that by a healthy dialogue between Christians and Moslems a new religious sensitivity, called ecumenism ... can give Nigeria peace and unity because dialogue is an eternal action."[77] Reflecting on the fallout of Nigeria's religious crisis in the 1980s, Anih called on people of all faiths, especially Christians, to "listen" and "dialogue" carefully and work with Muslims to achieve a common good. He insisted that this new ecumenism must lie in reconciliation, the acceptance of pluralism, and "bracketing" all destructive aspects of culture to achieve unity in diversity. After all, "the basic doctrine of all theologies is the sameness of divinity in all men [and women]."[78]

Some mainstream Muslim organizations attempted to encourage constructive dialogue between Muslim and Christian groups. For example, the Council of Ulama tried to corral diverse Islamic interests into a peace movement, but its ties to the "radical" Muslim Student Society hindered the organization's claims as a reliable broker of peaceful dialogue with Christian groups.[79] Other peace efforts initiated by federal and state authorities took the form of seminars, workshops, and conferences to foster religious dialogue between Christians and Muslims.[80] In 1987, the Babangida administration convened the National Council for Religious Affairs (NCRA) as a statutory body to promote peaceful coexistence. This body, however, enjoyed little success. In practice, the committee consisted of leaders of the NSCIA and CAN. When the latter alleged bias from federal authorities toward Northern Muslims and stopped participating in the body's deliberations, the committee became obsolete.[81]

Despite the peace initiatives, the divide between Christian and Muslim groups grew wider as the OIC controversy raged on with great intensity. Muslim leaders, most of them from emirate society, defended Babangida's decision to join the OIC, arguing that Nigeria is a majority Muslim country and thus should deepen its relationship with Muslim countries.[82] Muslim rebuttals to OIC critics further contended that the organization merely sought parity with Christian organizations; for example, Muslim activists argued that belonging to the OIC was no different from having diplomatic relations with the Vatican, as many countries did, including Nigeria.[83] However, the OIC's stated objectives revealed a major contradiction for a country with Nigeria's religious history: as noted by a former OIC secretary-general, the organization's main objectives are "to propagate Islam and acquaint the rest of the world with Islam, its issues and aspirations... [and affirm that] Islam is the only path which can lead [Muslims] to strength, dignity, prosperity, and a better future. It is the pledge and guarantee of the authenticity of the *Ummah*, safeguarding it from the tyrannical onrush of materialism."[84]

Christian leaders, for their part, argued that since OIC membership held the force of international treaty, Nigeria, like other OIC members, now would be duty-bound to provide financial resources to defend Islamic holy places, support Palestinian liberation movements, and promote global Islamic solidarity. In the end, the OIC affair and resultant controversy only hardened religious identities, especially as they reflected entrenched Hausa-Fulani Muslim power structures, Northern Christian minority resistance, and Southern Christian intelligentsia insistence on Nigerian state secularity.[85]

Embedded in the OIC conflict and contemporaneous national debate were the questions of how and by whom "Islam" and "secularity" were defined in a country where the vestiges of Western governance were steeped in Christian influences. The saga thus exposed a fundamental contradiction in the discourse of the Nigerian state and society over the meaning of religion in Nigeria's purported secular state. In his keynote address at the annual conference of the Nigerian Association for the Study of Religions in 1991, the eloquent Yoruba secretary-general of the NSCIA, Lateef Adegbite, argued that Nigerian Muslims who confront this contradiction fall into the following stark categories:

> state supremacists (who seek to place the state above all other social institutions including Islam); atheists and secularists (who claim that Nigeria is a secular state, which Muslims argue against because Islam forbids denying the presence of God); modernists (who undermine religion and [would like] to do away with it); rival religious groups (who feel threatened by Islam and want to harass Muslim leadership and drown Islamic voices); spoilers within (a house divided within itself, giving Islam a bad image); and media misrepresentation (local and international media aimed at distorting [the image of] Islam).[86]

While such specific religious dictates reflect strong conviction, they reify major ethno-religious fault lines in Nigeria's contentious politics.

During this period, another major bout of religious violence exploded on the national scene in Kafanchan, in Kaduna State, in March 1987, later spinning off to other parts of the state and several Northern communities. This wave of Christian-Muslim confrontations would mark the peak of the religious violence in Northern and Middle Belt states in the turbulent 1980s. Kafanchan, headquarters of the Jema local government, is located about three hundred kilometers south of the city of Kaduna. With a population of about eighty thousand, Kafanchan consists largely of Christian indigenous ethnic groups—the Jaba, Kagoma, Ninzom, Ayyu, Gwantu, Numana, and Godo-godo—as well as Hausa-Fulani Muslim "settlers." In this specific case, underlying Christian-Muslim tension turned into open attacks on churches when a recent Christian convert from Islam, Abubakar Bako, allegedly blasphemed against Islam at a Christian students' organization meeting at the city's College of Education.[87]

After a week of destruction, the Kaduna State military government convened a panel chaired by State Commissioner for Justice Hansen Donli to investigate the riots and to make recommendations to the state authorities. The Donli Panel noted: "From many submissions made, it was quite obvious that certain highly placed individuals and organizations, had in the past been in the habit of either making unguarded utterances or publishing provocative and sensitive materials in the media, capable of causing tension in the country."[88] However, the panel failed to secure the confidence of both Christian and Muslim groups. CAN claimed that the panel did little to address the plight of aggrieved Christians and kowtowed to powerful Muslim interests.[89] Representing Muslims' interests, the Council of Ulama called for Islamic solidarity, argued that the state governor should have done more to protect Muslims, and requested the release of Muslims detained in police custody. A Committee of Concerned Citizens claimed that the economic and social deprivation of the masses of Hausa-Fulani Muslims was the root cause of the violence, but Christian groups, the Kaduna State government, and the federal government dismissed the committee's claims. Eventually, the FMG (Federal Military Government) convened a judicial tribunal chaired by Justice Karibi-Whyte to try all those detained in the religious riots. In the end, little was done to provide either justice or reconciliation. Reflecting on these tragic riots many years later, the Rev. Dr. Matthew Hassan Kukah—a renowned Catholic theologian and later Catholic bishop of Sokoto—concluded that the crisis further consolidated the power base of the Northern Muslim elite.[90]

Sporadic religious violence continued in some Northern communities in the late 1980s as the Hausa-Fulani Muslim elite asserted its power base during the Babangida regime's transition to democratic government. Toward this end, Hausa-Fulani elites created the Northern Elders' Committee, consisting of emirs, politicians, businessmen, and senior administrators, to exert influence over the FMG. In the context of these efforts, internecine battles continued between Muslims and Christians, especially in Kaduna State, with its large indigenous Christian population. More widespread communal conflicts were reported during the 1987 local government elections. Christian leaders in Kaduna State and other Northern states with substantial Christian populations alleged that Muslims retained a stranglehold on state affairs, as exemplified by the OIC crisis, Nigeria's involvement in the Islamic Development Bank, and the unrelenting push for expanded sharia in Northern states.[91] Northern Christian leaders called for comprehensive reforms to ensure secularity and national unity, and for a prohibition against Nigerian membership in international religious organizations.[92]

During this period of intense religious conflict, intra-Muslim relations in the Northern states also suffered as reformists, particularly Abubakar Gumi (see chapter 4), rose to prominence. Gumi had been educated in elite Islamic schools; he came to know Hausa-Fulani Muslim notables such as Tafawa Balewa, Aminu Kano, Ibrahim Dasuki, and Shehu Shagari in his youth.[93] After attending Kano Law School, he briefly worked with the sardauna and as a scribe for the chief alkali, thereafter taking up a teaching position at his old school in the early 1950s. In 1955, Gumi was made imam of the sardauna's hajj group, and later, in 1957, he oversaw the pilgrimage of Nigerians to the hajj. As discussed earlier, these notable accomplishments won him the appointment as deputy grand qadi of the Northern Region just before independence, and in 1962 he was promoted to grand qadi. Gumi and the sardauna collaborated to found the JNI (Jama 'atu Nasril Islam) and established many Islamic schools in the Northern Region. After the sardauna's assassination, however, Gumi embraced a new Islamic reformism and questioned the authority of the masu sarauta. In the early 1970s, he criticized Gowon's military regime; this move won him support from populist elements in emirate states. In 1975 General Murtala Mohammed appointed Gumi grand mufti. Three years later, Gumi gave his blessing to a new movement, Jama't Izalat al Bid'a Wa Iqamat as Sunna, or Izala. Seeking to both revive and reform Nigerian Islam, Izala leaders preached a return to orthodoxy and decried Sufi thought as deviating from holy texts. He reserved the strongest criticism for the tijaniyya because of the association of the qadiriyya with Sokoto jihadists, whom he revered. Despite Sufism's long history—arising from twelfth- and thirteenth-century mysticism, with qadiriyya coming first and the tijaniyya arriving during the eighteenth century—Gumi claimed that such Sufi orders "are inconsistent with true Islam."[94] According to him, Sufis teach withdrawal from this world, practice mystical rites, canonize certain rulers, recognize saints, and organize the ummah into hierarchical, competing structures, all of which are unauthorized innovations to the Qur'an and the Prophetic tradition.[95]

Nevertheless, Izala gained prominence among relatively well-educated professionals in the public and private sectors, especially in the cosmopolitan cities of Kaduna and Jos. With a focus on religious orthodoxy, Izala emphasized strict interpretations of religious texts, especially the Qur'an and hadith, along with the widespread availability of classical texts in Hausa language.[96] Reflecting in his autobiography on the establishment of Izala, Gumi frames the organization as a regrettable necessity, given the corruption of some emirs who had broken from Sokoto's piety: "They had brought back to life all the corrupt practices against which Sheikh dan Fodio went to war with the former Hausa rulers. They had become kings with big palaces full of servants and courtiers, and required other people to bow down before them. They kept concubines and did not really fear God's anger."[97] Later, Gumi defends his Izala movement on grounds similar to those propagated by Usman dan Fodio and his followers during the Sokoto Jihad: "Certainly, one could draw a lot of parallels between the rise of some contemporary mass elements, like the Izala Movement, and the forces that overthrew the Hausa kings during the Jihad in 1804."[98] Indeed, it was from the tradition of the Sokoto Jihad that Izala established its moral authority to inscribe sharia into the Nigerian politico-religious project.[99]

Thus, Izala institutionalized criticism of Hausa-Fulani Muslim rulers and lambasted preachers who claimed to have direct connection to the Prophet. Within months, such activity had sparked a full-fledged crisis among Northern Muslims; attempts at reconciliation failed in 1979 and again in 1983, the second time despite President Shagari's personal intervention. Hausa-Fulani Muslim youths flocked to its teachings despite the emirate establishments' ambivalence toward the movement. Tensions, already fraught, were heightened when Saudi Arabia gave the prestigious King Faisal Award to Gumi in 1987 for his service to Islam. Nigerian Christians were against the award because it underscored the influence of Saudi Arabia in Nigerian politics; in addition, some emirs frowned at it because it elevated Gumi's brand of Islamic orthodoxy among Nigerian Muslims. Nevertheless, "intra-Sufi and Sufi–*Yan Izala* differences mounted" by the late 1980s,[100] resulting in the formation of Jundullahi (Soldiers of God) and the Fityan al-Islam (Muslim Youth or Heroes/Youth of Islam) by qadiriyya and tijaniyya, respectively. Despite these counters, members of Izala were widely seen as forward-thinking Muslims because they advocated female education and denounced entrenched traditional practices considered un-Islamic, such as customary bride prices. Despite Gumi's death in 1992, and eroding Izala membership, the movement remains influential among Northern Muslims.[101]

A Long Transition to Democracy

At the height of such political uncertainty in 1985 Babangida announced his transition program to a constitutional democratic government. Although the program was later subverted by Babangida himself,[102] the issues that dominated the discussion from military rule to a democratic government nevertheless provides a good illustration of Nigerian public discourse for almost four decades. The regime's contentious politics of democratic transition exposed the growing politicization of the Nigerian military by the late 1980s, revealing a clique of senior military officers' domination of the extractive agencies of the state.

Immediately after seizing power in 1985, Babangida appointed a Political Bureau to recommend a suitable democratic system for Nigeria. At its inauguration in January 1986, Babangida called on the panel to identify the problems that had led to previous failures of Nigerian civilian governments and to propose effective political response to sustain a democratic system in the long term.[103] Unlike the 1976 Constitution Drafting Committee, this was a fact-finding commission, responsible for appraising Nigeria's governance institutions and proposing viable solutions. Although many Nigerian civic groups were growing wary of military-sponsored transition programs, emirate elites actively participated in the Political Bureau discussions. Dominated by proscribed NPN party bosses from the Second Republic, Northern Muslim elite formed a political organization called the Committee of Elders to lobby the Political Bureau. The political class of Southern states (notably from the Igbo, Ibibio, Efik, Ijaw, and Yoruba communities) also lobbied the bureau. In one landmark gathering in early 1987, an organization called the Eastern Solidarity Group, consisting of politicians and traditional rulers from the Eastern states of Anambra, Imo, Rivers, and Cross Rivers, resolved to "advance eastern interests."[104] In the West, Yoruba politicians and obas started an ethnic association called the Egbe Ilosiwaju Yoruba (Yoruba Progressive Organization) to position the Yorubas for the next democratic government.[105]

The Babangida regime, in any case, rejected the Political Bureau's main recommendation: the establishment of a social democratic/socialist republic. This decision left the regime with no other option but to embrace the existing political arrangement. This further hardened Nigeria's neopatrimonial political structure, rationalized by dominant ethno-regional power relations. As the resultant crisis of political legitimacy intensified, the Nigerian political process was aggravated by a dramatic economic downturn brought on by falling oil prices, a staggering foreign debt burden, and shortages of foreign exchange.

This intensified existing disequilibria—between classes, between regions, and between community-based structures and the Nigerian state.[106]

Complicated by the economic crisis of the 1980s, religious identity in the Babangida years thus reflected intersections of ethnic, regional, and class interests. Babangida's initial policy of dialogue was steadily replaced by manipulative and repressive measures to ward off growing discontent.[107] This only alienated restless professional and civic organizations. As the regime restricted the political space and civil liberties of the urban citizenry, its policies were complicated by the failure of its economic liberalization program. It was clear by the late 1980s that it would be difficult to reconcile a structural adjustment program, imposed with the blessing of the International Monetary Fund, with the regime's faltering democratic transition program.[108]

Nonetheless, economic problems worsened, causing cutbacks in already dwindling social services, resulting in more unrest by early 1988. Small-scale, localized events, such as mobs of Muslim youths attacking churches, became frequent,[109] and religious intolerance continued into the early 1990s. The sultan of Sokoto, Sir Abubakar III, died in 1988, ending a fifty-year reign, and disputes over his succession caused riots that killed ten people before the appointment of Ibrahim Dasuki as sultan.

As the Babangida regime planned, the Constituent Assembly met in 1989 to review a new constitution. Christian activists argued that the legal system was now tilted toward advocates of expanded sharia in civil and criminal cases. Sharia advocates, on the other hand, were adamant that the opposite was the case and that Nigeria needed a federal sharia appeal court system, for which they had unsuccessfully fought in the previous decade. In language foreshadowing the sharia crisis that would overwhelm the country at the beginning of the twenty-first century, sharia advocates in the Constituent Assembly argued that in order to make justice equitable, Nigerian Muslims should have the constitutional right to be governed by sharia in civil and criminal cases. With the growing polarization between pro-sharia and anti-sharia factions, Babangida removed federal Islamic law from the Assembly's terms of reference.[110] Finally, while the Constituent Assembly increased the jurisdiction of sharia courts of appeal at the state level, it still limited these courts' powers to civil cases among Muslims. This constitution, which came to bear Babangida's name, was made into law but never enacted.[111]

Significantly, 1990 witnessed a failed coup by junior officers, mostly of Middle Belt and Northern Christian minority origin, that further deepened religious tensions, alongside the growing delegitimation of the Babangida regime. Sporadic religious riots in Bauchi continued from 1990 to 1991, reportedly killing two hundred people, and similar outbreaks in Katsina took forty lives. In 1991, Islamists clashed with the military in several Northern communities, while anti-Christian riots occurred in Kano.[112] Meanwhile, the Federal Military Government conducted a census that led to allegations of widespread census inflations across the federation.[113] In early 1992, ethno-religious conflict broke out in Kaduna and Taraba States, the latter a Tiv-Jukun conflict that lasted through the following two years. Later in 1993, the Babangida regime's transition program finally brought about a presidential election. A Yoruba Muslim from Ogun State, Moshood Abiola, won the presidency on the Social Democratic Party ticket. It was declared the freest election in Nigerian history, yet Babangida annulled the result, a move widely attributed to the fact that it would have shifted regional control over federal government from the Hausa-Fulani Muslim North to the South. Strong opposition against the military regime forced Babangida to step down. After a brief interim civilian government led by Ernest Shonekan, a Yoruba ally of Babangida, former Chief of Army Staff Sani Abacha staged a coup in November 1993, keeping power in the hands of Hausa-speaking Muslim officers.

The next five years were characterized by a level of state brutality unknown in postcolonial Nigerian history. Political dissidents and prodemocracy activists, including former military head of state Olusegun Obasanjo, were jailed on trumped-up charges of sedition for opposing the regime. And in 1995, Abacha executed Ogoni (Niger Delta Region) human rights activist Ken Saro Wiwa and his compatriots, amid global outrage.[114] In March 1996, Abacha took the unprecedented step of deposing Dasuki as sultan of Sokoto and replaced him with the more conservative Muhammadu Maccido, initially preferred by the Sokoto kingmakers.[115] Moreover, Abacha imprisoned the radical Muslim cleric Ibrahim Zakzaky in September 1996. Zakzaky's followers clashed with state security forces in Zaria in late 1996, and again in February 1997, when they tried to capture the Kano Central Mosque.[116] By this time, it was evident that the relationship between the Abacha regime and the Northern Muslim elite was significantly strained because the regime's excessive repression had shattered the equilibrium between the Northern Muslim political class and the political classes of other geopolitical zones in the country, effectively undermining the strategic political advantage of the emirate political class.

Abacha died suddenly in 1998, amid speculation of foul play, and the defense chief of staff, General Abdulsalami Abubakar, another Northern Muslim, became interim head of state. He immediately announced a transition to civilian rule. As prodemocracy activists insisted that the interim regime respect the outcome of the June 12, 1994, presidential election, President-elect Abiola died suddenly only a month after Abacha, and the Abubakar administration introduced another transition to democratic government program. The interim government reinstated political freedoms, released political dissidents—including Obasanjo, Zakzaky, and Dasuki—from prison. Finally, a Constitutional Drafting Committee was instated.

This committee's final proposal for a new constitution was based on the 1995 Abacha draft constitution, which had curtailed sharia.[117] Unlike the 1979 Constitution, this draft constitution came from a peculiar environment. It was formulated during the period when emirate power was declining and the military's image was being shattered. Nonetheless, elections were held, and former military head of state, Olusegun Obasanjo, a Yoruba Christian, was elected president on the ticket of the People's Democratic Party (PDP)—and Nigeria's Fourth Republic was born.[118]

CHAPTER SIX

RELIGIOUS REVIVAL
AND THE STATE: THE RISE
OF PENTECOSTALISM

Pentecostalism formed the most important religious movement that swept through Nigeria's Southern and Middle Belt states starting in the 1980s. It evolved from mission Christianity and African-initiated churches in the wake of the political ferment of the 1950s, grew exponentially during the national upheavals of the 1960s and 1970s, and further expanded because of the consequences of neoliberalism in the 1980s and 1990s. Jacob Olupona, a leading scholar of Christianity in Nigeria, argues persuasively that despite its deep religious roots, Pentecostalism is essentially a manifestation of and response to the complexities of modern transformations in the country:

> Pentecostalism is a phenomenon inseparable from modernity and should be seen as complementing the increasingly cosmopolitan character of business, ideas, and people. Studies in Pentecostalism should not only consider the issues of origin—that is, where and when Pentecostalism began—but also should address the influence of the movement on individuals and society.[1]

In his book *Nigerian Pentecostalism*, theologian Nimi Wariboko makes the critical connection between Pentecostalism and the material conditions of local people, arguing that the "Pentecostal epistemic" reveals a dialectical process between transcendence and temporal, sacred and profane, local and global, engaging major themes that are emblematic of Nigeria's rapidly changing society.[2] As the crisis of the Nigerian state deepened by the 1980s, mass conversion to Pentecostal churches from mainline Catholic and Protestant churches, as well as African-initiated churches, centered on material and spiritual empowerment. Consequently, Pentecostalism, despite its evocative piety, provides a pragmatic and moral response to the crisis of statism and neoliberalism.[3] Wariboko provides a compelling analysis of contending Pentecostal doctrines, distinguishing between various traditions including Holiness and Prosperity and showing how this remarkable religious movement transformed Nigerian public life, especially since the attainment of independence in 1960.[4] Furthermore, the renowned scholar of African Pentecostalism Ogbu Kalu argued that many social science—especially sociological—approaches to the study of Nigerian Pentecostalism are limited in their analytical perspective because they fail to seriously engage the religious experience of adherents of Nigeria's Pentecostal movement. He called for a greater engagement with religious beliefs and traditions.[5] Concomitantly, Ruth Marshall focused on the explicitly religious manner in which Nigerian Pentecostals interpret political developments and the manner in which they express their political opinions and activities.[6] Lamin Sanneh contends that one of the major issues facing new African Christian movements such as Nigerian Pentecostal movements lies in the inability of the secular state to effectively engage the religious questions that are central to the everyday lives of local people.[7] In this context, Pentecostalism provides an important medium for the articulation of religious, social, political, and economic conditions that shape local people's aspirations in contemporary Nigerian society. Consequently, Simeon Ilesanmi perceptively observed that Nigeria's Pentecostal movement reflects a complicated religious, social, and political process that is integral to the making of modern Nigerian society. He notes that Nigerian Pentecostalism "does not constitute an homogenous movement, but is rather the sum of a number of succeeding waves, each of which draws upon and transforms that which has gone before."[8] As the crisis of the Nigerian state intensified in the 1980s, Pentecostal Christianity did not only fill the gap left behind by the state, but also provided a powerful critique of the state's custodians. In its engagement with the wider Nigerian state and society, this movement has complicated the structural imbalance between Christians and Muslims in the three major Nigerian geopolitical regions that feature significantly in this study: the core North (the Hausa-Fulani region), the Southwest (the Yoruba region), and the Middle Belt.

Holiness Pentecostals in Historical Perspective

Nigeria's Holiness Pentecostal movement grew significantly in the context of the challenges confronting Nigerian society following independence in 1960.[9] Its followership grew exponentially during the Nigerian-Biafra Civil War (1967–1970) because the fluid theological structure of Pentecostal movements freely adapted to the disruptions precipitated by the war.[10] Equally significant was the fact that in the Igbo-speaking areas of southeastern Nigeria, the epicenter of the civil war, local people moved toward syncretistic prayer houses that combined Christianity with indigenous cosmology. In addition, the influence of mainline Protestant and Catholic churches eroded in southeastern Nigeria because many major Western countries, especially Britain, supported the Nigerian Federal Government's opposition to Biafra's insistence on secession from the country. More importantly, the war severely disrupted missionary work in Biafra-controlled areas and undermined the integrity of some established missionary institutions in Northern, Western, and Mid-Western states. In a context of national crisis, it is not difficult to see how and why indigenous religious beliefs would interact with forms of charismatism, creating new "social control models" in a moment of great uncertainty and insecurity.[11] Consequently, the crisis precipitated by the civil war encouraged the growth of "antistructural" Christian movements that had been a feature of Nigerian Pentecostalism, especially during the upheaval of the late colonial period.[12]

With the crisis of the 1980s and 1990s (see chapter 5), the deliverance doctrines of Pentecostalism gained momentum, attracting millions of disillusioned Nigerian Christians.[13] As Pentecostal leaders denounced the political alliances that had produced the insecurities of this period, their membership moved further away from prevailing social networks to form distinct moral communities. In many instances, religious practices transformed social orientation. Engaging innovative methods of responding to the material and spiritual needs of their growing adherents, Holiness churches contested the public space as the exclusive domain of secularism.[14] While materialism remained a function of everyday life, it was repackaged into specific Christian rules: prosperity flowed from personal moral integrity and not the economy of favors, and rewards come in both this life and the next. Leaders of mainline Christian denominations who had been preaching "progress" since the colonial era were "disarmed" because of their connection to the discredited political and social order.[15] Thus, leaders of Holiness groups denounced the old churches for their "traditionalism, the sustenance of the heritage from the missionary ancestors, [and] encrusted patriarchy."[16] In response, mainline church leaders responded rigidly to this moral challenge, imposing new codes of discipline within their ranks. Indeed, in many cases, mainline church leaders treated the younger generation who were attracted to the revivalist message of Pentecostalism as rebellious upstarts and in some cases expelled them from their churches.

A younger generation of charismatic clerics led the movement's remarkable growth and creative energy. Political independence in the early 1960s had seen thousands of young Nigerians in higher education, and with four new universities established between 1960 and 1962, university enrollment grew significantly in the years immediately after independence, particularly in Southern areas.[17] Many young people who had grown up with connections to African independent churches (AICs) such as the Aladura Church, with its syncretistic rituals, were attracted to the revivalist theology of the Pentecostal movement.[18] But despite this attempt to distance themselves from AICs, Olupona perceptively observes that "Pentecostal practices surreptitiously reflect traditional forms of African religious spirituality, including speaking in tongues, possession by the Holy Ghost, and an emphasis on the proximate, this world salvation, as evidenced by a focus on materiality, prosperity, and pragmatism."[19] Indeed, several notable Pentecostal churches traced their roots to AICs: for instance, in 1969 prominent Pentecostal church leaders such as Stephen Okafor, Raphael Okafor, and Arthur Orizu left Aladura churches to form the Hour of Freedom Evangelical Association, which grew rapidly in Igbo communities after the civil war.[20] Similarly, when a schism appeared in Christ Ascension Church, Mike Okonkwo, another prominent Pentecostal leader, led a group of "young rebels" and founded a Pentecostal church, the True Redeemed Evangelical Mission; in 1986 Okonkwo became the president of Nigeria's powerful Pentecostal national umbrella organization, the Pentecostal Fellowship of Nigeria (PFN).[21] More importantly, a network of evangelical students' organizations in Southern and Middle Belt states expanded the scope of the three dominant Christian spiritual associations in Nigerian universities—the Student Christian Movement (SCM), the Scripture Union (SU), and the Christian Union (CU)—in the first decade after independence in 1960.

The SCM had come to prominence in the 1940s, with returning Nigerian graduates from British universities, including Igbo statesman Sir Francis Akanu Ibiam and Yoruba leader Theophilus Ejiwumi; the latter had mentored many of the first generation of Christian students at the University of Ibadan. From the early 1960s, SCM branches were formed at the newly established University of Nigeria campus in Enugu and the University of Zaria (later Ahmadu Bello University). Indeed, as the only interdenominational Christian student organization in Nigerian universities, the SCM had established vibrant branches in the newly established Universities of Ife, Lagos, and at the Nsukka campus of the University of Nigeria by the mid-1960s.[22]

By contrast, the SU, established in England in 1867, arrived in Nigeria in 1884 as a nondenominational evangelical movement. It almost disappeared in Nigeria during the Second World War, and was revived by the evangelical fervor of several British teachers in the 1950s. Nigerian university students seized the helm of the SU resurgence by the early years of independence, and the movement grew significantly in the country's institutions of higher learning and secondary schools. In the 1970s the movement shifted focus to its Pilgrims' groups, established a vibrant youth evangelism program, and published a vast literature to propagate the faith among Nigeria's growing educated class.[23]

Similarly, the CU has its roots in Nigeria's colonial past. It began in 1910, having broken away from the SCM "for being spiritually and ethically tepid."[24] In the early years of independence, the CU grew in popularity, spreading at the University of Ibadan; the University College Hospital, Ibadan; the University of Lagos; and the University of Nigeria, Nsukka. By the late 1970s, CU had established the Christian Students' Social Movement of Nigeria, seeking to "enlighten [young] Christians on the possibility of their influence in national life."[25] With support from faculty mentors as chaplains, dedicated CU students actively recruited new members. In January 1970, the Tuesday Group, a CU-affiliated Pentecostal prayer network at the University of Ibadan, formed the World Action Team for Christ, spreading its message of intense Bible study, strict moral rectitude, and baptism in the Holy Spirit. In addition to forming the Calvary Ministries—an evangelical arm extending into Northern states—the group organized numerous retreats to deepen the faith among its members and spread its message throughout the country.[26]

An inadvertent tool for the evangelization of the Holiness movement among educated young Nigerians arrived in the form of the National Youth Service Corps (NYSC), a one-year mandatory program for national integration imposed by the Gowon regime in 1973. As evangelical NYSC recruits arrived at their postings in various regions of the country, they formed national evangelical organizations such as the Fellowship of Christian Students, New Life for All, and the Nigerian Fellowship of Evangelical Students. By the mid-1970s, NYSC evangelical members had established ten ministries in the Northern and Middle Belt cities of Jos, Kaduna, Kano, and Zaria, further projecting a Southern Christian consciousness into Northern and Middle Belt states. In the words of Kalu:

> Initially, these fellowships served as the ministerial formation sites.... The young people walked on foot along the railway line from one town to the other preaching, sleeping in open classrooms, without money, and dependent on the hospitality of strangers. They trusted that God would miraculously meet their needs. The millennialist beliefs added urgency to their evangelism and inspired one and all to be agents of God's work in these end-times.[27]

Significantly, these student movements served as a catalyst for the charismatic churches that proliferated during the economic and political crisis of the 1980s and 1990s in many urban Nigerian areas.

Matthews Ojo provides an insightful analysis[28] of a prominent Holiness church, the Deeper Christian Life Ministry (also known as Deeper Life Bible Church or Deeper Life), that traversed the Nigerian social landscape from the transformative years of the 1960s to the period of state decline in the 1990s. The founder of the Deeper Life Christian Ministry, William Folorunso Kumuyi, from Ogun State in the Yoruba Southwest, had been a member of various Anglican and Aladura congregations before converting to the Apostolic Faith Church in 1964. As a mathematics student at the University of Ibadan, Kumuyi was an active member of the CU and the SU. Following his graduation with honors in 1967, he earned a postgraduate diploma in education at the University of Lagos. It was from Kumuyi's Bible study group there that the Deeper Life Church movement emerged in 1973. Within two years, the group had become large enough to rent worship spaces and offices from the Redeemed Christian Church of God (RCCG), by that time a well-known Pentecostal church. Deeper Life began holding retreats across Southern Nigeria and by 1980 was active in some Northern states. While distancing itself from the earlier charismatic movement, Deeper Life grew tremendously in the 1980s and 1990s. No longer a small evangelical network, Deeper Life transitioned into a full-fledged church by establishing a full-time staff, regular Sunday services, and formal organizational structure by the early 1980s.[29] Insisting on its unique evangelical Christian identity, Deeper Life members embraced strict moral codes that shaped their corporate identity, distinguishing them from the plethora of Pentecostal churches that dominated the religious landscape in the 1980s and the 1990s.

The case of the RCCG, Nigeria's most prominent Pentecostal church movement by the early 1990s, provides another compelling illustration of the far-reaching impact of Holiness Pentecostalism in Nigerian society. Although Pastor Josiah Akindayomi had broken from AIC Cherubim and Seraphim in 1952 to found the RCCG, it was not until the early 1980s, just as Deeper Life gained prominence, that the movement expanded beyond its Yoruba base. In the 1960s and 1970s, RCCG members were sometimes looked down upon, identified with the perceived "fanaticism" of the SU, and pitied for their general poverty, a product of their doctrinal asceticism. The RCCG's transformation from a regional to a national and even global church came after the appointment of Pastor Enoch Adejare Adeboye, a former University of Lagos mathematician and confidant of Pastor Akindayomi, as general overseer in 1981. Under Pastor Adeboye's leadership, the RCCG embraced the strategy of earlier evangelical movements at university campuses and established a monthly prayer group, the Holy Ghost Camp. Embracing this general shift from fellowship-based Bible study to institutionalization through evangelism, the RCCG emerged as the largest Pentecostal church in Africa by the early 2000s. With its headquarters at the popular Lagos-Ibadan Expressway, the RCCG had, by the turn of the millennium, established about two thousand parishes in Nigeria, and had parishes in many African, European, North America, and Caribbean countries.[30]

The RCCG's statement of faith reveals a strong embrace of fundamentalist Christian doctrines drawn from the Old and New Testaments.[31] RCCG doctrines are defined in church manuals it publishes periodically. One such manual lays out the responsibilities of lay members to the church and defines steadfast adherence to church rules.[32] Church members are implored to fervently pray for their leaders and church missionaries. RCCG members are required to generously give from their financial resources and professional expertise to the church.[33] Such codes of conduct are binding on church staff members, too: a similar RCCG manual spells out qualifications for them, ranging from being born again to attributes needed for spiritual holiness. Staff members are charged with various activities central to the mission of the movement, such as submission to duly constituted authorities, personal hygiene, appropriate dressing, and commitment to Christian fellowship.[34] We now turn to an analysis of the Prosperity movement, the second type of Pentecostal church that has dominated the Nigerian Pentecostal movement since the 1980s.

The Rise of Prosperity Pentecostalism

Just as Holiness Pentecostal churches were growing in prominence, the mid-1980s brought another major development: a new trend among evangelicals that later would be known as the Prosperity Pentecostal church movement.

Significantly influenced by the charismatic style of postwar American evangelical churches, this movement harbored notable theological differences with the older Holiness movement, reflecting important distinction on the conception of the relationship between the believer and the world around him or her. In notable cases, Prosperity theology connects spiritual excellence and moral uprightness to the believer's material well-being. As the Word comes from a God of abundance, to be worthy of it one must give abundantly. To win converts to the movement, Prosperity churches sell goods and services, offer retreats, and market their message against the backdrop of neoliberalism.[35] Similar to their Holiness forebears, the ranks of Prosperity followers were predominantly young and relatively well educated. Unlike the earlier revival movements, however, Prosperity churches emerged from the onset with strong institutional frameworks. Furthermore, while mainstream churches and, to some extent, Holiness churches appear rigid, Prosperity churches freely adapt to Nigeria's changing conditions.

One of the first Prosperity churches was Benson Idahosa's Church of God Mission in Benin City, Edo State's major city. This was followed by Patrick Ngozi Anwuzia of Zoe Ministry International in Lagos and Tunde Joda's Christ Chapel, the last of which emerged on the national scene in 1985 and inspired the foundation of the Household of God Fellowship led by Kris Okotie and Powerline Bible Church. Other prominent Prosperity pastors include George Adewale Adegboye of the Ever Increasing Word Ministries (also known as Rhema Chapel, founded in 1987), and Alex Adegboye of World Alive Ministries, founded in 1993.[36]

Midsize churches of a tempered message, mediating Holiness and Prosperity strains, also sprang up in the turbulent 1990s.[37] These churches include Bishop Mike Okonkwo's Redeemed Evangelical Mission, Francis Wale Oke's Sword of the Spirit Ministries in Ibadan, and Tunde Bakare's Latter Rain Assembly in Lagos. Among the most successful of this hybrid type are megachurches such as Overcomers Assembly in Lagos and Bishop David Oyedepo's Living Faith Church Worldwide,[38] also widely known as Winners Chapel International. Living Faith's transformative religious and social roles has consistently responded to the pressing needs of local communities at a time of great uncertainty following the enduring economic crisis posed by neoliberal reforms since the 1980s. This powerful megachurch provides critical social services in education and health care, as well as support for building business enterprises.[39] Taking off in 1986 after the start of the Word of Faith Bible Institute, Winners' Chapel is a formidable religious and social force. The movement's student groups are active at over sixty university campuses throughout Africa. Bishop Oyedepo followed his initial success with the World Mission Agency and African Gospel Invasion Program that sent evangelical aid to many African countries. Winners' Chapel has collaborated with the Gilead Medical Center to provide medical resources to local people.[40] Thus, articulated in clearly defined educational and humanitarian commissions, Bishop Oyedepo's Living Faith Church has responded to Nigeria and several other African countries' educational, health care, and social welfare crises with comprehensive and efficient services in education, health care clinics, and many humanitarian projects. The church's educational institutions include two private universities, Covenant and Landmark, each of which has a comprehensive curriculum in the arts, humanities, sciences, social sciences, business, agriculture, engineering, and technology; a group of leading secondary schools, known as the Faith Academies, that spread across Nigeria and several African countries; and fifty-seven excellent elementary schools in Nigerian communities and several major African cities, notably Dar esalam, Tanzania, and Mombasa, Kenya.[41]

Moreover, from the onset, Living Faith Church Worldwide has actively provided humanitarian assistance to communities ravaged by war and natural disaster, such as Rwanda and Liberia, as well as humanitarian assistance to the Nigerian Red Cross and impoverished communities in Koma Hills in Adamawa State.[42] To underscore the significance of the church's educational and humanitarian mandate, Bishop Oyedepo in retrospect observes:

> Years ago, I caught a caption on one of my trips to the United States which to me was a fundamental philosophy behind the greatness of the American nation. It reads "America the home of the free, land of the brave." Truly only the brave ever become great. It is bravery that begets greatness. It is not just a dreamers world anymore. It is the darers world. It is bravery that moves men [and women] to think the unthinkable, dare the undareable and move the immovable.[43]

Rosalind Hackett further provides an insightful case study of the Mountain of Fire and Miracles Ministries (MFM), a deliverance church within the arc of the Prosperity gospel movement. Founded by molecular geneticist Dr. D. K. Olukoya, this church boasted one hundred thousand worshippers at its Sunday service by the beginning of 2000, and millions more members throughout the world. Hackett interrogates Pastor Olukoya's deliverance doctrine, arguing that it focuses attention on bad foundations, wastage of life, links to evil, and even family curses. To cure these spiritual ailments, Pastor Olukoya recommends "high-voltage prayer," specific intonations that invoke Jesus's name to save the afflicted from their "contamination" and ward off evil spirits. Such teachings describe the danger of everyday life in militaristic terms, empowering the afflicted to fight their own battles. Dark forces aligning against Christ and MFM are fought with continual prayer, tithing to the church, and numerous testimonials.[44]

Since holding onto their vast wealth is important to church leaders, Prosperity churches tend to have centralized administrative structures that rely on family members and trusted associates to oversee the management of their enormous resources.[45] There is the concern, however, that while Nigeria's Prosperity theology can inspire believers to transform their lives, they also focus excessively on material conditions. Nevertheless, Prosperity churches are remarkable actors in contemporary society and have served as critical engines for development since the economic downturn of the 1980s and 1990s.[46]

In sum, Holiness and Prosperity forms of Pentecostalism have thrived in the context of state crisis, especially in the aftermath of the civil war in the late 1960s and neoliberalism, starting in the 1980s. The dynamism of Nigeria's Pentecostal revolution, with its intersecting social and political currents, is connected to changing local conditions. As a new generation of Christians responded to a turbulent era in Nigerian society since independence, Pentecostal churches provided institutional framework to engage the uncertainties of Nigeria's complicated social and political conditions.

Constructing a Pentecostal Public Sphere

As the globalization of markets and media systems intensified in the 1990s, the ability of Nigerian authorities to shape moral and political discourses in local communities further eroded, giving Pentecostal movements ample room to extend their influence in national and transnational contexts. With access to resources derived from global networks, leaders of Pentecostal churches are less dependent on the custodians of the Nigerian state, allowing their members space to take charge of their social conditions.[47] Nigeria's Pentecostal movement has been at the center of shaping the country's public sphere in the global era, and it is well integrated with global popular culture, media, institutions, and technology. For example, popular American culture, notably African American expressive culture, has shaped how Nigerian evangelical churches disseminate their messages in both Nigerian-based churches and Nigerian diaspora branches that have sprung up in many British and US metropolitan areas since the economic crises of the 1980s and 1990s.[48] As Ebenezer Obadare notes, the growing influence of these external agents in shaping the style and doctrines of Nigeria's evangelical churches is indeed a reflection of "the weakening of the state and its institutions, [which translates] into freer access by foreign religious groups and personalities to their local counterparts.... The major external players in this respect have mostly come from the United States, the global influence of whose charismatic televangelists has become an academic staple."[49]

This trend was particularly expressed through Nigeria's media networks, starting in the 1980s. With regard to television and audio media, Pentecostal churches were not the first to use these critical media to evangelize; however, they pioneered their use as medium of mass proselytizing by exploiting vast industrial networks around the production, distribution, and consumption of gospel cassettes, videos, and CDs.[50] Reflecting on some of these developments, Kalu notes three factors that encouraged Pentecostal churches to use media to shape Nigerian public discourse:[51] the liberalization of the Nigerian state radio since the 1970s; the growth of television in Nigerian cities in the 1980s; and the influence of American televangelists on Nigerian Pentecostal pastors in the 1980s.[52]

The evolution of popular music and the global diffusion of musical genres exemplify these trends. Mainline Protestant and Catholic missionaries had long suppressed local musical trends because of their customary expression, but by the 1960s the "vernacularization" of music, liturgy, and media progressed together. Evangelical movement in the earlier years of Holiness Pentecostalism used popular musical trends to increase spirituality while avoiding the materialism of Nigerian society. Embracing popular musical genres initially took some adjustment for many Nigerian Pentecostal churches. For example, dances viewed as sensual were replaced with Pentecostal-friendly variants such as the "holy shuffle." Similarly, where original lyrics praised indigenous deities, evangelical musicians replaced them with instrumentals or tunes extolling the deliverance of Christ and the glory of God. This reshaping of popular musical trends to fit the message of local evangelism, helped by the general liberalization that dominated the early 1990s, threw the field open for entrepreneurs to capitalize on changing religious structures. The music industry became both a product and an agent of the Pentecostal revolution.[53]

Pentecostal churches' increasing use of the media since the 1980s was further reflected in the globalization of television, the explosion of the Nigerian film industry, and access to the Internet. For instance, in the 1990s Pastor Ashimolowo's Kingsway International Church Center had programs broadcast in twenty-one European countries, while God Digital (formerly the Christian Channel Europe) hosts the God Channel, the Revival Channel, the Worship Channel, and others reaching across Western Europe and into many African states. Similarly, a Pentecostal film industry developed into a range of subgenres, including religion-based dramatic forms, secular movies with heavy religious overtones, religious music videos, documentaries, and sermons. All these initiatives were designed to promote Pentecostal ministries' mission in an entertaining way. Mount Zion Faith Ministries International paved the way from Ile-Ife, when it made the first Nigerian Christian motion picture in 1994 and led the Nigerian Pentecostal film industry. Finally, Pentecostal churches' websites have created forums where members can interact with one another and have served as tools for proselytizing. Though their effectiveness has been questioned—some observers note that sustained strategies of proselytizing still depend on the personal interaction that is at the core of the Pentecostal witnessing tradition—these social-media efforts are invaluable in expanding the scope of Pentecostal church groups.[54] Nevertheless, the modernist implications of the Pentecostal church movement cannot be overstated, as eloquently noted by Ilesanmi:

> Its media-savvy pastors-cum-superstars regularly fill airwaves with their preaching and gospel music, and creating a new publishing niche for their tracts and manuals on self-improvement. Youthful congregations fill modern airconditioned tabernacles and chapels for all-night services. They come in search of the latest blessing and to participate in Christianized popular culture.[55]

Just as the new generation of evangelicals transformed the internal core of Pentecostal churches, so too have they altered these churches' relationships with the broader Nigerian public, especially since the late 1980s, when some leading Pentecostal ministers pushed for greater involvement of their movement in national politics. As Nigerian politics became more contentious in the 1980s and 1990s, socioreligious structures were politicized, and evangelical leaders began injecting their influence into the public sphere.[56] Idahosa, the leader of the Church of God Mission, was one such power broker in Edo State; and in 1992, the Rev. Peter Obadan, a prominent Pentecostal minister, was elected deputy governor in Edo State. The link between Pentecostalism (church) and the state (politics) was expressed in dramatic fashion in a statement attributed to Pastor Adeboye, RCCG's general overseer: the statement was widely publicized as prophesy of impending doom for Nigeria's military despot and the arrival of a new dawn in June 1998. General Abacha, the Northern Muslim military ruler, died suddenly, and military rule came to an end after Adeboye's prophesy; a presidential election (1999) ushered a civilian government into power, and Olusegun Obasanjo, a self-proclaimed Born-Again from the Yoruba region, became Nigeria's civilian leader.[57]

More important was the meteoric rise of the Pentecostal Fellowship of Nigeria (PFN)—the movement's national umbrella organization—in national politics.[58] By the time of its first biennial meeting in 1991, the organization had more than seven hundred registered affiliated member churches in Lagos State alone.[59] Within a decade of its existence, PFN had stamped its imprint on Nigeria's public landscape with an active national president, an efficient secretariat in Abuja, Nigeria's federal capital, and many branches in each state of the federation. The PFN frequently hosts high-profile events to discuss matters of pressing national significance. Furthermore, PFN is a constituent member of the larger Christian Association of Nigeria (CAN). In comparison to CAN, PFN possesses stronger institutional cohesion and has a more affirmative voice in national debates.

Despite the tendency to cooperate on matters of mutual interests, especially on issues of political significance, major Pentecostal groups continue to function as autonomous entities with distinct religious and political agendas. Wariboko, himself an ordained RCCG pastor, notes a clear distinction between his church (RCCG), Deeper Life, and Winners' Chapel.[60] This tendency for Pentecostal groups to pursue distinct agendas can be attributed to their independent evolution since the 1960s.[61] Thus Allan Anderson, in broader African context, notes, "Pentecostalisms are more important than Pentecostalism: the local dynamics of change and interpretation are more important than any overarching unity among different groups."[62]

With a focus on a theology that stresses rebirth and the free-forming spirit of the Pentecost, "Pentecostalism seeks to transform the mental and material cultures of communities and challenges extant religious structures as it seeks to transform the religious landscape."[63] In this context, Pentecostal churches have created a distance between themselves and AICs because of the latter's expressive reflection of indigenous religious practice. Furthermore, mainline church members, according to Kalu, are dismissed "as benchwarmers who have lost the power of the gospel that was very real in the early Jesus movement."[64] To be sure, Pentecostal churches inscribe charismatism within a particular evangelical tradition, but their emphasis on "history in the present" leads to antagonism with mainline Christianity.[65] As Kalu notes, "Just as Augustine, Luther and Calvin variously taught, experience of the *charismata* exists outside established dispensation, and thus spiritual rebirth necessitates new medium and methods of receiving it."[66] With these factors preventing a broad Pentecostal alliance, growth continued through the 1990s—but further splintering of the movement took place.[67] As Pentecostal churches grew in response to the destabilizing effects of neoliberalism in the 1990s, older Holiness churches questioned the perceived excesses of the Prosperity gospel and the proliferation of theologies that make prophetic claims and emphasize a pervasive demonic world.[68]

However, Pentecostal churches, irrespective of theological orientation, have posed important critiques of societal norms. On matters of gender, for example, Pentecostalism's fluid structure and doctrines provide ample space for empowerment and innovation. With the entrenched power of a male hierarchy in mainline Protestant and Catholic churches, mainline churches had largely left women ambivalent, keeping even elite women away from the leadership of their churches. In the Pentecostal movement, however, some notable female pastors, such as Archbishop Dorcas Siyanbola Olaniyi and Dr. Stella Ajisebute of Agbala Daniel Church and Water from the Rock Church in Ile-Ife, have played important roles in the movement since the 1980s. Both leaders are well educated, with doctorates in microbiology, and both have been eloquent voices for leadership roles for women in the Pentecostal movement.[69]

Finally, the exponential growth of Pentecostal churches has occurred alongside the resurgence of Islamic reformist movements, notably Izala (see chapter 5), since the 1980s. Inevitably, this has led to major confrontations, especially in non-Muslim areas of Northern states and in the Middle Belt,[70] where competition for converts had historically complicated social relations and rapidly changing demographic conditions have intensified communal tensions between predominantly Christian "indigenes" and Hausa-Fulani Muslim "settlers." With a movement away from the purification of the interior of the Christian community to conversion of local communities,[71] a network of groups known as the Northern Christian Association had intensified evangelization in Middle Belt and Northern non-Muslim minority communities starting in the 1970s.[72] Ultimately, this fervor of Pentecostal evangelism came up against the strong missionary impulse of Northern Muslim reformists who utilize the media, technology, and other methods to propagate the Muslim faith. For example, although Northern Muslim reformists had debated whether it was halal to read the Qur'an on the radio well into the 1960s, by the 1980s they had built a significant television and radio presence—as well as a film industry in Kano (Kannywood)—to counteract the expansion of the Pentecostal movement in Middle Belt states and in Northern states with substantial Christian populations, such as Kaduna and Niger States.[73] Indeed, even in the Yoruba states where it is widely believed that Christians and Muslims have historically forged common grounds of peaceful coexistence, Obadare has argued that Islamic reformism has taken on the strong proselytizing fervor often associated with Pentecostal churches. This trend, he contends, is beginning to erode the vaulted tradition of religious accommodation and tolerance in the region. Obadare concludes: "We see a revitalized Islam forging a response to a surging and increasingly hegemonic Pentecostalism. This revitalization, which ostensibly involves the incorporation of the demonstrably successful aspects of Pentecostal prayer is, nevertheless, not simply mimetic.... What we in fact see at play is a dynamic reformulation of Muslim identity, against (1) the external pressure exerted by Pentecostalism, and (2) internal prompts which more closely echo a historical cycle of decay and renewal."[74]

Pentecostal and Islamic reformist movements thus embody similar methods of propagating their faiths, despite their drastically different religious doctrines and perspectives on politics. Indeed, as previously discussed, following the turbulent decades after independence a new generation raised in the political culture of postcolonial Nigerian society has placed their faith in the competing visions of these two religious movements.[75] Extolling the reformist doctrines of these two movements to restructure the moral order of contemporary Nigerian society, Ruth Marshall insightfully argues:

> While initially concerned with the revitalization or restoration of their respective religious traditions, and largely inspired by the intensification of transnational relations, both movements arise from within the same social classes, are products of post-colonial educational institutions, and seek to create moral and political renewal and order from the chaos of the oil-boom years through religious revival. Their competing projects were bound to clash, and constant provocation from both sides has meant that the bid for converts and for political representation has taken increasingly violent forms.[76]

Thus, although these two movements are different in many respects, they are both inspired by a "quest for justice" and the transformation of society.[77] Conceived in the vortex of rapidly shifting demographic and ethno-religious conditions, the recurring conflict between Muslims and Christians in Middle Belt and Northern states resonates in the structural tensions between the mission of Pentecostal and Northern Islamic reformist movements. Elaborating further on the consequences of these developments in Northern and Middle Belt states, Paul Lubeck notes:

> What, then, had changed in the Middle Belt since Ahmadu Bello eliminated sharia criminal law in the compromise of 1960 (see chapter 4) in order to mollify Northern Christians? The answer lies in the politicization of religious identities among Christians and Muslims and, specifically, the

rising organizational power of CAN and the militancy of an evangelical and Pentecostal Christianity fueled by global networks. In 1970, "Pentecostals and charismatics *combined* represented less than 5% of Africans," but by 2006 Pentecostals alone represented 12% about 107 million [quoted from Pew Forum 2006a]. In Nigeria, where Pentecostal growth is rapid and their voice increasingly assertive, they represented 18% of the population and 48% of all Protestants, roughly equal to Nigerian Catholics and Anglicans combined.[78]

Nevertheless, as Pentecostal and Northern Muslim reformist movements confront each other, adherents of the latter seek to reconstitute the juridical state around their perception of a proper Islamic society (see chapters 7, 8, 9), while followers of the former favor radically restructuring the world around them into a pious Christian community. In the context of Nigeria's Middle Belt and Northern states, where Islam and Christianity are particularly integral to the rationalization of state power, the prevailing reformist ideologies of Pentecostal and Northern Islamic reformist movements has intensified the contradiction of the postcolonial nation-state. As the Pentecostal movement has transformed Nigerian society alongside the destabilizing effects of neoliberal reforms since the 1980s, this remarkable religious movement has had profound implications for the dialectical relations between national and transnational forces in the global era.

Pentecostalism: Transnational and Global Networks

Religious movements have always been important media for the articulation of African and black identity in African diaspora history, especially across the great waterways of the Atlantic world. As essential structure of society among African-descended populations in the Atlantic world, religion has not only engaged the quotidian issues confronting local communities, but has also responded to the vicissitudes of life among African diasporic peoples over the centuries.[79] Shaped by its own unique conditions, this trend persisted in the global era following the crisis of the state in many African countries in the 1980s, 1990s, and 2000s. In the context of globalism, trends in Nigerian transnational experience were to be found in migration flows of various types and intensities, characterized by links between homeland and diaspora, reflecting complex processes of movements of people, ideas, cultures, and religions.[80] With regard to the intersection between Pentecostal Christianity and transnationalism in the context of neoliberalism, Olupona notes:

Theories of transnationalism and globalization are essential to understanding how movement of people and ideas across borders shape Christianity in Africa. Former paradigms of assimilation, secularization, and the loss of identity are no longer sufficient to explain the complex web of geographic, cultural, and personal connections that bind people and places. In an age of technological advancement where people often have ready access and movement across global space, immigrants can maintain ties with their homelands and participate in various global networks of people and institutions.[81]

It would be useful to set the context for Nigeria's transnational Pentecostal networks by outlining the major features of globalization, especially as they affect a fragile African state such as Nigeria in the context of the economic and political crisis of the 1980s, 1990s, and 2000s. David Held and Anthony McGrew explain that globalization is "a process in which events, decisions, and activities in one part of the world can come to have significant consequences for individuals and communities in quite distant parts of the globe."[82] They perceptively define globalization as a process "which embodies a transformation of the spatial organization of social relations and transactions [that can be] assessed in terms of their extensity, intensity, velocity, and impact, generating transcontinental or interregional networks of activity."[83] Focusing particular attention on the religious dimensions of this global and transnational process, Ilesanmi contends that globalization's major thesis "is that the world is undergoing an irresistible mutation, tending towards shrinkage and interdependence, in which the media, economy, religions, migration are playing active and mutually reinforcing roles."[84]

With the growing contradictions of global capital by the 1970s, economic globalization led to the privatization of public services, the search for cheap labor, crisis of too much accumulation and too little consumption, and the collapse of space and time by the early 1990s.[85] This volatile global economic condition has complicated Nigeria's entrenched neopatrimonial political system, exposing the fragility of the country's economic, political, and social institutions. In an environment of economic and political crisis, this development triggered new transnational networks, shaped by the migration of millions of skilled and unskilled Nigerian workers to various parts of the world starting in the mid-1980s. As we shall soon observe, Nigeria's Pentecostal churches would play important roles in the transnational process that resulted from these economic and political disruptions.

Religious Revival and the State 155

Responding to the economic crisis that goes back to the 1980s, Nigeria's skilled workers sought out new destinations in the United Kingdom and in other English-speaking Western countries, especially the United States and Canada, as well as in South Africa, Botswana, and Gulf states. These Nigerian professionals were largely products of the Christian missionary educational institutions of Southern and central Nigeria that traces its origins to the turn of the twentieth century (see chapters 1 and 2). While these skilled Nigerian professionals have brought in vast financial remittances to their Nigerian homeland, bridging government shortfalls in the provision of essential goods and services, the overall cost of their migration has been a massive net loss of human capital for the developmental imperatives of the Nigerian state.[86] Thus, this migration of trained professionals has led to a serious brain drain and daunting challenges in Nigerian society.

Indeed, this process had its structural foundation in the thousands of Southern and central Nigerian Christians who had left in large numbers to pursue higher education in American, British, and Canadian universities since the late 1960s. Most had been supported by scholarships made possible via Nigeria's petro-dollar of the 1970s and early 1980s. From the beginning, the objective of this higher-education enterprise was simple enough: obtain university education in Western countries and return to professional careers guaranteed by the Nigerian state. However, with a drastic decline in petroleum revenue, a growing debt burden, and a deepening economic crisis in the 1980s, returning to Nigeria became a less attractive option for many of these young Nigerians and their families. With the imposition of structural-adjustment policies in the late 1980s, another wave of Nigerian professionals migrated to the United Kingdom, United States, and Canada in the 1990s, bringing with them branches of Pentecostal churches from their Nigerian homeland.

Over the years, these churches became critical public spaces for collective social action for Nigerian migrant populations during this period of uncertainty.[87] Nigerian Pentecostal churches have responded effectively to the religious and social need of these energetic Nigerian professionals and have provided a framework for them to negotiate alien social environments in many British, United States, and Canadian metropolitan areas.[88] Consequently, transnational Nigerian Pentecostal churches are popular because they provide distinctive social networks for their adherents to explore economic opportunities and social mobility.[89] Itinerant Pentecostal evangelists travel widely to spread their message to Nigeria's immigrant congregations abroad. Conversely, financial resources flow from these immigrant congregations to support Pentecostal churches in the homeland. Indeed, many Nigerian Pentecostal evangelists are courted by

Christian organizations in Western countries to fill the gap in pastoral personnel, bolster Christian missionary work, and help sustain church membership in Western countries. This is indeed a moment of notable historical irony: African evangelists are moving to the West as carriers of the Christian faith. Olupona labels this process the "reverse missions" of African Christian evangelizing to secular Western countries in the age of globalization.[90] Olupona's conceptualization of "reverse missions" further shows how Pentecostal doctrines transcend the narrow communal boundaries that had previously been the case for other charismatic churches, such as the AICs.[91] Thus, many Nigerian immigrant Pentecostal churches project a cosmopolitan image, appropriate to the ethos of transnational corporate bodies.[92] For example, Pentecostal immigrant groups such as the All Nations International Development Agency became important sources of humanitarian support in Nigeria in the early 2000s.[93]

From the above, it is clear that Nigeria's Pentecostal movements have navigated complicated transnational pathways[94] in the course of their evangelizing mission. As major actors in Nigerian politics and society, religious forces are embedded in the structures that transformed modern Nigeria. The complex social and political manifestations of these religious forces would assume a central role in the Nigerian state and society during the Olusegun Obasanjo civilian administration, when twelve Northern state governments imposed sharia as the state religion. The implications, actions, interactions, and constitutional dimensions of expanded sharia are extensively analyzed in the rest of the book.

CHAPTER SEVEN

EXPANDED SHARIA:
THE NORTHERN UMMAH
AND THE FOURTH REPUBLIC

Ahmed Sani, the governor of Nigeria's Northern Zamfara State, was fresh in office (October 1999) when he generated major political stirrings in Nigerian politics by signing two items of legislation into law: the first established new lower sharia courts and the second changed the jurisdiction of the Sharia Court of Appeal. Associated with this, Sani enacted into law a Penal Code that was integrated into sharia in January 2000. Several weeks later, the Zamfara State's government transferred the administration of sharia courts from the state chief justice to the grand qadi, who by this very official act was empowered to preside over a transformed Sharia Court of Appeal. These executive actions enjoyed overwhelming endorsement from the state legislature, and for the first time in Nigeria's postcolonial history, sharia courts gained authority over civil and criminal cases in a state located in the Federal Republic of Nigeria. In his announcement declaring the arrival of expanded sharia to the State House of Assembly, Sani insisted that this historic development established a new dawn not only for Zamfara State but for all Nigerian Muslims, affirming emirate Nigeria's reformist tradition going back to the Sokoto Caliphate.[1] To consolidate the policy, Sani enlisted the support of emirs and ulamas.² However, Paul Lubeck tells us that Zamfara did not draw direct moral authority from the Sokoto Jihad, nor did the policy initially have the rousing endorsement of the Hausa-Fulani political class:

> Zamfara was a renegade community, for its rulers had rejected the iconic Islamic eighteenth-century [and nineteenth-century] reform movement of Usman dan Fodio. For a number of reasons, "playing the sharia card," according to informed observers whom I interviewed, was a radical departure from the long-standing preferences of more established northern politicians, who specialize in constructing multi-ethnic coalitions to hold federal political power and control the distribution of petro-rents.³

Three months after Zamfara's announcement, the governor of another Northern state, Niger, announced that he, too, would sign into law a bill for expanded sharia.⁴ Over the next two years, nine more Northern state governors followed suit: Sokoto, Katsina, Kano, Jigawa, Yobe, Bornu, Bauchi, Kebbi, and Gombe. In addition, the governor of Kaduna State signed a more limited version of expanded sharia. Among Northern majority-Muslim states, only the Adamawa and Nasarawa governments did not embrace expanded sharia. Again, Lubeck provides a perspective on the conditions of extreme uncertainty that made the expansion of sharia so attractive to the masses of Northern Nigerian Muslims:

> There is no doubt that for the youths participating in the Muslim sphere in the eighties, the spectacular failure of Nigerian oligarchic rule confirmed what their cultural nationalist and anti-imperialist instincts told them was true. For these cohorts, the obvious failure of Western-imposed institutions to meet their material and spiritual needs confirmed that they should recommit themselves to *tajdid* [renewal] in order to implement sharia as an alternative path to realizing Muslim self-determination.⁵

These complicated questions with their implications for the configuration of state power throughout the country necessitates a discussion of the context in which Islamic law was vigorously contested at the beginning of Nigeria's Fourth Republic in 1999. These contestations over the meaning of sharia among contending ethno-religious and ethno-regional political classes and the constituencies they claim to represent in Nigeria's troubled nation-state also warrant a careful analysis of the legal and political implications of sharia reforms for Nigerian citizens, especially since the attainment of independence in 1960.

Legal and Political Contexts

We will recall that Muslim and customary laws have been supplanted by common law since the imposition of colonial rule at the beginning of the twentieth century. Islamic scholar Syed Khalid Rashid contends that over time this colonial policy not only undermined sharia's legitimacy under colonial rule, but also established the framework for the marginalization of Islamic law in the postcolonial era.[6] Additionally, various military regimes had used the area court system to further supplant Islamic law in Northern communities. Finally, we will also recall that the drafters of the 1979 Constitution had overcome the pressures from the Hausa-Fulani political class to establish federal and state sharia courts of appeal during Nigeria's second transition to civil-democratic government.[7] By the 1990s, opposition to the area court system had gained momentum, especially among Northern Muslim leaders. Detractors of the area court system charged that these courts lacked due process.[8] The area courts' bureaucracies were said to suffer from a host of administrative problems: by many accounts the courts were notoriously corrupt, with no systematic records of court decisions. Furthermore, relations between Islamic judges and Western-trained legal experts were often strained. The former considered the latter ignorant of local custom and overly bureaucratic, while the latter considered the former uninformed about basic legal principles. Many cases in these courts were decided ex parte (with only one party present), usually not in exigent circumstances. In many cases, judges used oaths to decide the case when a full trial was necessary.[9] Often, in Northern states, judges were Muslim clerics even though the courts administered many cases that did not possess any religious components. Beyond these structural problems, the area courts were poorly staffed—most of the legal assistants and court clerks were untrained.[10] Nevertheless, these courts adjudicated most of the cases involving Nigeria's poor, an arrangement perceived as legitimate because their authority was considered to reflect local custom and tradition. In short, informality made the area courts more accessible but also impeded justice and due process.

With such grossly inefficient administration of the area courts—and the Islamic and customary courts—outspoken sharia advocates seized on the democratic opening that followed military rule to press their case for legal reform. To most Northern Muslim critics of the prevailing system, however, the more pressing concerns went beyond the failures of the area courts; they complained that Islamic law needed greater representation within Nigeria's judiciary system. Islamic scholar Abdulmumini Adebayo Oba, for example, captures this sentiment when he called for the professionalization of Islamic courts and questioned the constitutional requirements that insist on Maliki *madhab* (school of thought) law as essential qualification for sharia judges. He demanded greater representation of sharia experts in the Nigerian judiciary and insisted on the separation of sharia from customary law to meet the religious needs of Muslims, including those from Southern and Middle Belt states. Similarly, Rashid suggested that sharia should be paramount in civil matters and that its appeals process should be specific to Islamic law.[11]

Particularly contentious were the sharia courts of appeal, first established by British colonial authorities as the Muslim Court of Appeal during the reforms of the decolonization process in the 1950s. Although they were superior courts of record, they hardly engaged the Constitution and were widely ignored by legal professionals trained under the common-law system. Other Muslim scholars proposed an overhaul of the Judicial Service Commission to reflect equality among competing legal systems.[12] For most reformers, autonomy and parity among the three legal systems was essential for any efficient and just legal reform.[13]

In failing to increase the scope of Islamic or customary law, the 1999 Constitution did little to address these problems. Indeed, as with previous constitutions, the Nigerian legal system remained decidedly under the authority of the common-law courts. New courts that were established at Nigeria's Federal Capital Territory in Abuja also affirmed the authority of the common-law courts. At the national level, a federal high court has broad jurisdiction on matters pertaining to the federation or between particular states. Appeals from this court or any of the superior state courts go to the Federal Court of Appeal, as do decisions from constitutional tribunals and any ad hoc commissions established by acts of the National Assembly. Finally, in addition to its role as the ultimate appellate bench, the Supreme Court is granted original jurisdiction on all cases pertaining to the existence of legal rights and any further remit bestowed by acts of the National Assembly (not including criminal matters).

As is evident from this system, Islamic and customary laws were highly circumscribed. Not only are the customary and sharia courts of appeal limited to personal law; they also can be appealed to the Federal Court of Appeal and ultimately the Supreme Court, which are both based on common law. Equally relevant to ensuing contestations, all common-law justices are required to have specific legal training and must be accredited, but judges of Islamic law only need "a recognized qualification in Islamic law from an institution acceptable to the National Judiciary Council."[14] The long-contested issue of English provisions being superior to those of sharia was thus firmly upheld in the 1999 Constitution, which creates a regulatory system anchored in common law. Consequently, when the Northern Muslim political class and Islamic clerics insisted on expanded sharia in the early years of the Fourth Republic, that posed a thorny constitutional problem. With Nigeria's entrenched ethno-religious structure, the insistence on expanded sharia exposed the contradictions between Islamic law and Nigeria's Western-derived Constitution. The analyses that follow will further underscore specific aspects of the constitutional challenges posed by expanded sharia to the Nigerian state in the early years of the Fourth Republic.

ISLAMIC LAW AND COMMON LAW

In the Northern Provinces during the colonial era, Oba identifies two phases of the evolution of Islamic law that contributed to the erosion of sharia in postcolonial Nigerian society. First, in the early years of colonial rule, he contends that British authorities embraced Islamic law as a necessity but limited its scope by classifying it as customary, steadily allowing common law to dominate its authority.[15] With the growing presence of Southern Christian immigrants and foreign immigrants (European and Lebanese) in the Northern Provinces by the 1930s,[16] common law rapidly gained supremacy over Islamic law. During this period, Islamic courts were also subjected to the oversight of British administrators. Most contentious was the restriction of sharia's jurisdiction to personal law.[17] Firmly established by the period of decolonization, the Repugnancy Clause established by British administrators in the early years of colonial rule was reviled by conservative Muslim clerics and emirs as the hallmark of colonial intrusion.[18]

Conceived during decolonization and the early decades of independence, the second phase effectively witnessed the formal subjugation of Islamic and customary law to the jurisdiction of common-law courts,[19] reflecting a profusion of cases where common, customary, and Islamic law conflicted with each other as well as with competing legal interpretations. Islamic law was increasingly flexible, despite claims of its divine origin by Muslim clerics, while customary law was so ill-defined that it could be shoehorned into competing juridical systems. With the exception of conflicts between Islamic law and common law in criminal cases, Islamic law often was adaptive to local conditions on personal cases where it retained jurisdiction. Consequently, as Nigerian society evolved in the postcolonial era, the three legal systems converged, diverged, and overlapped in various ways. By the time of the 1990s democratic transition, local people were choosing their preferred bench based on their identification with a particular religious or cultural group, and to many, the country appeared headed toward a mixed legal system.[20] Emerging from this legal blend, however, was a perception by a vocal voice in the Northern Muslim political class of an unjustifiable preference for common law in Nigeria's legal system. These advocates of sharia contend that common law is not normatively neutral because it is derived from Christian traditions.[21]

SECULARISM, MULTIRELIGIOSITY, AND STATE RELIGION

A second cause of conflict revolved around Nigeria's multireligious identity versus the constitutional principle of secularism, which prohibits state religion. While the former calls for a state structure that embraces a diversity of faiths, the latter asserts a complete absence of religious influence in state affairs. Christian opponents of sharia have long complained about sharia's endorsement of state religion, though they resisted attempts to strip state funding for churches and Christian schools.[22] By the time the sharia crisis exploded on the national scene in 1999, sharia advocates had latched onto the distinction, extending their argument for sharia from federal and state governments' undeniable support for Nigeria's two world religions. For example, at a Kwara State College of Islamic Studies seminar, sharia advocates concluded that religious and civil liberties do not come from man and thus cannot be bound by human law; as all rights are divinely granted, they can only be divinely governed. As Adegbite observes, "To the Muslims, the notion [of secularism] is anti-God, and we reject it totally and irrevocably. We are wholly committed to the sovereignty of Allah to whom we submit without reservation. That is Islam."[23] Or as Gumi had argued a decade before, in his autobiography:

> The roots of our instability lie deep in the concept of secularism, which eats away at the very cords which should bind us together as a nation. By divorcing our government from God we are at once encouraging selfishness and unfounded ambitions. The current system does not acknowledge God, which is why we lack direction.... Secularism, therefore, as the policy of operating government outside God's control, is alien to civilized human existence. We cannot expect to succeed in our affairs without abiding by the wishes of God, in spirit and in form.[24]

Furthermore, advocates of sharia felt it hypocritical for Christian opponents of Islamic law to claim that the Nigerian Constitution should be based on unassailable secularity. To these sharia advocates, the Nigerian state has never been secular, having its foundation in common law that is derived from Christian traditions.[25] Their insistence on expanded Islamic law would simply bring sharia on equal footing with common law, as both have religious moorings that need to be balanced for Nigerian jurisprudence to be acceptable to Muslims. Thus, sharia activists contended that since historically the government had favored Christian traditions and institutions (for example, through the Christian origins of common law and by subsidizing Christian missionary schools), the sharia policies of the twelve Northern states simply rectify the imbalance of many decades.[26] As a result of this history, Southern, Middle Belt, and Northern-minority Christians consistently have enjoyed significant advantages in Nigerian constitutional evolution, from which they project the myth of Western secularism that blocks Muslim religious and social aspirations.[27] In short, advocates of expanded sharia presented secularism as Western-derived, in direct conflict with Islam, and at its core fundamentally a political theology.[28]

The claims of sharia advocates seemed substantially bolstered in the numerous provisions of the Constitution providing for a Sharia Court of Appeal.[29] If it were simply the religious nature of sharia that was unconstitutional, sharia advocates argued, then how could the same document concede so much authority to Islamic law within the jurisdiction of the state governments? They further contend that the mere provision against state religion[30] did not guarantee secularity, or the absence of religion in government.[31] On this, Adegbite argued that expanded sharia did not amount to declaring a state religion because secular courts still existed in Northern sharia states.[32]

Nevertheless, opponents of sharia underscored the importance of secularity in the constitution, insisting the new laws violated section 10 of the 1999 Constitution. Harnischfeger provides the typical refrain: "Muslims' call for autonomy flies in the face of Nigeria's moderately secular tradition.... The Constitution does not allow elevating any religion to a state religion. Yet this principle is violated when governors in the North use state authority to Islamize public life."[33] This position flowed in part from the OIC debacle of the 1980s and the conflict over whether joining an Islamic organization, such as the Islamic Bank, amounted to declaring a state religion, as well as the 1978 and 1989 Constituent Assembly debates wherein pro-sharia advocates purportedly refused to differentiate between secularism as godlessness and secularism as religious neutrality.[34] Furthermore, many detractors of sharia argued that state resources would be directed to enforcing a religious code, which amounted to funding Islam.[35] Sharia proponents countered that these critics ignored the fact that the state was already heavily subsidizing and funding religious institutions, especially schools, pilgrimages, and other interests.[36]

Constitutional scholars, judges, and politicians in the end relied on specific circumstances to decide constitutional meaning.[37] Both "secular" and "religious" states are not the simple products of various stages of modernization; rather, they are stages in ongoing processes of state formation, overlapping with people's aspirations and struggles.[38] According to Islamic scholar Sanusi

Lamido Sanusi (who was installed as emir of Kano in 2014), the concept of justice that is held by progressive Muslims has been connected to Western scholarship since the Enlightenment, and the interpretations conferred on Islam represent a hermeneutical process of finding meanings in the Qur'an and the hadith.[39]

STATES' RIGHTS

The third constitutional issue involves the question of whether state governments have the powers to create, modify, and abolish courts in their spheres of influence. When Mamuda Aliyu Shinkafi, deputy governor of Zamfara State, defended sharia's legality, he noted that "any law that is enacted by the House of Assembly is constitutional."[40] While this is at best a curious constitutional pronouncement, more common was the narrower claim that, as Adegbite argued, states have the right to control their laws and their courts.[41] Importantly, Northern states retained the Sharia Court of Appeal and extended its jurisdiction. Exercised through these reforms, expanded sharia appeared to have exceeded constitutional guarantee by claiming authority over criminal cases.[42]

Southern, Middle Belt, and Northern-minority anti-sharia analysts found room to contest these changes by the Northern sharia states. Distinguished lawyers Rotimi Williams and Ben Nwabueze contended that Islamic and customary-law provisions in the Constitution are subject to the federal Penal Code, making a statewide shift to sharia illegal. Nwabueze further argued that, by the rules of statutory construction (the Constitution was written after the Penal Code), the application of a uniform federal Penal Code is necessary.[43] Nevertheless, constitutional scholars such as E. Essien argued that changes by the Northern states were in line with provisions of the Constitution: only an amendment to the Constitution can *take away* from the jurisdiction of a state's Sharia Court of Appeal, but any state can legislate to *add* to its original jurisdiction. More problematic, however, was the legal limbo in which high courts' jurisdiction was left hanging with the new role of expanded sharia in civil and criminal cases.[44]

WRITTEN LAW

Islamic law is essentially derived from the holy texts in Arabic about the life and teachings of the Prophet Muhammad. According to doctrine, these texts should not be translated from Arabic into any other language. Despite defending sharia's constitutionality, Justice Bello (former chief justice of the supreme court) had noted that the challenges of translating Islamic law from Arabic pose a serious problem for the constitutional requirement to codify Nigerian criminal laws.[45] On this measure, opponents of expanded sharia argued that

Islamic law is not compatible with chapter IV, section 36 (12) of the Constitution, which states that "a person shall not be convicted of a criminal offense unless that offense is defined and the penalty therefore is prescribed in a written law," and in this subsection, a written law refers to an act of the National Assembly or a law of a state, any subsidiary legislation, or instrument under the provisions of a law.[46] Many sharia activists rejected this argument because, as they see it, sharia has endured over a thousand years of textual interpretation and scholarly debates.[47]

FREEDOM OF RELIGION

The relevant constitutional provision on freedom of religion is found in chapter IV, section 38 (1) of the Constitution: "Every person shall be entitled to freedom of thought, conscience, and religion, including freedom to change his religion or belief, and freedom (either alone or in community with others, and in public or in private) to manifest and propagate his or her religion or belief in worship, teaching, practice and observance."[48] Many sharia activists read this provision to mean that the constitution gave Muslims access to all that Islam entails, including the requirement that Muslims be governed by sharia; in this reading, section 38 validates the constitutionality of expanded Islamic law. The speaker of the Plateau State House of Assembly, while denying that his state would implement Islamic law, argued that the "core Muslim North" had a right to sharia inherent in its Muslim identity.[49]

Along the same lines,[50] anti-sharia analysts argue that just as the Constitution grants freedom of religion, it also ensures freedom *from* religion, protecting citizens from state-sanctioned expanded sharia.[51] Defense lawyers in Kaduna and Niger states would make this case on behalf of their non-Muslim clients who were being prosecuted under sharia.[52] Advocates for sharia have argued that religious orthodoxy necessitated sharia, but legislators had made alterations to the law that seemingly violated their faith, making the new legislation no more "holy" than the previous. For instance, in many states, the sharia Penal Code was not written de novo but, rather, adapted from the old Northern Nigerian Code, itself a colonial compromise.[53]

CIVIL AND HUMAN RIGHTS

Particularly objectionable to opponents of expanded sharia was the concern that the twelve Northern states' expanded Islamic law abrogated constitutionally guaranteed civil and human rights of Nigerian citizens. These critics contend that the Northern states' sharia courts, in contrast to prevailing practices in common-law courts, contravene established norms of justice and lacked procedural standards. Consequently, they conclude that expanded Islamic laws are in violation of constitutional provisions protective of citizens' rights and due process.[54]

Anti-sharia analyst Simeon Nwobi's argument encapsulates the sentiments of most of these critics. He identifies three areas where strict application of sharia in criminal and civil cases contravened the civil and human rights guaranteed by the Nigerian Constitution. First, sharia's prohibition of commercial activities on products deemed *haram* (forbidden), such as alcohol, abrogates the constitutional rights of citizens to participate freely in the country's national economy.[55] Second, Nwobi claims that expanded sharia restricted Nigerians from moving freely within the country because it limits the social activities of people under its jurisdiction.[56] Finally, Nwobi judges that sharia prohibits conversion from Islam to any other religion, contradicting the Constitution.[57] The ban on "apostasy," while formally absent from the letter of Islamic law in most of the twelve Northern states, would be considered an essential rule once expanded sharia was instituted.[58] Anti-sharia advocates Masih and Salam further argued that preaching Christianity (and other religions) would be outlawed under sharia, which violates the "freedom to manifest and propagate [any] religion or belief in worship, teaching, practice, and observance," as would expanded sharia's abrogation of Christian education, a right guaranteed by the Constitution.[59] With these queries, *less* Islamic law was required for sharia to be constitutionally acceptable.[60]

Whatever the limits of the Fourth Republic's judicial framework, it was clear that Islamic reformers' wishes were not integrated into the prevailing Nigerian legal system. It was in this context that prominent Hausa-Fulani politicians and Muslim clerics pushed for reforms within their respective states. This led to expanded sharia policies instituted by the twelve Northern states.[61] To understand the impact of these reform policies in the Northern states, it is necessary to situate the push for sharia in Islamic thought and the construction of the Northern Nigerian ummah.

Islamic Thought and the Ummah

The extent to which Islamic thought impacted the sharia crisis is reflected in interpretations of scriptural texts and the variety of doctrines that have shaped Northern Nigerian Muslim identity over several centuries. Although religious clerics are not granted any special authority under Islamic doctrine, they are entrusted with interpreting legal texts through case studies, a practice known as *fiqh*.[62] Fiqh was codified by Imam al-Shafi'i in the eighth and ninth centuries.[63]

This "science of Islamic law" is divided into *usul* (the methodology of law, its sources, and scope) and *furu* (the study of substantive branches of law).[64] Fiqh is applied to the corpus of Islamic jurisprudential texts, and divided among primary and secondary sources. The first primary source is the Qur'an; it is composed of the text itself (with 114 *surah*, or chapters), legal commentary on the Qur'an (referred to as *tafsir*, carried out only by those who have attained advanced knowledge of the Qur'an), and the *sunnah* (documentation of the life of the Prophet, transmitted orally until Caliph Umar Ibn al-Aziz instructed scholars to write it down). As it varies in reliability, the *sunnah* is further split into *Sahih* (if the sources are trustworthy) and *Da'if* (if not), with accordingly different legal weight applied. The second primary source is the hadith, the record of the Prophet's and his companions' sayings and actions.[65] Secondary sources are essentially composed of legal interpretations, known as *ra'i* if by an individual and *ijma* if made by consensus—with the latter weighted more heavily. Other secondary sources include *istishab*, or legal presumption, such as of innocence or lawfulness of those activities not expressly forbidden. More controversial secondary sources are public interest (Malikis refer to this as *al-Masalih Mursalah*); earlier religious law from recognized prophets such as Moses and Jesus (*Shar min Qblana*); acts of Madinah people, since they lived with the Prophet (*Amal Ahl al-Madinah*); and local customs (*urf*).[66] Should this body of legal doctrine fail the scholar, *fiqh* dictates that he makes a *qiyas*, an analogical deduction based on available evidence for a legal problem to which no solution can be found in the texts.[67] Decisions must always follow five concerns: belief, moralities, devotions, transactions, and punishments. All acts are classified into one of five categories: obligatory, recommended, indifferent, prohibited, or distasteful.[68]

Islamic jurisprudence is informally divided between a divine half and a human half, the latter of which can change over time.[69] Thus, claims that Islamic law is universal and unchanging do not contradict assertions that it can be adapted to local circumstances. In this respect, the principle that shapes sharia is similar to that of common law, for which (until recently) divine law ruled and positive (human) law supplemented a legal baseline derived from Christianity. The major distinction between Islamic law and common law lies in the fact that the latter has sucked up its divine component.[70] However, this balance leaves room for disagreement over interpretation of the corpus, partly arising from differences in scholars' intellects, legal abilities, and readings of linguistic derivations.[71] As a whole, sharia forms a uniform, all-encompassing legal system: "Law, religious ethics, and morality form an integral part of the same normative process,"[72] therefore Islamic law is a necessary component of Islamic society.

Islamic law cases proceed with the presentation of the relevant parties in the case, followed by the oath, the presentation of the witnesses (if the accused denies the charges, witnesses are brought in and cross-examined), and eventually the rendition of judgment.[73] Depending on the case, two males, a male and two females, or two females are needed for witness testimony to prove guilt. Each must be of a certain "quality" with respect to gender, adherence to Islam, and age. With regard to judgment, specific sentences are not always provided for; instead sharia relies on judicial discretion.[74] Appeals are heard by the justice from the original decision, as opposed to the Western practice of a second judge (or panel of judges) reviewing the case.[75] The most serious criminal acts are classified as *hudud* offenses, of which there are eight: *zina* (adultery), *qadhf* (slander), *sariqa* (theft), *hirabah* (armed robbery), *shurb al-khamr* (consumption of alcohol), *jinayat* (homicide), *riddah* (apostasy and blasphemy), and *baghye* (rebellion). All have fixed penalties, and all but the last two were implemented in Northern Nigeria following the imposition of expanded sharia.[76]

Among contending Northern Nigerian Muslim groups, the reformism that shaped the agitation for sharia came out of the Izala movement. Providing the movement's dominant theological perspective since the 1980s, Izala had mobilized a new generation of Northern Muslims to articulate new Islamic legal tradition that challenged Nigeria's constitutional and political reform. Consequently, Lubeck argues that Nigeria's sharia movement was

> driven by a new generation of Islamic reformers who while drawing upon eclectic sources, are largely inspired by neo-Salafi legal models and discourses originating in the Gulf states and Saudi Arabia. The latter should be distinguished from the Salafi reformers of the nineteenth century, like Mohammed Abduh and Rashid Rida. Neo-Salafi doctrines privilege the Qur'an and Sunna of the Prophet, respect the companions of the Prophet, and reject subsequent innovations such as Sufism and Muslim modernist reasoning (*ijtihad*) for the public good (*maslahah*). While neo-Salafi reasoning relies heavily on Hanbali doctrines, it is important to emphasize that when scriptural legal movements travel through global networks and are applied by reformers living in large, complex societies, like those of Northern Nigeria, they become intermingled with each other. Therefore, while sharia reform was empowered by neo-Salafis, Nigeria's legal system remained largely Maliki because the existing sharia

judges adjudicating personal and family law were trained in the Maliki, not the Hanbali tradition.[77]

With such a well-defined jurisprudential tradition, the expanded sharia codes introduced by Nigeria's Northern state governments in 1999 and 2000 followed a fairly uniform format. Kaduna State's Penal Code provides a standard example of such reform. The new code acknowledges that only Muslims (and non-Muslims who consent) are subject to Islamic law, extending its jurisdiction to those who commit a sharia offense outside Kaduna when they reenter the state. Years are counted by both Islamic and Gregorian calendars, oaths must be in Allah's name, and several Arabic terms are defined. A list of possible punishments, such as caning and amputation, are outlined. With regard to doctrine, punishments are divided into four categories: hudud, diyya, qisas, and ta'zir. As would be expected from expanded sharia, corporal punishment and judicial discretion are elevated, while probation and fines are less common and degrees of punishment are less graduated.[78] In addition to this textual grounding, the philosophical disposition of Muslim clerics tied jurisprudence to the word of Allah. This barred any expedient revision of Islamic law, much less its replacement with an alien common-law jurisprudence.

To Muslim reformers, these changes were essential. The adoption of expanded sharia, one advocate of Islamic law claims, was "the essential foundation of the just Islamic society... one that follows the revelations and words of God."[79] When the Bauchi State government announced its expanded sharia policy, the governor reasoned that the decision was taken simply in fidelity to Islam.[80] A typical editorial of the Northern-centered *New Nigerian* reiterated that the law governing Muslims "cannot be adapted, altered, or dropped capriciously but must be followed absolutely."[81] It followed that any contradiction within the constitution that restricted access to expanded sharia on civil and criminal cases for Northern Muslims was prima facie invalid.

Similarly, as Murray Last argues, ideas inherent to emirate society have always pushed Muslim leaders to advocate for sharia in local communities. Because Islam is as much a civilization as a religion, it experienced various transformations as it spread across Sudanic Africa over many centuries. Since the imposition of colonial rule, its doctrines have acted as a buffer against Western conceptions of modernity and other global intrusions.[82] Moreover, "the sense of closure," Last argues, "is central to Islamic culture. Not only is the interior of a house strictly private... so too, in a sense, is the territory of the *jama'a* [Muslim faithful]. Not for nothing is the land of the Muslim *ummah* [Muslim polity] called *dar al-Islam*, the 'house' of Islam." The push to expand Islamic law in 1999 and 2000 represented "a way of keeping 'strangers' in their place, reminding them that [a community such as] Kano is not theirs and reasserting the right of Muslim dominance in a Muslim city."[83] Thus, sharia is an attempt to reestablish the *dar al-Islam* and assert Northern Nigeria's membership in a global Muslim community. In Last's words:

> *Shari'a* and *hisba* are proof to the wider *ummah* that "we Muslims" in Northern Nigeria are serious members of the *ummah*; that "we" are not to be pigeon-holed by foreigners simply as "Nigerians" and associated with doubtful dealings. It proves, too, that "we" are not aligned with the USA against "our" Muslim brothers and sisters in Iraq, Iran, or indeed Afghanistan. But while I argue that we should interpret *hisba* and the *shari'a* as aspects of this reaffirmation of a Muslim citizenship, I would argue also that it is not about cancelling Nigerian citizenship; it is just an attempt to develop and articulate a second nationality.[84]

He adds, "Putting things right in the *Jama'a* will lead Allah to aid the *Jama'a* significantly, albeit in His own time. Calling the *Jama'a* to order is thus a serious political act." Muslims from emirate society cite as an example of Allah's aid the end of Christian colonial rule in 1960 and the removal of various corrupt postcolonial regimes.[85] From the start, the imposition of expanded sharia was a reassertion of Northern Muslim identity; sharia thus became the unifying regional framework for the enunciation of a vision that connected the noble past articulated in the Sokoto Jihad with the future of a Northern Muslim community. Consequently, Brandon Kendhammer contends,

> As elites and ordinary citizens argued about what it meant to be a Muslim in a democratic society and about how Islamic injunctions might shape state policy, a discourse emerged connecting sharia implementation to broader, pan-Nigerian ways of talking about democracy. This discourse drew on symbols and images from Northern Nigeria's Muslim past, but also represented new and evolving coalitions of religious and political interests.[86]

These critical issues were vividly reflected in a landmark national conference on sharia sponsored by JNI in February 2000 and presided over by distinguished Nigerians, including Justice Mohammed Bello, former chief justice of the Federal Republic of Nigeria; a renowned academic, Professor Abubakar Mustapha, vice chancellor of the University of Maiduguri; and the Rev. Dr. Matthew Hassan Kukah, a prominent Northern Nigerian theologian and later Catholic bishop of Sokoto.[87] Offering incisive interventions in his keynote address, Justice Bello traced the course of Islamic law in Northern

Nigeria through two centuries and identified distinct stages of its evolution in the region following Usman dan Fodio's jihad in the early nineteenth century: the formation of the Sokoto Caliphate involved an expansive emirate system governed by Islamic law that lasted through the better part of the nineteenth century; Islamic law endured the imposition of the early colonial administrative system in the Northern Nigerian Protectorate. Thus, as the colonial system evolved, emirate rulers—emirs, alkalis, and ulamas—served both as agents of the British authorities and as embodiments of prevailing Islamic legal order. While acknowledging that the modern legal system eroded Islamic law, Justice Bello insisted that "with the exception of matters within the exclusive jurisdictions of Federal and State High Courts, [Northern Nigeria's] mode and conduct of life has always been governed by sharia."[88]

Given his reputation as Northern Nigeria's preeminent common-law jurist, many pro-sharia activists conveniently interpreted Justice Bello's nuanced endorsement of Islamic law as an unqualified support for sharia in Northern communities.[89] In regional newspapers, sharia advocates insist that Islamic law has long governed the public life of Northern Muslims. Expressing a popular Northern pro-sharia perspective, the emir of Ilorin, Alhaji Sulu Gambari, in the northern Yoruba region, on the southern fringe of the Caliphate, thought it unreasonable for "Christians to demand secularity in a region [the Hausa-Fulani emirate] long ruled by Islamic law."[90] While pledging support for Obasanjo's federal government, Northern ulamas noted that sharia "has been in existence in Nigeria, regulating the lives of Muslims in various states of the country for centuries."[91] One prominent pro-sharia commentator described the Northern states' insistence on expanded sharia as the modern manifestation of the Sokoto Jihad, and a critical step in defining the essence of the Northern Nigerian *ummah*.[92] Even high-ranking federal government officials from Northern states in the Obasanjo administration, though generally ambivalent on expanded sharia, supported their Northern Muslim compatriots. For example, in a BBC interview, Nigerian foreign minister Sule Lamido, an influential Hausa-Fulani Muslim, defended the sharia policies of the Northern states.[93]

For Muslim proponents of sharia, this restoration of the ummah required the reframing of expanded sharia to challenge the erosion of Islamic law since decolonization. At independence, the final "reconciliation" of Islamic law and common law had come in the Penal Code, which was embraced by the sardauna's NPC regional government, under the tutelage of outgoing British colonial officers. This public support for Islamic law not only challenges this alien legacy, but also situates Northern states in their proper place as legitimate Muslim communities.

The Ummah and the Common Good

In addition to articulating sharia as the essence of the ummah, powerful advocates of expanded sharia also packaged their support for sharia as the quest for the common good in emirate society. Ludwig observes that many Northern Muslim proponents of sharia defended the application of expanded Islamic law on the grounds that "the new laws have been enacted by democratically elected executive and legislative officials responding to the unquestionable desire of the vast majority of their constituents."[94] Governor Ahmed Sani of Zamfara State, a champion of expanded sharia, provides a good illustration of this line of argument. For Sani the democratic process was premised on implementing sharia because he had based his gubernatorial campaign on Islamic law. As opposition mounted against Zamfara's sharia policy, Sani replied: "When I was campaigning for this office, wherever I [went], I always start[ed] with '*Allahu Akbar*' (Allah is the greatest) to show my commitment to the Islamic faith. . . . As part of my programme for the state, I promised the introduction of sharia."[95] Sani told us additionally that sharia is essential for the organization of a just Islamic society, and would serve as an effective response to the corruption that Western conception of modernization had imposed on Zamfara communities.[96] He was backed by the state's chief justice of the Sharia Court of Appeal and by the Speaker of the State House of Assembly; these officials were convinced that sharia represents the Zamfara people's mandate.[97]

In an editorial in the *New Nigerian*, Bello Alkali, a prominent pro-sharia commentator, argued that the Zamfara State governor and legislators were popularly elected and that their sharia policy was a reflection of democracy, not an abrogation of it. In addition, he insisted that "the overwhelming population of Zamfara State had told [Governor Sani] they want sharia to govern their lives if the Almighty makes him the Governor."[98] In summation, Alkali argued that sharia would help reverse the moral and social crises endemic in Zamfara's society; contrary to the position of Northern, Southern, and Middle Belt Christians, sharia, he contends, is in keeping with constitutional provisions on freedom of religion and state's rights. Another *New Nigerian* editorial opined that expanded sharia would affirm the right of Muslims to be governed by Islamic law, as dictated by the Qur'an, sunnah, and hadith. The editorial outlined the functions of qualified judges and called for the establishment of a police force to enforce the new Islamic law.[99]

The sharia-as-justification-for-democracy argument later was used by advocates of Islamic law in Bauchi State[100] to turn the Katsina State government's position toward sharia,[101] and in Kano to declare that if non-Muslims (only

2 percent of the population there) were against sharia, they should leave the state.[102] In Katsina State, Governor Umaru Yar'adua, a confidant of President Obasanjo among PDP governors and later president of the federal republic, who earlier had been ambivalent about expanded sharia, reversed himself when he was confronted with sharia's popularity in his state.[103] In Kaduna State, with its substantial Christian population, the government established a statewide public opinion campaign,[104] which eventually led to sharia's enactment.[105] From the perspective of pro-sharia scholar Ibrahim Ado-Kurawa, Southern "secularists" and Christians were conspiring to crush the democratic aspirations of Northern Muslims.[106] Lateef Adegbite, the Yoruba secretary-general of the NSCIA, declared that since Northern Muslims had spoken through the democratic process, any opposition to sharia could only be seen as an attack on the popular will.[107] Consequently, for pro-sharia activists, Southern, Middle Belt, and Northern Christians' fierce opposition to sharia signifies intolerance and is antithetical to the democratic will.[108]

Supporters of the expanded sharia policies of the Northern states also argued that Islamic law represents a societal necessity. Beyond a straightforward binary of legal and illegal, sharia, they think, provides the only just legal system for mediating relations among Muslims. Many prominent emirate clerics had argued since decolonization in the 1950s that sharia's elimination from the Penal Code spelled the death knell of Usman dan Fodio's vision for the Sokoto Caliphate.[109] For its supporters, the extension of sharia beyond family cases thus represented a homogenizing force, eliminating the sectarianism that had plagued Northern communities since independence.[110] Furthermore, since the Constitution does not provide for social and economic rights, one prominent pro-sharia commentator pointed out that sharia's zakat tax levy on the wealthy would help reduce emirate society's grinding poverty.[111] Indeed, Lubeck observes that

> the poor members of the popular classes rallied around sharia because they hoped that the zakat tax on the affluent (2.5 percent of liable asset) would result in the redistribution of wealth.... In Kano, for example, approximately a million people turned out to celebrate the passing of sharia in 2000. The advantage of sharia, advocates argued, was that judgment would be swift, access improved, and citizen participation increased because Muslims already spoke the same language of sharia and understood its principles of justice, which was not true of Nigerian common law.[112]

Another pro-sharia commentator, Yakubu Yahaya Ibrahim, argued that expanded sharia would resolve the corruption inherent in the financial requirements of common law.[113] Of particular relevance to sharia is its critical role in the Penal Code,[114] where its proponents contend that the new expanded Islamic law will effectively check society's countless social ills.[115]

As riots between Muslims and Christians over the implementation of sharia later engulfed some Northern communities, pro-sharia commentators conveniently argued that the orgy of violence was evidence that the Penal Code should be reflected in Northern states' sharia laws.[116] Responding to detractors who criticized the harsh penalties in Islamic law, Governor Sani noted, "Sharia [is] always aimed at deterring human beings from committing crimes rather than executing punishment."[117] Praising Zamfara State's policy, Bello Adamu Sakkwato, a sharia advocate, agreed with the governor: "Justice, fair dealings, economic development, peace, and tranquility in all ramifications will ensue in the state."[118] Bashir Sambo, a renowned emirate judge, continued the optimistic viewpoint that sharia can solve all of Nigeria's problems,[119] echoing the observation in the 1980s of Ibrahim K. R. Sulaiman, a prominent Northern Muslim legal analyst, that sharia is the bastion of morality against the corruption inherent in common law.[120]

With the popularity of Sani's sharia initiative in many Northern states, prominent regional personalities from all walks of life and of diverse ideological perspectives showed their support for sharia. Barrister Abdullahi Jalo, a prominent regional attorney, called on Governor Habu Hashidu of Gombe State to follow Zamfara's example and introduce sharia in order to rid "the state of crime, prostitution, and other vices";[121] a leading emirate potentate Adamu Shanono, Baraden Abakpa commended Governor Sani's foresight and courage, claiming that this policy would reverse the social decay that was endemic in emirate society.[122]

Tied to this argument was the belief that sharia is inherently just and is built upon extensive textual and case law for the protection of minority rights. The *National Concord,* founded by Moshood Abiola as a pro-NPN newspaper during the Second Republic, editorialized that true sharia would lead to religious tolerance,[123] while an opinion piece in the *New Nigerian* said that sharia in Kaduna State would, in fact, protect the religious beliefs of the state's substantial Christian population.[124] Indeed, Sani personally assured Christians in his state that their freedom of worship would be protected under sharia.[125] Again, Adegbite wrote that if properly administered, sharia would deter crime, foster public order, and promote social justice.[126] Many pro-sharia letters to the editor of the *New Nigerian* were confident that sharia would reverse the Western values that have corrupted the morality of emirate society.[127] In the run-up to the implementation of the new Islamic laws, the Speakers of the Houses of Assembly of Northern states met to coordinate prohibitions on alcohol, prostitution, and gambling across their respective states.[128] When sharia came, many declared preemptively: "Peace and moral improvement had arrived."[129] Northern states immediately passed strict anti-vice measures such as the Zamfara State law that banned non-Muslim cultural resources, including videos, foreign films, and advertisements, all considered to have negative impact on Muslim youths.[130]

As pro-sharia commentators contended that expanded sharia is the panacea to the social problems in Northern communities, they also argued that the sharia revolution would encourage a renaissance in Islamic culture. This, they contend, would not only provide an effective response to the corrupting influence of Christian and secular education in Northern communities, but would also reverse the educational disparity between Northern and Southern states. Ado-Kurawa argued that Islamic education gave the Sokoto Caliphate its power, but colonial authorities elevated secular education and, even worse, missionary schooling in Northern communities.[131] Proponents of expanded sharia said the educational requirement inherent in the implementation of Islamic law would provide culturally relevant education for talakawa commoners and women.

These thoughts in part illustrate the context in which pro-sharia commentators imagined the significance of a revitalized sharia movement in the educational transformation of Northern states.[132] Indeed, the acerbic reaction of sharia's opponents to the reforms, its proponents contended, was simply an episode in secularist ignorance, particularly among anti-sharia Muslims, indicating the extent to which widespread educational reform was needed.[133] Most prominent was a campaign to establish an Islamic university as a center for advanced Islamic studies in Katsina.[134] So strong was the extent of local support in Katsina State that Katsina civil servants agreed to donate 5 percent of their annual salaries to fund its construction.[135]

With heavy emphasis on lionizing the precolonial Sokoto Caliphate, British colonial authorities, the previous allies of Hausa-Fulani Muslim rulers, were now denounced by sharia advocates as the destroyers of Islamic piety and the cause of Northern states' turn to the immorality seen in the West.[136] The return of Islamic law, which British colonialism destroyed would thus represent the revival of a noble Islamic heritage.[137] To sharia proponents, Western vice was the cause of social chaos and economic crisis.[138]

Sharia advocates also were aware that they needed to provide effective response to the strong Southern Christian opposition to sharia mounted through the powerful Lagos-Ibadan news media outlets, especially in the months after the launching of comprehensive sharia policies by Northern state governments. As a Yoruba, Lateef Adegbite, the NSCIA secretary-general, was well positioned to respond to the scathing attacks on sharia policies of the Northern states by the Southern intelligentsia. Interestingly, Adegbite emerged as one of the most articulate defenders of Northern sharia states, challenging the assault of Southern Christians against sharia.[139] In Zamfara State, where Sani particularly drew the rage of Southern Christians, Adegbite countered that the state's sharia policy was not only in keeping with the Constitution, but also would address the crisis of law and order.[140] Furthermore, in an opinion piece, Northern Muslim commentator Abdul Gaffar lashed out against Southern journalists—especially Yoruba journalists—for what he considered their bias against Muslims.[141]

Indeed, to confront what many Hausa-Fulani Muslim elites have long considered Southern and Middle Belt Christian propaganda against Islam, now manifested in the vitriolic campaign against sharia, the chairman of the Council of Ulama called on Muslims everywhere to defend their religion against its enemies. Similarly, at the announcement of his state's sharia policy, Kano State's governor called for a massive turnout for its inauguration—demonstrating to the country that sharia had widespread appeal among Northern Muslims.[142]

However, this overwhelming Northern Muslim support for expanded sharia was hardly a blind allegiance to the Hausa-Fulani political class. The erosion of the moral authority of the emirate political elite, especially under unpopular military regimes led by Northern generals, had left the masses of Northern Muslims disaffected with the Sokoto Caliphate's power structures.[143] Hausa-Fulani politicians and their emirs and Islamic clerics allies are good at preaching sharia, critics argued, but are an essential component of a national neopatrimonial system that can only be eradicated through fidelity to true Muslim values.[144] Moreover, while noting sharia's constitutionality, a group of "progressive" Northern Muslim analysts saw the mass campaign for expanded sharia as a distraction from the political and economic failings of the Nigerian political class.[145]

Northern Muslim Coalition for Expanded Sharia

Despite the ambivalence of a small minority of Northern Muslims for expanded sharia, the sharia movement clearly had popular appeal among most Northern Muslims.[146] Sharia also had the support of notable figures in emirate society's small but influential group of radical intellectuals who had shaped the progressive traditions of populist socialist parties, notably NEPU (Northern Elements Progressive Union) and the PRP (People's Redemption Party), since decolonization. For a movement that Southern modernists generally saw as atavistic, the sharia movement, at least initially, succeeded in unifying Northern Muslim public opinion of diverse ideological orientations around a common ethno-religious—Hausa-Fulani-Northern-Muslim—identity.[147] These disparate groups coalesced around a revived Northern People's Congress (NPC) in March 2000. Led by the sultan of Sokoto, Alhaji Muhammadu Maccido, the revived NPC morphed into a renewed Arewa (Hausa for "Northern") Consultative Forum (ACF), a political association of emirate leaders (with a minority of junior partners from nonemirate Northern communities) committed to asserting Northern interests. In fact, the initial success of this pan-Northern ACF was not unconnected to Northern perception of a visceral Southern and Middle Belt Christian opposition to the sharia movement. This was particularly apparent in the Southern Christian-dominated national press corps. Thus, a Northern "manifesto" declared that the "pastime" of Southern Christians was "to ridicule, vilify and scandalize Islam and sharia."[148] Added to this was Northern Muslim leaders' feeling that despite their strong support for Obasanjo in the 1999 presidential election, an administration led by a self-proclaimed Yoruba born-again Christian failed to confer on Northern Muslims the recognition commensurate to their support for him.[149] In this context, the ACF unified Northern Muslims behind sharia and argued that Hausa-Fulani Muslims have a moral obligation to defend the Northern state governments' sharia policies against their Southern and Middle Belt Christian adversaries. The influence of this intersecting Northern Muslim identity will be seen in the evolution of the debate discussed below.

The major challenge before older-generation ACF leaders was to bring into the Northern Muslim fold disaffected Muslim youths, who had become increasingly restless since the political and economic crisis of the 1980s.[150] Confronted by an uncertain future, this younger generation of Northern Muslims had been attracted to Islamic reformist movements (especially neo-Salafi movements) such as Izala. Thus, the strong Southern and Middle Belt Christian opposition to sharia further radicalized educated Northern Muslim youths in the Arewa Peoples Congress, the de facto militant wing of the ACF under Brigadier General Sagir Mohammed. The group's militancy grew out of allegations of the "silence of the so-called elders over the massive massacre of Northerners in [the Yoruba cities of] Lagos and Ibadan.... The younger generation is losing confidence in the leadership of the older generation."[151]

Nevertheless, the environment created by these militant Hausa-Fulani Muslim youth movements gave greater coherence to the sharia riots that engulfed many Northern cities during the early years of the Fourth Republic. In Kaduna State, where the sharia riots were particularly violent, Northern Muslim youths blocked some one hundred thousand Christian demonstrators against sharia, whose "otherwise peaceful protest" they "literally lit on fire."[152] When Southern and Middle Belt Christian students fled their Northern university campuses during the Kaduna riots in February 2000, their properties were looted by Muslim mobs.[153] Also, Hausa-Fulani Muslim youths targeted the Christian deputy governor, Stephen Shekari, for his earlier handling of the sharia riots as acting governor.[154] At a minor level, the sharia crisis spilled over into a few Yoruba communities, betraying the low-level rumblings of Yoruba Muslim activists against the decidedly anti-sharia opposition of Yoruba Christians. For example, months after the Kaduna sharia riots, Ijebu and Lagos (Yoruba) Muslim youths attacked Christians in their local communities.[155] Less violent but equally vociferous was the National Committee of Muslim Youth, which organized a rally titled "Iwo [an Oyo-Yoruba city] Land for Islam," which tried to instigate religious conflict in the city.[156] To be sure, riots incited by Christian youths also were reported in Northern, Southern, and Middle Belt communities during this period of religious and political turbulence.

Another crucial constituency was to be found among emirs and Muslim clerics, who were promptly co-opted into the newly established sharia courts. In exchange for the emirs' support for state policies, senior state officials rewarded them with state patronage.[157] For instance, Zamfara State's governor identified emirs and traditional chiefs as the first vector for the implementation of the government's sharia policy.[158]

Sharia advocates also drew inspiration from international supporters by linking Northern Nigeria's sharia reforms to a global history of Islamic law dating back centuries. These reformers justified the legal changes by pointing to global jurisprudential precedents. Thus, "the experiences of countries which practiced forms of sharia such as Sudan and Saudi Arabia were taken into account" in drafting legislation in the Northern states.[159] One editorial in the *National Concord* traced sharia from Prophet Muhammad, through early Islamic states in the Middle East, to precolonial Nigeria.[160] Partly as a result of widespread concerns that the extension of sharia into criminal cases would undermine the civil rights of religious minorities, sharia proponents drew on Algeria as a successful case of protections afforded to non-Muslims.[161] Ado-Kurawa, meanwhile, framed the reform effort as part of a global Islamist resurgence, comparing it to the Iranian Revolution of 1979. He called for a pan-Islamic movement to break free of Western domination, insisting on Muslims' triumphant victory and moral superiority.[162] Similarly, situating Nigeria in the Muslim world, another leading Muslim commentator, Syed Khalid Rashid, argues that Islamization is progress and Nigerians should abandon their irrational tendency to imitate the West.

Many pro-sharia intellectuals concur, noting that Western-oriented Nigerian Christians consistently associate Islam with backwardness. Many Northern Muslim commentators contend that Islam is under attack throughout the world and that Nigerian Muslims should seek solidarity in political linkages with fellow Muslims around the world. As John Paden notes, major Nigerian Muslim constituencies have international ties going back many centuries:

> Hausa-Fulani rulers are linked to Sudanic Africa; Sufi movements are strongly transnational (*tijani* are tied to Morocco and Senegal, *qadiri* to the Maghreb and Iraq); anti-innovation legalists are allied with Saudi Arabia; intellectual reformers have global educational contacts; anti-establishment syncretistic network with local groups in Niger, Chad and Cameroon; the Muslim Brotherhoods have supporters in Iran; and even urban youth and migrants have access to foreign radio.[163]

Consequently, the Zamfara State government made overtures to the broader Islamic world, and several Muslim countries pledged to train Zamfara's Islamic judges and provide resources for the state's sharia institutions.[164] Other Northern states also sought and received different forms of support from the Arab world. Several Northern Islamic judges received training in Saudi Arabia, while Iran, Libya, Mauritania, and Sudan lobbied the Nigerian federal government to promote sharia.[165] Such efforts were helped by the formalization of Nigeria's place in the global ummah through its membership in the OIC, going back to the 1980s. Running parallel was a less effective attempt by sharia activists to define Nigeria's anti-sharia movement as an extension of the West's assault on Islam.[166] After allegations of Christian-instigated violence in January 2000, Kwara State Muslims charged that weapons used during the riots were imported from groups seeking to destabilize Nigeria.[167] Such statements appear to have been intended to isolate the non-Muslim opponents of expanded sharia in Northern and Middle Belt states from international backers, especially from Western countries, a tactic that largely failed.

CHAPTER EIGHT

EXPANDED SHARIA:
RESISTANCE, VIOLENCE,
AND RECONCILIATION

The early years of the Nigerian Fourth Republic were marked by systemic conflict between the twelve Northern sharia states and Christian groups, primarily from Southern and Middle Belt states. The conflicts were episodic and unprecedented in the extents of bloodletting, even by Nigeria's tragic standards of religious violence. The crisis did encourage some introspection on the part of senior federal government officials, religious leaders, and political elites from all regions of the country. But on the whole, collective efforts at reconciliation were less than far-reaching; peace initiatives were severely compromised by distrust among contending ethno-religious blocs in the country.

The Case against Sharia: Christian and Nationalist Critiques

Anthony Olubunmi Okogie, the Catholic archbishop and national president of the Christian Association of Nigeria (CAN), was at the forefront of national debates against the imposition of expanded sharia in the Northern states.[1] Archbishop Okogie and many Christian leaders argued essentially that the Northern states' sharia policies were serious threats to the rights of Christian minorities in Northern Muslim states and that sharia would destroy Nigeria's fragile democratic transition, undermine its precarious federal structure, reify ethno-religious identities, and derail the country's developmental agenda. Archbishop Okogie was particularly concerned about the danger of a Muslim versus non-Muslim binary in Northern states, as he expressed it: "Any such law [sharia] will stand as a parallel law to the Constitution and therefore, is unacceptable. If Christians and other religions practiced in the country decide to have their own judicial systems, how many systems of laws will be in this one country?"[2] Okogie's views were further elaborated in a five-part newspaper series on sharia's implications by his successor as CAN president, Dr. Sunday Mbang, primate of the Methodist Church of Nigeria.[3] Mbang, Okogie, and many Christian leaders embarked on a national campaign to neutralize what they considered a dangerous political development.

Southern intellectuals also wrote extensively to register their fears about sharia. In fiery newspaper editorials, pamphlets, and conference papers, their viewpoints underlined that pro-sharia initiatives threaten the Constitution.[4] For example, Rotimi Williams, a legal luminary and Yoruba Christian who had chaired the 1979 Constitution Drafting Committee, argued that a "radical sharia movement" would impose an unbridgeable constitutional fault line between the Northern states and other states in the country, as well as between common law and sharia. He endorsed the thinking among human rights groups that the imposition of expanded sharia will fundamentally alter the prevailing concept of civil rights and civil liberties in Nigeria.[5] Olu Onagoruwa, a Yoruba Christian who was once Nigeria's federal minister of justice and attorney general, argued that the Nigerian Constitution trumps any other legal code.[6] Particularly problematic for Christian-educated elites was the idea of equality between common law and sharia as competing legal systems. As an editorial in the Lagos-based national newspaper the *Weekend Concord* put it: "Nigerian common law was created by Christians and was also imposed upon the Muslim community. But there is a difference: common law can change and adapt to the needs of the time. Sharia does not change since it is believed to be the word of Allah."[7] The irony was not lost on many other Christian critics of expanded sharia that the constitutional provisions that granted the Northern Muslim states the right to legislate on matters of jurisprudence was derived from common law that now would be prohibited under expanded sharia.[8]

Unique among Nigerian states, indirect rule in Kaduna State had subjugated non-Hausa-Fulani indigenes (mostly Christians by the late colonial period) to the control of emirate rulers. If not de jure, aspects of this colonial imposition had continued de facto during the postcolonial period as Nigeria went through various political transformations. For Christians in Kaduna State, expanded sharia meant a forced return to an oppressive legal system still fresh in the memories of local elders.[9] Following the colonial imposition of earlier decades, the lines of citizenship were being redrawn; "by defining political self-determination in religious terms and excluding others from central aspects of public legislation, Muslims redefine the *demos* that it is entitled to rule," to the exclusion of Christians in Kaduna State.[10] Clearly, such rigid legal interpretation precluded any compromise. Christians who were obviously concerned about the implications of expanded sharia argued that the modern process of Islamization that the Hausa-Fulani political class was determined to impose must be stopped at all cost. Claims like these had been commonplace in Nigeria's political discourse. We will recall that during the OIC crisis in the 1980s, Christian theologians and Southern commentators argued that Nigeria's membership in the OIC during the Babangida regime was an attempt by Hausa-Fulani Muslim rulers to dominate the country.[11] Anti-sharia analyst Moni Odo Ngban pointed out that the push for expanded sharia by emirate rulers was the final confirmation of a trend that went back to the NPC's northernization and Islamization policies of the 1950s and 1960s.[12] Moreover, since each Northern state implemented sharia differently, critics argued, the principle of Islamic unity was compromised, with serious legal and political implications for state affairs throughout the country.[13]

Opponents of sharia were also concerned that the reforms would undermine Nigeria's nascent democratic transition.[14] Although expanding Islamic law appeared to have popular appeal among Northern Muslims voters, opponents of sharia claimed that it would undermine Nigeria's democratic principles because sharia, by its very nature, stifles civil liberties and liberal values.[15] Indeed, some commentators suggested that the sharia movement was purposefully erected to subvert the shift in presidential power to a Southern Christian, the Egba-Yoruba Olusegun Obasanjo.[16] Consequently, Southern, Middle Belt and Northern minority Christians cloaked themselves as defenders of the Nigerian democratic republic, keeping faith with the country's nationalist and republican traditions, going back to the colonial period.[17] Expanded sharia, they asserted, would set a dangerous precedent, indicating that majoritarian rule allowed state governments to enact nefarious Islamic laws that would trample on the constitutional rights of Christian minorities.[18] In a cacophony of opposition to the Northern states' sharia policies, prominent Nigerians from various walks of life, most of them Christians, and even some "progressive" Muslims registered strong objection to what they considered an assault on the Nigerian Constitution and the country's vaunted "federal character." One influential Pentecostal leader, Archbishop Abraham Oyeniran of the United Global Church Association of Nigeria, opined: "There is no doubt that some people are bent on seeing an end to this democracy."[19] Aishat Ismail, Nigeria's minister for women's affairs and a Muslim women's rights activist, stated that the Northern states' sharia policies were a distraction from national development and democratic consolidation.[20]

Prominent journalists including Tope Adeboye and Fred Egbe[21] wrote essays that reproduced Southern anxieties, contending that expanded sharia policies would deepen sectarianism and ethno-religious violence[22] and accelerate Nigeria's disintegration along ethno-religious lines.[23] Southern-based Christian newsletters were strident in their criticism, depicting the Zamfara State sharia initiative as a "Legislative Monster."[24] Unsubstantiated reports had it that the Northern Muslim states of Nigeria had mobilized funds to promote sharia in Southern states with substantial Muslim populations and thereby expand the political trouble.[25] Many sharia foes were united in their concern that sharia would further reify ethno-religious identities and carve permanent fault lines in Nigeria's fragile federal state. They feared that, just as colonial authorities had reinforced Northern Muslim rule, expanded sharia would permanently define rigid communal divisions along Christian-Muslim lines, dangerously undercutting the dynamic process of social interaction that was beginning to emerge in the postcolonial era.[26] In addition, mixed parentage, and the presence of other religions (particularly indigenous religious traditions and religious syncretism) scuttled any attempt to divide Nigerians into neat Christian and Muslim enclaves. Overlapping identities muddied the water, particularly in the case of Middle Belt and Hausa Christians.[27]

Religious riots have been particularly severe since the 1980s in Kaduna State, where the population historically has been evenly divided between Muslim and Christian indigenes; and the state's Christian-Muslim divide is further complicated by the large proportion of Christian Southerners. The trend of religious conflict reemerged when the Kaduna State House of Assembly passed legislation to implement expanded Islamic law and thousands of Christians registered their opposition by flooding the government's exploratory committee with petitions.[28] This was followed by violent riots between Muslim and Christians.[29] Igbo Christian traders in urban areas have always been vulnerable targets in Northern sectarian attacks.[30] More than four hundred people were killed and property worth billions of naira destroyed following waves of attacks and counterattacks in the state.[31] Even the proposal by the Kaduna State government to create a new local government administration for Kataf communities (that is, non-Hausa-Fulani Christian indigenes) was stiffly resisted by

Hausa-Fulani communities, who argued that such a move would encroach on their land; indeed, it ignited fresh communal violence[32] in which more than three hundred people were killed and more than one thousand buildings were destroyed.[33] The Kaduna sharia riots exposed preexisting tensions, despite the state's seeming cosmopolitan outlook.

Yoruba Christian analyst Ben Oguntuase's account of the Kaduna riots captures the suffering of thousands of Nigerians caught in the sharia crossfire in Kaduna State. What began as a drive for Islamic law led to open communal violence and consequently a national debate on public safety and the constitutional rights of Nigerian citizens. Revealing the extent of the crisis, Oguntuase recounts:

> A soldier drove in a Mercedes Benz car into the station narrating how he was forced to seek refuge. Other vehicles started arriving with shattered windows. Then a man was brought in with a machete cut on his head. Two armed policemen escorted the victim to a hospital. It will be a miracle if the man survived. The cut was deep and part of his brain was already gushing out.... Four officers agreed to escort us, all... armed. We formed a 10-vehicle convoy. A young police officer in mufti [Northern civilian clothes] volunteered to lead the convoy on a motorcycle. We headed for the Nigerian Defense Academy. All the way, we were meeting resistance. The policemen fired sporadically into the air to clear the way. Red-hot roadblocks mounted by the rioters were all along the route. As we approached a crowd, the policemen would fire into the air, the crowd would disappear. As soon as the last vehicle passed, they would start hauling stones at the convoy. Along the way we saw at least five roasted bodies.[34]

Religious violence was so severe that critics of the state government's sharia policy called for the creation of separate neighborhoods based on fixed religious affiliations. But CAN condemned the idea as outrageous. Tony Uda, the organization's state chairperson, dismissed the proposal: "All those involved in such movements are promoting the disintegration of the nation."[35]

Overall, the riots did more than destroy lives and property; they deepened communal suspicion in the state and etched intolerance into national consciousness.[36] Economically, opponents of expanded Islamic law argued that the campaign for sharia was a costly program that diverted resources from pressing national priorities in economic development. Anti-sharia commentator Moni Odo Ngban said that sharia would further harm Northern Nigeria's already fragile economy, as new regulations on the region's weak industrial sector would put many out of work.[37] Bee Debki, another anti-sharia analyst, argued that the sharia program was a "political gimmick" with which the masses of the Northern Muslim poor were given the false hope of economic redistribution through the implementation of new sharia policies.[38]

Interparty dialogue may have produced positive outcomes on the sharia question. In Zamfara State, for example, the state's opposition party (the PDP) called on the ruling party (the APP) to drop its sharia program and face the challenge of community development.[39] General Zamani Lekwot, a Christian Kataf stalwart and previous military governor of Rivers State, lamented the north-south development gap and held that it was the government's responsibility to invest in education reform instead of sharia. Condemnation of the Zamfara State government reached greater heights in the Yoruba states. The Lagos-based *National Concord* mocked Governor Sani: "What has happened to all the lofty election campaign promises made to the Zamfara electorate about better health care, improved infrastructure, good potable water supply, qualitative education, and enhanced farming subventions? These pragmatic programmes are now thrown into the dustbin in the mad chase for a religious El-Dorado [sic]."[40]

Christian leaders were particularly concerned about the implications of sharia for the rights of Christian minorities in Northern states.[41] In the highly contentious case of Niger State, with its substantial Christian population, the Right Rev. Jonah G. Kolo, Anglican bishop of Bida in the state capital and the state CAN chairman, urged national Christian leaders to protect Niger State's Christian minorities against the state government's expanded sharia policy.[42] Representing Christians, CAN also opposed the Kano State government's sharia policy, arguing that the state's implementation of sharia policy would undermine the rights of non-Muslims.[43] A national Christian organization called the Eclectic Movement of Nigeria denounced the sharia-inspired attacks on Christians in Northern states.[44] And Archbishop Peter Akinola, primate of the Nigerian Anglican Church, called for the withdrawal of state funding to religious groups.[45]

As would be expected, Nigeria's vibrant Pentecostal movement posed the most vociferous Christian opposition to expanded sharia. Many Pentecostal leaders were strongly against applying sharia to criminal law because of its impact on their church members in Northern states. Nigeria's Pentecostal church movement reflected the shifting political, social, and economic realities that went hand in hand with moving from military rule to democracy. Drawing on new national and transnational networks, in which evangelical churches positioned themselves to engage in pressing national debates (see chapter 6), prominent Pentecostal leaders argued that expanded sharia was a cynical attempt to recover the North's loss of presidential power following the demise of General Abacha's regime.[46] As they had done to confront the Abacha threat, Pentecostal leaders mobilized their members to confront a new menace of Zamfara sharia with the spiritual force of prayer. They presented Zamfara Governor Sani as spearheading the evil mission to undermine Nigeria's destiny as a prosperous democratic republic.[47] The general superintendent of the Gospel Light Redemption Church, the Rev. Isaac Orihaki, attacked the federal legislature for not protecting Christian minorities against the sharia policies of the Northern states.[48]

The challenge from the Pentecostal movement was most severe in the Middle Belt states and among Northern Christian minorities. In the case of the Middle Belt, Lubeck's apt summary of how religious identity has shaped political conflicts since the nineteenth century is worth quoting at length:

> From the 1980s until today [2011], the borderline regions with their mix of Christians and Muslims have been the site of bloody inter-communal violence. Ironically paralleling the Islamization process, the process of Christianization has served to unify smaller ethnic groups in this region and facilitated the formation of the common Christian identity in opposition to a long-dominant Muslim rule. Christian memories of exploitation by Muslim slave raiders in the precolonial era and discrimination since independence stoke grievances that found an effective voice in militant Pentecostal Christianity. Historically, communal violence was based upon ethno-national (e.g. tribal) identities, but as religious identities became increasingly politicized and nurtured by militant global networks, religion gradually displaced ethnicity as an identity marker.... The specific disputes provoking these violent conflicts arose from many issues: conversion, land rights, migrant rights, political reputation, control over schools, accusation of blasphemy, political patronage, Nigerian membership in the Organization of Islamic Conference, state subsidies for the hajj and, of course, the place of sharia in the 1987/1988 constitution. In a classic example of mirror image victimization, each side accused the other of seeking to dominate, marginalize, and convert its opponents.[49]

The archbishop of Canterbury, Dr. Rowan Williams, visited Zamfara State, now widely recognized as the spiritual headquarters of Northern Nigeria's sharia movement. During his visit, Williams expressed misgivings about harsh sharia punishments. Governor Sani defended his state policy, insisting that Zamfara's expanded sharia policy enjoyed the support of the masses of local Muslims.[50] In addition to Christian leaders, many prominent political leaders from Southern states actively opposed the Northern states' expanded sharia policies because they infringed on the constitutional rights of non-Muslim minorities in Northern states.[51] Vice President Atiku Abubakar, a Northern Muslim from Adamawa (one of the two predominantly Muslim Northern states that did not impose expanded sharia), would drop the political bomb on the sharia matter when he said that the sharia riots were the upshot of political agendas: specifically, that Northern Muslim stalwarts were determined to frustrate the presidency of Obasanjo, a Southern Christian, and cast doubt on the legitimacy of his PDP federal government.[52]

Nigerian Nobel laureate Wole Soyinka was critical of the Northern states' sharia policies and rendered scholarly views that reaffirmed the popular Christian arguments on the preeminence of national state secularity and citizenship. Soyinka told the nation that expanded sharia ipso facto nullifies Nigeria's existing Penal Code and that it effectively threatened to destroy the legal essence of the Nigerian federal republic. More pointedly, Soyinka wanted President Obasanjo to take legal action against the twelve Northern states on grounds of criminal negligence; he said the governors were neglecting their official responsibility to protect Christian minorities, "indigenes," and Southern Christian immigrants caught in a vast network of religious irrationality.[53] When the bloody Kaduna State riots erupted, state PDP leaders condemned APP politicians for instigating the sharia movement for political gains. Since sharia prohibits interest rates, the new laws were also opposed by commercial banks. When those banks threatened to pull their services from Northern states following the promulgation of expanded sharia, the Zamfara State government announced that the state was on the verge of securing external assistance from Arab states to establish Islamic banks and that Saudi Arabia and Libya were potential business partners.[54]

Some interesting subdebates did occur among Christian groups and within Muslim leaderships. A minority of Christian leaders argued that religious institutions—including sharia courts—have important roles to play in stemming Nigeria's rapidly slipping morality. For example, Olubi Docasta of Zaria's Celestial Church of Christ argued that sharia could remedy the erosion of moral values and serve as an antidote for societal decay. Likewise, Frieder Ludwig points out that some Christian leaders contend expanded sharia is principally against "social vices" such as alcohol and gambling.[55] He writes:

> Conservative Nigerian Muslims and conservative Nigerian Christians often agree in the demand to ban "social vices," and in their list of such vices both sides tend to include the consumption of alcohol, gambling, and homosexuality—all issues which are tolerated within the Western

legal systems. In addition, since Christians also witnessed the collapse of law and order in Nigeria and often have personal experiences of crime and corruption, many of them favor severe punishments for criminals and advocate the death penalty and other harsh punishments.[56]

Other Christian critics thought that pro-sharia supporters were self-righteous[57] and that enforcement of new sharia laws would put undue pressure on Nigeria's already weak criminal justice system. Surprisingly, support for moderation in the pursuit of sharia came from an unlikely source in Sokoto State: the grand qadi, who saw that sharia-derived alcohol regulations were not enforceable,[58] in part because alcohol vendors in several Northern states had devised creative ways of packaging and selling alcoholic beverages.[59] Performance evaluations of post-sharia policies showed that "social vices" targeted for elimination did not disappear automatically; expanded sharia did not seriously undermine prostitution, gambling, and alcohol distribution in Northern states, particularly in areas frequented by members of the armed forces.[60] An article in the influential Britain-based periodical *Africa Confidential* indicated that there was a rise in crime but no visible reduction in poverty.[61] Harnischfeger summed up these apparent policy shortcomings of expanded Islamic law many years after sharia's imposition:

> Divine justice has not materialized, so the masses of the faithful feel betrayed. Most of them had greeted the proclamation of Sharia with enthusiasm; today they defy many of its laws. The official gender separation is ignored in most places, alcoholic drinks are readily available, and the usual vices are back, though relegated to some hidden corners. . . . Sharia has created legal insecurity; its criminal laws, dress codes and dietary taboos cover a wide area of social activities, but they are enforced only sporadically and arbitrarily.[62]

Some critics went further, not only divorcing sharia from the prevention of crime but also linking it to endemic corruption and political vice by embedding it in the legacy of military rule.[63] Nigerian Christian church leaders condemned sharia as not only violating the religious rights of Christians, but also leaving "unpunished the failings of the powerful and wealthy."[64] Harnischfeger contends that sharia allows for systematic corruption under the guise of centralized zakat (alms) collection.[65] The Southern Nigerian commentator Tee Mac sarcastically queried:

> How is it that an unknown cattle thief loses one arm for being caught and tried under sharia, yet Mariam Abacha [former military ruler Sani

Abacha's widow] lives comfortably in her huge mansion? And everybody knows that she is one of the main actors in a multi-million dollar stealing scam or looting of our treasury. Shouldn't all those around her who helped to defraud Nigeria of billions of dollars be tried in sharia courts in their respective states?[66]

For some observers, when the Southern-dominated National Human Rights Commission gave support to expanded sharia with the provision that it would be enforced "on Muslims only," the announcement struck a dismissive tone, something like "Let them do what they want with their people."[67] This attitude of disengaging from Northern Muslims is widely held by the Southern Christian intelligentsia, which argues Northern Islamic culture is antithetical to Southern Nigeria's modernist traditions.[68]

Anti-sharia critics noted many other areas of discrimination against Christians in emirate society.[69] Ludwig cites how Christian hospitals and schools had been converted to Islamic institutions since the 1980s. He also describes a history of violence against Northern Christians and their exclusion from state office.[70] When Niger State, with its significant Christian minority population, expanded sharia, Reverend Kolo, CAN's state chair, stated that "Christians have been witnessing systematic marginalization ... from senior state appointment."[71] One prominent Christian critic catalogued Zamfara State's discriminatory measures:

> no Christian held a position of authority in [Zamfara]. Even the Religious Affairs Ministry set up to look into relevant areas of the two religions had no Christian member/representative, yet there are more than 77 qualified professionals who are indigenes and of the Christian faith.... The radio station in the State has closed its doors to Christians. Commercials and paid adverts containing Christian literature are not aired.... There is no Christian pilgrims' welfare board. Other restrictions include churches not being allowed to be built on any land sold to them, and Christians being evicted from rented apartments and in some cases not getting houses to rent.[72]

Conversely, Sani maintained that sharia would not have an adverse effect on non-Muslims because he had established a good rapport with Christians, established a Christian Complaints Commission, supported Christian pilgrims, admitted Christian students to the state's university, supported Christian education, and encouraged dialogue between Christians and Muslims.[73] At the same time, however, Zamfara State paid the salaries of imams and funded the building and maintenance of mosques, while many Christians were forced to relocate outside the state, especially those who ran nonsanctioned businesses.[74] In other Northern states, Christian critics insisted that non-Muslims were subjected to justice under sharia.[75] Moreover, the resources of Northern state governments were used to promote various Muslim activities at the expense of Christian groups. As Ludwig writes:

> Katsina CAN leaders pointed out that the admission of Christians to public secondary schools in the state is very difficult if not impossible. Thus, Christians have to send their children to other states to get post-primary education. Moreover, Christians cannot enroll in the army and head major establishments or institutions. When the time comes for them to occupy higher positions, Muslim juniors are imposed on them or they are transferred to other places to occupy subordinate positions. There is no provision for Christian programs on the state radio and television stations. The ban on public preaching seems to apply only to Christians. Most importantly, application for building plots for Churches are seldom approved and Christians are often denied burial grounds.[76]

In addition to the task of dealing with cases of discrimination, most Christians found it difficult to tolerate the moral implications of what they considered a medieval penal code that was undermining the progress of their country. While Northern Muslims asserted sharia's humanity, Christians claimed that its draconian rules, outlined in the Penal Code, proved Islamic law promoted cruel and inhumane punishment.[77] This sentiment permeated the Southern Christian print media. For example, the Lagos-based *National Concord* editorialized: "The proclamation of sharia and the series of reports about public flogging of adults, the Governor's threat to expel the local military formation in the state and the specter of beheadings, amputations, honor killings and stoning to death which form part of Islamic *Hudud* gave a picture of Iran rather than a state in the Federal Republic of Nigeria."[78] Yoruba Christian commentator Fred Agbaje, in reference to Zamfara, drew on the Western concept of natural law to condemn the reforms.[79] Elsewhere, Southern Christian commentator Festus Obin thundered: "In this twenty-first century when every country on planet earth is working hard to be technologically recognized, it would be shameful for any geographical enclave or living space to contemplate the introduction of sharia, a fourteenth century code of conduct."[80]

Built into these condemnations was a streak of paternalism, often associated with the Western-oriented Southern Christian elite, especially from public intellectuals, who predominated in Nigeria's influential Lagos-Ibadan news corridor. The most scathing condescension by Southern Christians was reserved for one of emirate society's most dominant social institutions, the *almajiri* system of Qu'ranic education. They denounced this age-old system as a reflection of the decay of emirate urban life. To these detractors, almajiri retarded the development of Northern states, especially at a time when modern education was essential for the modernization of Nigerian society.[81] However, the almajiri system has a long history in Northern Nigeria, dating back decades before the Sokoto Jihad, and is integral to the contemporary Qu'ranic educational system, in which Muslim teachers (*mallams*) retain control over their student wards.[82] Many scholars have implicated the almajiri system in the wave of religious riots in Northern states from the 1980s onward, especially the 'Yan tatsine riots of the 1980s, the ethno-religious riots in Zangon-Kataf in the early 1990s, the sporadic religious riots in the 1990s, the sharia riots of 2000–2002,[83] and Boko Haram attacks since 2008. Indeed, allegations of the almajiri harassing female students at Kaduna Polytechnic in July 2000 appeared to confirm some of these critics' contentions.[84] Thus, many Southern, Middle Belt and Northern Christians viewed Northern Muslim commoners as being in need of liberation from their scheming rulers, who imposed a backward legal system to advance narrow political agendas.[85] One anti-sharia editorial in the Lagos-based *National Concord* notes: "The almajiris, urchins, the poor and the oppressed should now be rescued before it is too late."[86] However, this condescension from Southern Christian commentators is ironic, too: they are arguing that the Northern Muslim poor must be "saved" from the system enacted by the very political leaders they elected.

Substantial opposition also was mounted against expanded sharia through established national public agencies. A notable illustration of this was carried out through the National Youth Service Corp (NYSC), the mandatory national integration and development service program established by the Gowon regime in 1973. The NYSC promoted national integration by dispatching its new recruits to communities far removed from their birthplace. However, following Zamfara's sharia declaration, some Southern government officials expressed a lack of confidence in the Northern states' ability to ensure the constitutional rights of non-Muslims and discouraged NYSC recruits from their states from taking up their postings in Northern states.[87] Since this program had become critical to the provision of essential services to most states, Sani intervened, promising Zamfara's NYSC members permanent appointment in the state civil service.[88]

Expanded Sharia: National and Global Connections

In their analyses of Nigeria's post-1999 sharia movement, Paul Lubeck, Ronnie Lipshutz, and Erik Weeks argued that economic globalization and "global Islam" are "mutually constitutive forces." As globalization disrupts the relations between state and society, they contend, nation-states with strong ethnoreligious groups and weak state system such as Nigeria, experience uncertainty that can encourage the resurgence of Islamist movements. In Northern Nigeria, this process had, in fact, started with the reformism of Izala in the 1980s, especially among younger, upwardly mobile Muslims. Consequently, Lubeck, Lipshutz, and Weeks contend that reformist Islamic movements like Izala provided the impetus for Nigeria's sharia movement in the formative years of the Fourth Republic.[89]

With these national and global connections, the sharia crisis thus complicated the old ethno-regional and ethno-religious alliances that have sustained power configurations from decolonization in the 1950s to the period of military rule in the 1990s. Indeed, during the previous military regime, fringe militant Southern political movements had gained prominence as important ethno-regional movements opposing the perceived Hausa-Fulani Muslim domination of national politics. One such group was the Yoruba militia movement, the Oodua Peoples Congress (OPC). Formed in 1993 after General Babangida annulled Abiola's election as president, OPC embarked on a militant agitation program for "Yoruba freedom" that reached its peak in the late 1990s.[90] In response to such intense identity politics, several Niger Delta militia groups, especially Ijaw, also solidified their power during military rule in the 1990s on the injustice over the exploitation of oil from the Niger Delta region.[91] Following the trend set by these groups, many Christian organizations took on more decided opposition as the sharia crisis intensified in the Northern states. With the apparent weakness of Nigerian state authorities, Southern, Middle Belt and Northern Christian organizations forged global alliances to confront the Northern states' expanded sharia policies.

However, with the exception of Pentecostal churches, Nigerian Christian denominations seemed to gain little from their global connections. Thus, the Vatican worked for peace, but had little influence on the country's diverse Christian communities. Even worse, doctrinal differences drove a wedge between Nigerian and Western Protestant clergy, leaving the latter ineffective during the sharia crisis. For example, Nigeria's chief Anglican, Archbishop Akinola, was joined by his charismatic Ugandan colleague, Bishop Orombi, to lead a global opposition of conservatives in the Anglican Communion (mostly from the Global South) against the liberal theological doctrines of Western Anglican churches.⁹² While denouncing the liberalism of Western Anglican and Episcopalian churches, the outspoken Akinola also led a strong opposition against expanded sharia in Nigeria's Northern states.⁹³ The effect of these divergent ideological perspectives had been to separate Nigerian mainline churches from their potential allies in the West, crippling the latter's ability to have an important influence on Nigeria's sharia crisis. When the archbishop of Canterbury visited Zamfara State in his capacity as titular head of the global Anglican Church in February 2001, the impact of his lobbying for Christian rights was minimal.⁹⁴

Nevertheless, Nigerian opponents of sharia drew a contrast between Islamic and international law, particularly the global treaties and human rights agreements to which Nigeria is a signatory,⁹⁵ including the African Charter on Human and Peoples' Rights, the UN Universal Declaration on Human Rights, and the Committee on the Elimination of Discrimination against Women. Agitation by activists following the first court-ordered amputation in Zamfara State led the Committee for the Defense of Human Rights to petition the state government.⁹⁶ Furthermore, detractors of sharia challenged the claims of sharia advocates that expanded sharia had been effective in other countries.⁹⁷ For example, in an editorial in the Lagos-based weekly magazine *Tempo*, an analyst argued that many countries that experienced Islamist revolutions in recent decades were now retreating from it.⁹⁸

Equally, while expanded sharia seemed to have popular appeal in Northern Muslim states, many emirate leaders were ambivalent about the new policies because of their potential to destabilize the country. Indeed, misgivings for expanded sharia sometimes came from unexpected sources. For example, Ibrahim Zakzaky, the popular reformist Muslim cleric who led a militant opposition against the emirate establishment during the Abacha regime, claimed that strong Christian resistance meant that Nigeria was not ready for this type of reform; Sanusi Lamido Sanusi, an influential emirate potentate and Muslim scholar who was installed as emir of Kano in 2014, argued that sharia must stick to its primary thrust of social justice, which the current codifications had not done.⁹⁹ These discordant voices provide a glimpse into some Northern Muslim ambivalence over expanded sharia.

Religious Reconciliation and Coexistence

Despite the clarity of the battle lines between pro-sharia and anti-sharia advocates, especially in Kaduna State, a quiet transition took place in many of the twelve Northern states between October 1999, when Governor Sani first introduced expanded sharia, and late March 2000, when many on both sides of the conflict began to moderate their strong positions. This trend toward reconciliation after the devastation in Kaduna State was apparent when several Northern Muslim states decided to moderate some of sharia's harshest provisions and some Christian leaders grudgingly accepted that Islamic law reflected aspects of Northern Muslim identity.

With the devastating consequences of the religious rift, many antagonists and protagonists in the confrontation were compelled to moderate their position on Islamic law. Many Northern Muslim leaders were more ambivalent because of the cost of expanded sharia to national unity.[100] For example, following the announcement of Sokoto State's expanded sharia policy, the state government convened a committee of Muslim clerics led by the grand qadi to investigate its implementation. This committee recommended that state authorities postpone the implementation of sharia so that the government could educate local people about the new laws.[101] Although this plea went unheeded, state authorities took on a moderate position, especially with regard to implementing the policy for Christian minorities. Also, because of the political crisis, many Southern Christian elites were willing to concede if the official interpretation of sharia was more "progressive."[102] Thus, the fallout from the sharia riots, especially in Kaduna State, forced Christian leaders to embrace the idea of a more moderate sharia policy that would respect the rights of Christian minorities in Northern states. Consequently, the backlash from the sharia conflict temporarily encouraged some Christian leaders to embrace a more centrist position as the sharia crisis intensified.[103] Progressive Northern theologian Dr. Matthew Hassan Kukah of the Catholic Secretariat seemed to have accepted the idea of a partial expansion of sharia at a Jama'atu Nasril (JNI) seminar in February 2000. Even the relatively shrill Eclectic Movement released a ten-point statement that only denounced the violence of sharia riots, while acknowledging the precedent for Islamic law in the Nigerian judicial system.[104]

With the transfer of presidential power to Obasanjo, a Yoruba Christian, Southern Christians, especially Obasanjo's Yoruba coethnics, soon felt it beneficial to tone down their strong opposition to expanded sharia. Indeed, the unique Yoruba experience with Christianity and Islam was called upon in this regard.[105] With the tragic religious riots in the Northern and Middle Belt states, the remarks of a political scientist at Sokoto's Usman dan Fodio University effectively captured this softening conciliatory trend: "For the Hausa, Islam is a total way of living. For the Yoruba, it's not a total way of living. The cultural aspects of the Yoruba are stronger than religion, whether it's Christianity or Islam."[106] A *New York Times* journalist quoting him may have exaggerated the affinity between Yoruba Christians and Muslims: "Indeed, Yoruba Christians and Muslims marry each other without a second thought. It is not unusual for Yoruba to have members of both faiths in their families; some even practice both religions. But among Northerners, being a Christian Hausa is considered a contradiction in terms."[107] This relative balance between the world of Yoruba traditions and Islam is evident in the writings of prominent Yoruba Muslim intellectuals such as Lateef Adegbite, the Yoruba secretary-general of Nigeria's leading Islamic organization, Jamat-Ul-Islamiyya; and Tajudeen Gbadamosi, a renowned scholar of Islam at the University of Lagos.[108] Finally, the biggest catalyst to general moderation was one that moved all actors alike: after more than a decade of recurring conflict, the impasse created by the sharia crisis encouraged a rapprochement among various religious and political groups.

Consequently, many national and regional organizations intervened to find solutions to the conflict. For example, a coalition of civil society organizations joined forces with traditional rulers and religious groups to press for a comprehensive peace arrangement. Five Northern states simultaneously agreed to suspend their plans to implement their sharia projects in order to mitigate additional episodes of bloody religious clashes.[109] Additionally, interfaith efforts expanded considerably. In a public show of solidarity, Muslim groups invited Christians on pilgrimages to Mecca. CAN and JNI publicized a joint peace agreement that underscored the common brotherhood between Christians and Muslims, though it also condemned the political manipulations undergirding the sharia crisis.[110] National seminars and conferences were organized by various civic and religious organizations to chart pathways to reconciliation.[111] Several Pentecostal churches urged peaceful coexistence between Christians and Muslims.[112] The federal government established the Nigerian Inter-Religious Council, and Yusuf Ameh Obaje was appointed as national coordinator.[113] Several prominent intellectuals proposed an Academy of Peace to design a moral code for religious reconciliation between Nigerian Christians and Muslims.[114] One such regional dialogue included a Catholic priest, a Pentecostal theologian, and a Muslim cleric.[115] Indeed, Christians and Muslims throughout Nigeria joined in a cross-country initiative for peace; prominent Igbo Christians such as B. O. Nwabueze embarked on personal missions to engage Muslim organizations in dialogue;[116] and among leading Yoruba Muslims, Lateef Adegbite devoted extensive time to calls for peace and reconciliation.[117]

Catholic and Protestant bishops called on church leaders to teach reconciliation and peaceful coexistence between Christians and Muslims.[118] Pastor Adeboye, the influential leader of the powerful Pentecostal church the Redeemed Christian Church of God, counseled Christians against carrying out reprisals on mosques and Muslim institutions.[119] The celebrated human rights lawyer

Gani Fawehinmi, a Yoruba Muslim, sued for peace and advised the government to investigate the religious riots.[120] In a burst of uncharacteristic self-awareness, public figures on both sides of the sharia divide said they wanted an end to media sensationalism that exacerbated religious divisions in Northern states.[121]

One of the most dramatic consequences of the sharia imposition was the flight of local capital from Northern states. Zamfara State saw a massive exodus of Igbo traders. As a result also, local banks saw savings evaporate, numerous businesses vanish, and markets shrink.[122] Moreover, when sharia came into force, financial services were no longer able to charge or bear interest, which further displaced banks and other financial institutions from Northern states and brought to a halt businesses that depended on credit and loans. Additionally, everyday economic transactions were seriously impeded by sharia's strict requirement to separate local communities on the bases of gender; women of all faiths attempting to take *okada* (the motorcycle public transportation) were harassed by vigilante sharia enforcers, effectively barring half of the population from the only affordable means of transportation in Northern communities.[123] In Kaduna State, as a result of the riots, over forty thousand Southerners fled, including numerous students, leaving the state's universities empty, and skyrocketing gas prices prompted bus drivers to charge exorbitant prices for transit, adding to the general economic chaos.[124] State government losses were compounded when churches affected by the violence sued for damages, after state authorities promised to reimburse 20 percent of the reconstruction costs of destroyed places of worship.[125]

Nigeria's international image was of course compromised by the recurrent violence. Conscious of the harm to foreign investment, the federal government hired international public relations firms to reassure Western partners that Nigeria was still safe for business. Professor Tam David-West, a former petroleum minister from the Niger Delta region, captured the sentiments of most observers on the economic implications of the sharia crisis:

> The collective madness and sadism displayed on the screens of global television cannot be inviting signals for foreign investments in our limping economy. Only a compound fool or a mad entrepreneur will invest in a country with doubtful sociopolitical stability; a country so primitive in the manifestation of its hate. And no amount of foreign globetrotting or sweet sermons and beautiful assurances for investment in our economy can impress any serious prospective businessman. It's as simple as that. Is this the Nigeria that anyone should be proud of? Is this the Nigeria whose "positive" image (laundered, obviously) we want to sell to

the outside world, inviting them with open arms, to bask in the sunshine of a said fledgling democracy? We should all hide our heads in shame.[126]

Much of the debate that ensued following the imposition of sharia in the Northern states effectively tilted national attention toward the parlous state of political instability and massive economic disruption in pro-sharia states. Many analysts also said that sharia was a grossly misplaced priority given the severe underdevelopment of Northern states. In responding to criticisms,[127] Zamfara Governor Sani unveiled an ambitious state development policy. Many of the sharia states followed the Zamfara example, publicizing various social welfare programs. In fact, the Bauchi government suspended the implementation of its sharia policy because it diverted resources away from essential social services.[128] These policy pronouncements may have been motivated by political expediency rather than a genuine commitment to development, but at least the sharia conflict provoked a new discourse on governance in some Northern states.[129]

CHAPTER NINE

SHARIA POLITICS, OBASANJO'S
PDP FEDERAL GOVERNMENT,
AND THE 1999 CONSTITUTION

Following many years of repressive military rule, the euphoria that welcomed the arrival of Olusegun Obasanjo's PDP federal government turned into despair when the sharia crisis became a platform for prolonged religious violence in Northern states. With the federal government unable to provide security for Christian minorities in Northern states, Southern activists together with irate Christian leaders in Northern and Middle Belt states were dismayed that Obasanjo's federal government had no effective response to the crisis.[1] Rt. Rev. Peter Jatau, Anglican bishop of Kaduna, chastised Obasanjo's government for remaining silent while the state was consumed by religious violence. He blamed Obasanjo for inaction: "This ambivalence will not do. The President must tell the sharia people whether what they are doing is permitted in the Constitution. He must make a declaration now before it is too late."[2] Catholic archbishop Okogie advised Christian groups to shame the government into positive action.[3] Rev. Isaac Orihaki, general superintendent of the Gospel Light Redemption Church, a popular evangelical church, supported public reaction against Obasanjo's administration, but also argued that the federal legislature had been negligent in tackling the crisis.[4] Anger at the Obasanjo federal government reached a boiling point as sharia violence escalated in February and March 2000: Obumna Abiakam, a well-known attorney, sued President Obasanjo in court for negligence, arguing that the president had a duty to demonstrate that the Northern states' expanded sharia policies were unconstitutional.[5] Ben Nwakanma, a prominent Owerri lawyer (in the southeast Igbo region), also sued the government and asked for the resignation of the federal attorney general.[6] The Catholic archbishop of Owerri, the Rev. Dr. Anthony Obinna, expressed his disappointment in the federal government's failure to protect Igbo (Christian) settlers in Northern Muslim states.[7] Bishop Abraham Oyeniran, a prominent Pentecostal leader, also sued the government, saying that President Obasanjo's delay in dealing with the crisis had compromised public safety.[8] Equally revealing of public frustration about perceived federal government ineptitude, Nobel laureate Wole Soyinka blamed Obasanjo for allowing a legal dilemma to become an intractable political crisis.[9]

In hindsight, Obasanjo's tardiness in responding to the crisis might have been the product of a complex political calculus. Two factors, not mutually exclusive, seemed to have shaped Obasanjo's response as the crisis intensified in 2000 and 2001. The first can be observed in the contingent nature of party political alignment after the transition from military rule to democratic government at the turn of the century. Although the president is a Yoruba Christian, Yoruba political networks had long been suspicious of him; his election had largely been engineered without their support; instead, Obasanjo depended on political support from Northern Muslim power brokers as well as the political class of the Igbo, Niger Delta, Cross River, and Middle Belt regions. Obasanjo was hesitant to engage the fight on sharia, perhaps because of the fear that such a move would alienate his most coveted constituency in the core Northern states. Second, Obasanjo was reluctant to hand the sharia matter to the Supreme Court for a constitutional solution because it was assumed that a legal quashing of Northern Muslim aspirations would intensify the conflict, particularly along ethno-religious lines, if the Hausa-Fulani political class interpreted a decision as a product of Southern Christian political assertiveness.[10] According to Murray Last, such a move would cause "populist pandemonium" in the core Northern Muslim states.[11] Or, in Johannes Harnischfeger's formulation: "If a Christian [Southern Yoruba] president had attempted to outlaw sharia, this would have stirred up millions of [Northern] Muslims against the central government."[12] Besides, many Hausa-Fulani Muslims already viewed the Constitution itself as illegitimate, therefore a legal decision derived from that document probably would have had little moral authority and could have even backfired by deepening the divisions. Even worse, were Obasanjo to challenge sharia in the Supreme Court and lose, the result would have been disastrous.[13] He opted, instead, for a political solution, which he said would "end up without any victor or vanquished," co-opting the hugely successful reconciliation slogan that was adopted by Gowon's military regime after the civil war.[14] With so much at stake for their long-term interest, Obasanjo felt that Nigeria regional power brokers would ultimately embark on a political compromise to resolve the sharia crisis.

Sharia and the 1999 Nigerian Constitution: Contending Issues

Mohammed Bello, a former Nigerian chief justice and the most prominent Northern jurist, had once argued that while major provisions in the Nigerian Constitution limited the scope of sharia, many legal principles in the same document also empowered it.[15] Many Nigerian lawmakers at the national assembly agreed with Bello and cited his views in the debates that unfolded in the federal legislature.[16] Principally, the debates on sharia were not always defined along strict ideological, partisan, or ethno-religious lines; for example, while President Obasanjo, the Christian Yoruba PDP leader, felt that expanded sharia was largely unconstitutional, Balarabe Musa, the noted radical socialist governor of Kaduna State during the Second Republic, saw sharia as superior to the Constitution. These two renowned national figures held views on sharia that reflect the complexities of defining the sharia crisis along conventional ideological, religious, or regional lines. The fierce conflict hinged on whether the Constitution ultimately had authority over sharia or whether sharia retained an infallible legal authority over Nigeria's Muslim citizens. Former federal minister of justice Olu Onagoruwa, a Yoruba Christian, contended that as the Constitution was Nigeria's ultimate legal document, all other legal systems must defer to it. For Onagoruwa, therefore, by expanding sharia the twelve Northern state governments had subverted the Constitution, leaving the federal government no other choice but to challenge the constitutionality of sharia through appropriate legal channels. Similarly, interpreting Islamic jurisprudence, analyst Jemila Nasir noted that sharia (as "God's law") places sovereignty in Allah, violating the basic tenet that the Constitution is sovereign over the Nigerian state.[17] Conversely, Islamic legal scholar Abdulmumini Adebayo Oba writes: "Islamic law, having accepted the sovereignty of Allah and His Laws, cannot accept the 'supremacy' of the Constitution and the sovereignty of the people."[18] Furthermore, Governor Sani, the lightning rod for all those who opposed expanded sharia, underscored the supremacy of sharia over the legal affairs of

Nigerian Muslims. Affirming Sani's position, the emir of Ilorin, Alhaji Ibrahim Sulu Gambari, drew extensively from the Qur'an and hadith to challenge the secular state argument, contending that in Nigeria's religiously plural society, the Constitution gives Muslims the right to be governed by expanded sharia.[19] Indeed, Northern Muslim opposition to the secularity argument had consistently featured in these debates even before the sharia crisis of 1999. For instance, in a debate in the 1980s, Northern analyst Ibrahim Suleiman described the secularity of the Nigerian state in rather colorful language. Nigerian secularity, he proposed, is "a child, albeit a bastard, of Christianity ... [that] has become a sinister but convenient mechanism to blackmail Muslims and impede the progress of Islam."[20] Others simply traced the roots of common law to Christian traditions.[21]

Despite the strong Northern Muslim opposition to the idea of Nigerian state secularity, influential Southern Christian legal analysts continue to exercise considerable influence in the debate on the role of sharia. For example, legal scholar Vincent Nmehielle looks at section IV of the 1999 Constitution and proceeds to present two primary questions at the core of the debates on the sharia conflict.[22] He argues that the imposition of a comprehensive sharia policy in the Northern states undermines the role of the Constitution to mediate the jurisdiction between federal and state authorities. Nmehielle further contends that expanded sharia "encroaches on fundamental human rights guaranteed in the Nigerian Constitution and in various international treaties and conventions that Nigeria is party to."[23] He also observes: "Freedom of religion is not an absolute freedom, but one that is limited by another individual's freedom in that one person's freedom to practice his or her own religion cannot legally impede another's freedom."[24] Nmehielle concludes:

> The zeal and determination of the twelve northern governors to provide leadership to Nigerian Moslems through the implementation of the Sharia are insensitive to the balance required.... The political zeal of a particular leader on an issue that has overwhelming sectarian support must be expressed within the confines of the Constitution no matter how strong that zeal may be. It does not justify taking "unconstitutional measures" for the sake of providing sectarian leadership.[25]

Given the serious contradiction between the expanded sharia policies of the twelve Northern states and the 1999 Nigerian Constitution, the analyses that follow will explore major national challenges posed by expanded sharia to the Nigerian state and society in the Fourth Republic.

Sharia and Women's Rights in Historical Perspective

Nigeria's anti-sharia and human rights advocates have long been concerned that expanded sharia poses severe threats to the constitutional rights of women and girls, particularly since unrestricted Islamic law excludes women from public office, positions of authority, and personal interactions with men not their relatives. On this, expanded sharia contravenes the constitutional guarantee of equal rights to all Nigerian citizens.[26] One critical editorial in a Lagos-based newspaper, the *National Concord,* amplified this constitutional anomaly: "In our encounter with the Governor [of Zamfara], we were surprised when he said two women were equivalent to one man especially in serving as witnesses in a sharia court."[27] Even the most casual observer of Nigerian society would be aware that expanded Islamic law is not particularly attentive to women's rights in Northern communities and that the application of expanded sharia to the everyday lives of women is problematic in the context of a modernizing society. This systemic marginalization of women through expanded sharia has a long history in emirate Northern Nigeria, going back to the Sokoto Jihad in the early nineteenth century.

Historians of Northern Nigeria generally agree that local mythology recognized women's participation in the royal courts of many Hausa city-states; for example, Hausa oral traditions show that in a few notable cases, such as the warrior Queen Amina of Zaria, a few women retained considerable power in Hausa city-states.[28] Women's power, however, steadily eroded in public affairs with the growth of Islam from the sixteenth century, and was severely curtailed after the Sokoto Jihad in the nineteenth century.[29] However, it is noteworthy that there is some scattered information about the role of women in public affairs, despite the restrictions imposed by the reform of the jihadists in the early years of the Sokoto Caliphate. A perusal of the works of the founders of the new Islamic confederacy—notably Usman dan Fodio; his brother, Abdulahi; his son, Mohammed Bello; and his daughter, Nana Asma'u—confirm that some women performed important roles in the new emirate communities during the jihad and immediately after the establishment of the caliphate.[30] Kathleen McGarvey says that while women supported the military efforts of the jihadists through important domestic activities, such as nursing the wounded and feeding the fighting men in Usman dan Fodio's jihad, leading reformists also highlighted the need to incorporate women into the new emirate society.[31]

Nevertheless, Barbara Callaway argues that the institutionalization of sharia after the Sokoto Jihad significantly curtailed the rights of women in critical family matters such as marriage, divorce, inheritance, and custody of children.

As emirs and members of their courts dominated public institutions, Hausa women, as mothers and wives, were effectively relegated to the household, further marginalizing them. This process was particularly apparent in Hausa marriage practices that continued after the Sokoto Jihad. In many local communities, marriages are arranged, usually with a bride price. Although divorce was easy to obtain and carried little stigma, it generally favored husbands.[32]

Within the colonial system of indirect rule and the colonial cash-crop economy, women's autonomy in the public sphere was further curtailed. For example, the practice of wife seclusion seems to have grown in response to the new colonial economic system, in which rigid gender roles became an essential part of a cotton- and groundnut-export-oriented economy. In addition, as emirate society embraced greater religiosity in resistance to colonial rule, women's role outside of male-headed households was severely curtailed in local communities, and their voices were marginalized in the leadership of the two dominant Sufi orders in the region—the qadiriyya and the tijaniyya.[33]

This entrenched gendered structure continued in the relationship between men and women of all social classes since the period of decolonization in the 1950s. In postcolonial emirate communities, elite women, for example, who because of minor government reforms embrace careers in the modern professions, are sometimes alienated in a deeply patriarchal emirate society. In short, over the centuries, ideology, religion, marriage, law, and culture have systematically circumscribed women and girls' lives, effectively subordinating them to men and boys in Northern Nigerian Muslim society.[34]

Despite the entrenched patriarchal practices of emirate society, an increasing number of women and some male allies have consistently resisted male domination, especially since the late colonial period. During decolonization, resistance to the domination of the patriarchal masu sarauta was carried out by their rival, the Northern Elements Progressive Union (NEPU), especially in Isa Wali's commentaries in *Gaskiya*, the popular Hausa newspaper in the 1950s and 1960s. Wali insisted that in Islam, women and men have equal rights and the marginalization of emirate women had more to do with local cultural practices. While this position achieved limited success in the struggle against the dominant emirate political party, the Northern Peoples Congress (NPC), progressive political activists have drawn from this enduring tradition to shape contemporary social realities since the attainment of independence in 1960. For instance, NEPU's ideological successor during Nigeria's failed Second Republic (1979–1983), the Peoples Redemption Party (PRP), though dominated by a male leadership, embraced this perspective in its support for comprehensive education for both boys and girls in emirate society. In one form or the other,

Hausa-Fulani women's organizations have drawn from these narratives at the intersecting histories of marginalization and resistance, especially since the decolonization process.

Women made some important inroads into the public sphere of Northern Muslim society after the introduction of the Federal Military Government's Universal Primary Education (UPE) scheme and the 1979 constitutional reforms that gave Northern Nigerian women the right to vote.[35] After Nigeria signed the treaty of the Committee on the Elimination of Discrimination against Women (CEDAW) in 1984 (ratified in 1985), the Federation of Muslim Women's Association of Nigeria (FOMWAN) was established, and many Muslim women's groups emerged to articulate the concerns of Nigerian Muslim women.[36] However, in contemporary emirate society, Islam continues to impact social relations in divergent ways, and women consistently have developed creative strategies to counteract patriarchal traditions that are embedded in religious structures.[37] Thus, a key aspect of the discussion on expanded sharia is how to engage the rights of women, both within Islamic jurisprudence and the wider rights of citizenship guaranteed by the Constitution. Callaway argues that many Northern Nigerian women feel that progressive change is most expedient if they avoid Western feminist discourse and strategically articulate their resistance politics within the framework of Islamic law and practice.[38] This is the perspective taken by a group of Northern Muslim women who challenged the patriarchal voice that dominated the implementation of expanded sharia in the twelve Northern states, especially in two landmark zina cases where two talakawa women, Safiya Hussaini (October 2001) and Amina Lawal (March 2002), were charged with adultery as the sharia crisis raged on in Northern states.

Thus, the impact of expanded sharia on women's rights exploded onto the national and international scene following the sentence of death by stoning of these two women for the crime of zina (adultery, fornication) when they became pregnant outside of marriage in 2001 and 2002 respectively. The details surrounding these cases are complicated, but here it suffices to explain that both women were divorcées, and the men alleged to have fathered their unborn children denied paternity under oath and were acquitted because of lack of evidence to prosecute them in accordance with sharia. As the controversy engulfed the country, anti-sharia advocates, reinforced by the fierce opposition of Nigerian and international women's and human rights groups, argued that the death sentence underscored the main objections to expanded sharia: that is, the strict application of sharia to criminal law is incompatible with modern ideas of human and civil rights that have evolved in Nigerian jurisprudence since the colonial period. Nevertheless, these cases set the stage for "a vitriolic confrontation between international human rights and women's group and sharia advocates."[39]

Following many tense months, the two women were eventually acquitted on appeal through the hard work of a group of Nigerian women lawyers, some of them trained in both Islamic and common law. They engaged Islamic law to challenge the women's convictions. Indeed, so important were these cases that President Obasanjo, who until then had kept a low profile on the sharia crisis, lent support to the defense of the two women's constitutional rights.[40] Nevertheless, "a problematic area in the application of sharia lies in the control of the public behavior of girls and women. The sharia movement's organizational apparatus is partly based on the hisba [volunteer community police on public morality]." Controlled by "overzealous, conservative and narrowly trained ulama," the hisba has consistently regulated "the behavior of women, especially those who are poor, uneducated, and powerless."[41]

Debates on the rights of women under expanded Islamic law by Northern Muslim organizations is consistently advanced by groups such as FOMWAN and BAOBAB for Women's Human Rights. During many seminars and workshops to explore strategies to protect women's rights, members of these Northern Muslim organizations focused on Women's Human Rights against the backdrop of theological interpretations, especially in the context of the Qur'an and the hadith. They distanced their discourses from Western feminist thought and from the perceived liberal values of Southern Nigerian Christians. These Northern Muslim women's groups focused on exploring new analytical horizons in Muslim scriptural interpretation of the rights of women to life, equality, freedom of thought, and economic advancement.[42] Drawing on the concept of Islamic feminism, Margot Badran contends that rather than confront Islamic traditions, with its populism in Muslim society, Muslim women activists have challenged the conservatism of Muslim clerics by insisting on the rights of women (and girls) through more progressive interpretations of religious texts.[43] Consequently, Nigerian advocates for Muslim women's rights argue that the promotion of women's rights in Northern Nigeria will not be realized from international conventions' pronouncements such as CEDAW, which calls for the removal of legal discrimination against women from the perspective of Western-oriented international legal conventions. Strategic campaigns for women's rights must also take into account a dynamic process of local religious and social conditions that advance freedom and social justice for talakawa women.[44]

Sharia, Christianity, and the Discourse on National Disintegration

As the sharia crisis intensified from 2000 and 2002, Obasanjo's federal government cultivated leaders of thought across the country, especially former government leaders, emirs, ulamas, and Christian leaders, for religious reconciliation and national integration. Obasanjo convened the National Council of State (NCS), the advisory board composed of current and former heads of the federal government's three branches, to define a clear pathway for a resolution to the sharia crisis. As an initial response to the crisis, the federal government, evoking the support of the NCS, called on the pro-sharia Northern states to suspend the implementation of their sharia policies.

Former presidents Shehu Shagari and Muhammadu Buhari, both Hausa-Fulani Muslims, despite frustrations with the religious riots in Northern states,[45] denounced the federal government's interference in the affairs of the twelve Northern states. A much more confident Obasanjo would take things in stride; in a national broadcast after Shagari and Buhari's announcement, he reassured the nation: "I must not end this brief address without assuring all our fellow citizens of the firm determination of our Government to resist any attempt from any quarters to pursue a line that can lead to the disintegration of this country. Those who break our laws will be punished to the full extent of the law. There will be no sacred cows. And those that extend the hand of fellowship to their fellow citizens will find understanding and friendship."[46]

Nevertheless, the Zamfara State government questioned the legitimacy of the federal government to interfere in its affairs; this was followed by the Kano State governor's insistence that the federal government had no constitutional authority to interfere in his state's sharia policy.[47] However, the federal order was respected in Bornu, Jigawa, and Niger States, whose governors temporarily suspended their sharia policies, pending further dialogue with the federal government to find a lasting resolution to the crisis.[48] And with the resolve of Zamfara to implement sharia by carrying out actual amputations, federal Minister of Justice Kanu Godwin Agabi cautioned Governor Sani: "Life is sacred and should be treated sacredly."[49]

National support for the federal government began to build because Obasanjo now seemed determined to encourage national mobilization against sharia advocates in the twelve Northern states. As reflected in the theology of prominent Pentecostal leader, Pastor Kehinde Osinowo, many Christian leaders, following the arrival of the Fourth Republic, increasingly connected their theological disposition to Nigerian nationalism, linking Obasanjo's national political project with God's divine plan for Nigeria's progress. They contend that Obasanjo had first risen to power in the 1970s after Hausa Muslim military leader Mohammed's assassination, and successfully handed power to Shehu Shagari (a Hausa-Fulani Muslim) through a transition program to civil-democratic government after sixteen years of military rule. Imprisoned by General Abacha (a Hausa-speaking Muslim), Obasanjo reemerged as a democratically elected head of state with strong Northern Muslim support. Calling on Nigerian Christians to pray for the president, Osinowo claimed that the sharia crisis was "engineered" by Nigeria's spiritual enemies, who were determined to destabilize the country's nascent democracy.[50] Ebenezer Obadare captures this sentiment:

> To many Christians, Obasanjo's "second coming" was a spiritual metaphor, one that went beyond the ordinary fact of his fortuitous emergence as a beneficiary of a political compromise between the country's geo-political power blocs.... For Christians, it was a fulfillment of God's promise to liberate his children (southern Christians) from the yoke of northern (Muslim) leadership.... Obasanjo's messianic status had been enhanced by his personal circumstances before his election as president. Jailed by Abacha on charges of plotting to overthrow the government, Obasanjo languished in various jails in the country until his eventual release by General Abubakar following Abacha's death. Following his release, Obasanjo went public with the fact of his "spiritual rebirth" in prison.[51]

Nevertheless, Pastor Osinowo, like many other Pentecostal leaders, had by now situated Obasanjo as a leader of destiny at the center of Nigeria's political narrative, positioning the president in major historical landmarks such as the Civil War, successful service as military head of state, escape from General Abacha's clutches, and emergence as elected civilian president in 1999. Osinowo and other Pentecostal leaders called on Christians everywhere to focus their prayer on the spiritual warfare that confronted Obasanjo and the Nigerian state. Prophet Samuel Kayode Abiara, leader of the Christ Apostolic Church, Igbala-Itura, declared the sharia crisis a plot from Satan, while Bishop Margaret Odeleke of the same church called on devoted Christians to "chase the sharia demon out of Nigeria."[52] For Southern, Middle Belt, and Northern-minority Christians, Buhari and Shagari's public opposition of Obasanjo's moderate position was packaged into a populist Christian script. Christian critics contend that the Hausa-Fulani Muslim leaders' opposition to the administration's policy was a desperate attempt by the Northern Muslim oligarchy to dominate state affairs.

By April 2000, much of Obasanjo's Christian (especially Yoruba) support had arrived, and condemnation of his initial hesitance on the sharia crisis was effectively turned to praise for a leader they said was measured and far-sighted. Influential Pentecostal Yoruba minister Felix Oke argued that Obasanjo's caution was wise, praising him for exercising restraint given Nigeria's contentious ethno-religious politics.[53] In the midst of the sharia conflict, the powerful Pentecostal leader of the RCCG (the Redeemed Christian Church of God), Pastor Adeboye, predicted Obasanjo's triumph, while another prominent Pentecostal leader, Pastor Tunde Bakare, preferred Christian vigilance through prayer to challenge sharia. Indeed, several Pentecostal leaders called for prayers to prevent religious wars that could lead to the disintegration of Nigeria. Obasanjo's cautious response to the sharia crisis was intertwined with "God's master plan to take Nigeria to its prophetic destiny where justice, peace, love, unity, progress, power and prosperity would be induced by holiness reigning supreme."[54] In support of Obasanjo's rule, a prominent Pentecostal leader named Pastor Fidelis Omoni sent a scripted message to Governor Sani of Zamfara in the biblical tradition of Jeremiah's prophecy: "Your days as Governor are numbered." He called on Sani to repent of his sins.[55] The Nigerian Baptist Convention's fiftieth anniversary meeting was similarly highlighted with exhortations of support for Obasanjo.[56]

This resurgence of Christian support for the president coincided with a sustained public discussion of the political machinations behind the sharia movement. Southern Christian suspicion of Northern Muslims was translated into the straightforward conclusion that the sharia crisis was precipitated by the Hausa-Fulani Muslim elite's master plan to contain Southern ascendancy, embodied in Obasanjo's presidency.[57] The Yoruba International Network, a diaspora organization with branches in New York and Washington, DC, argued that a corrupt Hausa-Fulani Muslim aristocracy, seeing its power erode, responded by imposing expanded sharia to strategically mobilize Northern Muslims against Southern Christians.[58] The governor of Ogun State in the Yoruba Southwest, Olusegun Osoba, argued that the conspiracy aimed not just to undermine Obasanjo, but to derail Nigeria's progress.[59] Many other prominent Yoruba politicians agreed.[60] This had been the official position of the president's party: at a leadership meeting to assess the cause of the Kaduna riots, PDP leaders concluded that some Northern power brokers masterminded the violent attacks to undermine Obasanjo, a Southern Christian president.[61] The plethora of anti-sharia analysts from the Southern and Middle Belt states, as well as Northern-minority Christians, chimed in to register their condemnation of the Northern Muslim political class. In Debki's account, insistence on expanded Islamic law is a reflection of the eroding power of oppressive Hausa-Fulani Muslim rulers.[62] Nwobi contended that the violent rage of sharia activists against vulnerable Christian minorities in Northern states reflected the desperation of a fading Northern Muslim hegemony;[63] Shehu, another anti-sharia activist, noted that the frenzied call for expanded sharia is not an expression of religious piety, but a strategic political maneuver;[64] and Emekwue, an analyst from the Igbo southeastern region, disparaged the agenda of sharia advocates as a push-back on the slipping emirate control over their local masses.[65]

Furthermore, many prominent national personalities were genuinely concerned about the prospects of national disintegration. Olu Falae (a Yoruba Christian), the national AD/APP leader who had won the Yoruba vote against Obasanjo in the 1999 presidential election, argued that the application of sharia to criminal law amounted to Northern secession from the federal republic.[66] Following the killing of Igbo Christians in Kaduna's sectarian crisis, Governor Orji Uzor Kalu "warned that his government could no longer guarantee the safety of any Northerner living in his state if the killings of Easterners [Igbo Christians] living in the North continued."[67] Adetunji Adeleke, former governor of Osun State in the Yoruba region, lamented that "some ex-leaders were using their enormous wealth to cause confusion and disaffection."[68]

The sharia crisis also complicated religious and ethnic relations among Middle Belt Christians and Muslims.[69] Despite the intensification of the unifying force of Christianity in reaction to the encroaching influence of Hausa-Fulani Muslim power in the region,[70] Middle Belt local communities have continued to experience recurring ethnic factionalism under growing political, demographic, and economic stress, especially since the neoliberal reforms of the 1990s. Harnischfeger notes:

> In order to withstand the superior strength of the Hausa and Fulani, who number about 40 million people in Nigeria, leaders of the Middle Belt Forum have called upon their people to develop a distinct Middle Belt identity. During clashes between Christians and Muslims, some solidarity appeared as members of different minorities fought shoulder to shoulder. But apart from such short-term alliances, neighboring villages or ethnic groups are caught in escalating conflicts over land resources. The so-called "ethnic nationalities" are so fragmented internally, that they are not able to act as political units in defence of a common "national" interest. Moreover, the Tangale, Dadiya, Tiv or Jukun have found no means of settling boundary disputes among themselves. So their demand to handle land affairs autonomously has little chance of realization.[71]

The push for Middle Belt Christian unity during the sharia crisis, however, carried more than symbolic weight. Emirate attempts to assert a unified Northern Muslim agenda pushed against the aspirations of a unifying Christian identity. Obasanjo's political fortunes significantly improved thanks to the unified support of Southern and Christian electorates. Conversely, Northern Muslims leaders were beginning to feel the political pressure that persistent religious riots were inflicting on Northern communities. Overall, however, as Obasanjo's Christian supporters grew throughout the country, his core Northern Muslim support eroded during the sharia crisis.[72]

Expanded Sharia, Communalism, and the Resurgence of Ethno-religious Violence

Citizenship is not portable in Nigeria—and this runs against the letter and spirit of the Nigerian Constitution. Under the British colonial indirect rule system, people without deep roots in the "traditional" structure of ancestral hometowns and city-states were commonly considered "native settlers" with less access to land-rights claims and public offices. In Northern and Middle Belt states, indirect rule hardened these claims by formally establishing non-Hausa quarters in *sabon garuruwa* (singular: *sabon gari*), or "new towns," for Southern Christians who had migrated to the region as traders, artisans, and lower-level civil servants. Consequently, most Northern Nigerian communities—and other regions in the country—ignore the full rights of residency for all citizens enshrined in the Nigerian Constitution. Instead, it is one's lineage, substantiated by ascribed claims to ancestors, that serves to establish full rights of residency. Such distinctions form a strong, if complex, primary identity, with ethnicity, class, and local origin intersecting to divide communities into "indigenes" and "nonindigenes." Indeed, the growing migration of Southern Christians to Northern and Middle Belt communities in the postcolonial era continues to complicate this process; and demographic transformations between Northern Muslim states and predominantly Christian Middle Belt states in recent decades intensified tensions between native "indigenes" and settler "nonindigenes" across urban areas in these states.[73]

However, as previously discussed, the most visible nonindigenes were usually economic migrants, often Igbo Christian traders from the Southeast, who were resented for their more prosperous economic conditions. This reference by Abubakar Gumi in his autobiography captures the feeling of resentment by Hausa-Fulani Muslim "indigenes" against Igbo Christian "settlers" or "nonindigenes": "One could hardly buy a sack of corn in the market except from an Igbo man, nor could one take one's bicycle to be mended other than to an Igbo mechanic.... The Northerner [Hausa-Fulani Muslim] was always something less than a citizen in his own country."[74] In Kano, such characterization of Igbo "nonindigenes" or "settlers" as objectified migrants was further complicated by the city's population explosion. Kano's population grew from 250,000 people in 1961 to 2.8 million inhabitants in 2006, and 95 percent of this population is Hausa-Fulani Muslims.[75] Against this backdrop, and in addition to sharia-induced violence, tensions would erupt between "indigenes" and "nonindigenes" over access to scarce resources in Northern and Middle Belt states.

Recurring religious violence in Bauchi State in 2001 seems to have been aggravated by the September 11, 2001, terrorist attacks in the United States. On September 12, 2001, internecine strife exploded in several communities in the state, reportedly leading to the killing of more than three thousand people.[76] Reflecting on the origins of the killing, one observer wrote: "Districts in which the Christians have driven out the Muslim inhabitants have been given new names such as Jesus Zone, New Jerusalem or Promised Land. Similarly, the Muslims have renamed their quarters, indicating to whom they belong: Jihad Zone, Saudi Arabia or Seat of [Osama bin] Laden."[77] In October 2001, about five hundred people were killed in Zaki-Biam in Benue State in retaliation for the murder of nineteen soldiers by Tiv militiamen who had apparently been mistaken for their Jukun rivals from Taraba State, with whom they had been fighting over access to farmland.[78] This crisis, in addition to its ethnic overtones, occurred against the backdrop of strained military-civilian relations in various troubled spots in the country, especially the Niger Delta region. As the sharia crisis ravaged the Northern and Middle Belt states, Nigeria's news media were fed with a continuous narrative of sectarian violence.

Tensions again erupted in 2002 when Nigerian federal forces began to crack down on sharia-related disturbances. Political violence again occurred in the Middle Belt cities of Jos and Yelwa in May, and religious conflict exploded in Jigawa State, where Muslim youths destroyed many churches.[79] This wave of riots was sparked by an article written in a Lagos-based national magazine, *ThisDay*, about the Miss World pageant that was scheduled to be held in Abuja, Nigeria's federal capital. Isiome Daniel, a Southern Christian, had reportedly blasphemed against the Prophet Muhammad in the newspaper article.[80] As riots raged in several Northern cities, Muslim youths attacked churches, killing more than two hundred people, displacing thousands, and destroying property worth millions of dollars.[81] As Human Rights Watch later reported,

Many people believed that if the Miss World contest had never been planned to take place in Nigeria, and even if the article in *ThisDay* had not been written or published, some other incident would have been seized upon instead, and sooner or later, violence would have erupted due to the same caustic mix of Northern power politics, hometown loyalties, economic slowdown, and ethnic differences.[82]

A BBC journalist noted the economic implications of Nigeria's sectarian violence: "[Many young men have] no jobs and no education, and frustrations over economic hardship leave them prey to political opportunists who want to foment violence."[83]

In the midst of so much violence, efforts toward peace were ongoing in 2002 and 2003, especially in Kaduna, home to some of the worst violence in the country. These efforts were led by the Reverend James Wuye and Imam Muhammad Ashafa, who had brokered the peace from the Miss World fiasco. Together they founded interfaith organizations, held workshops, and wrote pamphlets to encourage reconciliation between Christians and Muslims. Though both had been "radicals," they had become leaders of a burgeoning peace movement as early as 1992, after the Zango Kataf riots. Referring to the communal violence as politically motivated, they pushed for reconciliation among the warring parties.[84] Despite such efforts, in February 2004, communal violence again erupted in Shendam, Yelwa Local Government area, in Plateau State, with 78 Christians killed and several churches destroyed. On May 2, Christians retaliated and roughly 660 Muslims were killed, and 60,000 people displaced.

The National Assembly passed emergency power regulations in June 1, 2004, giving an interim military governor of Plateau State, Major General Mohammed Chris Alli, sweeping powers to deal with emergency situations in Plateau State. After establishing security, he set up special courts for all violence that had been committed since 2001 in Plateau State, and 1,284 suspects eventually were prosecuted.[85] Alli also developed the Plateau Peace Program, encouraging dialogue between leaders of religious and ethnic groups, as well as a statewide peace conference. Alli encouraged warring militants to surrender their weapons by granting amnesty to those who did so. In 2005, state and federal authorities uncovered similar dynamics of political violence in Kebbi State, along with a high prevalence of sexual assault.[86] However, while religious violence continued, a Human Rights Watch study found that the initial enthusiasm for sharia had eroded: "Many Muslims who had initially supported sharia have become disillusioned with the manner in which it has been implemented. They told

Human Rights Watch that this was not 'real sharia' but 'political sharia,' but [were] fearful of being labeled 'anti-Islamic' if they said so publicly."[87]

Though the sharia crisis had largely subsided, unfortunate national and global events triggered a rash of religious explosions in the last years of the Obasanjo administration, revealing enduring tensions between Christians and Muslims in Northern and Middle Belt states. In February 2006, for example, riots broke out in Northern cities after the publication of a Danish cartoon mocking the Prophet Muhammad. In Maiduguri, the Bornu State capital, riots by irate Muslim youths led to the deaths of more than five hundred people. Then, in June of the same year, another polarizing incident occurred when a Christian woman in Niger State reportedly preached to Muslim youths. When Muslim clerics expressed strong objection, a mob of Muslim youth clubbed her to death while she was in police protection.[88]

Elsewhere, in Ilorin, the southernmost post of the Sokoto Caliphate in the predominantly Northern Yoruba region, the sharia crisis opened up old claims between Hausa-Fulani Muslim rulers and descendants of the former Yoruba ruling lineages of the precaliphate era over the traditional "ownership" of the city.[89] This conflict over the legitimacy of "traditional" structures and symbols of local power are embedded in the distributive resources of the state. In a specific Northern context, Harnischfeger outlines the process of these fierce contestations for power as expressed through the prism of the ethno-religious identities of "indigenes" and "nonindigenes":

> When land disputes are brought to court, the ethnic and religious preferences of the judge are often decisive, and in cases of armed conflict, when police or army units intervene, it may be even more crucial to have one's own people among the decision-makers. Consequently, the migrants have a vital interest in wresting positions of authority.... As soon as the migrants constitute a critical mass within the population, they direct their efforts to occupying key positions in the district administration. In this way they, or their leaders, gain access to the state revenues that flow from the capital into the coffers of the local government councils.[90]

Furthermore, focusing on the Middle Belt region, Harnischfeger offers an insightful perspective on how shifting demographic conditions intensified these ethno-religious tensions during the sharia crisis. Largely dominated by the diverse ethnic groups in the region, such as Berom, Dadiya, Tangale, Tarok, Tiv, Tula, and Waja, most of whom had been converted to Christianity by the 1950s, religious and ethnic conflict complicated the sharia crisis in the region. Concomitantly, as Hausa-Fulani Muslims had migrated southward to the Middle Belt region since the late colonial period, the demographic balance in the region had steadily tilted in their direction. These new settlers contested property rights with the "indigenous"—non-Hausa-Fulani communities. As Hausa-Fulani Muslim migrants and their descendants transformed the region's demography, Muslims as "non-indigenes," by their sheer numbers are well positioned to dominate some Middle Belt local authorities. This situation was further exacerbated by communal conflicts among the non-Muslim "indigene" communities over the distribution of state resources, especially over land claims and control of local government agencies. Consequently, Harnischfeger argues: "[Hausa-Fulani Muslims] can send for relatives from their homelands, enlarge their enclaves, and claim further stretches of land. In many places this has brought them right up to the fields tilled by the local population, leading to disputes over boundaries. Out of all the groups of settlers [one observer notes] it is the Muslims [Hausa-Fulani] that want to claim the ownership of Jos.... The Igbo and Yoruba have never claim[ed] Jos nor care[d] to take over political power."[91]

As is apparent from the foregoing discussion, ethnicity, long associated with religious labels, was tied into these overlapping political and economic interests of communal groups as the sharia crisis intensified.[92] Thus, enduring religious conflicts further polarized Christians and Muslims in Middle Belt states, hardening religious and ethnic identities across the region. Thus, many "indigenes" of the Middle Belt's major city, Jos, maintained their independence from perceived Muslim hegemony by asserting their Christian identity. This trend is not new. As Last writes, as far back as the formal unification of the Northern and Southern Protectorates of Nigeria in the early colonial period, the "implicit boundary...between dar al-Islam and dar al-harb, remained; certainly the antagonism between the two worlds persists even to this day, some would say in a new, fiercer form than before as the creation of well-financed local governments has sharply raised the value of being 'indigenous,' as against the old value associated with 'becoming Hausa.'"[93]

Consequently, as discussed in the cases above, ethnicity was subsumed under religious identity to rationalize collective political action as the sharia crisis exposed communal fault lines and fissures. While Hausa-Fulani Muslims called for expanded sharia, indigenous ethnic groups—most of them Christians—mounted fierce opposition against an institution they considered anathema to the traditions of their local communities. This underlying sense of insecurity encouraged recurring violence as the fallout of the sharia crisis continued.[94]

For example, when communal riots broke out in Jos in 2000, killing 165 and wounding 928, it was sparked by the appointment of a Hausa-Fulani Muslim to head a federal agency in a predominantly Christian area.[95]

While ethnic nationalism served as a centrifugal force in Southern states, it is religion that has filled this role in Northern states, complicated by ethnic identity in the Middle Belt region. Since decolonization, Islam has provided a structural framework on which intra- and intercommunal conflict is contested and mediated. Sufi orders are strong social identities, and elite groups draw strongly on Islamic practices to sustain their political legitimacy in various communities.[96] Indeed, shifting demographic conditions have further driven "a wedge between the younger generation and the old guard of former rulers and emirate leaders, who refused to hand over northern power. Their frustration eroded the political and cultural legitimacy of emirate society from the bottom up."[97]

Despite deep communal divisions along religious and ethnic lines, some leaders, because of the delicate position they occupy in society, had to walk a tight line during this period of persistent crisis. For example, the police commissioner in Zamfara State, Ahmed Abdulkadir, a Muslim and Alhaji, refused to use the Nigerian police force to enforce the new sharia law in the state. He declared: "We will not enforce any law that goes contrary to and is in conflict with Nigerian law because we have sworn to defend the country and the citizens as a whole," referring to the institutional mandate of the Nigerian Police Force as a federal agency.[98] Similarly, in Kaduna, Deputy Speaker of the House of Assembly Gideon Gwani, a Kataf Christian, had to walk a tightrope, demanding Christians' inclusion on the state's sharia exploratory committee while agreeing with expanded Islamic law for Muslims: with a relatively large Christian population, particularly in the south of Kaduna, Gwani was forced to make overtures to both sides.[99] This occurred despite persistent animosity between Hausa-Fulani Muslims and the largely Christianized Kajes and Katafs, who had been subordinated to the Hausa-Fulani emirate structure through the indirect rule system.

This is, of course, not to argue that ethnicity was not an important factor in the sharia conflict. Clearly, ethnic divisions mattered in varying degrees to social and political actors. Yet even if ethnic identities motivated violence, this certainly did not amount to the all-consuming importance accorded it by some commentators.[100] With these enduring structures of society, the imposition of expanded sharia and the attendant struggle over its constitutionality were rooted in ideas of the past that continue to influence power relations through time and space.

Policing Sharia in Northern States

Despite the enthusiasm for expanded sharia, the complexities of Nigerian society curtailed the impact of the Northern states' sharia policies on emirate communities during the Obasanjo administration.[101] Significantly, this limitation in the implementation of the new sharia policies was vividly expressed in the activities of the hisba, the local Muslim militia established to enforce the new sharia laws in the twelve Northern states.[102] Ludwig notes that hisba law enforcement groups had been in existence in some Northern states before 1999; however, they were elevated in emirate society only after the spread of expanded sharia in 2000.[103] Under the caliphate, hisba was used to keep the peace in many emirate communities and uphold "proper" Muslim practices and moral standards stipulated by Islamic law.[104] With the introduction of expanded sharia, hisba, following in the tradition of state-sponsored "civic groups" in Northern Nigeria, was expanded to defend sharia policies.[105] Last suggests that hisba resulted from "widespread unease" among Muslims, brought on by a feeling of vulnerability to attack from "outsiders." Consequently, because it was recognized as the only viable legal instrument for the enforcement of sharia, hisba had the primary responsibility to secure *dar al-Islam* within the Nigerian state and society.[106]

Kano State developed its hisba program most extensively among the twelve Northern states. From 2000 to 2002, hisba flourished in Kano as an unofficial militia force under Governor Rabiu Musa Kwankwaso before being institutionalized at the state, senatorial, district, and village levels in 2003. At the village level, there were three divisions: advisory, management, and hisba corps. Within smaller communities, operations were further divided based on the *zauren sulhu* unit, "such as streets/areas, markets, schools, and transport stations." To show the importance of women's issues in the new laws, state authorities stipulated that the women's division of this militia force should be at least 10 percent of the overall hisba force. The main duties for the nine thousand Kano State hisba corps members included ensuring sharia compliance in commerce, defending sharia court decisions, reporting on interference with Islamic justice, keeping records of prison inmates with pending criminal cases, preventing social vice, enforcing modesty standards, and educating the public about the new sharia policy. These extensive statutory duties clearly indicate the significance of the hisba force in Kano State's new sharia policy. To achieve these extensive legal responsibilities, the state government established a radio station, Muryar Hisba (The Voice of Hisba), to disseminate information to the public.[107]

While Kano State's hisba was by far the most elaborate, it was not the only one at work in the Northern states. During the ethno-religious crisis in Jos, Nigeria's principal Middle Belt city (where sharia had not been enacted), hisba corps operating in the city distributed relief materials to victims of communal riots. Kaduna and Katsina States also established hisba boards to supervise the activities of a myriad of religious and social groups, and Zamfara State passed laws in 2003 that created official organizations, including hisba, to educate the public about the state's sharia policy. Across Northern states, members of hisba boards and commissions were drawn from government ministries, emirs' courts, and local Muslim clerics. These newly appointed state officials drew salaries and benefits as civil servants. In short, their official duties included encouraging "proper" Islamic behavior, discouraging corruption, mediating civil disputes, and assisting with traffic control and emergency relief, as well as coordinating their activities with the federal police forces and other state security agencies.[108]

However, as the hisba forces took on more law-enforcement responsibilities, it became apparent that they generally lacked the professional expertise to discharge their duties.[109] This was complicated by growing tensions between hisba officers and the Nigerian federal police force, the main source of law enforcement in the country. With respect to this tension between the state government–sanctioned hisba and the federal police force, Last observes: "Given that the legality of the sharia *vis-a-vis* the Federal Constitution is itself a contested issue, the police are reluctant to get involved in any action the hisba may get up to. Similarly, prisons and [teaching] hospitals are federal institutions; prisons therefore are unwilling to house prisoners found guilty of crimes under sharia, just as doctors are unwilling to amputate limbs as the sharia requires."[110]

Despite such distinctions, hisba soon became the central component of many Northern governments' extraconstitutional police power.[111] Indeed, Kano State sought funds from abroad to support its hisba institutions, in breach of the Constitution.[112] After several years of disagreement, in 2006, the inspector general of the Nigerian Police Force accused the Kano State government of developing an illegal state police force. Federal authorities subsequently banned the Kano State hisba and other sharia-enforcement agencies and arrested some of their leaders,[113] a move that the state governor deemed unconstitutional. More importantly, conflicts between hisba and federal law enforcement authorities only reinforced entrenched ethno-religious identities, solidifying divisions between Christians and Muslims in Northern and Middle Belt states. As power over security came under the control of federal authorities in later years, the federal police assumed greater regulatory control over sharia in Northern states.[114] Indeed, by the end of Obasanjo's second term in office in 2008, federal policing had been re-established in Kano State, not simply as a reassertion of federal power but, rather, as a practical response to pressing challenges of security in local communities.[115]

With growing frustration in the implementation of expanded sharia, a new militant Muslim reformist group, Boko Haram (which means "Western civilization forbidden"), emerged to insist on the establishment of an Islamic state in Nigeria by the end of Obasanjo's presidency. Like Mohammed Marwa, the charismatic leader of Maitatsine (see chapter 5), Boko Haram's founder, Mohammed Yusuf, preached a messianic neo-Salafi revivalism that denounced Hausa-Fulani Muslim rulers as an essential component of Nigeria's decadent political class.[116] Accompanied by lethal violence unprecedented in Nigerian history, the militancy of Boko Haram in the years following the Obasanjo administration reflects the deepening crisis of the Nigerian nation-state, revealing unbridled political corruption by the holders of state power, flagrant abuse of power by the country's security system, massive erosion of essential social services, recurring religious violence in the Northern and Middle Belt states, and the abjection of talakawa commoners.[117] Additionally, the threat of Boko Haram, like that of previous fringe militant Islamic movements in Northern Nigeria, is intimately connected to prevailing religious, social, political, and economic conditions in the region.[118] In this context, Boko Haram's militancy did not cause Nigeria's political crisis in the years after Obasanjo's presidency; rather, it reflects the endemic crisis of governance, especially in Northern states. Indeed, this crisis was further aggravated by ineffectual federal and state governments' security policies in Boko Haram's strongholds in the northeastern states of Bornu, Yobe, and Adamawa. While it is inconceivable that the entrenched political structure that fuels Boko Haram's militancy can be overturned in the short term, well-focused social and security policies orientation by the federal authorities—in collaboration with Northern state governments—can erode the extensive social space captured by Boko Haram in northeastern Nigeria. All told, Boko Haram emerged out of the failure of the restorative vision of Islamic reformism promised by expanded sharia in the early years of the Fourth Republic.

The Limits of Sharia: An Overview

It was in this context of political strains that Nigeria began its first-ever transition from one democratically elected administration to another in 2007. During this period of transition, two important developments were particularly notable:

first, with limited constitutional intervention from the federal government, the impact of expanded sharia in Northern Muslim communities waned considerably, and second, sharia's application varied significantly throughout the twelve Northern states. To bring this long and tragic episode of Nigeria's sharia saga to an end, I briefly review some notable outcomes of the Northern states' sharia programs when Obasanjo completed the second term of his presidency in 2007.

By the end of Obasanjo's presidency, Zamfara continued to provide the vision for all those committed to implementing expanded sharia. Governor Sani was reelected in 2003, and his former deputy, Mahmud Shinkafi, succeeded him in 2007. With a tiny Christian minority, a major problem that confronted the state's sharia agenda was the restriction placed on women that kept them from taking okada—the motorcycle taxis that are relied on for their ubiquity, speed, and low cost and are thus the state's major means of public transportation. CAN worked with the state government to devise a system to circumvent the restriction: Zamfara state authorities issued Okada taxi drivers "Association of Christian Motorcycle Operators" cards that helped taxi operators drive non-Muslim women without harassment from hisba officers and other state authorities.[119] Overall, despite its strict sharia laws, Zamfara State's reforms were the most politically effective and bureaucratically successful.[120]

In Kano State, Governor Kwankwaso, a moderate, implemented sharia gradually because of Kano city's massive size and cosmopolitan character. However, the governor underestimated the forces behind sharia: as discussed above, Islamic clerics there established a robust hisba. In 2003 Kwankwaso had lost reelection to conservative Ibrahim Shekarau of the All Nigeria Peoples Party (ANPP), who won reelection in 2007. As of 2008, the governor and Abubakar Rabo Abdulkarim, head of the state hisba board, attempted to extend sharia's jurisdiction to *sabon garuruwa* and compelled all students in the state—including those in Christian schools—to comply with the Muslim dress code.[121]

In Katsina State, Umaru Musa Yar'Adua served two terms as governor before being elected president in 2007 (he died three years into his term). Another PDP stalwart, Ibrahim Shema, replaced him. Sharia implementation here did not rival that in Zamfara or Kano, but was nevertheless a major reform. Despite the limitations of Katsina's sharia policy, Christian opposition was poorly organized and splintered. Additionally, the governor was a member of Obasanjo's party, and voting for him kept a hardliner ANPP candidate—who would have pushed implementation further—out of office.

Compromise between a Muslim majority and Christian minority generally prevailed in Bauchi State. Governor Ahmadu Adamu Mu'azu was slow in implementing sharia and took care to balance it with pro-Christian policies. He appointed Christians to senior positions in the Ministry of Justice and high courts, refused to expand sharia to Tafawa Balewa and Bogoro (Christian areas), and made it possible for residents in the state to access the courts of their choice. He also urged Islamic judges to be cautious on adultery cases, and expressed disapproval on punishments that violate contemporary norms of human rights. The reason for these countervailing measures lies in the strong opposition of Bauchi's substantial Christian minority to expanded sharia. Despite Governor Mu'azu's best efforts, Christian minorities consistently contested the state government's sharia policy. In one notable case in 2002, twenty-one Christian nurses were fired from their positions at the Federal Medical Center in Azare for refusing to comply with Muslim dress code; they won their positions back in a legal battle that lasted two years. Although Mu'azu won reelection in 2003, sharia remained a polarizing issue, and in 2007, the majority-Muslim state elected a conservative, Isa Yuguda, of the pro-sharia ANPP. After this election, Yuguda, the Sharia Commission, and other Islamic groups pressed for more comprehensive sharia.[122]

The policy of moving toward sharia with safeguards for non-Muslims worked best in Kaduna State. Following the wave of ethno-religious violence, Governor Ahmed Mohammed Makarfi of the PDP won reelection in 2003 and was elected a senator in 2007. His successor, Namadi Sambo, also a Muslim PDP, was elevated to the vice presidency of the federation when Goodluck Jonathan, a Christian from the Niger Delta, became president following Yar'Adua's death. Patrick Ibrahim Yakowa, Sambo's deputy governor, was subsequently elevated to the office of governor, to which he was elected; he was the first Christian from Southern Kaduna State to hold the office. Unlike Zamfara State, where sharia was the new baseline and common law only reigned in military and police barracks, Kaduna State limited Islamic law to predominantly Muslim areas, with common law the baseline everywhere else.[123] Kaduna sharia court judges were screened more carefully than their common-law counterparts, and separate bureaus for Christian and Islamic matters were established. Each had a permanent secretary, and the two frequently met to discuss state policies. In Kaduna State, then, because of its evenly divided Christian and Muslim population and the religious violence that immediately followed the announcement of expanded sharia, the state government adopted a moderate sharia policy.

Among the twelve Northern states, Gombe State exemplifies the limitations of sharia during the Obasanjo years. ANPP governor Abubakar Habu Hashidu followed fellow Muslim governors in other Northern states by establishing a tripartite legal system organized around magistrate, customary, and sharia courts from September 2000 and May 2001. The last to implement sharia, he tried to balance religious representation by creating a Sharia Committee and installing an Anglican bishop on the Customary Courts Committee. However, he lost reelection to PDP candidate Mohammed Danjuma Goje in 2003, who dropped sharia entirely and went on to win reelection in 2007. Among the Northern states to enact expanded sharia, Gombe has one of the largest Christian populations. It is no surprise that Gombe was one of the states where the implementation of sharia was least successful.[124]

CONCLUSION

In April 2014, Boko Haram became a global household name following the militant Islamist group's abduction of 276 schoolgirls from a secondary school in Chibok, a remote town in Nigeria's northeastern state of Bornu. Although Boko Haram had been unleashing terror on Nigerian civilians and state officials since 2008, this tragic event called world attention to the intense danger of Islamic extremism in Nigerian society. While it is true that this radical group's brutal activities do not represent the myriad role of Muslim groups in Nigerian society, it would be shortsighted to dismiss Boko Haram as an aberration in Muslim Northern Nigeria. Despite the unique context in which it exploded on the Nigerian public scene, Boko Haram is another example of militant Northern Muslim movements insisting on the radical transformation of the state in Northern Nigeria, going back several centuries. In the context of contemporary Nigerian politics, Boko Haram's horrific attacks have put a global spotlight on the deepening crisis of the nation-state, revealing the damaging consequences of the sharia crisis, neopatrimonialism, and neoliberalism in the context of the post-9/11 "global war on terror." Interestingly, Boko Haram's founder, Mohammed Yusuf—who was murdered in 2009 by Nigerian security forces—had criticized the custodians of state power in a way that curiously resembled critiques by previous militant Islamist groups analyzed in detail in this book, notably neo-Mahdi in the early colonial period and 'Yan tatsina under military rule in the 1980s. These groups had fought Nigerian colonial and postcolonial regimes, denouncing them as illegitimate and corrupt. However, at the other end of the spectrum of the world religions—either challenging or affirming the legitimacy of the holders of state power—is the myriad of mainstream Muslim and Christian movements that have sought to transform Nigerian society through peaceful means since the imposition of colonial rule at the turn of the twentieth century. For over two centuries, this broad range of political and social activities by Muslim and Christian structures has consistently reflected the complicated role of these world religious movements in the making of modern Nigeria.

Focusing on the social, political, and economic transformation of the diverse people of Nigeria since the turbulent nineteenth century, in this book I have analyzed how the entangled histories of Islam and Christianity are embedded in structures of society and how these religious forces profoundly shaped the colonial and postcolonial Nigerian state and society. Muslim and Christian movements not only have been dynamic in shaping the contours of the nation-state but also have been foundational in the making of modern Nigerian society. Specifically, Islamic reformist and evangelical Christian movements were integral to the social structure and ideological framework on which the modern Nigerian state and society were grafted after the imposition of colonial rule at the turn of the twentieth century. The intersections of contending regional and global religious movements were decisive in transforming Nigeria into a modern state and society—and these religious structures themselves were transformed by the enduring social, political, and economic imperatives of Nigeria's diverse communities.

Although the imbrications of these religious forces had an enduring impact on the structures of Nigerian society, their intersecting currents also greatly influenced a complicated political process, shaping power configurations in the modern Nigerian state. With fierce power struggles in a fragile nation-state,[1] the interactions between Christian and Muslim movements have consistently transformed Nigerian social relations since the imposition of colonial rule at the turn of the twentieth century. In the Hausa-Fulani Muslim North, Islamic structures anchored on the Sokoto Caliphate sustained the transformation of emirate society. In the Middle Belt and Yoruba Southwest, however, it was Christianity that provided a crucial framework for articulating a pathway to modernity within a structurally imbalanced Nigerian state and society.

Rather than seeing Islam and Christianity as anachronistic and atavistic, in my estimation, Nigeria's varied communities' encounters with these world religious movements have been pivotal to creating tapestries that reflect dialectical tensions between tradition and modernity, local and global, national and transnational, since the turbulent nineteenth century. At various stages of Nigeria's political history, these complicated religious forces have evolved in multilayered local, national, and transnational contexts. Their dynamic manifestations have influenced power configurations in a colonial context, shaped power relations during decolonization, helped mold Nigeria's problematic postcolonial nation-state, and responded to the forces of globalism at the turn of the twenty-first century. Overall, in postcolonial Nigeria, Muslim and Christian movements, along with their various segmented identities—Sufi, neo-Salafi, Protestant, Catholic, Pentecostal, and African-initiated church movements—are integrated into the fabric of Nigerian society, exposing the fault lines of the country's entrenched ethno-regional, ethno-religious, and neopatrimonial nation-state.

It would be presumptuous to suggest that the extensive Muslim and Christian currents that transformed Nigeria's diverse communities could fully be analyzed in a single book. Nevertheless, I have sought to offer a detailed analysis of major Muslim and Christian movements that are integral to the processes of social change in three critical regions where they have repeatedly intersected over the past two centuries. Although the nineteenth-century Sokoto Jihad in the Hausa-Fulani region of Northern Nigeria and the Christian missionary movement in Southern Nigeria were independent religious currents, their convergence at the turn of the twentieth century, propelled by British imperial objectives, provided dynamic structures, ideologies, and doctrines that profoundly transformed Nigeria. The Sokoto Jihad provided a structural framework and legitimating ideology for Hausa-Fulani Muslim rulers to articulate the hierarchies of power[2] in Northern and central Nigeria's diverse communities, while, starting in the mid-1800s with the arrival of Christian missions and propelled by favorable regional conditions, Christian evangelization rapidly transformed social relations in many Southern Nigerian communities.

Following the conquest of the Sokoto Caliphate and the Kanem-Bornu Empire, British administrators co-opted the caliphate's politico-religious structure as the fulcrum of the colonial administrative system of indirect rule in the Northern Nigerian Protectorate. By embracing Hausa-Fulani Muslim rulers, British administrators strengthened the authority of the potentates of the Sokoto Caliphate while simultaneously marginalizing other centers of Muslim authority in Northern Nigeria. More importantly, British rule entrenched the hegemony of Hausa-Fulani Muslim rulers over non-Muslim communities in the protectorate. This expedient system intensified contestations of power, prompting Middle Belt Christian-educated elites to resist Hausa-Fulani Muslim domination.

Given the significance of mission Christianity in Britain's Southern Nigerian Provinces—and Northern Nigeria's Middle Belt communities—the trajectory of social transformation was vastly different in these regions under British colonial rule. Starting with Atlantic Yoruba communities, and fueled by British imperial objectives, Christian missions embarked on the transformation of Southern and Middle Belt communities by the end of the nineteenth century. Indeed, by the early decades of colonial rule, mission Christianity had established a framework for rapid social change in key Southern Nigerian communities. In Yoruba coastal communities, doctrines of modern advancement and progress shaped profoundly by Yoruba Christian returnees from Sierra

Leone—and to a lesser extent Afro-Brazilian and Afro-Cuban repatriates—and embedded in Yoruba traditions of industry were adapted to the rapidly changing social conditions of the turn of the twentieth century. Indeed, the monumental transformation of Yoruba communities during this period was propelled by the desire of Yoruba missionaries and Christian converts to re-imagine a new world following several decades of turbulence in much of the nineteenth century. Consequently, the devastations of the nineteenth-century Yoruba wars gave way to the development imperatives of a Yoruba Western-educated Christian elite within only a few decades of colonial rule in Yoruba communities.[3] In this context, the impact of mission Christianity in local communities was far-reaching, though Yoruba cosmology did not wither away.[4] As mission Christianity further expanded under colonial rule, new charismatic Christian movements emerged to enrich religious life in Yoruba communities. In turn, this process accelerated the pace of Yoruba ethno-national consciousness under British colonial rule. This process would sustain a formidable Yoruba ethno-national identity in the context of the formation of the Nigerian postcolonial state.

The enduring structures, practices, ideologies, and legacies of the Sokoto Caliphate in emirate society and mission Christianity in Southern and Middle Belt communities were essential factors in Nigeria's decolonization process from 1946 to 1960, when the country gained independence from Britain. As Nigeria embarked on constitutional reforms, the contentious relations between Southern nationalists and Northern Muslim rulers revealed major fault lines between the Northern and Southern Provinces, now reconstituted in three newly established regional governments—the Northern Region (the old Northern Provinces), and Eastern Region and Western Region (the old Southern Provinces). While predominantly Christian Southern nationalists insisted on acceleration to independence, Northern Muslim rulers were inclined to slow down the pace of political change because of their vulnerability to the modern development that Christian missions had encouraged in Southern Nigeria. Consequently, while Southern nationalists called for a strong central government to encourage the integration of Northern Muslim society into the rest of the country, Hausa-Fulani rulers insisted on strong regional government structures to protect the Muslim North from the onslaught of Southern Christian elite. In the end, assuaging the fears of Hausa-Fulani Muslim rulers, British authorities opted for a federal system that strengthened the regional governments at the expense of the central government. This regionalization of state power had broad implications for the role of religion in Northern Nigeria's diverse communities, especially in the immediate years after the attainment of independence.

In addition to the structural and constitutional divide between the Northern and Southern Provinces, the decolonization process also intensified enduring political contradictions between Hausa-Fulani Muslim rulers and Christian minorities of the Northern Provinces. Indeed, the volatile mix of religious and ethnic identities, along with changing demographic conditions in the region, were essential elements in the struggle for state power and control over the distributive resources of the state during decolonization.[5] As decolonization intensified, Christian missionary influence provided essential ideological and structural frameworks for the disparate non-Muslim ethnic minority groups in central and northeastern Nigeria to resist Hausa-Fulani Muslim domination. Unlike the multitude of "tribal," "pagan" religions of the Northern Nigerian Protectorate in the early years of colonial rule, Christian missionary impact provided an effective universal institutional node of resistance to unite diverse ethnic groups against the real and imagined threat of Hausa-Fulani Muslim domination that had been consolidated under the colonial system of indirect rule. These developments shaped so profoundly by Muslim and Christian identities not only were essential to the articulation of ethno-religious alliances during decolonization, but also provided a framework for Middle Belt and Northern Christian minority resistance to the Hausa-Fulani Muslim political class after Nigeria's independence. Consequently, the enduring structures of the Sokoto Caliphate, the indirect rule system, and the Christian missionary impact all combined to shape competing political interest among various communal groups after decolonization. The structures and ideological orientations of these political alliances continue to have serious implications for governance and development in postcolonial Nigerian politics.[6]

In this fragile postcolonial nation-state system, contending and competing religious movements have consistently promoted divergent ideologies and doctrines that fuel recurring religious violence in Nigeria's Northern and Middle Belt states. Complicated by the insistence of a Southern Christian intelligentsia for the secularization of the Nigerian state, religious-based conflicts—such as the controversy over Nigeria's membership in the Organization of Islamic Conference and the 'Yan tatsine crisis in the 1980s—have intersected with ethnic identities to fuel ethno-religious violence in Northern and Middle Belt states. These enduring religious conflicts were further ignited by the politics of sharia during Nigeria's Fourth Republic—after military despotism in the late 1990s.

With the growing neopatrimonialism of the holders of state power and the devastation of neoliberalism in the 1980s and 1990s, the insistence on expanded sharia by a new generation of Hausa-Fulani political elite provided an alternative vision for the governance of emirate society. The popularity of expanded sharia in the twelve Northern states earlier in the Fourth Republic reflects the extent of the alienation of Hausa-Fulani Muslims from the rest of the country and reveals the depth of the crisis of the Nigerian nation-state. Hausa-Fulani advocates of sharia contend that pious Muslim traditions, embodied in expanded sharia, were continually assaulted by Nigeria's Western-oriented state in several ways. First, under colonial rule, sharia was subordinated to English common law by British authorities. Second, sharia's influence suffered because of the modernizing effects of Christian missions in non-Muslim sections of Northern and Middle Belt regions; and, finally, sharia was assailed by the secularist agenda of various Nigerian postcolonial civilian and military governments. Overall, the sharia crisis served as a structural platform for the expression of ethno-religious and ethno-regional struggles between Muslims and Christians in Northern and Middle Belt states and between the dominant political classes in Northern and Southern states. These recurring political alliances and conflicts illuminate numerous struggles for state power among major ethno-regional political classes in the country. Thus, during the early years of the Fourth Republic, the Hausa-Fulani Muslim elite insisted that expanded sharia reflect Northern Muslim traditions and stem eroding moral values. In turn, the political elite within Southern, Middle Belt, and Northern Christian minorities contended that expanded sharia was irreconcilable with Nigeria's constitutional integrity not only because it promotes Northern Muslim sectarianism but also, more importantly, because it violates the liberal traditions enshrined in the Nigerian Constitution. The crisis of sharia during the Fourth Republic certainly reveals the depth of the structural imbalance in Nigerian state and society and highlights the massive gulf between Northern Muslims states, on the one hand, and Southern and Middle Belt states, on the other. With serious implications for the safety of Christian minorities in Northern states, along with growing ethno-religious confrontations in Middle Belt states—where rapidly changing demographic conditions have transformed communal relations since the late colonial period—recurring ethno-religious violence has emerged as an essential element of power politics in Northern and Middle Belt states. The structures, ideologies, and doctrines in this dynamic process have become an essential component of postcolonial Nigerian politics.

At its most extreme level, Muslim militancy has encouraged political violence in Northern communities, especially since the 1980s. Islamic radicalism has a long history in the Northern Nigerian region, going back to the resistance of fringe Muslim movements to British rule, notably neo-Mahdist groups, at the turn of the twentieth century. Concomitantly, militant Islam has had many violent manifestations in postcolonial Northern Nigeria, notably 'Yan tatsine militant opposition to Nigerian state authorities in the 1980s and Boko Haram's bloody attacks on churches, state agencies, emirate rulers, and civilians (mostly Northern Christian minorities) since the collapse of expanded sharia in 2007. To be sure, the recurrence of these radical Muslim movements indicates a profound crisis of the postcolonial Nigerian nation-state: in the specific case of Boko Haram, its militancy does not simply reveal the extent of the crisis of national governance; it shows the eroding legitimacy of traditional Muslim rulers in Northern communities because of their essential role as a critical component of Nigeria's neopatrimonial state system.[7] Furthermore, since militant Islamist groups such as Boko Haram have consistently exploited the pressure for sharia to stake their claims in Northern Muslim communities, the custodians of the Nigerian state have had to confront a major constitutional dilemma between Nigerian state secularism and a clamor for an Islamic theocracy in postcolonial Northern Nigeria. Additionally, given the marginalization of Northern Muslim youths, especially with the social consequences of neoliberalism since the 1980s, militant Islamic groups, increasingly embracing radical neo-Salafi doctrines, insist on a Muslim state that would be governed by expanded sharia, as the alternative to Nigeria's problematic Western-oriented secular political system.[8] At the same time, since the militant Islamic group Boko Haram has flourished in the context of deepening state crisis and the "global war on terror," Nigerian state authorities have demonstrated limited capacity to control vast territories in Muslim Northern Nigeria, especially in the northeastern states of Bornu, Yobe, and Adamawa.

Focusing on a concerted response to the serious threat of Boko Haram to the Nigerian state following several years of government ineptitude, the *New York Times* op-ed piece of Nigeria's president-elect, Muhammadu Buhari, in April 2015 to commemorate the one-year anniversary of Boko Haram's abduction of the Chibok schoolgirls captures the extent of the crisis posed by the radical Islamic group to the Nigerian state. Buhari's op-ed is worth quoting at length:

> My administration would welcome the resumption of a military training agreement with the United States, which was halted during the previous administration. We must, of course, have better coordination with the military campaigns of our African allies, like Chad and Niger. But, in the end, the answer to this threat must come from within Nigeria. We must start by deploying more troops to the front and away from civilian areas in central and southern Nigeria where for too long they have been used by successive governments to quell dissent.... There are many reasons why vulnerable young people join militant groups, but among them are

poverty and ignorance. Indeed Boko Haram—which translates in English, roughly, as "Western Education Is Sinful"—preys on the perverted belief that the opportunities that education brings are sinful. If you are starving and young, and in search of answers as to why your life is so difficult, fundamentalism can be alluring.... So we must be ready to offer the parts of our country affected by this group an alternative. Boosting education will be a direct counterbalance to Boko Haram's appeal. In particular we must educate more young girls, ensuring they will grow up to be empowered through learning to play their part as citizens of Nigeria and pull themselves up and out of poverty.[9]

Finally, in the predominantly Christian Southern and Middle Belt states, this crisis of the nation-state also has encouraged the explosion of Pentecostal—and other charismatic—Christian movements. Similar to the resurgence of Islamic reformism in Northern states, the exponential rise of Pentecostal movements in Southern, Middle Belt, and Northern minority communities reflects disruptions of the postcolonial era, expressed profoundly through the Nigerian Civil War, statism, and neoliberalism. In an environment of unbridled political corruption, enduring uncertainty, and prolonged economic insecurity, Pentecostalism has emerged as a heuristic movement that mediates tensions between the temporal and the transcendent. This remarkable movement has empowered its adherents, nurturing a vision that anticipates the future in the context of globalization and transnationalism. Like the Islamic reformism that propelled expanded sharia in Northern Muslim states, the explosion of Pentecostalism was religion's response to the crisis of the nation-state in Southern, Middle Belt, and Christian minority communities in Northern states. While Pentecostalism generally operates outside the purview of formal state agencies, its remarkable capacity to bridge the religious and secular, tradition and modernity, and national and global speaks not only to its resourcefulness but also to its deep engagement with the dialectical tensions between state and society. What is significant about the "reformism" of Nigeria's Pentecostal movement is how it differs from the reformism of Northern Nigeria's neo-Salafi movement. The reformism of Nigeria's neo-Salafi movement drew its legitimacy from scriptural texts that insist on imposing a righteous Muslim theocracy that would transform the inner core of the Nigerian state, while the "reformism" of Pentecostal churches evokes the gift of the Holy Spirit that proclaims a new Christian moral order for its adherents.

The dynamism of Nigeria's Muslim and Christian movements refutes predictable ideas that religious structures inherently are retarding forces against modern transformation. The Nigerian experience reveals that these religious movements have been integral to the processes of state-society formation since the turbulent nineteenth century. Thus, it stands to reason that the doctrines of these religious forces are intricately connected to and deeply embedded in the structures of the Nigerian state and society. For more than two centuries, Islam and Christianity—in what we may refer to as mirror-image dialectical tensions—consistently have confronted, strategically contested, occasionally accommodated, and referentially shadowed each other as they have transformed Nigeria's social and political landscape.

The process of colonial rule in Nigeria, exemplified by the Lugardian system of indirect rule and the amalgamation of the Northern and Southern Provinces in the early twentieth century, provided the basis for the articulation of Muslim and Christian movements in the drive for state power. On one side of the mirror, Islam provides the structural framework for consolidating Northern Hausa-Fulani Muslim identity in modern Nigerian politics and society. As this hegemony crystalizes, Christianity—on the other side of the mirror—provides a strong framework to articulate an ethno-religious resistance ideology in the political theaters of Nigeria's Northern and Middle Belt regions.

Rather than focus on a theoretical perspective that suggests a Western constitutional solution to Nigeria's multifaceted crises, I have delved into the deep structural and historical roots of Islam and Christianity in the Nigerian political process since the transformative nineteenth century. Since Christianity and Islam are structural elements of Nigerian society, I contend that their prominence in the public sphere is a response to the deepening crisis of the nation-state. Until the custodians of the Nigerian state sustain a durable constitutional and political framework to effectively respond to the country's entrenched ethno-religious and ethno-regional fault lines,[10] the endemic religious crisis in Nigeria's Northern and Middle Belt states will continue to tragically undermine the viability of Africa's most populous and complicated nation-state.

NOTES

INTRODUCTION

1. Kukah, *Religion, Politics, and Power in Northern Nigeria*; Falola, *Violence in Nigeria*.
2. Braudel, "Histoires et sciences sociales."
3. Davidson, *The African Genius*.
4. For landmark anthropological and sociological studies that provided critical theoretical foundation for the study of religion in African societies immediately after independence in the 1960s, see Horton, "African Conversion"; Horton, "On the Rationality of Conversion: Part One." Horton, "On the Rationality of Conversion: Part Two"; see also Peel, "Religious Change in Yorubaland"; Peel, "Conversion and Tradition in Two African Societies." For further anthropological analysis in historical contexts, especially in a southern African experience, see Jean Comaroff and John Comaroff, *Of Revelation and Revolution*. I would like to thank Deji Ogunnike for sharing his superb knowledge on conversion from indigenous African religions to world religions with me. My brief reference to the extensive scholarly discussions on this subject by leading Africanists has more to do with the limited relevance of this subject to my own interest at the intersection of religion and state making, and does not do justice to Ogunnike's critical insight on these important works.
5. It is instructive to note that Robin Horton and John Peel were teaching as young scholars at the University of Ife (now Obafemi Awolowo University), Nigeria, when they made their theoretical breakthroughs in the 1970s. Their theoretical works were informed by a careful critique of the dominant anthropological scholarship on African indigenous religions in the immediate postwar period. Their interdisciplinary works in the humanities and the social sciences drew on rigorous readings of philosophical, anthropological, sociological, and historical studies, as well as on extensive field research in Southern Nigerian communities.
6. Horton, "African Conversion," "On the Rationality of Conversion: Part One," and "On the Rationality of Conversion: Part Two."
7. Horton asserts that prior to the rapid social, economic, and political transformations of the nineteenth century, the worship of the "cult of the Supreme Being" had been largely distant to most local people in their simple and isolated milieu in earlier moments in history. See ibid.
8. Ibid.
9. Peel, *Aladura*.

10 Ranger, "The Local and the Global in Southern African Religious History."
11 Ibid.
12 Goody, *The Logic of Writing and the Organization of Society*.
13 Lewis, *Islam in Tropical Africa*.
14 Hefner, "Introduction: World Building and the Rationality of Conversion," 25.
15 Braudel, "Histoires et sciences sociales."
16 Peel, "Inequality and Action."
17 Moses Ochonu's book, *Colonialism by Proxy*, is the most authoritative study on the history of Middle Belt consciousness in the making of modern Northern Nigeria.
18 A. D. Smith, "The Nation, Invented, Imagined, and Reconstructed."
19 Patricia Williams shows how prominent Christian missions in the Northern Nigerian Provinces, notably the Sudan Interior Mission and the Sudan United Mission, aided the formation of the regional political party that articulated the interest of Christian minorities in the Northern Region in 1950. See Williams, "The State, Religion, and Politics in Nigeria," 269–270; see also Ilesanmi, *Religious Pluralism and the Nigerian State*. For an insightful comparative example based on resistance politics in the African American experience, see Kelly, *Race Rebels*.
20 Ibid.
21 Peel, *Religious Encounter and the Making of the Yoruba*; see also Peel, *Ijeshas and Nigerians*.
22 Johnson, *History of the Yorubas*.
23 For insightful historical and theoretical studies, see Robertson, "Histories and Political Opposition, Ahafo, Ghana"; Ranger, "The Invention of Tradition Revisited."
24 Joseph, *Democracy and Pre-Bendel Politics in Nigeria*.
25 Marshall, *Political Spiritualities*.

CHAPTER 1: ISLAM AND CHRISTIANITY IN THE MAKING OF MODERN NIGERIA

1 Although these underlying communities had acquired Hausa culture and language over the years, they were not considered "legitimate" Hausa communities by the seven original Hausa city-states. For a detailed account, see M. G. Smith, *Government in Zazzau, 1800–1950*.
2 Ochonu, *Colonialism by Proxy*, 24.
3 Umar, "Hausa Traditional Political Culture, Islam, and Democracy," 180.
4 Gusau, *A Case for Shari'ah in Nigeria*.
5 Umar, "Hausa Traditional Political Culture, Islam, and Democracy."
6 Ibid., 182.
7 Kendhammer, "Muslim Talking Politics," 61.
8 Larémont, *Islamic Law and Politics in Northern Nigeria*, 41–43.
9 Lubeck, "Nigeria," 254.
10 For detailed discussion, see Hunwick, "The Nineteenth Century Jihad."
11 Umar, "Hausa Traditional Political Culture, Islam, and Democracy," 181.

12. Badru, "Historical Foundations and Basic Philosophy of Islam"; see also Badru, "The Hausa Speaking People of West Africa."
13. See Hodgkin, *Nigerian Perspectives*; Ilesanmi, *Religious Pluralism and the Nigerian State*.
14. Frank Salamone provides an insightful analysis of the Toronkawa clan in Hausa society. He contends that by the time of the Sokoto Jihad, the Toronkawa were well integrated into Hausa society, serving as respected clerical advisers to Hausa rulers, including the emir of Gobir. In the eighteenth and nineteenth centuries, Toronkawa Muslim clerics had a strong understanding of the regional and global Islamic world, and during the time of the Sokoto Jihad prominent Toronkawa clerics articulated their Muslim reformist doctrines to engage other regional reformist movements and to confront crippling European imperialism. Drawing on the works of Murray Last and Joyce Hendrixson, Salamone further argues that Toronkawa clan identity, which reflected more of a Muslim clerical identity before the Sokoto Jihad, took on a wider Fulani identity in the context of the jihad's monumental transformations in the nineteenth century. For detailed discussions, see Salamone, "Ethnic Identities and Religion." See also Last, *The Sokoto Caliphate*; Hendrixson, "The Changing Significance of Ethnicity and Power Relations, Sokoto, Nigeria."
15. Musa, *The Da'awah Approach of Shaikh Uthman Danfoidiyo*.
16. Crowder, *The Story of Nigeria*, 94.
17. Ballard, "'Pagan Administration' and Political Development in Northern Nigeria," 1–14, quoted from Ochonu, *Colonialism by Proxy*, 49.
18. Peters, *Islam and Colonialism*.
19. Umar, "Hausa Traditional Political Culture, Islam, and Democracy," 183.
20. See, for example, Hunwick, "The Nineteenth Century Jihad."
21. Hiskett, "Kitāb Al-Farq," 570–571.
22. Al-Hajj, "The Writings of Shehu Uthman dan Fodio," 38.
23. Hefner, "September 11 and the Struggle for Islam," 1.
24. Al-Hajj, "The Writings of Shehu Uthman dan Fodio," 61.
25. Ibid., 65.
26. Sulaiman, *The Islamic State and the Challenge of History*, 34.
27. Ibid.
28. Salamone, "Religion and Resistance in Pre-colonial and Colonial Nigeria," 202.
29. Sulaiman, *The Islamic State and the Challenge of History*, 40–41.
30. Ibid., 48.
31. Ibid., 36–37.
32. With the defeat of the sarki of Gobir, many prominent Fulani Muslim clerics obtained the blessing of Usman dan Fodio as flagbearers of the Sokoto Jihad against Hausa and other local rulers throughout the region. The military success of these flagbearers led to the establishment of many emirates under the spiritual leadership of the caliph (sultan) of Sokoto.
33. Hiskett, *The Sword of Truth*.
34. Ochonu, "Colonialism within Colonialism," 102.

35 Ibid.
36 Oba, "Islamic Law as Customary Law," 817–850.
37 Schacht, "Islam in Northern Nigeria," 123–146.
38 Ado-Kurawa, *Shari'ah and the Press in Nigeria*, chapter 5.
39 Sodiq, "A History of Islamic Law in Nigeria."
40 Last, "The Search for Security in Muslim Northern Nigeria," 44.
41 For example, Ikenga Ozigboh underscores the contradictions between the theoretical prescription of the founders of the Sokoto Jihad and the management of state affairs by rulers of the various emirates. He concluded that abuse of power was rife in many emirs' courts throughout the caliphate. For detailed analysis, see Ozigboh, *An Introduction to the Religion and History of Islam*, 142.
42 Harnischfeger, *Democratization and Islamic Law*, 44–50.
43 Bello, "Sharia and the Constitution."
44 Lovejoy and Hogendorn, *Slow Death for Slavery*.
45 Harnischfeger, *Democratization and Islamic Law*, 49–50.
46 Kukah, *Religion, Politics, and Power in Northern Nigeria*, especially chapter 2.
47 Crowder, *The Story of Nigeria*, 99.
48 Resident E. J. Arnett, "Intelligence Report," Sokoto Province, June 8, 1918.
49 Ibid.
50 Ibid.
51 Ochonu, "Colonialism within Colonialism," 98.
52 Hiskett in Balewa, *Shaihu Umar*, 15.
53 Schacht, "Islam in Northern Nigeria."
54 Ozigboh, *An Introduction to the Religion and History of Islam*, 133–152.
55 Kalu, "Constructing a Global Pentecostal Discourse," 39.
56 For a concise overview of the scholarship on Christian missionary impact on African communities, see Strayer, "Mission History in Africa," 1–15.
57 Kalu, "The Distorted Lens of Edinburgh 1910," 135.
58 By the turn of the nineteenth century, Western Christian evangelical missionaries were combining their missionary work with imperial mercantile interest in Asia and Africa. This process profoundly shaped the work of Western and African missionaries in Nigeria by the mid-nineteenth century. For detailed analysis, see Ajayi, "Introduction," xxviii.
59 Quoted in Bassey, "Missionary Rivalry and Educational Expansion in Southern Nigeria," 511.
60 Ajayi, "Introduction," xxviii.
61 Ajayi, "Henry Venn and the Policy of Development," 60.
62 Ajayi, "Introduction," xxxvi.
63 See, for example, Flint, "The Growth of European Influence in West Africa."
64 Ajayi, *Christian Missions in Nigeria 1841–1891*.
65 Ibid., 55.
66 Ajayi, "Introduction," xxxvi.
67 For an insightful account, see Dike, "Origins of the Niger Mission, 1841–1891."
68 Oduyoye, "The Church in Yorubaland."

69 The religious practices of Old Oyo legitimated the political authority of its rulers within the city-state and in its relations with their many tributary communities in the Yoruba region and beyond in the seventeenth and eighteenth centuries, when Old Oyo's power reached its zenith. With a dominant military force, Old Oyo extracted tributes from subordinate communities and controlled a vast network of trade routes. At its zenith, Old Oyo had a strong politico-religious system that included a ritual king, the Alaafin, and a powerful council of kingmakers, the Oyo mesi. For detailed analysis, see Crowder, *The Story of Nigeria*; see also Law, *The Oyo Empire*.
70 Ajayi, "Introduction."
71 See Crowder, *The Story of Nigeria*.
72 Although Ibadan controlled some Ife communities, Ile-Ife, the mythical cradle of Yoruba civilization, continued to enjoy the respect of emerging Yoruba powers such as Ibadan. The ooni of Ile-Ife, the traditional spiritual head of Yoruba rulers, was considered the embodiment of Orisa, the pantheon of Yoruba deities. The disruption of the ooni's religious authority effectively undermined the legitimacy of the traditional order among Yoruba obas (monarchs). For a detailed account, see Olupona and Gemignani, *African Immigrant Religions in America*.
73 Ajayi, "Introduction."
74 Ibid.
75 Kalu, "The Distorted Lens of Edinburgh 1910."
76 Akintoye, *A History of the Yoruba People*.
77 Ibid., 352–356; for a detailed historical analysis of the social impact of liberated Yoruba slaves from Sierra Leone on Yoruba communities in the nineteenth century see Kopytoff, *A Preface to Modern Nigeria*.
78 Sanneh, "The CMS and African Transformation," 175.
79 Ayandele, *Holy Johnson*, 85; see also Ayandele, *The Missionary Impact on Modern Nigeria*.
80 *Church Missionary Gleaner*, 1848, 1850, 1851.
81 Amadi, "Church-State Involvement in Educational Development in Nigeria," 483–484.
82 Adebiyi, "Anglican Church and Education," 184–185.
83 Ibid.
84 CMS Original Papers, Yoruba Mission, 1907.
85 Atanda, *Baptist Churches in Nigeria*.
86 Following the pioneering works of Bowen, many prominent Southern Baptist missionaries served meritoriously in Yoruba communities in the first half of the twentieth century. For example, Dr. Loy Connell Smith, a staff physician, and his wife, Eunice, worked for many years at the Baptist Hospital, Ogbomosho; James Christopher Pool served as principal of the Nigerian Baptist Theological Seminary for several decades; for thirty-three years, James Sidney and Doris McGee served at the Baptist College, Iwo, and played important roles in the founding of the Ekiti Baptist High School, Igede, following the example of earlier Baptist secondary schools in the Yoruba region such as the Baptist Academy, Lagos; Baptist Boys

High School, Abeokuta; Olivet Baptist High School, Oyo; Regan Memorial Girls High School, Lagos; and Baptist High School, Iwo. For detailed information, see Loy Connell Smith and Eunice Andrews Smith Bland Papers, 1958–1999; Pool Family Papers, 1928–1998; Roberson Family Papers, 1917–1977; McGee Family Papers, 1957–2013; Logan Family Papers, 1952–1994; Taylor Family Papers, 1950–1975, David M. Rubenstein Rare Books and Manuscript Library, Duke University, Durham, NC.

87 Atanda, *Baptist Churches in Nigeria, 1850–1950*, 122–152.
88 Amadi, "Church-State Involvement in Educational Development in Nigeria," 483.
89 Bassey, "Missionary Rivalry and Educational Expansion in Southern Nigeria," 514.
90 Samuel Crowther Jr. (son of Reverend Crowther) was one of the pioneers of modern medicine in Nigeria. After his medical training in England, he established a dispensary in Abeokuta. In January 1861, Henry Venn encouraged the appointment of a Cambridge-trained physician, Dr. A. A. Harrison, as "political agent and to take care of the health of the missionaries as well as to teach some gifted young men the elements of medical and surgical science." Obadiah Johnson, brother of Samuel Johnson (author of the famous *History of the Yorubas*), was also sponsored by the CMS to train to become a physician in England. For detailed discussion, see Adebiyi, "Anglican Church and Education," 78–179.
91 CMS Original Papers, Niger Mission, 1932.
92 Ajayi, "Bishop Crowther," 90.
93 The CMS established several printing presses in Lagos and Abeokuta in the mid-nineteenth century. Through these printing presses, Rev. Henry Townsend, a prominent CMS missionary, published pamphlets of hymns, catechism, and prayer books. In 1859, Townsend published the *Iwe Irohin*, a fortnightly journal in Yoruba, providing news for a growing reading public in Lagos. In 1860, he started the English supplement that contained an advertisement column. In 1862, Robert Campbell, another missionary, founded the Anglo-African Press in Lagos. For detailed account, see Adebiyi, "Anglican Church and Education," 177.
94 Akintoye, *A History of the Yoruba People*, 359.
95 O. Ojo-Ade, "Afro-Brazilians in Lagos."
96 Ajayi, "Henry Venn and the Policy of Development," 64–65.
97 CMS missionaries also established modern agricultural and industrial ventures in many of their stations. Adebiyi notes that by 1863, "there were five firms with resident agents in Abeokuta, two of them were Africans and three of them Europeans." These CMS industrial centers encouraged the cultivation and exportation of cotton. By 1861, there were several hundred gins in Abeokuta, Ibadan, Ijaiye, and around the Niger region. See Adebiyi, "Anglican Church and Education," 176–178.
98 CMS Mission 2, Bishop Patterson, CMS Missionary Account, Bishop Cecil Peterson, typescript interview, Mss. Afr. s. 2302, Rhodes House Library, University of Oxford (hereafter RHL).
99 Enwerem, *A Dangerous Awakening*.
100 Ojo-Ade, "Afro-Brazilians in Lagos," 237.

101 Ibid., 219–221; see also Kopytoff, *A Preface to Modern Nigeria*.
102 For detailed analysis, see Afolabi, *Afro-Brazilians*.
103 Ojo-Ade, "Afro-Brazilians in Lagos."
104 Chidester, "African Christian Communities," 350.
105 Peel, "Religious Change in Yorubaland"; see also Horton, "African Conversion."
106 Akintoye, *A History of the Yoruba People*.
107 See Johnson, *History of the Yorubas*.
108 Kolapo, "CMS Missionaries of African Origin and Extra-Religious Encounters," 110.
109 See Peel, *Religious Encounter and the Making of the Yoruba*.
110 Akintoye, *A History of the Yoruba People*, 357–358.

CHAPTER 2: ISLAM AND COLONIAL RULE IN NORTHERN NIGERIA

1 Moses Ochonu provides an insightful account of the meeting between Sultan Mohammed Bello and these British explorers. In extensive discussions with the British visitors, Sultan Bello impressed on them the basis for the moral authority of the Sokoto Caliphate over the diverse communities in the region, especially adherents of indigenous religions. For detailed discussion, see Ochonu, *Colonialism by Proxy*.
2 Umar, "Hausa Traditional Political Culture, Islam, and Democracy," 178–179.
3 For an overview, see Lugard, *The Dual Mandate in British Tropical Africa*.
4 Umar, "Hausa Traditional Political Culture, Islam, and Democracy," 186.
5 The qadiriyya is a Sufi tariqa (order) within Sunni Islam that was inspired by Syed Abdul Qadar Gilani Al Amoli (1077–1166 CE). Although the order professes strong adherence to Islamic theological traditions, it also exhibits mystical Sufi practices around the Muslim world where it had evolved over the centuries. For an overview, see Esposito, *The Oxford History of Islam*.
6 Oladimeji, "An Appraisal of the Place of Shari'ah in the Nigerian Constitution."
7 Schacht, "Islam in Northern Nigeria," 123–146.
8 Salamone, "Ethnic Identities and Religion," 52–53.
9 Reynolds, "Good and Bad Muslims," 601–618.
10 The tijaniyya is a Sufi tariqa (order) within Sunni Islam that originated in North Africa (contemporary Algeria) in the late eighteenth century, but gained currency in West Africa, especially in contemporary, Senegal, the Gambia, Mauritania, Mali, Guinea, Niger, Chad, Sudan, and Northern Nigeria. For detailed discussion, see Esposito, *The Oxford History of Islam*.
11 The rapid growth of the tijaniyya order in Northern Nigeria was largely due to the work of Sheikh Ibrahim Niass from Senegal in Kano in the 1940s and 1950s. The influence of Sheikh Niass on Northern Nigerian Muslims is analyzed in chapters 4 and 5 of this book. See Kendhammer, "Muslims Talking Politics," 77.
12 Reynolds, "Good and Bad Muslims," 603–604.
13 Ibid., 607.

14 Ibid., 609–611.
15 Ibrahim, *Sayyid 'Abd al-Rahman al-Mahdi*.
16 G. J. Lethem, Confidential File (file 9/1923), Correspondence of District Officer to the Resident, Bornu Province, September 22, 1923, RHL.
17 Ibid.
18 Ibrahim, *Sayyid 'Abd al-Rahman al-Mahdi*.
19 Ibid.
20 G. J. Lethem, Confidential File (file 9/1923).
21 Ibid.
22 Ibrahim, *Sayyid 'Abd al-Rahman al-Mahdi*.
23 G. J. Lethem, Islamic Propaganda, Mss. British Empire, S276, 13, 1924, 72–75, RHL.
24 Ibid., 13.
25 Ibrahim, *Sayyid 'Abd al-Rahman al-Mahdi*.
26 Kendhammer, "Muslims Talking Politics," 66.
27 Lovejoy and Hogendorn, "Revolutionary Mahdism and Resistance to Colonial Rule in the Sokoto Caliphate, 1905–06."
28 Kendhammer, "Muslims Talking Politics," 69.
29 G. J. Lethem, Intelligence Report, Islamic Propaganda in Northern Nigeria, Mss. British Empire, S276, 41–43, 46–47.
30 Ibid.
31 G. J. Lethem, Intelligence Report, Islamic Propaganda, 11, 5, Mss. British Empire, S276, Nazaru, Maiduguri, August 1924, RHL, 58–93.
32 Ibid.
33 G. J. Lethem, Confidential Document, Islamic Propaganda, Mss. British Empire, S276, 13/10, ff. 1–38, 42/1923, Maiduguri, November 15, 1924, RHL.
34 G. J. Lethem, Acting Resident, Bornu Province, 42/1923 of 9/6/1924, 231/123, Maiduguri, October 15, 1924, Mss. British Empire, RHL, 123.
35 Ludwig, "Christian-Muslim Relations in Northern Nigeria since the Introduction of Shari'ah in 1999," 606–607.
36 Larémont, *Islamic Law and Politics in Northern Nigeria*, 94.
37 Ado-Kurawa, *Shari'ah and the Press in Nigeria*.
38 Sodiq, "A History of Islamic Law in Nigeria."
39 Last, "The Search for Security in Muslim Northern Nigeria," 48–49.
40 Ludwig, "Christian-Muslim Relations in Northern Nigeria," 607.
41 Larémont, *Islamic Law and Politics in Northern Nigeria*, 108–111.
42 Ado-Kurawa, *Shari'ah and the Press in Nigeria*, especially chapter 5.
43 Okereafoezeke, *Law and Justice in Post-British Nigeria*, 164.
44 Anderson, quoted in Ludwig, "Christian-Muslim Relations in Northern Nigeria," 607.
45 Yusuf, *Nigerian Legal System*, chapter 6.
46 Ludwig, "Christian-Muslim Relations in Northern Nigeria," 607.
47 Yadudu, "Colonialism and the Transformation of the Substance and Form of Islamic Law in the Northern States of Nigeria," 28.

48 Mukoro, "The Interface between Customary Law and Local Government Legislation in Nigeria," 141.
49 Tabi'u, "Constraints in the Application of Islamic Law in Nigeria."
50 Kendhammer, "Muslims Talking Politics," 75.
51 Larémont, *Islamic Law and Politics in Northern Nigeria*, 114.
52 Musa, *Shari'ah in a Multi-Faith Nigeria*.
53 *Licensed to Harm: Framework of the Area Courts*.
54 Doi, "The Impact of English Law and Concepts on the Administration of Islamic Law in Nigeria."
55 Larémont, *Islamic Law and Politics in Northern Nigeria*, 111–112.
56 Ado-Kurawa, *Shari'ah and the Press in Nigeria*.
57 Obilade, "Jurisdiction in Customary Law Matters in Nigeria," 227.
58 Schacht, "Islam in Northern Nigeria," 124.
59 Ochonu, *Colonialism by Proxy*, 45.
60 Diaries of Administrative Officer, J. W. Watt, Mss. afr., 117, 1960, RHL.
61 CMS Original Papers, Niger Mission, 1907.
62 Larémont, *Islamic Law and Politics in Northern Nigeria*, 116–117.
63 Commander J. H. Carrow, Kano Province Annual Report, 1910, RHL.
64 Commander J. H. Carrow, Kano Province Annual Report, 1909, RHL.
65 Temple, Resident, Kano Province Annual Report, 1909, RHL, 2–5.
66 Ibid., 6.
67 Ibid., 8–9.
68 Ibid.
69 Commander J. H. Carrow, typescript of interview, 1966, RHL.
70 Ibid.
71 Commander J. H. Carrow, Native Administration, Sokoto Province, RHL, 1933–1935.
72 Commander J. H. Carrow, Native Administration, Kano Province, RHL, 1933–1935.
73 Ibid.
74 Commander J. H. Carrow, typescript of interview, 1966, RHL, 1933–1935.
75 Touring Diary, Assistant District Officer J. C. Guy, Katagum Division, Bauchi Province, Mss. afr., RHL.
76 The Jakada caliphate-era representatives of the emirs in tributary communities were used as tax collectors by emirs, chiefs, and village heads during the colonial period.
77 Arnett, Resident, Sokoto Province, Annual Report, June 1918, RHL.
78 In this instance, relationships between local people and sarauta notables, as well as between Hausa-Fulani Muslim rulers and tributary communities, reflected a novel interpretation of preexisting sociopolitical relations. See Jacob, Report on Taxation, Mss. afr. t. 16, RHL, 132–140.
79 Matthews, Handing Over Notes, Assistant District Officer H. F. Matthews, Agaie-Lapai Division, November 7, 1919, Mss. afr. s. 783, box 2/6, RHL.

80 Crampton, *Christianity in Northern Nigeria*, 54–55.
81 Kastfelt, "African Resistance to Colonialism in Adamawa."
82 Papers of Assistant District Officer Letchworth, RHL.
83 Circular, Native Administration, Governor Hugh Clifford, 1923, RHL.
84 Circular: number 89/285/1920, from the Secretary, Northern Provinces, to the Resident, Bornu Province, Kaduna, 23 September, 1920; Dikwa District, 10 May 1922, Lethem 15/3, RHL.
85 Lethem, Former Administrative Officer, 192 Ferry Rd, Edinburgh, Scotland; Circular, numbers 49–203, Kaduna, 29 June, 1920, from the Secretary, Northern Provinces, G. R. Matthews to the Resident Bornu Province; Confidential memorandum, Resident, Bornu Province, Potiskum, August 31, 1923; Correspondence, District Officer, G. J. Lethem to the Resident, Bornu Province, 15/3, 1923, September 25, 1923; Resident, Bornu Province to District Officer Lethem, file number 231/123, Maiduguri, October 15, 1923.
86 Assistant District Officer, Letchworth, Nasarawa Division, 1926, RHL.
87 Ochonu, *Colonialism by Proxy*, 4.
88 Reorganization of East Tangale District, Gombe, Assistant District Officer J. A. E. Morley, Mss. British Empire, s. 27, RHL, August 1945.
89 Birks, Assistant District Officer, Waja Native Authority, Gombe Division, 1945, RHL, 1–5.
90 Assistant District Officer H. M. Brice-Smith to the Resident of Kano Province, C. L. Temple, Mss. afr. s. 230, March 1915; C. L. Temple, Resident, Kano Province, Annual Report, for the year ending 31 December 1909, Mss. afr. s. 230, RHL.
91 Typescript of interview, Hedley H. Marshall Esq., Former Attorney General of Northern Nigeria (interview conducted by A. H. M Kirk-Greene in Oxford on May 15, 1970), Mss. afr. s. 2339, RHL.
92 For an outline of Governor Cameron's colonial policy, see Cameron, *The Principle of Native Administration and Their Application*.
93 Institute of Administration, Northern Nigeria, Local Government Wing, lecture note series, November 1954, Mss. afr. s. 1961, RHL.
94 Robert Huessler, a historian of colonial Northern Nigeria, notes that Cameron's tendency to treat local administration in colonial Northern Nigeria as a theoretical exercise distracted junior colonial administrators from pressing matters of native administration. See Carrow-Heussler Papers on Northern Nigeria, Mss. Afr. s. 1489, Oxford University Colonial Records Project, Institute of Commonwealth Studies, Queen Elizabeth House, 1965–1972; Carrow's letter, 5 April 1965, Dorset, England.
95 Larémont, *Islamic Law and Politics in Northern Nigeria*, 113.
96 Papers of Assistant District Officer Letchforth, RHL.
97 See Carrow-Heussler Papers on Northern Nigeria.
98 British colonial policy only allowed Christian missionaries to establish mission stations in the non-Muslim areas (the so-called pagan communities in the Middle Belt and in the emirates) of the Northern Provinces.

CHAPTER 3: CHRISTIANITY AND THE TRANSFORMATION
OF COLONIAL SOUTHERN AND NORTHERN NIGERIA

1. Shankar, *Who Shall Enter Paradise*, 5.
2. This provided a rationale for the transition from indigenous Yoruba religions to mission Christianity in the context of the rapid social and political transformation of the turn of the twentieth century. See Peel, *Religious Encounter and the Making of the Yoruba*.
3. Laitin, *Hegemony and Culture*.
4. Peel, "Religious Change in Yorubaland," 292–306.
5. In Yoruba communities during the early years of colonial rule, Aladura, like many other African-initiated Christian churches, emerged as a syncretistic union of indigenous religion and Christianity. For detailed analysis, see Peel, *Aladura*.
6. Mann, *Marrying Well*.
7. See, for example, Horton, "African Conversion," 219–235.
8. Berry, *Cocoa, Custom, and Socioeconomic Change in Rural Western Nigeria*.
9. The spread of Christianity in Africa in the nineteenth century resulted from the activities of Christian missions and spread along the pathways of Western imperial interests of the time. While African and European missionaries had made inroads into many Yoruba communities by the late nineteenth century, it was not until the imposition of colonial rule at the turn of the twentieth century that missionaries effectively established their influence on Yoruba communities. For detailed analysis, see Peel, "Religious Change in Yorubaland," 373–399.
10. Ajasin, *Ajasin*, 4.
11. It is important to note that the pattern of the spread of mission Christianity varied in the Yoruba region as well as in other parts of southern Nigeria. In the specific case of the Yoruba, Peel notes that various factors affected the growth of Christianity in the region, including earlier arrival of Islam and the social significance of Christianity at the turn of the twentieth century. See Peel, "Religious Change in Yorubaland."
12. Conversion to mission Christianity was more than a straightforward religious experience in the Yoruba region. With Christianity's connection to Western imperial power, this world religion provided a framework for local people to engage the rapidly changing conditions of this transformative moment in Ibadan, Ijebu, and other Yoruba communities. For a critical theoretical explanation, see Horton, "African Conversion."
13. Morgan, *Akinyele's Outline of History of Ibadan*.
14. Falola, *Ibadan*, 335.
15. Lloyd, *Africa in Social Change*, especially chapter 2.
16. Falola, *Ibadan*.
17. By the early nineteenth century, Yoruba indigenous cosmology was steadily engaging Islam, brought to Yoruba towns by Hausa traders and the influence of the Sokoto Jihad. Throughout the nineteenth century, Islamic practices mixed with Yoruba traditional worldview to shape the changing social condition of a turbulent century. For detailed analysis, see Gbadamosi, *The Growth of Islam among*

Yoruba Muslim; see also Olupona and Gemignani, *African Immigrant Religions in America*.

18 Peel, "Religious Change in Yorubaland."
19 For a detailed analysis, see Peel, "Conversion and Tradition in Two African Societies."
20 Webster and Boahen, *History of West Africa*, 231.
21 Ayandele, *The Ijebu of Yorubaland*, 227.
22 Peel, "Conversion and Tradition in Two African Societies."
23 Ayandele, *The Ijebu of Yorubaland*, 235–238.
24 Ibid., 230–232.
25 Ibid., 233–271.
26 Ibid.
27 Haynes, *Religion and Politics in Africa*, 53–57.
28 The conflict between Saro CMS missionaries and a new generation of English CMS missionaries captures this problem in the late nineteenth century. In this regard, the popular pan-Africanist Edward Blyden provided a strong defense for Saro CMS missionaries in the conflict with European CMS missionaries, who were not only dominating the leadership of the CMS, but also shaping the direction of missionary work in Nigeria in the late nineteenth century. For a detailed analysis of Blyden's role in this crisis, see Lynch, *Edward Wilmot Blyden*.
29 Reverend Canon Wright's Letter to his mother, September 16, 1929, RHL.
30 Atanda, *The New Oyo Empire*.
31 Reverend Canon R. A. Wright's letter to his mother, October 25, 1929, RHL.
32 Reverend Canon R. A. Wright's letter to his mother, May 7, 1929, RHL.
33 Reverend Canon R. A. Wright's letter to his mother, July 2, 1929, RHL.
34 Reverend Canon R. A. Wright's letter to his mother, January 12, 1930, RHL.
35 Reverend Canon R. A. Wright's letter to his mother, November 21, 1929, RHL.
36 Reverend Canon R. A. Wright's letter to his mother, May 15, 1930, RHL.
37 Ibid.
38 Kalu, "Christianity in Africa," 344–347.
39 Kalu, "Who Is Afraid of the Holy Ghost?," 87.
40 Marshall, *Political Spiritualities*.
41 Kalu, "African Pentecostalism in Global Perspective," 27.
42 See Kalu, "Christianity in Africa," 337–343.
43 Kalu, "The Distorted Lens of Edinburgh 1910," 133–148.
44 Kalu, "Black Joseph," 3.
45 For a detailed discussion, see Ranger, "Religious Movements and Politics in Sub-Saharan Africa."
46 Asaju, "Globalization, Politicization of Religion, and Religious Networking," 188–189.
47 Kalu, "Constructing a Global Pentecostal Discourse," 39.
48 Asaju, "Globalization, Politicization of Religion, and Religious Networking," 181–203; Olupona, "Globalization and African Immigrant Communities in America," 67–81; Anderson, "Globalization and Independent Pentecostals in

Africa," 133–154; Kalu, "Constructing a Global Pentecostal Discourse," 40–42; Adogame, "Online for God," 223–224.
49   Kalu, "Constructing a Global Pentecostal Discourse," 41.
50   Ibid., 41–42.
51   Marshall, *Political Spiritualities*, 56.
52   M. A. Ojo, "Deeper Christian Life Ministry," 142–143.
53   Afolayan, "The Church in Northern Nigeria."
54   Shankar, *Who Shall Enter Paradise*, xviii.
55   Kastfelt, "Christianity, Colonial Legitimacy, and the Rise of Nationalist Politics in Northern Nigeria."
56   Shankar, *Who Shall Enter Paradise*, xxviii.
57   Ayandele, "The Missionary Factor in Northern Nigeria," 58.
58   *West Africa*, January 19, 1924, 1691, "De Foucauld of the Sahara, a great son of France and view of French Muslim policy and problems," Mss. Afr. s.783, 1/11, 1922 (published posthumously), RHL.
59   Haynes, *Religion and Politics in Africa*, 38–39.
60   See Ayandele, "The Missionary Factor in Northern Nigeria," 138–139.
61   Salamone, "Ethnic Identities and Religion," 54.
62   Kukah, *Religion, Politics, and Power in Northern Nigeria*, especially chapter 1.
63   Barnes, "Religious Insults," 65–66.
64   Ibid., 67.
65   For a detailed analysis of Walter Miller and Ethel Miller's missionary work in Northern Nigeria, see Barnes, *Making Headway*.
66   Haynes, *Religion and Politics in Africa*.
67   Barnes, *Making Headway*; see also National Archives, Kaduna (SNP), 17–16694.
68   Reverend Maguire, typescript of interview conducted by Andrew Barnes, RHL, April–June 1993.
69   Ibid.
70   Ibid.
71   Ibid.
72   Ibid.

CHAPTER 4: THE POLITICS OF RELIGION IN NORTHERN NIGERIA DURING DECOLONIZATION

1   National issues surrounding balanced development and governance dominated the deliberations of regional delegates during Nigeria's first constitutional conference (1946) in London, which was chaired by Sir Arthur Richards, governor of Nigeria from 1943 to 1947. See Arthur Richards, former governor of Nigeria, typescript of interview, 1969, RHL.
2   Ostien, *A Study of the Court Systems of Northern Nigeria*.
3   Harnischfeger, *Democratization and Islamic Law*.
4   Resident Letchworth, Resident, Northern Provinces, typescript of interview, 1969, RHL.

5   Ado-Kurawa, *Shari'ah and the Press in Nigeria*; Kenny, "Shari'a and Christianity in Nigeria."
6   Institute of Administration, Northern Nigeria, Local Government Wing, lecture series, November 1954, Mss. Afr. s., 1971 (2), RHL; see also Northern Nigerian Native Administration Law of 1954.
7   Casey, "'Policing' through Violence," 110.
8   Harnischfeger, "Sharia and Control over Territory," 443.
9   Marshall, former attorney general of the Northern Region of Nigeria, typescript of interview, No. 8, 1969, RHL.
10 Marshall, former attorney general of the Northern Region of Nigeria, typescript of interview, No. 7, 1969, RHL.
11 Marshall, former attorney general of the Northern Region of Nigeria, typescript of interview, no. 8, 1969, RHL.
12 Macpherson, former governor of Nigeria, typescript of interview, 1969, RHL.
13 The Northern Region British Attorney General Hedley Marshall underscores the dominant power of the Sardauna in the Northern Regional executive council during the period of self-rule. He notes that the Sardauna "ran the whole of the Northern Region as if it were a native authority and he the Emir.... When we first started the Executive Council it was like a native authority meeting and Sir Bryan Sharwood-Smith [the Regional Governor] was the Resident or the District Officer." See Marshall, former Attorney General of the Northern Region of Nigeria, typescript of interview, No. 9, 1969, RHL.
14 Larémont, *Islamic Law and Politics in Northern Nigeria*, 135–140.
15 Crampton, *Christianity in Northern Nigeria*, 88; Ilesanmi, *Religious Pluralism and the Nigerian State*, 132.
16 Macpherson, former governor of Nigeria, typescript of interview, No. 10, 1969, RHL.
17 Gumi, *Where I Stand*, 102–103.
18 Marshall, former attorney general of the Northern Region of Nigeria, typescript of interview, No. 10, 1969, RHL.
19 Enwerem, *A Dangerous Awakening*, 51; see also Bello, *My Life*.
20 Larémont, *Islamic Law and Politics in Northern Nigeria*, 134.
21 Kendhammer, "Muslims Talking Politics," 79–80.
22 Ilesanmi, *Religious Pluralism and the Nigerian State*, 139.
23 Nigerian Constitution Conference, Sir Kenneth Maddocks, Mss. Afr. s. 11794. Secret and Personal Documents, 30 July 1953, signed by A. E. T. Benson Esq. CMG, Nigerian Secretariat, Lagos, 1953.
24 Diamond, *Class, Ethnicity, and Democracy in Nigeria*, 81–82.
25 Whitaker, *The Politics of Tradition*.
26 Nigerian Constitution Conference, Sir Kenneth Maddocks, Mss. afr. s. 11794, Secret and Personal Documents, 30 July 1953, signed by A. E. T. Benson Esq. CMG, Nigerian Secretariat, Lagos, 1953.
27 Abubakar Tafawa Balewa, whom Governor Macpherson considered a "splendid" and amiable personality, also called for the construction of major roads that

would connect Northern communities with river transit systems of the Niger and Benue Rivers to facilitate trade with the Eastern and Western Regions. See Resident Letchworth, former Resident, Bornu Province, typescript of interview, 1969, RHL.

28 For two impressive books on the role of this preeminent Yoruba leader, Obafemi Awolowo, in local and national politics, see Nolte, *Obafemi Awolowo and the Making of Remo*; Adebanwi, *Yoruba Elites and Ethnic Politics in Nigeria*.

29 For a detailed analysis of Awolowo's assessment of Nigeria's geopolitical configuration, see Awolowo, *Path to Nigerian Freedom*.

30 Nigerian Constitution Conference, Sir Kenneth Maddocks, Mss. afr. s. 11794, Secret and Personal Documents, 30 July 1953, signed by A. E. T. Benson Esq. CMG, Nigerian Secretariat, Lagos, 1953.

31 The Action Group supported the move, and equally important, in expressions of legal opinion, the chief justice of Nigeria, Sir John Verity, threw his weight behind a proposal that insisted on the security of Nigerian citizens domiciled in communities outside their home region. See Marshall, former attorney general of the Northern Region of Nigeria, typescript of interview, No. 7, 1969, RHL.

32 See Ostien, *A Study of the Court Systems of Northern Nigeria*.

33 The opposition of the Bornu Youth Movement to the NPC reflected old animosity between Hausa-Fulani Muslim rulers and Kanuri Muslim rulers that can be traced to the assault of Sokoto Jihadists on Kanem-Bornu in the early nineteenth century. Although Sokoto Jihadists failed to bring Kanem-Bornu under their control, the antipathy between Hausa-Fulani Muslim rulers and Kanem-Bornu persisted into the twentieth century. See Ilesanmi, *Religious Pluralism and the Nigerian State*, 139–140.

34 Whitaker, *The Politics of Tradition*, 322; see also Harnischfeger, *Democratization and Islamic Law*, 60–61.

35 Marshall, former attorney general of the Northern Region of Nigeria, typescript of interview, No. 8, 1969, RHL.

36 In reaction to claims of growing NPC domination of ethnic and religious minorities in Middle Belt areas of the Northern Region, the United Middle Belt Congress (UMBC), a party established in 1952 to promote the interest of the diverse peoples of the Middle Belt in the Northern Region, strongly petitioned the Willink Commission, a commission of inquiry established by the British authorities in 1957 to investigate claims of political domination of minorities by the major political parties in the three regions of the federation. Although the Willink Commission acknowledged that there were legitimate grounds for concern of NPC domination of Middle Belt minorities, the commission nevertheless rejected the UMBC's call for the creation of a Middle Belt state out of the Northern Region. Consequently, the Willink Commission contended that there was viable legal mechanism within the prevailing constitutional order to address the concerns of Middle Belt minorities within the regional political system. For detailed account, see Great Britain, Colonial Office, *Nigeria: Commission Appointed to Enquire into the Fears of Minorities and Means of Allaying Them*.

37 Institute of Administration Northern Nigeria, Local Government Wing, Lecture Notes Series, November 1954, Mss. Afr. s. 1871 (2), 1954.

38 Kukah, *Religion, Politics, and Power in Northern Nigeria*, especially chapter 1.
39 Paden, *Religion and Political Culture in Kano*; see also Paden, *Faith and Politics in Nigeria*, 27–28.
40 Sharwood-Smith, Mss. afr. s. 2103, SG, 3228/1957, Governor's Office, Northern Region, Kaduna, February 20, 1957.
41 Ibid.
42 Ibid.
43 Hickey, Catholic Mission in Northern Nigeria (Gongola), typescript of interview, 1969, RHL.
44 CMS Missionary File, Bishop Cecil Patterson, Mss. afr. s. 2302, RHL.
45 Ibid.
46 Ibid.
47 Customary Law and Its Application to English Law, RHL.
48 Ibid.
49 Conference on the Future of Law in Africa, December 1959–January 1960, Mss. afr. s. 1193, RHL.
50 Ibid.
51 Ibid., "Introduction, Relationship between Islamic Law and Customary Law in Africa, Emphasis on Northern Nigeria," Professor J. N. D. Anderson, School of Oriental and African Studies, University of London, 1959.
52 Doi, "The Impact of English Law and Concepts on the Administration of Islamic Law in Nigeria."
53 Conference on the Future of Law in Africa.
54 Ibid.
55 Oba, "Islamic Law as Customary Law," 831–832.
56 Ibid.
57 Conference on the Future of Law in Africa.
58 Ado-Kurawa, *Shari'ah and the Press in Nigeria*, especially chapter 5.
59 Ostien, *A Study of the Court Systems of Northern Nigeria*.
60 Oba, "The Sharia Court of Appeal in Northern Nigeria," 862–863.
61 Doi, "The Impact of English Law and Concepts on the Administration of Islamic Law in Nigeria."
62 Ostien, *A Study of the Court Systems of Northern Nigeria*.
63 Ibid.
64 Ibid.
65 Conference on the Future of Law in Africa.
66 Kukah, *Religion, Politics, and Power in Northern Nigeria*, especially chapter 2.
67 Conference on the Future of Law in Africa.
68 J. N. D. Anderson, *Islamic Law in Africa*.
69 Conference on the Future of Law in Africa.
70 Ibid.
71 For detailed analysis, see Great Britain, Colonial Office, *Nigeria: Report of the Commission Appointed to Enquire into the Fears of Minorities and Means of Allaying Them*; see also Vickers, *Ethnicity and Sub-Nationalism in Nigeria*.

72 Marshall, former attorney general of the Northern Region of Nigeria, typescript of interview, May 15, 1970, Mss. afr. s. 2339, RHL.
73 Conference on the Future of Law in Africa.
74 Indeed, in the early period following independence (1963), the sardauna disciplined the powerful emir of Kano, Alhaji Mohammed Sanusi, for not complying with regional government policies.
75 Marshall, former attorney general of the Northern Region of Nigeria, typescript of interview, May 15, 1970, Mss. afr. s. 2339, RHL.
76 Ibid.
77 See J. N. D. Anderson, "Introduction."
78 Edu et al., *The Sharia Issue: Working Papers for a Dialogue.*
79 Marshall, former attorney general of the Northern Region of Nigeria, typescript of interview, No. 7, RHL.
80 Ibid.
81 Ibid.
82 Ibid.
83 Ibid.
84 Musa, *Shari'ah in a Multi-Faith Nigeria.*
85 Ludwig, "Christian-Muslim Relations in Northern Nigeria since the Introduction of Shari'ah in 1999," 608.
86 Yadudu, "Colonialism and the Transformation of the Substance and Form of Islamic Law in the Northern States of Nigeria," 29.
87 Marshall, former attorney general of Northern Region of Nigeria, typescript of interview, 1969, RHL.
88 Ibid.
89 Ibid.
90 Ibid.
91 Conference on the Future of Law in Africa.
92 Marshall, former attorney general of the Northern Region of Nigeria, typescript of interview, RHL.
93 Yusuf, *Nigerian Legal System*, chapter 5.
94 Ostien, *A Study of the Court Systems of Northern Nigeria.*
95 Oba, "The Sharia Court of Appeal in Northern Nigeria," 863.
96 Gumi, *Where I Stand*, 77.
97 Marshall, former attorney general of the Northern Region of Nigeria, typescript of interview, RHL.
98 Conference on the Future of Law in Africa.
99 Ibid.
100 Ibid.
101 For landmark analyses on the role of the political classes of the three regions in the politics of decolonization, see Coleman, *Nigeria*, and Sklar, *Nigerian Political Parties.*

CHAPTER 5: RELIGION AND THE POSTCOLONIAL STATE

1. The United Middle Belt Congress (UMBC), the party that represented the interest of Christian minorities in the Middle Belt communities of the Northern Region, evolved from a non-Muslim associational interest group, the Non-Muslim League, founded in 1949. In 1950, this group became the Middle Zone League, the quasi-political party that was the forerunner for UMBC founded in 1952. For an excellent analysis of the role of UMBC in Northern Nigerian politics during decolonization and in the early years of independence, see Ochonu, *Colonialism by Proxy*, especially chapter 7. For pioneering works, see Coleman, *Nigeria*; Dudley, *Parties and Politics in Northern Nigeria*.
2. Diaries of Administrative Officer, J. W. Watt, Mss. Afr. 117, 1960, RHL.
3. See Dudley, *Parties and Politics in Northern Nigeria*; see also Ochonu, *Colonialism by Proxy*.
4. Moses Ochonu notes that NPC authorities freely used strategies of cooptation and state repression during UMBC-inspired Tiv uprising in 1963–1964 and in the Tiv-Hausa conflict in Makurdi in the early 1960s. See Ochonu, *Colonialism by Proxy*, 206.
5. Afigbo, "The National Question in Nigerian History, Politics and Affairs."
6. Tayob, "Sub-Saharan African Islam," 428.
7. Kendhammer, "Muslims Talking Politics," 84.
8. Ibid., 85.
9. Enwerem, *A Dangerous Awakening*, 52.
10. Ochonu, *Colonialism by Proxy*, 194.
11. Paden, *Religion and Political Culture in Kano*, 182–186.
12. Ibid.
13. Lubeck, "Nigeria."
14. Kendhammer, "Muslims Talking Politics," 86.
15. Paden, *Faith and Politics in Nigeria*, 33.
16. Enwerem, *A Dangerous Awakening*, 62.
17. Paden, *Faith and Politics in Nigeria*, 33.
18. Dudley, *Instability and Political Order*.
19. For detailed analysis of the factors that led to the carving out of a region, the Mid-West Region, from the Western Region during the AG crisis of 1962–1966, see Post and Vickers, *Structure and Conflict in Nigeria*.
20. For an overview of the crisis that led to the Nigerian Civil War, see Kirk-Greene, *Crisis and Conflict in Nigeria*.
21. *Broadcast to the Nation by His Excellency Major-General J. T. U. Aguiyi Ironsi, Head of the National Government and Supreme Commander of the Armed Forces, Tuesday, May 24, 1966.*
22. Dudley, *Instability and Political Order*.
23. During the horrific attacks on Igbo Christians in Northern cities, Hausa-Fulani Muslims conflated Igbo and Christian in a peculiar way. They contended that the Hausa-Fulani ummah had been assaulted because of the assassination of the two most prominent Northern Muslim leaders—Sir Ahmadu Bello, premier of the Northern Region, and Sir Abubakar Tafawa Balewa, prime minister of the Federal

Republic of Nigeria—by predominantly Igbo Christian military officers. The effects of these assassinations were further aggravated by the imposition of policies considered inimical to Hausa-Fulani Muslim interest by a military government led by an Igbo Christian military head of state, Major-General Aguiyi Ironsi. These factors provided the rationalization for strong anti-Igbo (and to a lesser extent anti–Southern Christian) sentiments in the Northern Region. These attacks on Igbo Christians in Northern cities led to the crisis that culminated in the Nigerian-Biafra Civil War of 1967–1970.

24 With this special relationship between Governor Katsina and Northern emirs, the Northern Military Governor replaced native authority councillors in the Northern Provinces with nominees of emirs.

25 Acting on instructions from military authorities in Lagos, Katsina twice summoned the emirs to the regional capital in Kaduna, where he assured them that the Federal Military Government would carefully consider their recommendations. See "Soldiers and the Sultan," *West Africa*, June 11, 1966.

26 Shankar, *Who Shall Enter Paradise*, 139.

27 Dudley, *Instability and Political Order*, 136–139.

28 Ibid.

29 Despite their compromise with the Gowon administration, Hausa-Fulani Muslim rulers, according to Abubakar Gumi, strongly resented the carving out of states—especially Benue-Plateau and Kwara (the new Middle Belt states)—from the Northern Region. See Gumi, *Where I Stand*, 125.

30 Kukah, *Religion, Politics, and Power in Northern Nigeria*, especially chapter 2.

31 It is significant to note that Yakubu Gowon, Nigeria's new military head of state, is a Christian from the Middle Belt, with deep cultural affinity with Hausa-Fulani Muslims. As a Christian minority from the Middle Belt section of the Northern Region, Gowon, a Sandhurst graduate, projected himself as a voice of reconciliation, even as Nigeria's federal troops unleashed a vicious war against the secessionist Republic of Biafra, dominated by Igbo communities, from 1967 to 1970.

32 Kukah, *Religion, Politics, and Power in Northern Nigeria*.

33 Governor Macpherson, typescript of interview, 1970, RHL.

34 Enwerem, *A Dangerous Awakening*, 153–159.

35 Ibid., 153–154.

36 Ibid., 76.

37 For a comprehensive analysis of CAN, see Enwerem, *A Dangerous Awakening*.

38 Paden, "Islam and Democratic Federalism in Nigeria," 1–10.

39 Following the recommendation of a Customary Courts Reform Committee, the government also reinstated customary and area courts in states where they had been removed, and affirmed their authority in states where they had remained. These military government decisions were justified on the grounds that Islamic and customary courts remained the dominant medium of legal administration for the masses of Nigerians. For detailed discussion of customary and area court reforms under the military in the 1970s, see Collett, "Recent Legislation and Reform Proposals for Customary and Area Courts in Nigeria," 165.

40   In many Northern states, military initiatives at legal reform had eroded the authority of Islamic law during the turbulent period of the Civil War in the late 1960s. Before the outbreak of the war, many of these military state governments had replaced the native courts with "area" courts and folded Islamic law into the jurisdiction of customary law. Significantly, in 1967, the Military Government's Area Courts Edict limited the scope of sharia and simplified the rules of personal jurisdiction in customary law. For detailed analysis, see Obilade, "Jurisdiction in Customary Law Matters in Nigeria," 228–229.
41   Kenny, "Shari'a and Christianity in Nigeria."
42   Laitin, "The Sharia Debate and the Origins of Nigeria's Second Republic."
43   Ibrahim, "Religion and Political Turbulence in Nigeria."
44   In 1976, General Mohammed was assassinated by a group of dissident army officers, notably Middle Belt Christians, loyal to the ousted former military ruler, General Gowon. This abortive coup further revealed the deep ethnic and religious divisions among Nigerian military officers in the 1970s. After the assassination of General Mohammed, the chief of staff of the Supreme Headquarters, Lieutenant General Olusegun Obasanjo, a Yoruba Christian, succeeded to the position of head of state and supreme commander of the armed forces.
45   Diamond, "Nigeria."
46   The National Movement reflected an alliance of powerful emirs with a younger generation of influential Northern senior civil servants and businessmen who had consolidated their power base during the intervening years of military rule. See D. Williams, *President and Power in Nigeria*.
47   D. Williams, *President and Power in Nigeria*.
48   The editor of the acclaimed weekly magazine *West Africa*, David Williams, underscored the Makaman's crucial role in Shehu Shagari's nomination as the NPN presidential candidate in 1979. See ibid.
49   It was not unusual, for example, in his official capacity as president of the federal Republic of Nigeria and as the Turaki in the sultan of Sokoto's court, for Shehu Shagari to pay courtesy calls on Northern emirs and Southern traditional rulers. He also conferred prestigious national awards on them during his tenure as president. See ibid.
50   As part of the military's transition program to democracy, seven new states were created by the Mohammed/Obasanjo regime in 1976, bringing the number of states in the federation to nineteen.
51   Abdulraheem, "Politics in Nigeria's Second Republic."
52   Ibid.
53   Ibid.
54   Clarke, *Local Practices, Global Controversies*.
55   For a penetrating analysis of religious violence in Nigerian politics, see Falola, *Violence in Nigeria*.
56   John Hunwick argues that the growing politicization of religion was intimately connected to the structural challenges confronting the Nigerian state in the 1970s

and 1980s. For detailed analysis, see Hunwick, "An African Case Study of Political Islam."
57. Abubakar, "Ethnic Identity, Democratization, and the Future of the African State."
58. Joseph, *Democracy and Pre-Bendel Politics in Nigeria.*
59. Lubeck, "Islamic Protest under Semi-industrial Capitalism."
60. Bienen, "Religion, Legitimacy, and Conflict in Nigeria."
61. Boer, *Nigeria's Decades of Blood.*
62. Kenny, "Shari'a and Christianity in Nigeria."
63. Boer, *Nigeria's Decades of Blood.*
64. Ibid.
65. Ibid.
66. *Africa Confidential,* April 10, 1985.
67. Many analysts believed that the Babangida regime's decision to join the OIC was intended to placate Northern emirs and Muslim clerics. See "Time to Withdraw from OIC," *Challenge,* no. 4, 1986.
68. *Catholic Bishops' Stand on the O.I.C. Issue.*
69. Adigwe, "Nigeria Joins the Organization of Islamic Conference."
70. In the pamphlet, which became a blueprint for a vocal anti-OIC movement, Monsignor Adigwe observed that the secrecy in which the Babangida regime handled the OIC matter not only widened suspicion between Christians and Muslims, but also had serious implications for the status of Nigeria as a secular state. See ibid., 1–5.
71. Ibid., 17.
72. *Address Delivered at the Inaugural Meeting of the Committee on Nigeria's Membership of the Organization of Islamic Conference by Major General Ibrahim Badamosi Babangida, CFR, President of the Federal Republic of Nigeria and Commander-in-Chief of the Armed Forces, in Abuja on Monday, 3rd February, 1986.*
73. Representatives of the Nigerian Military Government at the OIC conference in Fez, Morocco, include Northern Muslim stalwarts such as Rilwanu Lukman, federal minister of petroleum; Abubakar Alhaji, federal permanent secretary in the Ministry of National Planning, and Abdulkadir Ahmed, governor of the Central Bank. See Adigwe, "Nigeria Joins the Organization of Islamic Conference," 6.
74. *Statement of the Consultative Committee on Nigeria's Full Membership in the OIC.*
75. Vatican Council II, *Declaration on the Relations of the Church to Non-Christian Religions,* No. 3.
76. Arinze, *Progress in Christian-Muslim Relations Worldwide.*
77. Anih, *The Cathedral and the Mosque,* 44–45.
78. Anih, *An Introduction to the Fundamentals of Religious Ecumenism in Nigeria,* 133, and *Religious Ecumenism and Education for Tolerance.*
79. *Military Rule and Religion as a Political Platform: Politics of a Secular State and the Babangida Agenda,* Lagos.
80. Ibid.
81. Paden, "Islam and Democratic Federalism in Nigeria," 1–10.
82. Onaiyekan, *Religion.*

83 Ibid.
84 Kenny, "Shari'a and Christianity in Nigeria," 351.
85 Ibid.
86 Lateef Adegbite, keynote address delivered at the opening ceremony of the Sixteenth Annual Conference of the Nigerian Association for the Study of Religions, October 8, 1991, Ilorin, Nigeria.
87 Isyaku, *The Kafanchan Carnage*.
88 *General Observations and Recommendation of the Donli Panel*, 2.
89 *Reaction of the Christian Association of Nigeria to the Report and Recommendation, Submitted by the Committee to Investigate Causes of Riots and Disturbances in Kaduna State*, 1.
90 Kukah, *Religion, Politics, and Power in Northern Nigeria*, especially chapter 6.
91 *Catholic Bishops of Nigeria*.
92 Ibid.
93 Gumi, *Where I Stand*, 14–22.
94 Ibid., 135.
95 For an insightful analysis of Izala-Sufi conflict, see Lomeier, *Islamic Reform and Political Change in Northern Nigeria*.
96 Paden, *Faith and Politics in Nigeria*, 29.
97 Ibid., 108.
98 Ibid., 189.
99 Kane, "Izala," 490–512.
100 Larémont, *Islamic Law and Politics in Northern Nigeria*, 159.
101 Ibid., 154–160.
102 Oyediran, "Transition without End."
103 *Report of the Political Bureau* (1986), 2.
104 *West Africa*, July 2, 1987.
105 *Report of the Political Bureau*.
106 O. Vaughan, *Nigerian Chiefs*, especially chapter 9.
107 For a comprehensive analysis of economic and political liberalization under the Babangida regime, see Ihonvbere, *The Politics of Adjustment and Democracy*.
108 Mustapha, "Structural Adjustment and Agrarian Change in Nigeria."
109 Kenny, "Shari'a and Christianity in Nigeria."
110 Oba, "Islamic Law as Customary Law," 831–832.
111 Essien, "The Jurisdiction of State High Courts in Nigeria," 271.
112 Kenny, "Shari'a and Christianity in Nigeria."
113 Emekwue, *Democracy and Religion*.
114 Amnesty International, *Nigeria*.
115 Paden, "Islam and Democratic Federalism in Nigeria," 1–10.
116 Ibid.
117 Ostien, *A Study of the Court Systems of Northern Nigeria*.
118 In recognition of the annulled June 12 presidential election that would have ushered in Nigeria's third democratic system, "The Third Republic," Nigerian political analysts generally referred to the post-Abacha constitutional democratic period as

the Fourth Republic. The aborted democratic transition that would have ushered in the Abiola presidency is placed in the chronology of Nigerian political history as a historic moment in the country's constitutional democratic system.

CHAPTER 6: RELIGIOUS REVIVAL AND THE STATE:
THE RISE OF PENTECOSTALISM

1   Olupona, "The Changing Face of African Christianity," 181.
2   Wariboko, *Nigerian Pentecostalism*.
3   Marshall, "Power in the Name of Jesus."
4   Wariboko, *Nigerian Pentecostalism*.
5   For a detailed analysis see Kalu, Wariboko, and Falola, *African Pentecostalism*.
6   For a detailed analysis see Marshall, *Political Spiritualities*.
7   Sanneh, *The Crown and the Turban*.
8   Ilesanmi, "From Periphery to Center," 1.
9   Marshall, *Political Spiritualities*, 68.
10 Kalu, "Pentecostalism and Mission in Africa," 283.
11 Ibid., 284.
12 Ibid.
13 Marshall, *Political Spiritualities*, 103–104.
14 See Marshall-Fratani, "Mediating the Global and the Local in Nigerian Pentecostalism," 278–315.
15 Marshall, *Political Spiritualities*, 110–111.
16 Kalu, "Who Is Afraid of the Holy Ghost?," 88.
17 M. A. Ojo, "The Contextual Significance of Charismatic Movements in Independent Nigeria," 141.
18 Kalu, "Pentecostalism and Mission in Africa," 285.
19 Olupona, "The Changing Face of African Christianity," 182.
20 Ibid., 283–285.
21 Ibid., 285.
22 M. A. Ojo, "The Contextual Significance of Charismatic Movements in Independent Nigeria," 177.
23 Ibid., 182.
24 Ibid., 178.
25 Ibid., 187.
26 Kalu, "Pentecostalism and Mission in Africa," 285–286.
27 Ibid., 288.
28 M. A. Ojo, "The Contextual Significance of Charismatic Movements in Independent Nigeria," 69–71.
29 M. A. Ojo, "Deeper Christian Life Ministry," 152.
30 Kalu, "Pentecostalism and Mission in Africa."
31 thekingsparish.org/statementsoffaith.html, The Redeemed Christian Church of God, The King's Parish, Walthamstow, London E17 5QX. Accessed April 12, 2014.

32. Redeemed Christian Church of God, "Illustrating the Fundamental Beliefs in the Bible."
33. Ibid.
34. *Pentecostal (The Redeemed Christian Church of God) Doctrine*, Library of Congress.
35. Ayegboyin, "New Pentecostal Churches and Prosperity Theology in Nigeria," 158–160.
36. Ibid., 158.
37. Ibid., 157–158.
38. Marshall, *Political Spiritualities*, 81–82.
39. Wariboko, *Nigerian Pentecostalism*.
40. Ayegboyin, "New Pentecostal Churches and Prosperity Theology in Nigeria," 155–179.
41. Oyedepo, *On Eagle's Wings*, 175–228; see also *The Mandate*.
42. Oyedepo, *On Eagle's Wings*, 229–240.
43. Ibid., 185.
44. Hackett, "Is Satan Local or Global?," 111–131.
45. Ayegboyin, "New Pentecostal Churches and Prosperity Theology in Nigeria," 155–179.
46. Wariboko, *Nigerian Pentecostalism*.
47. Marshall-Fratani, "Mediating the Global and the Local in Nigerian Pentecostalism."
48. Kalu, "Black Joseph," 326–330.
49. Obadare, "Religious NGOs, Civil Society and the Quest for the Public Sphere in Nigeria," 148.
50. Kalu, "Holy Praiseco," 100–102.
51. Ibid.
52. Kalu, "Pentecostalism and Mission in Africa," 281–282.
53. Ibid.
54. Adogame, "Online for God," 224–235.
55. Ilesanmi, "From Periphery to Center," 3.
56. Asaju, "Globalization, Politicization of Religion, and Religious Networking," 183.
57. Marshall, *Political Spiritualities*, 215–218.
58. Asaju, "Globalization, Politicization of Religion, and Religious Networking," 187.
59. A. Anderson, "Globalization and Independent Pentecostals in Africa," 139.
60. Wariboko, *Nigerian Pentecostalism*.
61. Danfulani, "Globalization, Fundamentalism and the Pentecostal/Charismatic Movement in Nigeria," 47–48.
62. A. Anderson, "Globalization and Independent Pentecostals in Africa," 133–135.
63. Kalu, "African Pentecostalism in Global Perspective," 27.
64. Ibid., 7.
65. Marshall, *Political Spiritualities*, 53–54.
66. Kalu, "Holy Praiseco," 92–96.
67. Marshall, *Political Spiritualities*, 239–242.
68. Kalu, "Constructing a Global Pentecostal Discourse," 52.

69 Bateye, "Female Religious Leadership in Nigerian Pentecostalism," 214.
70 Larkin and Meyer, "Pentecostalism, Islam and Culture," 299–302.
71 Kalu, "Holy Praiseco," 104.
72 Marshall, *Political Spiritualities*, 225.
73 Kalu, "Pentecostalism and Mission in Africa," 291–293.
74 Obadare, "The Muslim Response to the Pentecostal Surge in Nigeria," 13.
75 For detailed analyses, see Kane, "Izala," 508; Larkin and Mayer, "Pentecostalism, Islam and Culture," 290.
76 Marshall, *Political Spiritualities*, 219.
77 Ibid., 13–14.
78 Lubeck, "Nigeria," 266.
79 Zeleza, "Africa and Its Diaspora." See also Larkin and Meyer, "Pentecostalism, Islam and Culture."
80 Zeleza, "Africa and Its Diaspora," 145.
81 Olupona, "The Changing Face of African Christianity," 183–184.
82 Held and McGrew, *Globalization/Anti-globalization*.
83 Ibid.; see also Scholte, "Defining Globalization."
84 A critical reading of the extensive scholarship on economic globalization and the global South is essential to developments on religion, state formation, and transnationalism in the age of globalization. World systems scholar Immanuel Wallerstein contends that globalization is another turning point in the crisis of global capital regardless of its unique qualities. As this crisis deepens, globalization provides new infrastructure for capitalism to reinvent itself so that it can reorder social relations at national and global levels. Nevertheless, most historical sociologists will agree that the phenomenon we now call globalization is integral to late capitalism. But what we are concerned with here is the most recent manifestation of globalization: the postwar variant that has its foundation in the quadrupling of the world economy before the global economic meltdown of 2007. For detailed analyses, see Wallerstein, "Contemporary Capitalist Dilemma." See also Vaughan, "Africa, Transnationalism, and Globalization," 17–37; Ilesanmi, "From Periphery to Center."
85 Wallerstein, "Contemporary Capitalist Dilemma."
86 Federici and Caffentzis, "Globalization and Professionalization in Africa."
87 Marshall-Fratani, "Mediating the Global and the Local in Nigerian Pentecostalism."
88 Ibid. The most successful Nigerian Pentecostal immigrant churches with worldwide reach are the RCCG (Redeemed Christian Church of God), Church of the Pentecost, Living Faith Worldwide (Winners' Chapel), Deeper Life, and Lighthouse. Many other Pentecostal churches, notably Kingsway International in London, Embassy of the Blessed Kingdom of God in the Ukraine, All Nations Church in Toronto, and the House of Praise in Toronto, also have had a great impact on Nigerian immigrant populations in many European and North American cities.
89 Larkin and Meyer, "Pentecostalism, Islam, and Culture," 292–295.
90 Olupona, "The Changing Face of African Christianity," 188.
91 Ibid.

92 For detailed analysis, see Miller, "E. A. Adeboye."
93 Olupona, "Globalization and African Immigrant Churches in America," 67–68.
94 Olupona and Gemignani, *African Immigrant Religions in America*.

CHAPTER 7: EXPANDED SHARIA: THE NORTHERN UMMAH AND THE FOURTH REPUBLIC

1 "Nigeria Will Lead World Back to God," *National Concord*, October 11, 1999.
2 "Zamfara Organizes Seminar for Royal Fathers on Shari'a," *New Nigerian*, February 9, 2000.
3 Lubeck, "Nigeria," 245.
4 "Niger Set to Send Sharia Bill to Assembly," *National Concord*, January 18, 2000.
5 Lubeck, "Nigeria," 253.
6 Rashid, *Islamic Law in Nigeria*.
7 For detailed discussion, see Jinadu, "Federalism, the Consociational State, and Ethnic Conflict in Nigeria," 71–100; see also Laitin, "The Sharia Debate and the Origins of Nigeria's Second Republic," 411–430.
8 Odinkalu and Civil Liberties Organisation, *Justice Denied*.
9 Ibid.
10 Ibid.
11 Rashid, *Islamic Law in Nigeria*.
12 Sambo, *Shari'a and Justice*.
13 Oba, "The Sharia Court of Appeal in Northern Nigeria," 900.
14 Ibid.
15 Ibid., 817–850.
16 Yusuf, *Nigerian Legal System*.
17 Oba, "The Sharia Court of Appeal in Northern Nigeria," 895.
18 Doi, "The Impact of English Law and Concepts on the Administration of Islamic Law in Nigeria," 25–56.
19 Sambo, *Shari'a and Justice*.
20 Yusuf, *Nigerian Legal System*.
21 Kukah, *Religion, Politics, and Power in Northern Nigeria*.
22 Ludwig, "Christian-Muslim Relations in Northern Nigeria since the Introduction of Shari'ah in 1999," 617.
23 "Winds against Shari'a's Soul," *National Concord*, July 14, 2000.
24 Gumi, *Where I Stand*, 127.
25 See Muhibbu-Din, *Shari'ah in a Multi-Faith Nigeria*.
26 *A Memorandum on the 1999 Constitution to the Government and National Assembly*.
27 Gusau, *A Case for Shari'ah in Nigeria*.
28 Harnischfeger, *Democratization and Islamic Law*, 224.
29 Not least chapter VII, part 2, article B, section 275 (1), which guarantees, "There shall be for any State that requires it a Sharia Court of Appeal." See *Constitution of Nigeria*, 1999.

30 Chapter I, part 2, section 10 states, "The Government of the Federation or of a State shall not adopt any religion as State Religion." See *Constitution of Nigeria*, 1999.
31 Oba, "Islamic Law as Customary Law," 817–850.
32 Edu et al., *The Sharia Issue: Working Papers for a Dialogue*.
33 Harnischfeger, *Democratization and Islamic Law*, 13.
34 Kenny, "Shari'a and Christianity in Nigeria," 338–364.
35 Byang, *Shari'a in Nigeria*.
36 "The Way Forward," *National Concord*, May 5, 2000.
37 Durham, "Nigeria's 'State Religion' Question in Comparative Perspective," 145.
38 Hackett, "Rethinking the Role of Religion in the Public Sphere," 86–89.
39 Sanusi, "The West and the Rest," 257.
40 "Pending Cases in Zamfara to Be Heard in Shari'a Courts," *National Concord*, January 17, 2000.
41 There is substantial constitutional evidence for such an argument, particularly in chapter VII, part 2, article B, section 277 (1) of the Nigerian Constitution, which reads in part, "The Sharia Court of Appeal of a State shall, in addition to such other jurisdiction as may be conferred upon it by the law of the State, exercise such appellate and supervisory jurisdiction in civil proceedings involving questions of Islamic personal Law which the court is competent to decide." See *Constitution of Nigeria*, 1999; see also Edu et al., *The Sharia Issue: Working Papers for a Dialogue*.
42 Edu et al., *The Sharia Issue: Working Papers for a Dialogue*.
43 Ibid.
44 Essien, "The Jurisdiction of State High Courts in Nigeria," 264.
45 Edu et al., *The Sharia Issue: Working Papers for a Dialogue*.
46 *Constitution of Nigeria*, 1999.
47 Ado-Kurawa, *Shari'ah and the Press in Nigeria*.
48 *Constitution of Nigeria*, 1999.
49 "Core North Has a Right to Shari'a Law—Speaker," *New Nigerian*, February 2000.
50 Edu et al., *The Sharia Issue: Working Papers for a Dialogue*.
51 Nasir, "Women's Human Rights in Secular and Religious Legal System."
52 Harnischfeger, *Democratization and Islamic Law*, 15.
53 Ibid., 89–93.
54 Ibid., 174–178.
55 For example, the subject of citizen's economic rights is defined in chapter II, section 16 of the Constitution, part of which asserts that "the state shall ... without prejudice to the right of any person to participate in areas of the economy within the major sector of the economy, protect the right of every citizen to engage in any economic activities," and section 17, which reads in part, "The State shall direct its policy toward ensuring that ... all citizens, without discrimination on any group whatsoever, have the opportunity for securing adequate means of livelihood." See Nwobi, *Sharia in Nigeria*.

56 Nwobi contends that this would violate chapter IV, section 41 (1) of the Constitution: "Every citizen of Nigeria is entitled to move freely throughout Nigeria and to reside in any part thereof." See *Constitution of Nigeria*, 1999; see ibid.

57 Chapter IV, section 38 (1) of the 1999 Constitution reads in part, "Every person shall be entitled to freedom of thought, conscience, and religion, including freedom to change his religion or belief." See *Constitution of Nigeria*, 1999.

58 Quoted in Ludwig, "Christian-Muslim Relations in Northern Nigeria since the Introduction of Shari'ah in 1999," 613–614.

59 Section 38 (3) of the 1999 Constitution notes: "No religious community or denomination shall be prevented from providing religious instruction for pupils of that community or denomination in any place of education maintained wholly by that community or denomination." See *Constitution of Nigeria*, 1999.

60 Odinkalu and Civil Liberties Organisation, *Justice Denied*, 1992.

61 Legislative provisions among the twelve Northern states varied from state to state, with sharia courts in each state having their own distinct characteristics. However, these provisions in all twelve Northern states include the creation of sharia courts, the enactment of a penal code based on Islamic law, and the expansion of the jurisdiction of the Sharia Court of Appeal. In all of these states, sharia courts replaced the old area courts as courts of first instance in Islamic legal matters. Now under the supervision of the grand qadi, the courts have jurisdiction in criminal cases on all matters involving Muslims; in civil cases, sharia courts have jurisdiction on Muslims as well as on consenting non-Muslims. Appeals in sharia courts of first instance could only be adjudicated in superior sharia courts, with ultimate appeals only to the Sharia Court of Appeal. Significantly, the Sharia Court of Appeal for the first time since its creation now has jurisdiction in criminal cases. See Oba, "The Sharia Court of Appeal in Northern Nigeria," 883–884.

62 Yesufu, *World Inter-Religious Crisis*, especially chapter 2.

63 Ado-Kurawa, *Shari'ah and the Press in Nigeria*, 2000.

64 Oba, "Islamic Law as Customary Law," 819.

65 Ado-Kurawa, *Shari'ah and the Press in Nigeria*.

66 Oba, "Islamic Law as Customary Law," 820.

67 Ado-Kurawa, *Shari'ah and the Press in Nigeria*.

68 Oba, "Islamic Law as Customary Law."

69 Ladan, "Women's Rights and Access to Justice under Sharia in Northern Nigeria."

70 Oba, "Islamic Law as Customary Law," 822.

71 Ado-Kurawa, *Shari'ah and the Press in Nigeria*.

72 Oba, "Islamic Law as Customary Law."

73 Mahmud, *Notes on Islamic Civil Law Procedure*, 1–14.

74 Bello, "Sharia and the Constitution."

75 Oba, "The Sharia Court of Appeal in Northern Nigeria," 892.

76 Larémont, *Islamic Law and Politics in Northern Nigeria*, 211–216.

77 Lubeck, "Nigeria."

78 *Kaduna State Shari'ah Penal Code*, 2001.

79 "The Meaning of Prophethood, Messengership, and Sainthood," *New Nigerian*, February 4, 2000.
80 "Bauchi Moves to Adopt Shari'a," *National Concord*, October 25, 1999.
81 "The Right Belief Is Based on Shari'a," *New Nigerian*, January 21, 2000.
82 Callaway and Creevey, *The Heritage of Islam*.
83 Last, "The Search for Security in Muslim Northern Nigeria," 47.
84 Ibid., 60.
85 Ibid., 58.
86 Kendhammer, "Muslims Talking Politics," 13.
87 "National Shari'a Seminar Opens Today," *New Nigerian*, February 11, 2000.
88 Justice Mohammed Bello, GCON, CON, "Shari'a and the Constitution," *New Nigerian*, February 15, 2000.
89 See Edu et al., *The Sharia Issue: Working Papers for a Dialogue*.
90 Sulu Gambari, "Understanding Shari'a Law," *New Nigerian*, February 16, 2000.
91 "Violence Erupts in Sokoto," *National Concord*, March 8, 2000.
92 "Governor Mu'azu, a Word on Shari'a," *New Nigerian*, February 16, 2000.
93 Typescript of interview on BBC News Program *HardTalk* with Sule Lamido, November 12, 2000.
94 Ludwig, "Christian-Muslim Relations in Northern Nigeria since the Introduction of Shari'ah in 1999," 611.
95 "Sharia Implications for Nigeria," *National Concord*, February 2, 2000.
96 *New Nigerian*, January 30, 2000.
97 "Sharia Implications for Nigeria," *National Concord*, February 2, 2000.
98 A. Bello Alkali, "The Zamfara Initiative," *New Nigerian*, January 4, 2000.
99 Bello Adamu Sakkwato, "Shari'a in Zamfara: Problems and Prospects," *New Nigerian*, January 5, 2000.
100 Danlami M. B. Takko, "Governor Mu'azu, a Word on Shari'a," *New Nigerian*, February 16, 2000.
101 "Ugly Face of Contradiction," *New Nigerian*, January 12, 2000.
102 "We Didn't Suspend Sharia," *National Concord*, March 3, 2000.
103 "Ugly Face of Contradiction," *New Nigerian*, January 12, 2000.
104 "Shari'ah," *New Nigerian*, January 3, 2000.
105 "Govt Will Not Hesitate to Implement Shari'a," *National Concord*, December 12, 1999.
106 Ado-Kurawa, *Shari'ah and the Press in Nigeria*.
107 See Muhibbu-Din, *Shari'ah in a Multi-Faith Nigeria*; see also *A Memorandum on the 1999 Constitution to the Government and National Assembly* (2000).
108 "Understanding Shari'a Law," *New Nigerian*, February 16, 2000.
109 Gumi, *Where I Stand*, 79.
110 Harnischfeger, "Sharia and Control over Territory," 438.
111 Ladan, "Women's Rights and Access to Justice under Sharia in Northern Nigeria."
112 Lubeck, "Nigeria," 269.
113 Ibrahim, *Shari'ah and Muslims in Nigeria*.
114 "Shari'a in the North: Fear of the Unknown," *New Nigerian*, February 27, 2000.
115 "Governor Mu'azu, a Word on Shari'a," *New Nigerian*, February 16, 2000.

116 "It's the Key to Nigeria's Salvation—Shari'a Implementation Committee Member," *Weekend Concord*, July 1, 2000.
117 "We're Not against Shari'a," *New Nigerian*, January 30, 2000.
118 "Shari'a in Zamfara: Problems and Prospects," *New Nigerian*, January 5, 2000.
119 Sambo, *Shari'a and Justice*.
120 Sulaiman, in Rashid, *Islamic Law in Nigeria*.
121 "Jalo Wants Hashidu to Introduce Shari'a," *New Nigerian*, January 3, 2000.
122 "Zamfara Governor Hailed over Shari'a," *New Nigerian*, January 3, 2000.
123 "In Search of a Peaceful Society," *National Concord*, June 30, 2000.
124 "Shari'a Committee in Kaduna Hailed," *New Nigerian*, January 25, 2000.
125 "In Zamfara, Tension over Shari'a," *National Concord*, October 21, 1999.
126 "Adegbite Sheds More Light on Shari'a," *New Nigerian*, February 1, 2000; see also "Sharia: No State Can Be Declared Islamic, Says Adegbite," *National Concord*, January 31, 2000.
127 *New Nigerian*, February 1, 2000.
128 "Northern States Embrace Ban on Alcohol," *National Concord*, September 1, 1999.
129 See Musa, *Shari'ah in a Multi-Faith Nigeria*.
130 "Zamfara Retains NYSC Members," *National Concord*, January 25, 2000.
131 Ado-Kurawa, *Shari'ah and the Press in Nigeria*.
132 Gurin, *The Concept of Honesty in Islam*.
133 Sambo, *Shari'a and Justice*.
134 "Katsina Islamic Foundation: Islamic University Project," *New Nigerian*, January 5, 2000.
135 "Workers Donate 5% of Salaries to Islamic University," *National Concord*, March 6, 2000.
136 Ado-Kurawa, *Shari'ah and the Press in Nigeria*.
137 Sambo, *Shari'a and Justice*.
138 "Shari'a in the North: Fear of the Unknown," *New Nigerian*, February 27, 2000.
139 "Sharia Not Aimed at Obasanjo," *Sunday Concord*, July 23, 2000.
140 "Shari'a: No State Can be Declared Islamic, Says Adegbite," *National Concord*, January 31, 2000.
141 Abdul-Gaffar, "The Noise on Sharia," *National Concord*, October 29, 1999.
142 "Muslims Urged to Defend Islam," *National Concord*, June 14, 2000.
143 Yusuf, *World Inter-Religious Crisis*.
144 See Muhibbu-Din, *Shari'ah in a Multi-Faith Nigeria*.
145 Mohammed, Adamu, and Abba, *Human Living Conditions and Reforms of Legal Systems*.
146 Tayob, "The Demand for Shari'ah in African Democratisation Processes," 45.
147 "Towards a Northern Renaissance," *New Nigerian*, January 30, 2000.
148 "The Way Forward," *National Concord*, May 5, 2000.
149 "We Need One Party State," *National Concord*, August 2, 1999.
150 "Governor Mu'azu, a Word on Shari'a," *New Nigerian*, February 16, 2000; see also "Give Shari'a a Chance," *New Nigerian*, February 8, 2000.
151 "Of Elders Fora and the North," *New Nigerian*, February 21, 2000.

152. "Shari'a: Days of Rage, Blood, and Death in Kaduna," *Weekend Concord*, February 25, 2000.
153. "More People Flee Kaduna . . . Students Vacate Campuses . . . Soldiers Drafted to Kano," *Sunday Concord*, February 27, 2000.
154. "Shari'a: From Zamfara to Kaduna," *Weekend Concord*, February 26, 2000.
155. "Community Leaders Alert on Imminent Religious Violence," *National Concord*, April 10, 2000.
156. "No Religious Crisis in Iwo—Muslim Youths Declare," *National Concord*, July 8, 2000.
157. "Zamfara Governor Hailed over Shari'a," *New Nigerian*, January 3, 2000.
158. "Zamfara Organizes Seminar for Royal Fathers on Shari'a," *New Nigerian*, February 9, 2000.
159. Ludwig, "Christian-Muslim Relations in Northern Nigeria since the Introduction of Shari'ah in 1999," 610.
160. *National Concord*, June 6, 2000.
161. Muhammadu Sanusi Garba, "Unnecessary Fears of the Shari'a" (editorial), *New Nigerian*, January 6, 2000.
162. Ado-Kurawa, *Shari'ah and the Press in Nigeria*.
163. Paden, "Islam and Democratic Federalism in Nigeria," 1–10.
164. "Obasanjo Worried over Shari'a," *National Concord*, October 18, 1999.
165. David, "Islamic Law May Spread in Nigeria."
166. Bello Adamu Sakkwato, "Shari'a in Zamfara: Problems and Prospects," *New Nigerian*, January 5, 2000.
167. "Kwara Muslims Allege Arms Importation," *New Nigerian*, January 5, 2000.

CHAPTER 8: EXPANDED SHARIA: RESISTANCE, VIOLENCE, AND RECONCILIATION

1. "Okogie, Others React to Adoption of Shari'a," *National Concord*, October 18, 1999.
2. Ibid.
3. "Sharia Implications for Nigeria," *National Concord*, March 3, 2000.
4. Edu et al., *The Sharia Issue: Working Papers for a Dialogue*.
5. Craig Keener, "Mutual Mayhem: A Plea for Peace and Truth in the Madness of Nigeria," *Christianity Today*, November 2004.
6. *Weekend Concord*, February 26, 2000.
7. "Religious Leaders and Violence," *Weekend Concord*, March 4, 2000.
8. "Sharia: Our Stand," *National Concord*, March 10, 2000.
9. "Peace and Stability in Kaduna State," *National Concord*, May 30, 2000.
10. Harnischfeger, "Sharia and Control over Territory," 431.
11. Adigwe, "Nigeria Joins the Organization of Islamic Conference, O.I.C."
12. Ngban, *Is Shari'ah the Law of God?*
13. Harunah, *Shari'ah under Western Democracy in Contemporary Nigeria*.
14. William Wallis, "Sharia Debate Reignites Violence in Nigeria," *Christian Science Monitor*, May 26, 2000.

15 Byang, *Shari'a in Nigeria*.
16 Debki, *The Tragedy of Sharia: Cry and the Voice of Masses*.
17 "Spiritual War over Obasanjo," *Weekend Concord*, September 25, 1999.
18 "CAN Dismisses Kure's Claim," *New Nigerian*, January 23, 2000.
19 "Clergyman Sues for Peace over Shari'a," *Sunday Concord*, June 25, 2000.
20 "Shari'a Will Fail," *National Concord*, January 26, 2000.
21 "Shari'a Will Lead to Confusion," *National Concord*, October 26, 1999.
22 "Shari'a: Why Christian Leaders Are Worried," *Weekend Concord*, October 23, 1999.
23 "Shari'a: Why the Opposition?," *New Nigerian*, January 3, 2000.
24 "The Two Nigerias," *National Concord*, January 21, 2000.
25 "Zamfara Plans to Sponsor Shari'a in S-West, East," *National Concord*, February 17, 2000.
26 "Human Rights and Shari'a in Nigeria," *National Concord*, June 15, 2000.
27 "Shari'a: Why Christian Leaders Are Worried," *Weekend Concord*, October 23, 1999.
28 "Kaduna Shari'a Panel in Dilemma," *New Nigerian*, February 25, 2000.
29 "Shari'a: Days of Rage, Blood, and Death in Kaduna," *Weekend Concord*, February 26, 2000.
30 "More People Flee Kaduna... Students Vacate Campuses... Soldiers Drafted to Kano," *Sunday Concord*, February 27, 2000.
31 "Fear Grips Kano as Death Toll Hits 400 in Kaduna; Britain Forewarned FG, U.S. Worried; Criminal Part of Shari'a Unconstitutional," *National Concord*, February 26, 2000.
32 "100 Killed... As Kaduna Riot Rages—Commissioner Missing," *National Concord*, May 24, 2000.
33 "Kaduna Riot Toll Hits 300: 1,000 Houses Burnt; Presidency Summons Governor," *National Concord*, May 25, 2000. In February 2000, a peaceful protest in Kaduna State had escalated into widespread killings. Anti-sharia activist Bee Debki provides a summary of the human toll and suffering that resulted. Specifically, she claimed that Muslims torched churches and escalated the crisis in Rigasa; killed Christian minorities in Tudun Wada; looted properties and burned houses including a Baptist Theological Seminary in Kawo; killed a pastor in Kwaru/Badarawa; were repelled by strong Christian resistance in Sabo after a fierce struggle; killed Christians in Kachia; burned a church in Barnawa. Debki's list indicates the extent of the violence in Kaduna State; corroborating reports putting the death toll in Kaduna State at about two thousand. Thousands of Christian students from Southern and Middle Belt states studying at Ahmadu Bello University, Zaria, the Federal College of Education, and Kaduna State Polytechnic fled en masse from the state. For detailed discussion, see Debki, *The Tragedy of Sharia*.
34 "Kaduna Riot: A Refugee's Story," *National Concord*, March 6, 2000.
35 "CAN Pleads with Riot Victims," *National Concord*, March 6, 2000.
36 "Shari'a, a Monstrous Spoiler?," *National Concord*, July 24, 2000.

37 Ngban, *Is Shari'ah the Law of God?*
38 Debki, *The Tragedy of Sharia*.
39 "Zamfara Government Is Neglecting Development," *National Concord*, February 7, 2000.
40 "Shari'a: Reversion to Primitivity," *National Concord*, January 27, 2000.
41 "Shari'a: Why Christian Leaders Are Worried," *Weekend Concord*, October 23, 1999; "Shari'a, an Attempt to Destabilize Civil Rule," *National Concord*, October 20, 1999.
42 "Christians, Muslims at Loggerheads over Shari'a in Niger," *National Concord*, January 17, 2000.
43 "Tension in Kano . . . over Shari'a," *National Concord*, January 15, 2000.
44 "Christians Not Opposed to Shari'a for Muslims," *National Concord*, April 18, 2000.
45 Nigerian federal and state governments have long subsidized the country's two world religions, especially through the extensive funding of religious-based educational institutions, health institutions, and annual pilgrimages to Mecca and Jerusalem.
46 *Africa Confidential*, July 12, 2002.
47 "Church Leaders Hit Zamfara Governor over Shari'a, Say: 'It Is a Decision from Hell!,'" *Weekend Concord*, October 30, 1999; "Cleric Advises Obasanjo on Shari'a," *National Concord*, October 19, 1999.
48 "Shari'a Riots: Cleric Lambasts Senate, Governors," *National Concord*, November 2, 1999.
49 Lubeck, "Nigeria," 265–266.
50 "Archbishop Visits Zamfara," BBC, February 3, 2001, http://news.bbc.co.uk/2/hi/africa/1152031.stm.
51 For example, Southern notables such as Lam Andesina, AD governor of Oyo State; Professor B. O. Nwabueze, leader of Ndigbo, the preeminent Igbo interest group; Kayode Eso, former justice of the Supreme Court; and prodemocracy activist Arthur Nwankwo strongly denounced expanded sharia. See *National Concord*, July 10, 2000.
52 "Kaduna Riots Planned in Kano," *National Concord*, April 17, 2000.
53 "Sharia: Obasanjo Has Failed Nigeria," *Weekend Concord*, July 15, 2000; "Winds against Sharia's Soul," *National Concord*, July 14, 2000; "Let Sharia States Have Their Ways," *Sunday Concord*, July 16, 2000.
54 "Sharia Scare: Banks May Pull Out of Zamfara," *National Concord*, October 26, 1999.
55 Ludwig, "Christian-Muslim Relations in Northern Nigeria since the Introduction of Shari'ah in 1999," 615.
56 Ibid., 631–632.
57 "Shari'a: Why Christian Leaders Are Worried," *Weekend Concord*, October 23, 1999.
58 "Shari'a Takes Off in Zamfara," *New Nigerian*, January 23, 2000; see also "Sokoto Backs Down on Shari'a," *National Concord*, January 17, 2000.

59 "Alcohol Consumers Beat Shari'a ... Take Liquor out of Cellophane Bags," *National Concord*, July 31, 2000.
60 "First Week of Shari'a in Zamfara," *Weekend Concord*, February 5, 2000. One writer reported no noticeable drop in crime or corruption in sharia states. See Jessi Herman, "A Divided Nigeria," Institute for Global Engagement, November 30, 2001, http://www.globalengage.org.
61 "Shariacracy on Trial."
62 Harnischfeger, *Democratization and Islamic Law*, 29.
63 Ibid., 124–126.
64 "Nigerian Bishops Decry Adoption of Shari'a Law," *National Catholic Reporter*, October 4, 2002.
65 Harnischfeger, *Democratization and Islamic Law*, 128–184.
66 "Shari'a for the Abachas," *Weekend Concord*, July 22, 2000.
67 "Apply Shari'a on Muslims Only," *New Nigerian*, February 2, 2000.
68 Nwobi, *Sharia in Nigeria*.
69 Shehu, *Sharia*.
70 Ludwig, "Christian-Muslim Relations in Northern Nigeria since the Introduction of Shari'ah in 1999," 612–613.
71 "Xtians, Moslems at Loggerheads over Shari'a in Niger," *National Concord*, January 17, 2000.
72 "Sharia Implications for Nigeria," *National Concord*, March 1, 2000.
73 Ludwig, "Christian-Muslim Relations in Northern Nigeria since the Introduction of Shari'ah in 1999," 621–631.
74 Herman, "A Divided Nigeria."
75 Richard Dowden, "Death by Stoning," *New York Times Magazine*, January 27, 2002.
76 Ludwig, "Christian-Muslim Relations in Northern Nigeria since the Introduction of Shari'ah in 1999," 630.
77 Obed Minchakpu with Compass Direct, "Islamic Law Raises Tensions," *Christianity Today*, January 10, 2000.
78 "Sharia Implications for Nigeria," *National Concord*, February 29, 2000.
79 "Human Rights and Shari'a in Nigeria," *National Concord*, June 12, 2000.
80 "Lessons from the Kaduna Tragedy," *Sunday Concord*, April 2, 2000.
81 "Many Ills of the Almajiri System," *New Nigerian*, January 25, 2000.
82 Awofeso, Ritchie, and Degeling, "The Almajiri Heritage and the Threat of Non-State Terrorism in Northern Nigeria," 311–325.
83 Ibid., 315–325.
84 "Almajiris Harass Poly Girl over Shari'a," *National Concord*, July 10, 2000.
85 "Many Ills of the Almajiri System," *New Nigerian*, January 25, 2000.
86 *National Concord*, April 7, 2000.
87 "Of NYSC Members and Shari'a States," *Sunday Concord*, July 16, 2000.
88 "Zamfara Retains NYSC Members," *National Concord*, January 25, 2000.
89 Lubeck, Lipshutz, and Weeks, "The Globality of Islam."
90 "A Harvest of Crises and Ethnic Conflicts," *Sunday Concord*, May 28, 2000.
91 "Of Elders Fora and the North," *New Nigerian*, February 21, 2000.

92 For example, this was expressed in the strong opposition of conservatives, led by Archbishop Akinola, to the ordination of Bishop Gene Robinson, a gay American Episcopalian priest from New Hampshire.
93 Mindy Belz, "Daniels of the Year," *World*, December 16, 2006.
94 "Archbishop Visits Zamfara," February 3, 2001, BBC News, http://news.bbc.co.uk/2/low/africa.1152031.stm. This disconnect was further reflected five years later when Pope Benedict referenced a fourteenth-century Byzantine emperor's negative comment about the Prophet Muhammad. Against the backdrop of September 11, 2001, attacks in the United States and the "global war on terror," his speech incited Muslim mobs to attack Christians in Northern Nigerian cities. Elsewhere, riots raged over the killing of Palestinian leaders by the Israeli army and the American treatment of Iraqi prisoners.
95 "Sharia: Implications for Nigeria (5)," *National Concord*, March 6, 2000.
96 "Emirs Summon Zamfara Gov over Amputation," *National Concord*, April 3, 2000.
97 "Shari'a and Women's Rights," *Weekend Concord*, May 20, 2000.
98 "Regional Reports," *World Press Review*, May 2000.
99 Harnischfeger, *Democratization and Islamic Law*, 205–210.
100 Auwalu Yaduda, "Issues on Constitutional Amendments (III)," *New Nigerian*, February 15, 2000.
101 "Sokoto Backs Down on Shari'a," *National Concord*, January 17, 2000.
102 "Human Rights and Islamic Concept," *National Concord*, August 17, 1999; "Press Conference Addressed by Citizen's League for Peace and Democracy on the Kaduna Crisis," March 30, 2000, Library of Congress.
103 "Yobe Raises Committees on Shari'a," *New Nigerian*, January 3, 2000.
104 "Xtians Not Opposed to Shari'a for Muslims," *National Concord*, April 18, 2000.
105 See Laitin, *Hegemony and Culture*.
106 "Deep Political and Religious Rifts Disrupt the Harmony of Nigerian Towns," *New York Times*, March 26, 2000.
107 Ibid.
108 "Accountability in Islam: Societal Action," *National Concord*, April 14, 2000.
109 "Nigeria: In God's Name," *Africa Confidential*, March 3, 2000.
110 "Restraint on Shari'a," *National Concord*, April 27, 2000.
111 "LIFE: Building Bridges across Religious Divide," *National Concord*, May 23, 2000.
112 "Obasanjo Sued over Shari'a," *New Nigerian*, March 2, 2000.
113 "Inter-Religious Council to End Ethnic Clashes," *New Nigerian*, January 21, 2000.
114 Edu et al., *The Sharia Issue: Working Papers for a Dialogue*.
115 "Day Muslims and Christians Stormed Seminary for Shari," *Weekend Concord*, May 7, 2000.
116 Edu et al., *The Sharia Issue: Working Papers for a Dialogue*.
117 "Nigerians Urged to Embrace Religious Harmony," *National Concord*, April 10, 2000.

118. "Religious Attacks: CAN Cautions Members against Retaliating," *National Concord*, March 12, 2000.
119. "Muslims Not Your Enemies," *National Concord*, March 6, 2000.
120. "Fawehinmi Advocates National Confab over Kaduna Riot," *National Concord*, February 25, 2000.
121. "The Fear of Fear and Political Disequilibrium," *Weekend Concord*, April 15, 2000.
122. "Shari'a Scare: Banks May Pull Out of Zamfara," *National Concord*, October 26, 1999.
123. "Christians Kick against New Law in Zamfara," *Sunday Concord*, July 30, 2000.
124. "More People Flee Kaduna ... Students Vacate Campuses ... Soldiers Drafted to Kano," *Sunday Concord*, February 27, 2000.
125. "Shari'a Riot: Churches to Sue PDP, Others," *National Concord*, May 1, 2000.
126. "Sharia Riots: Shame of a Nation," *Weekend Concord*, March 11, 2000. Indeed, other religious riots in Jos in September 2001 left the people of Nigeria's principal Middle Belt city emotionally broken and property worth millions of dollars destroyed in 2001.
127. *National Concord*, August 19, 1999.
128. "Bauchi Backs Down on Shari'a," *Sunday Concord*, July 23, 2000.
129. "Sokoto Backs Down on Shari'a," *National Concord*, January 19, 2000.

CHAPTER 9: SHARIA POLITICS, OBASANJO'S PDP FEDERAL GOVERNMENT, AND THE 1999 CONSTITUTION

1. "Obasanjo's Action Too Little, Too Late," *Weekend Concord*, March 2, 2000.
2. "Shari'a May Bomb Nigeria Out of Existence," *Weekend Concord*, February 26, 2000.
3. "Kaduna Mayhem: Beginning of the Beginning," *National Concord*, February 28, 2000.
4. "Shari'a Riots: Cleric Lambasts Senate, Governors," *National Concord*, March 2, 2008.
5. "Obasanjo Sued over Shari'a," *New Nigerian*, March 2, 2000.
6. "Cleric Warns against Killing of Igbos," *National Concord*, March 8, 2000.
7. Ibid.
8. "Clergyman Sues for Peace over Shari'a," *Sunday Concord*, June 25, 2000.
9. "Shari'a: Obasanjo Has Failed Nigeria," *Weekend Concord*, July 15, 2000.
10. "Shari'a: That Fear of the Supreme Court," *Weekend Concord*, April 1, 2000.
11. Last, "The Search for Security in Muslim Northern Nigeria," 59.
12. Harnischfeger, *Democratization and Islamic Law*, 107.
13. "Shariacracy on Trial."
14. "Deep Political and Religious Rifts Disrupt the Harmony of Nigerian Towns," *New York Times*, March 26, 2000.
15. "Shari'a and the Constitution," *New Nigerian*, February 15, 2000.
16. "Islamic Law Raises Tensions," *Christianity Today*, January 20, 2000.
17. Nasir, "Women's Human Rights in Secular and Religious Legal System."

18 Oba, "The Sharia Court of Appeal in Northern Nigeria," 895.
19 "Understanding Shari'a Law," *New Nigerian*, February 18, 2000.
20 Ibrahim Suleiman, *Nigerian Sunday Triumph*, April 24, 1986, quoted in Hunwick, "An African Case Study of Political Islam," 150.
21 Laitin, "The Sharia Debate and the Origins of Nigeria's Second Republic," 419.
22 Nmehielle, "Sharia Law in the Northern States of Nigeria."
23 Ibid., 749.
24 Ibid., 750.
25 Ibid., 739–740.
26 "Female Workers in Zamfara," *National Concord*, January 10, 2000.
27 "Sharia: Implications for Nigeria," *National Concord*, March 6, 2000.
28 Callaway, *Muslim Hausa Women in Nigeria*.
29 Callaway and Creevey, *The Heritage of Islam*.
30 Mack, "Muslim Women's Knowledge Production in the Greater Maghreb."
31 McGarvey, *Muslim and Christian Women in Dialogue*, 93–94.
32 Vaughan and Banu, "Muslim Women's Rights in Northern Nigeria," 1–7.
33 Ibid.
34 Callaway, *Muslim Hausa Women in Nigeria*.
35 Ibid.
36 Paden, "Islam and Democratic Federalism in Nigeria."
37 Callaway and Creevey, *The Heritage of Islam*.
38 Callaway, *Muslim Hausa Women in Nigeria*.
39 Lubeck, "Nigeria," 272.
40 Harunah, *Shari'ah under Western Democracy in Contemporary Nigeria*.
41 Lubeck, "Nigeria," 270.
42 Nana Asm'u, Usman dan Fodio's daughter, is a central figure for scholars and activists who insist on the agency of Muslim women in the Sokoto Caliphate. Beverly Mack's work is an exemplar on this important subject. Through the remarkable works of Nana Asm'u, Mack notes that some women contributed to education in Northern Muslim communities in ways that are not often associated with them after the Sokoto Jihad. Mack's works are important for those who argue against the notion that sharia in Northern Muslim communities renders women helpless. For detailed analysis, see Mack, "Muslim Women's Knowledge Production in the Greater Maghreb."
43 For example, Margot Badren's critical reading of scriptural text, especially the Quran and Hadith, insists on the agency of Muslim women in emirate society. See Badren, "Sharia Activism and Zina in Nigeria in the Era of Hudud."
44 Behrouz, "Transforming Islamic Family Law."
45 "Sharia: Staccato of Extreme Views in the Hour of National Grief," *Sunday Concord*, March 5, 2000.
46 "Sharia Riots Worst Bloodletting since Civil War: Obasanjo Broadcast," *National Concord*, March 2, 2000.
47 "Zamfara, Kano Insist on Sharia," *National Concord*, March 2, 2000.
48 "Borno Split over Sharia," *National Concord*, March 15, 2000.
49 "Lesson from Zamfara Amputation," *Sunday Concord*, April 7, 2000.

50. "Spiritual War over Obasanjo . . . to Abort His Mission," *Weekend Concord*, September 25, 1999.
51. Obadare, "Pentecostal Presidency?," 669.
52. "Sectarian Crises: Abaria Begins Prayer Crusade to Free Nigeria," *National Concord*, March 21, 2000.
53. "Obasanjo's Handling of Shari'a Perfect," *Weekend Concord*, April 22, 2000.
54. Ibid.
55. *The State of the Nation* 2, no. 2 (March 2000).
56. "Shari'a Bill," *National Concord*, April 20, 2000.
57. "Sharia: Ex-Head of State Indicted," *Sunday Concord*, March 12, 2000.
58. "Sovereign National Conference Now," *Sunday Concord*, March 12, 2000.
59. "Shari'a Bill," *National Concord*, April 20, 2000.
60. "Shari'a Will Crumble," *National Concord*, July 3, 2000.
61. "Kaduna Riots Planned in Kano," *National Concord*, April 17, 2000.
62. Debki, *The Tragedy of Sharia*.
63. Nwobi, *Sharia in Nigeria*.
64. Shehu, *Sharia*.
65. Emekwue, *Democracy and Religion*.
66. "Shari'a Declaration Amounts to Secession," *New Nigerian*, February 2, 2000.
67. "Violence Erupts in Sokoto," *National Concord*, March 8, 2000.
68. "Kaduna Riots Planned in Kano," *National Concord*, April 17, 2000.
69. "Never Again Shall North Dominate Middle-Belt," *Weekend Concord*, June 3, 2000.
70. Ludwig, "Christian-Muslim Relations in Northern Nigeria since the Introduction of Shari'ah in 1999," 617.
71. Harnischfeger, "Sharia and Control over Territory," 451–452.
72. "Sharia: Ex-Head of State Indicted," *Sunday Concord*, March 12, 2000.
73. Essien, "The Jurisdiction of State High Courts in Nigeria," 265.
74. Gumi, *Where I Stand*, 120.
75. Hills, "Policing a Plurality of Worlds," 49.
76. Ludwig, "Christian-Muslim Relations in Northern Nigeria since the Introduction of Shari'ah in 1999," 603.
77. Harnischfeger, "Sharia and Control over Territory," 446.
78. Norimitsu Onishi, "Nigeria Army Said to Massacre Hundreds of Civilians," *New York Times*, October 30, 2001.
79. Obed Minchakpu, "Muslim Youths Destroy 10 Nigerian Churches," *Compass Direct News*, 2002.
80. "Nigeria Miss World Strife Goes On," *CNN News*, November 27, 2002.
81. "Reports on Ethnic Relations."
82. *This Day*, November 2002.
83. "Analysis: Nigeria's Shari'a Split," *BBC News*, January 7, 2003, http://news.bbc.co.uk/2/hi/africa/2632939.stm, accessed April 2009.
84. Mike Crawley, "Two Men Create Bridge over Nigeria's Troubled Waters," *Christian Science Monitor*, February 28, 2003.

85 Ludwig, "Christian-Muslim Relations in Northern Nigeria since the Introduction of Shari'ah in 1999," 618–619.
86 "Revenge in the Name of Religion."
87 Ibid.
88 Obed Minchakpu, "Mob in Nigeria Stones Woman for Evangelizing," *Compass Direct News,* July 8, 2006.
89 "Kwara Muslims Allege Arms Importation," *New Nigerian,* January 5, 2000.
90 Harnischfeger, "Sharia and Control over Territory," 445.
91 Ibid., 441–448.
92 Nwobi, *Sharia in Nigeria.*
93 Last, "The Search for Security in Muslim Northern Nigeria," 47.
94 "Death Toll Rises in Religious Clashes," *National Catholic Reporter,* September 28, 2001.
95 "Nigerian Religious Riots Leave Hundreds Dead," *Christianity Today,* October 17, 2001.
96 Bienen, "Religion, Legitimacy, and Conflict in Nigeria," 50–60.
97 Warner, "The Sad Rise of Boko Haram," 3.
98 "Sharia: Unheeded Doomsday Warnings," *Weekend Concord,* March 2, 2000.
99 "Shari'a: House Committed Oversight," *New Nigerian Weekly,* February 2, 2000.
100 "Democracy and Development in Africa," *New Nigerian,* January 22, 2000.
101 Suberu, "Religion and Institutions."
102 Vandu, "The Talibanization of Northern Nigeria."
103 Ludwig, "Christian-Muslim Relations in Northern Nigeria since the Introduction of Shari'ah in 1999," 612.
104 Adamu, "Gender, *Hisba* and the Enforcement of Morality in Northern Nigeria," 136.
105 Gwarzo, "Activities of Islamic Civic Associations in the Northwest of Nigeria," 292–293.
106 Last, "The Search for Security in Muslim Northern Nigeria."
107 Adamu, "Gender, *Hisba* and the Enforcement of Morality in Northern Nigeria," 143–144.
108 Ibid.
109 Ibid., 141.
110 Last, "The Search for Security in Muslim Northern Nigeria," 56.
111 Adamu, "Gender, *Hisba* and the Enforcement of Morality in Northern Nigeria," 141.
112 Vandu, "The Talibanization of Northern Nigeria."
113 Ibid.
114 Adamu, "Gender, *Hisba* and the Enforcement of Morality in Northern Nigeria," 146.
115 Hills, "Policing a Plurality of Worlds," 50.
116 Cook, "Boko Haram," 6.
117 Human Rights Watch, *Spiraling Violence,* especially 6–15.
118 Loimeier, "Boko Haram."

119 Ludwig, "Christian-Muslim Relations in Northern Nigeria since the Introduction of Shari'ah in 1999," 622.
120 Vandu, "The Talibanization of Northern Nigeria."
121 Ludwig, "Christian-Muslim Relations in Northern Nigeria since the Introduction of Shari'ah in 1999," 623–624.
122 Ibid., 629.
123 Harnischfeger, "Sharia and Control over Territory," 433.
124 Ludwig, "Christian-Muslim Relations in Northern Nigeria since the Introduction of Shari'ah in 1999," 627–628.

CONCLUSION

1 See Coleman, *Nigeria*.
2 For detailed analysis, see Peel, "Inequality and Action."
3 For penetrating analysis of Yoruba hometown, religion, ethnicity, and politics, see Laitin, *Hegemony and Culture*.
4 See Peel, "Religious Change in Yorubaland."
5 For a comprehensive analysis of the role of the Nigerian ethno-regional political class and the struggle for state power, see Diamond, *Class, Ethnicity, and Democracy in Nigeria*.
6 For an insightful theoretical explanation of the processes of Nigerian state-society formation, see Joseph, *Democracy and Pre-Bendel Politics in Nigeria*.
7 For an insightful analysis that effectively captures the historical, sociological, and political context for Boko Haram's bloody attacks on state institutions, emirate rulers, and vulnerable northern Christian minorities, see Warner, "The Sad Rise of Boko Haram"; see also Walker, "What Is Boko Haram?"; Adesoji, "The Boko Haram Uprising and Islamic Revivalism in Nigeria," 95–108; Campbell, *Nigeria*, especially chapter 9; and Verini, "The War for Nigeria."
8 In 2014, following presidential directives, the office of the National Security Adviser of the Federal Republic of Nigeria promulgated a comprehensive policy to confront the serious security threat of Boko Haram. The policy is defined in the following documents: *The National Counter-Terrorism Strategy*; *Nigeria's CVE Program: Changing Minds and Influencing Communities*; and *Presidential Initiatives for the North East*, Publications of the Office of the National Security Adviser, Federal Republic of Nigeria, 2014.
9 Muhammadu Buhari, "We Will Stop Boko Haram," *New York Times*, April 14, 2015.
10 For an illuminating perspective on the critical role of communal identity in modern state formation, see A. D. Smith, "The Nation, Invented, Imagined, and Reconstructed."

BIBLIOGRAPHY

PRIMARY SOURCES

Rhodes House Library, University of Oxford

Anderson, J. N. D., School of Oriental and African Studies, University of London. "Introduction: Relationship between Islamic Law and Customary Law in Africa, Emphasis on Northern Nigeria." Conference on the Future of Law in Africa, December 1959.

Arnett, E. J., Resident. "Intelligence Report." Sokoto Province, June 8, 1918.

Assistant District Officer H. M. Brice-Smith to the Resident of Kano Province, C. L. Temple. Mss. Afr. March 1915.

Birks, D. T. M., Assistant District Officer. *Waja Native Authority*. Gombe Division, 1945.

Carrow J. H., Commander. "Interview by A. H. M. Kirk-Greene." Typescript, 1966.

———. *Kano Province Annual Report, 1909*.

———. *Kano Province Annual Report, 1910*.

———. *Native Administration, Kano Province*.

———. *Native Administration, Sokoto Province*.

———. Typescript.

Carrow-Heussler Papers on Northern Nigeria. "Commander Carrow's Letter, April 5, 1965: Dorset, England." Colonial Records Project, Institute of Commonwealth Studies, Queen Elizabeth House, 1965–1972. Mss. Afr. s. 1489.

Clifford, Hugh, Governor. "Circular." Native Administration, 1923.

Conference on the Future of Law in Africa, December 1959–January 1960. Mss. Afr. s. 1193.

"Correspondence." District Officer, G. J. Lethem to the Resident, Bornu, 15/3, September 25, 1923.

Customary Law and Its Application to English Law. CO/537 6/59.

De Foucauld of the Sahara, a Great Son of France and of View of French Muslim Policy and Problems. *West Africa*, January 19, 1924. Mss. Afr. s. 783, 1/11, 1922. Published posthumously.

Great Britain. Colonial Office. *Nigeria: Report of the Commission Appointed to Enquire into the Fears of Minorities and Means of Allaying Them; Presented to Parliament by the Secretary of State for the Colonies by Command of Her Majesty July 1958*. Norwich, UK: HM Stationery Office, 1958.

Guy, J. C., Assistant District Officer, Katagum Division. *Touring Diary*. Bauchi Province. Mss. Afr.

Hickey, Raymond. *Typescript of Interview,* Catholic Mission in Northern Nigeria (Gongola).

Institute of Administration, Northern Nigeria, Local Government Wing. Lecture Note Series, November 1954. Mss. Afr. s. 1871.

———. Lecture Note Series, November 1954. Mss. Afr. s. 1871 (2), 1954.

Jacob, S. M. Report on Taxation. Mss. Afr. T. 16.

Letchworth, Assistant District Officer. *Nassarawa Division, 1926.*

Letchworth, Resident. Typescript of interview, former Resident, Bornu Province, 1969.

———. Typescript of interview, Resident, Northern Provinces, 1969.

Lethem, G. J. Confidential Document, Islamic Propaganda. Mss. British Empire. Maiduguri, November 15, 1924.

———. Confidential File.

———. Intelligence Report, Islamic Propaganda, 11, 5. Mss. British Empire. Nazaru, Maiduguri, August 1924.

———. Intelligence Report, Islamic Propaganda in Northern Nigeria, LMSS. Mss. British Empire.

———. Islamic Propaganda. Mss. British Empire (Lethem) 13, 1924.

———, Acting Resident. 42/1923 of 9/6/1924, 231/123. Bornu Province, Maiduguri, October 15, 1923.

———, District Officer to the Resident. Confidential Correspondence (file 9/1923). Bornu, September 22, 1923.

———, Former Administrative Officer. 192 Ferry Road: Edinburgh, Scotland.

"Circular, Number 49–203, Kaduna, June 29, 1920." From the Secretary, Northern Provinces, G. R. Matthews to the Resident Bornu Province.

———, Resident. "Circular: Number 89/285/1920." From the Secretary, Northern Provinces, to the Resident, Bornu Province, Kaduna, September 23, 1920, 15/3 (Dikwa District: May 10, 1990).

Letters of the Reverend Canon R. A. Wright to His Mother.

Macpherson, Sir John Stuart, Former Governor of Nigeria. Typescript of interview, 1969.

———. Typescript of interview, 1970.

———. Typescript of interview, No. 10, 1969.

Maddocks, Sir Kenneth. "Secret and Personal Documents, 30 July 1953, signed by A. E. T. Benson Esq. CMG, Nigerian Secretariat." Nigerian Constitution Conference. Mss. Afr. s. 11794. Lagos, 1953.

Maguire, Reverend. Typescript of interview conducted by Andrew Barnes.

———. Typescript of oral interview, April–June 1993.

Marshall, Hedley H., Former Attorney General of Northern Nigeria. Typescript of interview, 1969.

———. Typescript of interview, No. 7, 1969.

———. Typescript of interview, No. 8, 1969.

———. Typescript of interview, No. 9, 1969.

———. Typescript of interview, No. 10, 1969.

———. Interview conducted and transcribed by A. H. M. Kirk-Greene in Oxford on May 15, 1970. Mss. Afr. s. 2339.

Matthews, H. F., Assistant District Officer, Agaie-Lapai Division. Handing Over Notes, November 7, 1919. Mss. Afr. s. 783, box 2/6.

Morley, J. A. E., Assistant District Officer. *Re-Organization of East Tangale District.* Gombe, August 1945. Mss. British Empire.

Northern Nigerian Native Administration Law of 1954.

Papers of Assistant District Officer Letchworth.

Patterson, Bishop Cecil. "C.M.S. Missionary Account (CMS Mission 2)." *Interview.* Mss. Afr.

———. C.M.S. Missionary File. Mss. Afr. s. 2302, 1969.

———. Typescript of interview. Mss. Afr. s. 1680.

Resident. Confidential Memorandum. Bornu Province, Potiskum, August 31, 1923.

Richards, Arthur, former Governor of Nigeria. Typescript of interview, 1969.

Sharwood-Smith, Bryn. Mss. Afr. s. 2103, SG, 3228/1957, Governor's Office, Northern Region, Kaduna. February 20, 1957.

Temple, C. L. *Kano Province Annual Report, 1909.*

———, Resident. *Annual Report, 41, for the year ending December 31, 1909, Kano Province.* Mss. Afr. s. 230.

———. *Kano Province Annual Report, 1909.*

Watt, J. W. Diaries of Administrative Officer. Mss. Afr. 117, 1960.

Wright, Reverend Canon. Letter to His Mother, May 7, 1929.

———. Letter to His Mother, July 2, 1929.

———. Letter to His Mother, September 16, 1929.

———. Letter to His Mother, October 25, 1929.

———. Letter to His Mother, November 21, 1929.

———. Letter to His Mother, January 12, 1930.

———. Canon. Letter to His Mother, May 15, 1930.

Documents from the Library of Congress, Washington, D.C.

Catholic Bishops of Nigeria (pamphlet).

General Observations and Recommendation of the Donli Panel. Kaduna, 1987.

Herman, Jessi. "A Divided Nigeria." Institute for Global Engagement, unpublished manuscript, November 30, 2001.

Kaduna State Shari'ah Penal Code.

Ngban, Moni Odo. *Is Shari'ah the Law of God? Why Christians Reject It: The Implications on a Nation.* Self published, 2001.

"Press Conference Addressed by Citizen's League for Peace and Democracy on the Kaduna Crisis." (press release) March 30, 2000.

Reaction of the Christian Association of Nigeria to the Report and Recommendation Submitted by the Committee to Investigate Causes of Riots and Disturbances in Kaduna State. 1987.

Church Missionary Society Digital Archive

Church Missionary Gleaner. 1848, 1850, and 1851.
"Niger Mission." CMS *Original Papers*, 1907.
"Niger Mission." CMS *Original Papers*, 1932.
"Yoruba Mission." CMS *Original Papers*, 1907.

University of Ibadan Library, Africana Collection

Address Delivered at the Inaugural Meeting of the Committee on Nigeria's Membership of the Organization of Islamic Conference by Major General Ibrahim Badamasi Babangida, CFR, President of the Federal Republic of Nigeria and Commander-in-Chief of the Armed Forces, at Abuja, February 3, 1986.

Adegbite, Lateef, Secretary-General, Nigerian Supreme Council for Islamic Affairs. Keynote Address, delivered at the opening ceremony of the 16th Annual Conference of the Nigerian Association for the Study of Religions, October 8, 1991, Ilorin, Nigeria.

Broadcast to the Nation by His Excellency Major-General J. T. U. Aguiyi Ironsi, Head of the National Government and Supreme Commander of the Armed Forces, Tuesday, 24 May, 1966. Lagos: Government Printer, 1966.

Committee of Concerned Citizens (Nigeria). *The Sharia Issue: Working Papers for a Dialogue*. Nigeria: Committee of Concerned Citizens, 2002.

Constitution of Nigeria, 1999.

Licensed to Harm: Framework of the Area Courts, pamphlet, undated.

Onaiyekan, John, ed. *Religion: Peace and Justice in Nigeria. Breaking New Grounds, Communiqué of the Catholic Bishops' Conference of Nigeria, February 1989 and related Documents*. Lagos: Ilorin Diocese Catechetical Resource Centre, 1989.

Report of the Political Bureau. Lagos: Federal Government Printer, 1986.

Family Papers of Southern Baptist Convention Missionaries at the David M. Rubenstein Rare Books and Manuscript Library, Duke University

Logan Family Papers, 1952–1994
McGee Family Papers, 1957–2013
Pool Family Papers, 1928–1998
Roberson Family Papers, 1917–1977
Loy Connell Smith and Eunice Andrews Smith Bland Papers, 1958–1999
Taylor Family Papers, 1950–1975

Records of the Sudan Interior Mission International, Wheaton College, Illinios

BGG Reel number 99 and SIM Reel number SR-19, 1912–1971, (Nigeria) Kano-Karu

Publications of the Office of the National Security Adviser, Federal Republic of Nigeria

The National Counter-Terrorism Strategy
Nigeria's CVE *Program: Changing Minds and Influencing Communities*
Presidential Initiatives for the North East. Published by the Office of the National Security Adviser, Federal Republic of Nigeria, 2014.

Publications of Pentecostal Churches

Adeboye, E. A. *Open Heavens: A Daily Guide to Close Fellowship with God.* Redemption Camp, Ogun State: Open Heavens International, 2013.
Aransiola, Moses. *Praying for National Transformation: Securing Divine Visitation for Nigeria.* Ibadan: Gethsemane, 2008.
———. *Prophetic Destiny of Africa.* Ibadan: Gethsemane, 2008.
Fadele, James O. *Your 4 Fathers and Their Kingdom.* Greenville, TX: Fadel, 2014.
Oyedepo, David O. *The Mandate: A Timeless Operational Manual.* Canan Land, Ota: Dominion, 2012.
———. *On Eagle's Wings: My First 30-Year Adventure in Ministry.* Canan Land, Ota: Dominion, 2013.
———. *Ruling Your World: A Recipe for Impactful Living.* Canan Land, Ota: Dominion, 2005.
———. *The Unlimited Power of Faith: Operating in a World of Unlimited Possibilities.* Canan Land, Ota: Dominion, 2011.
———. *Winning Prayer.* Canan Land, Ota: Dominion, 2008.
Oyedepo, Faith A. *Overcoming Anxiety.* Canan Land, Ota: Dominion, 2008.
Pentecostal Doctrine, The Redeemed Christian Church of God, undated.
Redeemed Christian Church of God. *Illustrating the Fundamental Beliefs in the Bible.* Ibadan: Feyisetan Press, 1998.
Thekingsparish.org. The Redeemed Christian Church of God, The King's Parish, Walthamstow, London E17 5QX, accessed April 12, 2008.

Newspapers and Magazines

Africa Confidential
BBC News Africa
BBCNews, HARDtalk
Christian Science Monitor
Christianity Today
Compass Direct News
National Catholic Reporter
National Concord
New Nigerian
New Nigerian Weekly
New York Times
New York Times Magazine
Sunday Concord
Weekend Concord
World
World Press Review

SECONDARY SOURCES

Abdullah, Zain. "Towards an African Muslim Globality: The Parading of Transnational Identities in Black America." In *West African Migrations: Transnational and Global Pathways in a New Century,* edited by Mojubaolu Olufunke Okome and Olufemi Vaughan. New York: Palgrave Macmillan, 2011.

Abdulraheem, Tajudeen. "Politics in Nigeria's Second Republic." DPhil thesis, University of Oxford, 1990.

Abimbola, Adesoji. "The Boko Haram Uprising and Islamic Revivalism in Nigeria." *Afrika Spectrum* 45, no. 2 (2010): 95–108.

Abimbola, Wande. *Ifa: An Exposition of the Literary Corpus.* Ibadan: Oxford University Press, 1976.

Abubakar, Dauda. "Ethnic Identity, Democratization, and the Future of the African State: Lessons from Nigeria." *African Issues* 29, nos. 1 and 2 (2001): 31–36.

Adamu, Fatima L. "Gender, *Hisba* and the Enforcement of Morality in Northern Nigeria." *Africa* 78, no. 1 (2008).

Adebanwi, Wale. *Yoruba Elites and Ethnic Politics in Nigeria: Obafemi Awolowo and Corporate Agency.* Cambridge: Cambridge University Press, 2014.

Adebiyi, P. A. "Anglican Church and Education." In *The Anglican Church in Nigeria,* edited by Akinyele Omoyajowo. Ibadan: Macmillan Nigeria, 1994.

Adesoji, Abimbola. "The Boko Haram Uprising and Islamic Revivalism in Nigeria." *Africa Spectrum,* 45, no. 2 (2010): 95–108.

Adigwe, Hypolite A. "Nigeria Joins the Organization of Islamic Conference, O.I.C.: The Implications for Nigeria." Paper presented at the Symposium on OIC, Bigard Memorial Seminary Enugu, March 15, 1986.

Adogame, Afe. "Engaging the Rhetoric of Spiritual Warfare: The Public Face of Aladura in Diaspora." *Journal of Religion in Africa* 34, no. 4 (1998): 278–315.

———. "Online for God: Media and Negotiation and Africa New Religious Movement." In *Who Is Afraid of the Holy Ghost? Pentecostalism and Globalization in Africa and Beyond.* Trenton, NJ: Africa World Press, 2011.

Ado-Kurawa, Ibrahim. "Nigeria: State of the Nation." In *Shari'ah and the Press in Nigeria: Islam versus Western Christian Civilization.* Kano, Nigeria: Kurawa Holdings, 2000.

———. *Shari'ah and the Press in Nigeria: Islam versus Western Christian Civilization.* Kano, Nigeria: Kurawa Holdings, 2000.

Afigbo, A. E. "The National Question in Nigerian History, Politics and Affairs." In *Nigerian History, Politics and Affairs: The Collected Essays of Adiele Afigbo,* edited by Toyin Falola. Trenton, NJ: Africa World Press, 2005.

Afolabi, Niyi. *Afro-Brazilians: Cultural Production in a Racial Democracy.* Rochester, NY: University of Rochester Press, 2009.

Afolayan, Funso. "The Church in Northern Nigeria, 1842–1992." In *The Anglican Church in Nigeria (1842–1992),* edited by Akinyele Omoyajowo. Lagos: Macmillan Nigeria, 1994.

Ajasin, M. A. *Ajasin: Memoirs and Memories.* Lagos: Ajasin Foundation, 2003.

Ajayi, J. F. Ade. "Bishop Crowther: A Patriot to the Core." In *Tradition and Change in Africa: The Essays of J. F. Ade Ajayi*, edited by Toyin Falola. Trenton: Africa World Press, 2000.

———. *Christian Missions in Nigeria 1841–1891: The Making of a New Elite*. Evanston, IL: Northwestern University Press, 1965.

———. "Henry Venn and the Policy of Development." In *Tradition and Change in Africa: The Essays of J. F. Ade Ajayi*, edited by Toyin Falola. Trenton: Africa World Press, 2000.

———. "Introduction." In *The Anglican Church in Nigeria (1842–1992)*, edited by Akinyele Omoyajowo. Ibadan: Macmillan Nigeria, 1994.

Akintoye, S. Adebanji. *A History of the Yoruba People*. Dakar, Senegal: Amalion, 2010.

Al-Hajj, M. A. "Hayatu Said: A Revolutionary Mahdist in the Western Sudan." In *Sudan in Africa*, edited by Y. F. Hasan. Khartoum: Khartoum University Press, 1971.

———. "The Writings of Shehu Uthman dan Fodio." *Kano Studies* 1, no. 2 (1974).

Aliyu, Abubakar Y., ed. *The Role of Local Government in the Social, Political, and Economic Development of Nigeria*. Zaria: Ahmadu Bello University, 1982.

Alkali, Muhammad, Nur Abubakar, Kawu Monguno, and Ballama Shettima Mustafa. "Overview of Islamic Actors in Northwestern Nigeria." Working Paper No. 2, Nigeria Research Network, Oxford Department of International Development, Queen Elizabeth House, University of Oxford, January 2012.

Amadi, E. Lawrence. "Church-State Involvement in Educational Development in Nigeria, 1842–1948." *Journal of Church and State* 19, no. 3 (1977): 481–496.

Amnesty International. *Nigeria: Time to End Contempt for Human Rights*. November 6, 1996.

Anderson, Allan. "Globalization and Independent Pentecostals in Africa: A South African Perspective." In *Who Is Afraid of the Holy Ghost? Pentecostalism and Globalization in Africa and Beyond*, edited by Afe Adogame. Trenton, NJ: Africa World Press, 2011.

Anderson, J. N. D. "Conflict of Laws in Northern Nigeria: A New Start." *International and Comparative Law Quarterly* 8, no. 3 (July 1959): 442–456.

———. *Islamic Law in Africa*. London: Frank Cass & Co., 1955.

Anih, Stan. *The Cathedral and the Mosque Can Co-exist in Nigeria*. Enugu, Nigeria: Stan Anih, 1984.

———. *An Introduction to the Fundamentals of Religious Ecumenism in Nigeria*. Enugu, Nigeria: SNAAP, 1990.

———. *Religious Ecumenism and Education for Tolerance*. Enugu, Nigeria: SNAAP, 1992.

Arinze, Francis A. (Cardinal). *Progress in Christian-Muslim Relations Worldwide*. Jos, Plateau State: Augustinian Publications Nigeria, 1988.

Asaju, Dapo. "Globalization, Politicization of Religion, and Religious Networking: The Case of the Pentecostal Fellowship in Nigeria." In *Who Is Afraid of the Holy Ghost? Pentecostalism and Globalization in Africa and Beyond*, edited by Afe Adogame. Trenton, NJ: Africa World Press, 2011.

Atanda, J. A., ed. *Baptist Churches in Nigeria: Accounts of Their Foundation and Growth, 1850–1950*. Ibadan: University of Ibadan Press, 1988.

———. *The New Oyo Empire: Indirect Rule and Change in Western Nigeria 1894–1934*. London: Longman, 1973.

Awofeso, Niyi, Jan Ritchie, and Pieter Degeling. "The Almajiri Heritage and the Threat of Non-State Terrorism in Northern Nigeria: Lessons from Central Asia and Pakistan." *Studies in Conflict and Terrorism* 26, no. 4 (2003): 311–325.

Awolowo, Obafemi. *Path to Nigerian Freedom*. London: Faber, 1947.

Ayandele, E. A. *Holy Johnson, Pioneer of African Nationalism, 1836–1917*. Africana Modern Library 13. New York: Routledge, 1970.

———. *The Ijebu of Yorubaland, 1850–1950: Politics, Economy and Society*. Ibadan: Heinemann Educational Books, 1992.

———. "The Missionary Factor in Northern Nigeria, 1870–1919." In *The History of Christianity in West Africa: The Nigerian Story*, edited by Ogbu Uke Kalu, Ibadan: Daystar, 1978.

———. *The Missionary Impact on Modern Nigeria, 1842–1914: A Political and Social Analysis*. London: Longman, 1966.

Ayantuga, Obafemi, "Ijebu and Its Neighbours, 1851–1914." PhD diss., University of London, 1965.

Ayegboyin, Deji. "New Pentecostal Churches and Prosperity Theology in Nigeria." In *Who Is Afraid of the Holy Ghost? Pentecostalism and Globalization in Africa and Beyond*, edited by Afe Adogame. Trenton, NJ: Africa World Press, 2011.

Azikiwe, Nnamdi. *Zik: A Selection from the Speeches of Azikiwe*. Cambridge: Cambridge University Press, 1961.

Badren, Margot. "Sharia Activism and Zina in Nigeria in the Era of Hudud." In *Gender and Islam in Africa: Rights, Sexuality, and Law*, edited by Margot Badren. Bloomington: Indiana University Press, 2012.

Badru, Pade. "The Hausa Speaking People of West Africa." in *Encyclopaedia of Africa and the Middle East*, 127–129. Santa Barbara, CA: ABC-CLIO, 2011.

———. "Historical Foundations and Basic Philosophy of Islam." In *Islam in Sub-Saharan Africa: Changing Gender Relations and Political Reforms*, edited by Pade Badru and Brigid Sackey. New York: Rowman & Littlefield, 2012.

Balewa, Sir Abubakar Tafawa, Alhaji. *Shaihu Umar: A Novel about Slavery in Africa*. Edited by Beverly Mack. Translated by Mervyn Hiskett. Princeton, NJ: Markus Wiener Publishers, 1989.

Barnes, Andrew E. *Making Headway: The Introduction of Western Civilization in Colonial Nigeria*. Rochester, NY: University of Rochester Press, 2009.

———. "Religious Insults: Christian Critiques of Islam and Colonial Government in Northern Nigeria." *Journal of Religion in Africa* 14, no. 1 and 2 (2004): 62–81.

Bassey, Magnus O. "Missionary Rivalry and Educational Expansion in Southern Nigeria, 1885–1932." *Journal of Negro Education* 60, no. 1 (1991).

———. *Missionary Rivalry and Educational Expansion in Nigeria, 1885–1945*. Lewiston, NY: Edwin Mellen, 1999.

Bateye, Bolaji. "Female Religious Leadership in Nigerian Pentecostalism: Embers or Gale?" In *Who Is Afraid of the Holy Ghost? Pentecostalism and Globalization in Africa and Beyond*, edited by Afe Adogame. Trenton, NJ: Africa World Press, 2011.

BBC News. Interview with Sule Lamido. *HardTalk*, November 12, 2000.

Behrouz, Andra Nahal. "Transforming Islamic Family Law: State Responsibility and the Role of Internal Initiative." *Columbia Law Review* 103, no. 5 (2003): 1136–1162.

Bello, Mohammed, former Chief Justice of Federal Republic of Nigeria. "Sharia and the Constitution." In *The Sharia Issue: Working Papers for a Dialogue*, edited by S. L. Edu et al., 5–13. Lagos: Committee of Concerned Citizens, 2000.

Bello, Sir Ahmadu. *My Life*. Cambridge: Cambridge University Press, 1962.

Berry, Sara S. *Cocoa, Custom, and Socioeconomic Change in Rural Western Nigeria*. Oxford: Clarendon, 1975.

Bienen, Henry. "Religion, Legitimacy, and Conflict in Nigeria." *Annals of the American Academy of Political and Social Science* 483, no. 1 (January 1986): 50–60.

Boer, Jan H. *Nigeria's Decades of Blood, 1980–2002*. Vol. 1 of *Studies in Christian-Muslim Relations*. Belleville, ON: Essence, 2003.

Braudel, Fernand. "Histoire et sciences sociales: La longue durée." *Réseaux: Communication-Technologie-Société* 5, no. 27 (1987): 7–37.

Byang, Danjuma. *Shari'a in Nigeria: A Christian Perspective*. Jos, Nigeria: Challenge, 1988.

Callaway, Barbara J. *Education and the Emancipation of Hausa Muslim Women in Nigeria*. Working Paper for Women in International Development 129. East Lansing: Michigan State University Press, 1986.

———. *Muslim Hausa Women in Nigeria: Tradition and Change*. Syracuse, NY: Syracuse University Press, 1987.

Callaway, Barbara J., and Lucy Creevey. *The Heritage of Islam: Women, Religion, and Politics in West Africa*. Boulder, CO: Lynne Rienner, 1993.

Cameron, Donald C. *The Principle of Native Administration and Their Application*. Lagos: Government Printers, 1934.

Campbell, John. *Nigeria: Dancing on the Brink*. Lanham, MD: Rowman & Littlefield, 2013.

Casey, C. "'Policing' through Violence: Fear, Vigilantism, and the Politics of Islam in Northern Nigeria." In *Global Vigilantes: Perspectives on Justice and Violence*, edited by David Pratten and A. Sen. London: Hurst; and New York: Columbia University Press, 2007.

Catholic Bishops' Stand on the O.I.C. Issue. Lagos: Catholic Secretariat Publications, September 1986.

Chidester, David. "African Christian Communities." In *The Oxford Handbook of Global Religions*, edited by Mark Juergensmeyer. New York: Oxford University Press, 2006.

Clarke, Kamari Maxine. *Local Practices, Global Controversies: Islam in Sub-Saharan African Contexts*. MacMillan Center Working Paper Series. New Haven, CT: MacMillan Center, 2005.

Coleman, James S. *Nigeria: Background to Nationalism*. Berkeley: University of California Press, 1958.

Coles, Catherine, and Beverly Mack, eds. *Hausa Women in the Twentieth Century*. Madison: University of Wisconsin Press, 1991.

Collett, Adrian. "Recent Legislation and Reform Proposals for Customary and Area Courts in Nigeria." *Journal of African Law* 22, no. 2 (Autumn 1978): 161–187.

Comaroff, Jean, and John Comaroff. *Of Revelation and Revolution*, volume 1: *Christianity, Colonialism, and Consciousness of a South African People*. Chicago: University of Chicago Press, 1991.

Cook, David. "Boko Haram: A Prognosis." James A. Baker III Institute of Public Policy, Rice University, unpublished manuscript, December 16, 2010.

Crampton, E. P. T. *Christianity in Northern Nigeria*. London: Geoffrey Chapman, 1979.

———. "Christianity in Northern Nigeria." In *Christianity in West Africa: The Nigerian Story*, edited by Ogbu Kalu. Ibadan: Daystar, 1978.

Creech Jones, Arthur. *Labour's Colonial Policy*. London: Fabian Colonial Bureau, 1947.

Crowder, Michael. *The Story of Nigeria*. London: Faber & Faber, 1966.

Danfulani, Umar Habila Dadem. "Globalization, Fundamentalism and the Pentecostal/Charismatic Movement in Nigeria." In *Who Is Afraid of the Holy Ghost? Pentecostalism and Globalization in Africa and Beyond*, edited by Afe Adogame. Trenton, NJ: Africa World Press, 2011.

David, P. "Islamic Law May Spread in Nigeria." *Washington Report on Middle East Affairs* 19, no. 3 (April 2000).

Davidson, Basil. *The African Genius*. Athens: Ohio University Press, 2004.

Debki, Bee. *The Tragedy of Sharia: Cry and Voice of Masses. Kaduna Crisis from an Eye Witness*. Kaduna, Nigeria: Bee Debki, 2000.

Diamond, Larry. *Class, Ethnicity, and Democracy in Nigeria: The Failure of the First Republic*. London: Macmillan, 1988.

———. "Nigeria: The Uncivic Society and the Descent into Praetorianism." In *Politics in Developing Countries: Comparing Experience with Democracy*, 2nd ed., edited by Larry Diamond, Juan J. Linz, and Seymour Martin Lipset. Boulder, CO: Lynne Rienner, 1995.

Dike, K. Onwuka. "Origins of the Niger Mission, 1841–1891." A paper read at the Centenary of the Mission of Christ Church, Onisha, on November 13, 1957. Ibadan: Published for CMS Niger Mission by Ibadan University Press, 1962.

Doi, Abdur Rahman I. "The Impact of English Law and Concepts on the Administration of Islamic Law in Nigeria." In *African and Western Legal Systems in Contact*, translated by T. Akinola Aguda et al., 25–56. Bayreuth African Studies Series. Bavaria, Germany: Bayreuth University, 1989.

Dudley, B. J. *Instability and Political Order: Politics and Crisis in Nigeria*. Ibadan: Ibadan University Press, 1970.

———. *Parties and Politics in Northern Nigeria*. London: Frank Cass, 1968.

Durham, W. Cole, Jr. "Nigeria's 'State Religion' Question in Comparative Perspective." In *Comparative Perspectives on Shari'ah in Nigeria*, edited by Philip Ostien, Jamila M. Nasir, and Franz Kogelman, 144–177. Ibadan: Spectrum Books, 2005.

Edu, S. L., et al., eds. *The Sharia Issue: Working Papers for a Dialogue*. Lagos: Committee of Concerned Citizens, 2000.

Emekwue, Henry. *Democracy and Religion: Sharia in Nigeria*. Enugu, Nigeria: SNAAP, 2000.
Enwerem, Iheanyi M. *A Dangerous Awakening: The Politicization of Religion in Nigeria*. Ibadan: Institut Francais de Recherche en Afrique, 1995.
Esposito, John L., ed. *The Oxford History of Islam*. New York: Oxford University Press, 1999.
Essien, E. "The Jurisdiction of State High Courts in Nigeria." *Journal of African Law* 44, no. 2 (2000).
Falola, Toyin. *Ibadan: Foundation, Growth and Change, 1830–1960*. Ibadan: Bookcraft, 2012.
———. *Religious Militancy and Self Assertion: Islam and Politics in Nigeria*. London: Avebury, 1996.
———. *Violence in Nigeria: The Crisis of Religious Politics and Secular Ideologies*. Rochester, NY: University of Rochester Press, 1998.
Falola, Toyin, and Julius Ihonvbere. *The Rise and Fall of Nigeria's Second Republic*. London: Zed Press, 1985.
Falola, Toyin, and Dare Oguntomisin. *The Military in Nineteenth Century Yoruba Politics*. Ile-Ife: University of Ife Press, 1982.
Federici, Sylvia, and George Caffentzis. "Globalization and Professionalization in Africa." *Social Text* 22, no. 2 (Summer 2004): 81–99.
Flint, J. E. "The Growth of European Influence in West Africa in the Nineteenth Century." In *A Thousand Years of West African History*, edited by A. Ade Ajayi and Ian Espie. London: Nelson, 1969.
Galadima, Justice Suleiman. "Marriage and Inheritance Laws in a Plural Society—Nigerian Experience." *Journal of Private and Public Law* 1, no. 1 (2008): 86–99.
Gbadamosi, T. G. O. *The Growth of Islam among Yoruba Muslim*. London: Longman, 1978.
Goody, Jack. *The Logic of Writing and the Organization of Society*. Cambridge: Cambridge University Press, 1986.
Gumi, Sheikh Abubakar, with Ismaila Abubakar Tsiga. *Where I Stand*. Ibadan: Spectrum Books, 1992.
Gurin, Aminu M. *The Concept of Honesty in Islam: Its Role in Fostering Discipline in Nigeria*. Occasional Publication of the National Orientation Agency, no. 1. Zaria, Nigeria: Centre for Islamic Legal Studies, Institute of Administration, Ahmadu Bello University.
Gusau, Nababa Sanda. *A Case for Shari'ah in Nigeria*. Kaduna, 1994.
Gwarzo, Tahir Haliru. "Activities of Islamic Civic Associations in the Northwest of Nigeria: With Particular Reference to Kano State." *Africa Spectrum* 38, no. 3 (2003): 289–318.
Hackett, Rosalind I. J. "Is Satan Local or Global? Reflections on a Nigerian Deliverance Movement." In *Who Is Afraid of the Holy Ghost? Pentecostalism and Globalization in Africa and Beyond*, edited by Afe Adogame. Trenton, NJ: Africa World Press, 2011.
———. "Rethinking the Role of Religion in the Public Sphere: Local and Global Perspectives." In *Comparative Perspectives on Shari'ah in Nigeria*, edited by Philip Ostien, Jamila M. Nasir, and Franz Kogelman. Ibadan: Spectrum Books, 2005.

Harnischfeger, Johannes. *Democratization and Islamic Law: The Sharia Conflict in Nigeria*. New York: Campus Verlag, 2008.

———. "Sharia and Control over Territory: Conflicts between 'Settlers' and 'Indigenes' in Nigeria." *African Affairs* 103, no. 412 (2004): 431–452.

Harunah, Hakeem B. *Shari'ah under Western Democracy in Contemporary Nigeria: Contradictions, Crises, and the Way Forward*. Ikeja, Nigeria: Perfect Printers, 2002.

Haynes, Jeffrey. "Popular Religion and Politics in Africa." *Third World Quarterly* 16, no. 1 (1995): 89–108.

———. *Religion and Politics in Africa*. London: Zed Books, 1996.

Hefner, Robert W. "Introduction: World Building and the Rationality of Conversion." In *Conversion to Christianity: Historical and Anthropological Perspectives on a Great Transformation*, edited by Robert W. Hefner. Berkeley: University of California Press, 1993.

———. "September 11 and the Struggle for Islam." New York: Social Science Research Council, 2002.

Held, David, and Anthony McGrew. *Globalization/Anti-Globalization: Beyond the Great Divide*. 2nd ed. Cambridge: Polity, 2007.

Hendrixson, Joyce. "The Changing Significance of Ethnicity and Power Relations, Sokoto, Nigeria." *Studies in Third World Societies* 11 (1980): 51–93.

Hills, Alice. "Policing a Plurality of Worlds: The Nigeria Police in Metropolitan Kano." *African Affairs* 111, no. 442 (January 2012): 46–66.

Hiskett, Mervyn. "Kitāb Al-Farq: A Work on the Habe Kingdoms Attributed to 'Uthman Dan Fodio." *Bulletin of the School of Oriental and African Studies* 23 (1960): 570–571.

———. *The Sword of Truth: The Life and Times of the Shehu Usuman Dan Fodio*. New York: Oxford University Press, 1973.

Hodgkin, Thomas. "Madhism, Messianism, and Marxism in the African Setting." In *African Social Studies: A Radical Reader*, edited by Thomas Hodgkin, Monthly Review Press, New York (1977): 306–323.

———. *Nigerian Perspectives: An Historical Anthology*. London: Oxford University Press, 1960.

Horton, Robin. "African Conversion." *Africa* 41, no. 2 (1971): 85–108.

———. "On the Rationality of Conversion: Part One." *Africa*, 45, no. 3 (1975): 219–235.

———. "On the Rationality of Conversion: Part Two." *Africa*, 45, no. 4 (1975): 373–399.

Human Rights Watch. *"Political Sharia"? Human Rights and Islamic Law in Northern Nigeria*. International Crisis Group, Northern Nigeria: Background to Conflict, December 20, 2010.

———. *Spiraling Violence: Boko Haram Attacks and Security Force Abuses in Nigeria*. October 11, 2012.

Hunwick, John. "An African Case Study of Political Islam." *Annals of the American Academy of Political and Social Sciences* 525 (November 1992): 143–155.

———. "The Nineteenth Century Jihad." In *On Thousand Years of West African History*, edited by F. Ade Ajayi and Ian Espie. London: Nelson, 1969.

Ibrahim, Hassan Ahmed. *Sayyid 'Abd al-Rahman al-Mahdi: A Study of Neo-Mahdism in the Sudan, 1899–1956*. Islam in Africa 4. Leiden, Netherlands: Brill Academic, 2004.

Ibrahim, Jibrin. "Religion and Political Turbulence in Nigeria." *Journal of Modern African Studies* 29, no. 1 (March 1991): 115–136.

Ibrahim, Yakubu Yahaya. *Shari'ah and Muslims in Nigeria*. Kaduna, Nigeria: Fisbas Media Services, 1991.

Ihonvbere, Julius. *Nigeria: The Politics of Adjustment and Democracy*. New Brunswick, NJ: Transaction, 1994.

Ilesanmi, Simeon O. "From Periphery to Center: Pentecostalism Is Transforming the Secular State in Africa." *Harvard Divinity Bulletin* 35, no. 4 (Autumn 2007).

———. *Religious Pluralism and the Nigerian State*. Athens: Ohio University Press, 1997.

Imam, Ayesha M. "Ideology, the Mass Media, and Women: A Study of Radio Kaduna, Nigeria." In *Hausa Women in the Twentieth Century*, edited by Catherine Coles and Beverly Mack. Madison: University of Wisconsin Press, 1991.

Isyaku, Bashir. *The Kafanchan Carnage*. Zaria, Nigeria: Bashir Isyaku, 1991.

Jinadu, L. Adele. "Federalism, the Consociational State, and Ethnic Conflict in Nigeria." *Publius* 15, no. 2 (1985): 71–100.

Johnson, Samuel. *The History of the Yorubas: From the Earliest Times to the Beginning of the British Protectorate*. Lagos: CMS (Nigeria) Bookshops, 1921.

Joseph, Richard A. *Democracy and Pre-Bendel Politics in Nigeria: The Rise and Fall of the Second Republic*. Ibadan: Spectrum Books, 1987. Reprint, Cambridge: Cambridge University Press, 2013.

July, Robert. *The Origins of Modern African Thought: Its Development in West Africa during the Nineteenth and Twentieth Centuries*. New York: Praeger, 1967.

Kalu, Ogbu Uke. "African Pentecostalism in Global Perspective." In Kalu, Wariboko, and Falola, *African Pentecostalism*.

———. "Black Joseph: Early African American Charismatic and Pentecostal Linkages and Their Impact on Africa." In Kalu, Wariboko, and Falola, *African Pentecostalism*.

———. "Christianity in Africa: A Synopsis." In Kalu, Wariboko, and Falola, *African Pentecostalism*.

———. "Constructing a Global Pentecostal Discourse: An African Example." In *African Pentecostalism: Global Discourses, Migrations, Exchanges and Connections*, edited by Wihelmina J. Kalu, Nimi Wariboko, and Toyin Falola. Trenton, NJ: Africa World Press, 2010.

———. "The Distorted Lens of Edinburgh 1910." In *African Pentecostalism: Global Discourses, Migrations, Exchanges and Connections*, edited by Wihelmina J. Kalu, Nimi Wariboko, and Toyin Falola. Trenton, NJ: Africa World Press, 2010.

———. "Holy Praiseco: Negotiating Sacred and Popular Music and Dance." In *African Pentecostalism: Global Discourses, Migrations, Exchanges and Connections*, edited by Wihelmina J. Kalu, Nimi Wariboko, and Toyin Falola. Trenton, NJ: Africa World Press, 2010.

———. "Pentecostalism and Mission in Africa, 1970–2000." In Kalu, Wariboko, and Falola, *African Pentecostalism*.

———. "Who Is Afraid of the Holy Ghost? Presbyterians and Early Charismatic Movement in Nigeria, 1966–1975." In *Who Is Afraid of the Holy Ghost? Pentecostalism and*

Globalization in Africa and Beyond, edited by Afe Adogame. Trenton, NJ: Africa World Press, 2011.

Kalu, Wihelmina J., Nimi Wariboko, and Toyin Falola, eds. *African Pentecostalism: Global Discourses, Migrations, Exchanges and Connections.* Trenton, NJ: Africa World Press, 2010.

Kane, Osuman. "Izala: The Rise of Muslim Reformism in Northern Nigeria." In *Accounting for Fundamentalism: The Dynamic Character of Movements,* edited by Martin F. Marty and R. Scott Appleby. Chicago: University of Chicago Press, 1994.

———. *Muslim Modernity in Postcolonial Nigeria: A Study of the Society for the Removal of Innovation and Reinstatement of Tradition.* Leiden: E. J. Brill, 2003.

Kastfelt, Niels. "African Resistance to Colonialism in Adamawa." *Journal of Religion in Africa* 8, no. 1 (1976): 1–12.

———. "Christianity, Colonial Legitimacy, and the Rise of Nationalist Politics in Northern Nigeria." In *Legitimacy and the State in Twentieth Century Africa: Essays in Honor of A. H. M. Kirk-Greene,* edited by Terence Ranger and Olufemi Vaughan. London: Macmillan, 1993.

Kelly, Robin, D. G. *Race Rebels.* New York: Free Press, 1994.

Kendhammer, Brendan. "Muslims Talking Politics: Framing Islam and Democracy in Northern Nigeria." PhD diss., University of Wisconsin, Madison, 2010.

Kenny, Joseph. "Shari'a and Christianity in Nigeria: Islam and a 'Secular' State." *Journal of Religion in Africa* 26, no. 4 (1996): 338–364.

Kirk-Greene, A. H. M., ed. *Crisis and Conflict in Nigeria: A Documentary Source Book, 1966–1969.* London: Oxford University Press, 1971.

———. *The Principle of Native Administration in Nigeria: Selected Documents, 1900–1947.* London: Oxford University Press, 1965.

Kolapo, Femi J. "CMS Missionaries of African Origin and Extra-Religious Encounters at the Niger-Benue Confluence, 1858–1880." *African Studies Review* 43, no. 2 (2000): 87–110.

Kopytoff, Jean H. *A Preface to Modern Nigeria: The "Sierra Leonians" in Yorubaland, 1830–1890.* Madison: University of Wisconsin Press, 1965.

Kukah, Matthew H. *Religion, Politics, and Power in Northern Nigeria.* Ibadan: Spectrum Books, 1993.

Ladan, Muhammad Tawfiq. "Women's Rights and Access to Justice under Sharia in Northern Nigeria." Paper presented at a conference on Islamic Legal System and Women's Rights in Northern Nigeria, Abuja, Nigeria, October 27–30, 2002.

Laitin, David D. *Hegemony and Culture: Politics and Change among the Yoruba.* Chicago: University of Chicago Press, 1986.

———. "The Sharia Debate and the Origins of Nigeria's Second Republic." *Journal of Modern African Studies* 20, no. 3 (September 1982): 411–430.

Larémont, Ricardo Rene. *Islamic Law and Politics in Northern Nigeria.* Trenton, NJ: Africa World Press, 2011.

Larkin, Brian, and Brigit Meyer. "Pentecostalism, Islam and Culture: New Religious Movements in West Africa." In *Themes in West African History,* edited by Emmanuel Kwaku Akyeampong. Oxford: James Currey, 2006.

Last, Murray. "The Search for Security in Muslim Northern Nigeria." *Africa* 78, no. 1 (2008): 41–63.

———. *The Sokoto Caliphate*. London: Longman, 1967.

Law, Robin. *The Oyo Empire, c.1600–c1836: A West African Imperialism in the Era of the Atlantic Slave Trade*. Oxford: Clarendon, 1974.

Lewis, I. M. Introduction to *Islam in Tropical Africa*. Edited by I. M. Lewis. Bloomington: Indiana University Press, 1980.

Lloyd, P. C. *Africa in Social Change*. London: Penguin, 1972.

Loimeier, Roman. "Boko Haram: The Development of a Militant Religious Movement in Nigeria." *Africa Spectrum* 47, nos. 2–3 (2012).

———. *Islamic Reform and Political Change in Northern Nigeria*, Evanston, IL: Northwestern University Press, 2011.

Lovejoy, Paul, and J. S. Hogendorn. "Revolutionary Mahdism and Resistance to Colonial Rule in the Sokoto Caliphate, 1905–06." *Journal of African History* 31 (1991): 217–244.

———. *Slow Death for Slavery: The Course of Abolition in Northern Nigeria, 1897–1936*. Cambridge: Cambridge University Press, 1993.

Lubeck, Paul. "Islamic Protest under Semi-industrial Capitalism: 'Yan Tastine Explained." *Africa* 55, no. 4 (1985): 369–389.

———. "Nigeria: Mapping a Sharia Restorationist Movement." In *Sharia Politics: Islamic Law and Society in the Modern World*, edited by Robert W. Hefner. Bloomington: Indiana University Press, 2011.

Lubeck, Paul, Ronnie Lipshutz, and Erik Weeks. "The Globality of Islam: Sharia as a Nigerian 'Self-Determination' Movement." Queen Elizabeth House Working Paper Series 106. Queen Elizabeth House, University of Oxford, 2003.

Ludwig, Frieder. "Christian-Muslim Relations in Northern Nigeria since the Introduction of Shari'ah in 1999." *Journal of the American Academy of Religion* 76, no. 3 (September 2008): 602–637.

Lugard, Fredrick D. *The Dual Mandate in British Tropical Africa*. Edinburgh: Blackwood, 1929.

Lynch, Hollis R. *Edward Wilmot Blyden: Pan-Negro Patriot, 1832–1912*. Oxford: Oxford University Press, 1967.

Mack, Beverly. "Muslim Women's Knowledge Production in the Greater Maghreb: The Example of Nana Asm'u of Northern Nigeria." In *Gender and Islam in Africa: Rights, Sexuality, and Law*, edited by Margot Badren. Bloomington: Indiana University Press, 2011.

Mahmud, Alkali Alhaji Abubakar. *Notes on Islamic Civil Law Procedure*. Yola, Nigeria: Al Abumahdi, 1997.

Mann, Kristin. *Marrying Well: Marriages, Status, and Social Change among the Educated Elite in Colonial Lagos*. Cambridge: Cambridge University Press, 1985.

Marshall, Ruth. *Political Spiritualities: The Pentecostal Revolution in Nigeria*. Chicago: University of Chicago Press, 2009.

———. "Power in the Name of Jesus: Social Transformation and Pentecostalism in Western Nigeria Revisited." In *Legitimacy and the State in Twentieth Century Africa:*

Essays in Honor of A. H. M. Kirk-Greene, edited by Terence Ranger and Olufemi Vaughan. London: Macmillan, 1993.

Marshall-Fratani, Ruth. "Mediating the Global and the Local in Nigerian Pentecostalism." *Journal of Religion in Africa* 28, no. 3 (1998): 278–315.

McGarvey, Kathleen. *Muslim and Christian Women in Dialogue: The Case of Northern Nigeria.* Vol. 42, Religions and Discourse. Oxford: Peter Lang, 2009.

A Memorandum on the 1999 Constitution to the Government and National Assembly. Abuja, Nigeria, 2000.

Miller, Lisa. "E. A. Adeboye: A Pentecostal Preacher from Nigeria Has Made Big Plans to Save Your Soul." *Newsweek's* 50 Most Influential People in 2008, December 19, 2008.

Mohammed, Abubakar Siddique, Sa'idu Hassan Adamu, and Alkasum Abba. *Human Living Conditions and Reforms of Legal Systems: The Talakawa and the Issue of the Shari'ah in Contemporary Nigeria.* Zaria, Nigeria: Centre for Democratic Development, Research and Training, 2000.

Mohammed, Bello. "Sharia and the Constitution." In *The Sharia Issue: Working Papers for a Dialogue,* edited by S. L. Edu et al., 5–13. Lagos: Committee of Concerned Citizens, 2000.

Morgan, Kemi. *Akinyele's Outline of History of Ibadan.* Part III. Ibadan: Caxton, 1972.

Muhibbu-Din, M. A., ed. *Shari'ah in a Multi-Faith Nigeria.* Ibadan: Association of Teachers of Arabic and Islamic Studies (NATAIS), 2005.

Mukoro, Akpomuvire. "The Interface between Customary Law and Local Government Legislation in Nigeria: A Retrospect and Prospect." *Journal of Social Sciences* 26, no. 2 (2011): 139–145.

Musa, Sulaiman. *The Da'awah Approach of Shaikh Uthman Danfodiyo.* Kaduna, Nigeria: Alkausar Printing and Publishing Co., 1994.

———. *Shari'ah in a Multi-Faith Nigeria: The Effects of British Colonial Administration on the Shari'ah Legal System in Northern Nigeria.*

Mustapha, Abdul Raufu. "Structural Adjustment and Agrarian Change in Nigeria." In *The Politics of Structural Adjustment in Nigeria,* edited by Adebayo Olukoshi. London: James Currey, 1993.

Nasir, Jemila. "Women's Human Rights in Secular and Religious Legal System." Paper presented at a conference on Islamic Legal System and Women's Rights in Northern Nigeria, Abuja, Nigeria, October 27–30, 2002.

"Nigeria: In God's Name." *Africa Confidential* 41, no. 5 (March 3, 2000).

"Nigeria Miss World Strife Goes On." *CNN News,* November 27, 2002, http://archives.cnn.com/2002/WORLD/africa/11/27/nigeria.fatwa/index.html., accessed March 2007.

Nmehielle, Vincent O. "Sharia Law in the Northern States of Nigeria: To Implement or Not to Implement, the Constitutionality in the Question." *Human Rights Quarterly* 26, no. 3 (2004): 730–759.

Nolte, Insa. *Obafemi Awolowo and the Making of Remo: The Local Politics of a Nigerian Nationalist.* Edinburgh, UK: Edinburgh University Press, 2009.

Nwobi, Simeon Okezuo. *Sharia in Nigeria: What a Christian Must Know*. Abuja, Nigeria: Totan, 2000.

Oba, Abdulmumini A. "Islamic Law as Customary Law: The Changing Perspective in Nigeria." *International and Comparative Law Quarterly* 41, no. 4 (2002): 817–850.

———. "The Sharia Court of Appeal in Northern Nigeria: The Continuing Crises of Jurisdiction." *American Journal of Comparative Law* 52, no. 4 (Autumn 2004): 859–900.

Obadare, Ebenezer. "In Search of a Public Sphere: The Fundamentalist Challenge to Civil Society in Nigeria." *Patterns of Prejudice* 8, no. 2 (2004): 177–198.

———. "The Muslim Response to the Pentecostal Surge in Nigeria: The Rise of Charismatic Islam." *Journal of Religious and Political Practice*, forthcoming, 2016.

———. "Pentecostal Presidency? The Lagos-Ibadan 'Theocratic Class' and the Muslim 'Other.'" *Review of African Political Economy* 110 (2006): 665–678.

———. "Religious NGOs, Civil Society and the Struggle for a Public Sphere in Nigeria." *African Identities* 5, no. 1 (2007): 135–153.

Obilade, Akintunde. "Jurisdiction in Customary Law Matters in Nigeria: A Critical Examination." *Journal of African Law* 17, no. 2 (1973): 227–240.

Ochonu, Moses. *Colonialism by Proxy: Hausa Imperial Agents and Middle Belt Consciousness*. Bloomington: Indiana University Press, 2014.

———. "Colonialism within Colonialism: The Hausa-Caliphate Imaginary and British Colonial Administration of the Nigerian Middle Belt." *African Studies Quarterly* 10, no. 2 (2008).

Odinkalu, Ansel Chidi, and Civil Liberties Organisation (Lagos). *Justice Denied: The Area Courts System in the Northern States of Nigeria*. Ibadan: Kraft Books, 1992.

Oduyoye, Modupe. "The Church in Yorubaland, 1842–1892." In *The Anglican Church in Nigeria*, edited by Akinyele Omoyajowo. Ibadan: Macmillan Nigeria, 1994.

Ojo, Matthews A. "The Contextual Significance of Charismatic Movements in Independent Nigeria." *Africa* 58, no. 2 (1988): 175–192.

———. "Deeper Christian Life Ministry: A Case Study of the Charismatic Movements in Western Nigeria." *Journal of Religion in Africa* 17, no. 2 (1988): 141–162.

Ojo, Olatunji. "Afro-Brazilians in Lagos: Atlantic Commerce, Kinship, and Transnationalism." In *Back to Africa: Afro-Brazilian Returnees and Their Communities*, edited by Kwesi Kwaa Prah. Cape Town, South Africa: Centre for Advanced Studies of African Society, 2009.

Ojo-Ade, Femi. "Afro-Brazilians in Lagos: A Question of Home or Exile." In *Back to Africa: Afro-Brazilian Returnees and their Communities*, edited by Kwesi Kwaa Prah. Cape Town, South Africa: Centre for Advanced Studies of African Society, 2009.

Okereafoezeke, Nonso. *Law and Justice in Post-British Nigeria: Conflicts and Interactions between Native and Foreign Systems of Social Control in Igbo*. Westport, CT: Greenwood, 2002.

Oladimeji, Lateef. "An Appraisal of the Place of Shari'ah in the Nigerian Constitution." Presented at the 21st National Conference of the Nigerian Association of Teachers of Arabic and Islamic Studies.

Olupona, Jacob K. "The Changing Face of African Christianity: Reverse Mission in Transnational and Global Perspective." In *Transnational Africa and Globalization*, edited by Mojubaolu Olufunke Okome and Olufemi Vaughan. New York: Palgrave Macmillan, 2012.

———. "Globalization and African Immigrant Communities in America." In *Who Is Afraid of the Holy Ghost? Pentecostalism and Globalization in Africa and Beyond*, edited by Afe Adogame. Trenton, NJ: Africa World Press, 2011.

———. *Kingship, Religion, and Rituals in a Nigerian Community: A Phenomenological Study of Ondo Yoruba Festivals*. Stockholm: Almuiist and Wiksell, 1991.

Olupona, Jacob K., and Regina Gemignani, eds. *African Immigrant Religions in America*. New York: New York University Press, 2005.

Ostien, Philip. *A Study of the Court Systems of Northern Nigeria with a Proposal for the Creation of Lower Sharia Courts in Some Northern States*. Jos, Nigeria: Centre for Development Studies, University of Jos, 1999.

Oyediran, Oyeleye. "Transition without End: From Hope to Despair—Reflections of a Participant Observer." In *Dilemmas of Democracy in Nigeria*, edited by Paul A. Beckett and Crawford Young. Rochester, NY: University of Rochester Press, 1997.

Ozigboh, Ikenga R. A. *An Introduction to the Religion and History of Islam*. Enugu, Nigeria: Fourth Dimension, 1988.

Paden, John N. *Ahmadu Bello, Sarduna of Sokoto: Values and Leadership in Nigeria*. Zaria: Hudahuda, 1986.

———. *Faith and Politics in Nigeria: Nigeria as a Pivotal State in the Muslim World*. Washington, DC: U.S. Institute of Peace Press, 2008.

———. "Islam and Democratic Federalism in Nigeria." *Africa Notes, Center for Strategic and International Studies*, no. 8 (March 2002).

———. *Religion and Political Culture in Kano*. Berkeley: University of California Press, 1973.

Peel, J. D. Y. *Aladura: A Religious Movement among the Yoruba*. London: Oxford University Press, 1968.

———. "Conversion and Tradition in Two African Societies: Ijebu and Buganda." *Past and Present* 77, no. 1 (1977): 108–141.

———. *Ijeshas and Nigerians: The Incorporation of a Yoruba Kingdom, 1890s–1970s*. Cambridge: Cambridge University Press, 1983.

———. "Inequality and Action: The Forms of Ijesha Social Conflict." *Canadian Journal of African Studies* 14, no. 3 (1980): 473–502.

———. "Religious Change in Yorubaland." *Africa* 37 (1967): 292–306.

———. *Religious Encounter and the Making of the Yoruba*. Bloomington: Indiana University Press, 2003.

Peters, Rudolf. *Islam and Colonialism: The Doctrine of Jihad in Modern History*. The Hague: Mouton; Berlin: De Gruyter, 1979.

Phillips, Barnaby. "Archbishop Visits Zamfara." BBC *News*, February 3, 2001, http://news.bbc.co.uk/2/hi/africa/1152031.stm., accessed March 2007.

Post, Kenneth, and Michael Vickers. *Structure and Conflict in Nigeria, 1960–1966.* London: Heinemann, 1973.

Ranger, Terence. "The Local and the Global in Southern African Religious History." In *Conversion to Christianity: Historical and Anthropological Perspective on a Great Transformation,* edited by Robert W. Hefner. Berkeley: University of California Press, 1993.

———. "Religious Movements and Politics in Sub-Saharan Africa." *African Studies Review* 29 (1986).

———. "The Invention of Tradition Revisited: The Case of Africa." In *Legitimacy and the State in Twentieth Century Africa: Essays in Honour of A. H. M. Kirk-Greene,* edited by Terence Ranger and Olufemi Vaughan. London: Macmillan, 1993.

Rashid, Syed Khalid, ed. *Islamic Law in Nigeria: Application and Teaching.* Lagos: Islamic Publications Bureau, 1986.

"Religion of Peace: Followers Torch Christian Churches: Hundreds Seek Refuge as Mobs Riot over Alleged 'Insult' to Muhammad." *World Net Daily,* September 23, 2006.

"Reports on Ethnic Relations" (ten articles). November 2002, http://www.ethnonet-africa.org/data/Nigeria/rep1102.htm, accessed March 2007.

"Revenge in the Name of Religion." Human Rights Watch, May 26, 2005, http://www.hrw.org/reports/2005/05/25/revenge-name-religion-0, accessed April 2007.

Reynolds, Jonathan. "Good and Bad Muslims: Islam and Indirect Rule in Northern Nigeria." *International Journal of African Historical Studies* 34, no. 3 (2001): 601–618.

Robertson, A. F. "Histories and Political Opposition, Ahafo, Ghana." *Africa* 43 (1973).

Salamone, Frank A. "Ethnic Identities and Religion." In *Religion and Society in Nigeria: Historical and Sociological Perspectives,* edited by Jacob K. Olupona and Toyin Falola, Ibadan: Spectrum Books, 1991.

———. "Religion and Resistance in Pre-colonial and Colonial Nigeria." In *Religion and Society in Nigeria: Historical and Sociological Perspectives,* edited by Jacob K. Olupona and Toyin Falola. Ibadan: Spectrum Books, 1991.

Sambo, Bashir. *Shari'a and Justice: Lectures and Speeches.* Zaria, Nigeria: Sankore Educational Publishers, 2003.

Sanneh, Lamin. "The CMS and African Transformation: Samuel Ajayi Crowther and the Opening of Nigeria." In *The Church Mission Society and World Christianity, 1799–1999,* edited by Kevin Ward and Brian Stanley. Grand Rapids, MI: William B. Eerdmans, 1999.

———. *The Crown and the Turban: Muslim and West African Pluralism.* Boulder, CO: Westview, 1997.

Sanusi, Sanusi Lamido. "The West and the Rest: Reflections on the Intercultural Dialogue about Shari'ah." In *Comparative Perspectives on Shari'ah in Nigeria,* edited by Philip Ostien, Jamila M. Nasir, and Franz Kogelman, 251–302. Ibadan: Spectrum Books, 2005.

Schacht, Joseph F. "Islam in Northern Nigeria." *Studia Islamica* 8 (1957): 123–146.

Scholte, Jan Aart. "Defining Globalization." *World Economy* 31, no. 11 (November 2008): 1471–1502.

Shankar, Shobana. *Who Shall Enter Paradise: Christian Origins in Muslim Northern Nigeria, ca. 1890–1975*. Athens: Ohio University Press, 2014.
"Shariacracy on Trial." *Africa Confidential* 42, no. 17 (August 31, 2001).
Shehu, Emman Usman. *Sharia: The Fate of Northern Christians* (Church and Society Margazine), 2000.
Sklar, Richard. *Nigerian Political Parties: Power in an Emergent African Nation*. Princeton, NJ: Princeton University Press, 1963.
Smith, A. D. "The Nation, Invented, Imagined, and Reconstructed." *Millennium* 26 (1991).
Smith, M. G. *Government in Zazzau, 1800–1950*. London: Oxford University Press, 1960.
Sodiq, Yushau. "A History of Islamic Law in Nigeria." *Islamic Studies* 31 (Spring 1992): 85–108.
State of the Nation 2, no. 2 (March 2000).
Strayer, Robert. "Mission History in Africa: New Perspective on an Encounter." *African Studies Review* 19 (1976): 1–15.
Suberu, Rotimi T. "Religion and Institutions: Federalism and the Management of Conflicts over Sharia in Nigeria." *Journal of International Development* 21, no. 4 (2009): 547–560.
Sulaiman, Ibraheem. *The Islamic State and the Challenge of History: Ideals, Policies, and Operation of the Sokoto Caliphate*. East-West University Islamic Studies. New York: Mansell, 1987.
Syed Khalid Rashid, ed., *Islamic Law in Nigeria: Application and Teaching*, Lagos: Islamic Publications Bureau, 1986.
Tabi'u, Mohammed. "Constraints in the Application of Islamic Law in Nigeria." In *Islamic Law in Nigeria: Application and Teaching*, edited by S. Khalid Rashid. Lagos: Islamic Publications Bureau, 1986.
Tayob, Abdulkader I. "The Demand for Shari'ah in African Democratisation Processes: Pitfalls or Opportunities?" In *Comparative Perspectives on Shari'ah in Nigeria*, edited by Phillip Ostien, Jamila M. Nasir, and Franz Kogelmann, 27–57. Ibadan: Spectrum Books Limited, 2005.
———. "Sub-Saharan African Islam." In *The Oxford Handbook of Global Religions*, edited by Mark Jeurgensmeyer. Oxford: Oxford University Press, 2011.
"Time to Withdraw from O.I.C." *Challenge*, no. 4 (1986).
Umar, Muhammad S. "Hausa Traditional Political Culture, Islam, and Democracy: Historical Perspectives on Three Political Traditions." In *Democracy and Prebendalism in Nigeria: Critical Interpretations*, edited by Wale Adebanwi and Ebenezer Obadare. New York: Palgrave Macmillan, 2013.
Vandu, Chippla. "The Talibanization of Northern Nigeria." February 10, 2006, http://chippla.blogspot.com, accessed March 2007.
Vatican Council II. *Declaration on the Relations of the Church to Non-Christian Religions*, No. 3.
Vaughan, Olufemi. "Africa, Transnationalism, and Globalization: An Overview." In *Transnational Africa and Globalization*, edited by Mojubaolu Olufunke Okome and Olufemi Vaughan. New York: Palgrave Macmillan, 2012.

———. *Nigerian Chiefs: Traditional Power in Modern Politics, 1890s–1990s*. Rochester, NY: University of Rochester Press, 2000.

Vaughan, Olufemi, and Suraiya Zubair Banu. "Muslim Women's Rights in Northern Nigeria." Africa Program Occasional Papers Series. Washington, DC: Woodrow Wilson International Center for Scholars, 2014.

Verini, James. "The War for Nigeria: A Bloody Insurgent Tears at the Fabric of Africa's Most Populous Nation." *National Geographic*, December 17, 2013.

Vickers, Michael. *Ethnicity and Sub-Nationalism in Nigeria: Movement for a Mid-West State*. African Studies Series 3. Oxford: Worldview, 2000.

Walker, Andrew. "What Is Boko Haram?" United Institute of Peace, Special Report (June 2012): 1–16.

Wallerstein, Immanuel. "Contemporary Capitalist Dilemma, the Social Sciences, and the Geopolitics of the Twenty-First Century." *Canadian Journal of Sociology* 23, 2/3, (1998): 141–158

Wariboko, Nimi. *Nigerian Pentecostalism*. Rochester, NY: University of Rochester Press, 2014.

Warner, Zach. "The Sad Rise of Boko Haram." *New African*, April 2012,

Webster, J. B., and A. Adu Boahen. *History of West Africa: The Revolutionary Years—1815 to Independence*. New York: Praeger, 1967.

Whitaker, C. S., Jr. *The Politics of Tradition: Continuity and Change in Northern Nigeria, 1946–1966*. Princeton, NJ: Princeton University Press, 1970.

Williams, David. *President and Power in Nigeria: The Life of Shehu Shagari*. London: Frank Cass, 1982.

Williams, Patricia A. "The State, Religion, and Politics in Nigeria." PhD diss., University of Ibadan, 1988.

Yadudu, Auwalu H. "Colonialism and the Transformation of the Substance and Form of Islamic Law in the Northern States of Nigeria." *Journal of Law and Religion* 9, no. 1 (1991): 17–47.

Yesufu, Tijani M., ed. *World Inter-Religious Crisis: An Islamic Initiative for Peace*. Lagos: West Africa Book Publishers, 2005.

Yusuf, Ahmed Beita. *Nigerian Legal System: Pluralism and Conflict of Laws in the Northern States*. Delhi, India: National Publishing House, 1982.

Zeleza, Paul. "Africa and Its Diaspora: Remembering South America." *Research in African Literatures* 40, no. 4 (Winter 2009): 151–159.

INDEX

Abacha, Mariam, 189–90
Abacha, Sani, 126, 137, 150, 187, 208, 254n118
Abduh, Mohammed, 169
Abdulkadir, Ahmed, 216, 253n73
Abdulkarim, Abubakar Rabo, 220
Abeokuta, 26, 29–32, 36, 75, 238n86, 238n93, 238n97; evangelizing in, 27, 28, 69; middle class and, 35; Western medicine in, 238n86, 238n90
Abiakam, Obumna, 200
Abiara, Prophet Samuel Kayode, 208
Abiola, Moshood, 137–38, 175, 193, 255n118
Abubakar, General Abdulsalami, 137–38
Abubakar, Vice President Atiku, 188
Abubakar, Sir, III, 117, 123, 127, 136
Abuja, 161, 212
Achimuga, Peter, 105
Action Group (AG), 94, 116, 118, 123, 247n31
Adamawa, 20, 42, 58, 82, 85, 97, 147, 159, 188; Boko Haram and, 219, 229
Adamawa Province, 85, 97
Adeboye, Pastor Enoch Adejare, 145, 150, 196, 209
Adeboye, Tope, 184
Adegbite, Lateef, 131, 163–65, 174–77, 196, 254n86
Adeleke, Adetunji, 210
Adetiloye, Bishop J. A. (Anglican), 128
Adigwe, Monsignor Hypolite A., 127–28, 253n70
Ado-Ekiti, 28, 30, 34
Ado-Kurawa, Ibrahim, 174, 176, 179
adultery (*zina*), 48, 54, 169, 205–6, 221

Afigbo, Adele, 113
Africa, 99, 145; Christian missions in, 83, 84, 236n58; Christian student groups in, 146; colonial, 78, 80; diaspora and African history and, 154; European civilizing mission in, 80; Nigeria and, 1; spread of Christianity in, 155, 243n9
African-initiated churches (AIC), 37, 81, 139, 142, 151, 157. *See also* Aladura
Afro-Brazilian returnees (Aguda), 36
Agabi, Kanu Godwin, 207
Agbaje, Fred, 191
Agbebi, Reverend Mojola, 31
Ahmad, Muhammad, 43–44
Ahmadu Bello University (University of Zaria), 126, 143, 264n33
Ajasin, Michael, 71–72
Ajayi, J. F. Ade, 25, 33
Akinola, Archbishop Peter (Anglican), 186, 193–94, 267n92
Akintoye, S. Adebanji, 34, 38
Akoko, 27, 28
Akure, 28, 34
Aladura (Those Who Pray) (African-initiated Christian church), 3, 70, 81, 82, 142, 144, 243n5
Algeria, 15, 92, 179, 239n10
Alkali, Bello, 173
Allah: sovereignty of, 16, 17, 18, 19, 163, 173, 201; word of, 170, 182
All Nigeria Peoples Party (ANPP), 220, 221
Alli, Maj. Gen. Mohammed Chris, 213
Amina, Queen of Zaria, 203
Anderson, Allen, 151

Anderson, Norman, 104–5
Anglicans, 30, 37, 97, 98, 128, 186, 193–94
Anih, Dr. Stan, *The Cathedral and the Mosque*, 130
Arabian Peninsula, 100, 101
Arabic, 16, 17, 37, 67, 93, 108, 165, 170
Arewa Consultative Forum (ACF), 178
Arewa Peoples Congress, 178
Argungu riots in, 115
Arinze, Cardinal Francis, 129–30
Ashafa, Imam Muhammad, 213
Asm'u, Nana, 203, 269n42
assassinations, 115, 116, 118, 133, 208, 250n23, 252n44
Akinyele, I. B., *Iwe Itan Ibadan*, 73
Atlantic Yoruba communities, 1, 8, 225
Attahira, Muhammadu, I, 45
Awolowo, Obafemi, 94, 118, 123, 233n5
Ayegumbiyi, Thomas, 30
Azikiwe, Nnamdi, 94, 124
Ibn al-Aziz, Caliph Umar, 168

Babangida, Ibrahim, 127, 130, 132, 137, 193; OIC and, 128, 253n67, 253n70; regime of, 126, 135–36, 183
Badagry, 28, 32
Badran, Margot, 206
Bakare, Pastor Tunde, 209
Bako, Abubakar, 132
Balewa, Sir Abubakar Tafawa, 91, 94, 133, 246–47n17; assassination of, 116, 250n23; as prime minister, 250–51n23; *Shaihu Umar*, 23
Baptists, 27, 28, 30, 37, 73, 264n33; Southern, 30, 31, 237–38n86
Barnes, Andrew, 84, 86
Barth, Heinrich, 39
Bassey, Magnus, 32
Batley, Sybil K., 33
Bauchi, 20, 56, 59, 60, 100; expanded sharia and, 159, 173, 198, 220–21; riots in, 136–37, 212
Bayero, Emir Abdullahi, 54–55
Bell, Governor Hesketh, 65

Bello, Sir Ahmadu, 91–92, 113–14, 153; assassination of, 115, 116, 250n23
Bello, Sultan Atiku, 20
Bello, Justice Mohammed, 165, 171–72, 201
Bello, Sultan Mohammed, 17–21, 39, 47, 239n1; works of, 20
Bendel State, 123
Benedict XVI, Pope, 267n94
Benson, A. E. T., 93–94
Benue-Plateau State, 82, 86, 87, 118, 119, 212, 251n29
Benue River, 5, 25, 39, 94, 247n27
Berom, 214
Berry, Sara, 71–72
Biafra, Republic of, 119, 129, 141, 251n31. See also Nigerian-Biafra Civil War
Bible, 33, 34, 72, 143, 144, 145
Bida emirate, 31, 39–40, 105
Birks, D. T. M., 62–64
Boko Haram ("Western civilization forbidden"; "Western Education Is Sinful"), 219, 223, 230, 272n8; attacks by, 192, 229, 272n7
Bonnke, Richard, 126
Bornu, 21, 43–46, 97, 105, 124, 126, 159, 207, 214; Boko Haram in, 219, 223, 229; Bornu Youth Movement in, 95, 247n33
Bouche, Father Pierre, 32
Bowen, Thomas Jefferson, 31, 237–38n86
Brazil, Yoruba returnees and, 27, 28, 34, 36
Brice Smith, H. M., 64
British rule, 1, 2, 8–9, 76–80, 225; Christianity under, 5, 8, 83; Christian missions and, 25, 82–85, 97, 242n98; empire making and, 78; hegemony of, 37; imposition of, 13, 14; Islam and, 55, 74, 242n94; Mahadism and, 42–47; Northern Nigerian Colonial Service, 100; in Northern Nigerian Protectorate, 6; paternalism of, 76; Al Rahman and, 44–45; sharia and, 176, 228; Sokoto Caliphate and, 5–6; in south, 4; welfare and healthcare and, 82, 83; women and, 204. See also colonialism; decolonization; indirect rule

Brown, Chief Justice Sir Algernon, 106
Buhari, Muhammadu, 126, 127, 207, 208, 229
Burmi, Battle of, 45
Buxton, Thomas Fowell, 24

Callaway, Barbara, 203
Callow, Captain G., 42
Cameron, Donald, 65–67, 242n92, 242n94
Cameroon, 127, 180
Canterbury, Archbishop of, 187, 194
Carrow, J. H., 51, 53–55, 66
Catholicism, Catholics, 36, 37, 82, 95, 98, 128, 152, 195; bishops, 127, 128–29, 132, 181, 196; Catholic Brothers and, 83, 85–88; Catholic Missions and, 30, 85, 98; collaboration with Protestants, 120–21; missionary work of, 32, 73, 97, 120; Muslims and, 129; priests, 32, 130; social issues and, 86–87, 97, 121; Vatican, 129, 130, 193; Vatican II, 128, 129
Chad, 127, 180, 229, 239n10
Chibok, 223
Chidester, David, 36
Christian Association of Nigeria (CAN), 132, 181, 185, 186, 190, 196; formation of, 121; in Katsina, 191; NCRA and, 130; okada and, 220; PFN and, 151
Christian Council of Nigeria, 81, 83, 98, 120
Christianity, 1, 4, 7, 72–76, 243n9; adaptation of, 69–70; charismatic, 80–82, 91, 142, 144, 146, 149, 151, 154, 157, 226, 230; colonial rule and, 8, 83; conversion to, 2–4, 37, 113, 243n12; doctrine and theology of, 3, 36, 37, 164; identity frameworks of, 4; modernization and, 74; social significance of, 223–28, 243n11; structure and, 2, 141; struggles with Islam, 83, 84, 129, 153, 207–11, 230–31; universal language of, 67; as world religion, 4, 5, 129, 243n12; Yoruba region and, 24–26, 70–72; *See also* evangelicals, evangelism; missions, missionaries; world religions; *other "Christian" entries; and under names of denominations*

Christian missionary work, 13, 24–28, 102, 225; ambivalence in, 76–80; by Catholics, 30, 32, 73, 85, 85–88, 97, 98, 120; colonial policy and, 82–85, 98; education and, 34, 82, 164; Muslims and, 69, 83, 84, 121; war and, 141; Western literacy and, 33. *See also* Church Missionary Society; missions, missionaries
Christians: anxiety of, 124; identity of, 10, 36–38; Igbos as, 250–51n23; "indigenes" as, 125, 152; as migrants, 49, 113, 156; as military officers, 252n44; as minorities, 181–82, 227, 251n31; Obasanjo and, 208–11; relations amongst, 97–98; relations between Muslims and, 127–34; rights of, 127, 181, 186; security needs of, 199; sharia and, 182, 207–11, 220–22; violence against, 126, 136, 210, 264n33, 267n94; Yoruba as, 7, 138, 179, 182, 185, 195, 252n44
Christian Union (CU), 142, 143
Church Missionary Society (CMS), 24–25, 27–30, 32, 82, 83, 98, 238n90, 238n97, 244n28; in Atlantic Yoruba, 1, 7; bookshops and printing presses of, 34, 238n93; in Eastern Region, 97; Niger Diocese of, 35; reports of, 50
Church of God Mission, 146, 150
citizenship, citizens, 188, 247n31, 259n41; civil rights and, 166–67, 179, 182, 183, 205; freedom of movement of, 211, 260n56
civil war. *See* Nigerian-Biafra Civil War
Clapperton, Captain Hugh, 39
Clarkson, Thomas, 24
Clifford, Governor Sir Hugh, 59–60, 65, 67
CMS. *See* Church Missionary Society
cocoa cultivation, 71–72
colonialism, 72–76; Mahdism and, 43; mission Christianity and, 9, 87, 243n9; Yoruba society and, 70–72. *See also* British rule; decolonization; indirect rule
Committee for National Unity and Progress, 124
Committee of Elders, 135

Index 297

Committee of Friends, 123, 124
Committee on the Elimination of Discrimination against Women (CEDAW), 205, 206
commoners, 15, 93. See also *talakawa*
common law. See law, English common
community, communities, 2, 5, 13, 19
Constituent Assembly (1978), 164
Constituent Assembly (1989), 136, 164
constitutional conferences, 89; first (1946), 245n1; of 1951, 89–90
constitutional democratic system, 255n118
Constitution of 1922: court reform under, 49
Constitution of 1951. *See* Macpherson Conference and Constitution
Constitution of 1954, 90, 95. *See also* London Constitution Conference
Constitution of 1960, 90
Constitution of 1979, 121–22, 138, 182
Constitution of 1987–88, 187
Constitution of 1999: rights and freedoms in, 211, 258n29, 259n55, 260n56; religion in, 259n30, 259n41, 260n57, 260n59; sharia and, 161, 201–2
conversion, 233n4: analyses of, 2–4; by Muslims, 37, 132; of pagans, 113; socioeconomic environment and, 5, 243n12
cosmologies, 3, 4; indigenous, 9, 37, 243n17
cotton industry, 204, 238n96
Council of Ulama, 130, 132, 177
courts. *See* Islamic law and courts; sharia; and *"law" entries*
Crampton, E. P. T., 58
Criminal Procedure Code, 48, 49, 85, 106, 109, 161; Islamic law and, 89, 106–7, 162, 169; sharia and, 122, 124, 136, 153, 158, 165–67, 170, 179, 186, 205, 210, 260n61
Cross River, 123, 124, 135, 200
Crowder, Michael, 17, 22
Crowther, Dr. Samuel, Jr., 238n90
Crowther, Reverend Samuel Ajayi, 25, 29, 32–33, 34, 238n90
Cuba, 28, 34
cult of Supreme Being, 3, 233n7

Dadiya, 210, 214
Dahomey Kingdom, 28, 31
Daniel, Isiome, 212
Dasuki, Ibrahim, 115, 123, 128, 133, 136–38
Daura, 14
David-West, Tam, 197
Debki, Bee, 185–86, 209–10, 264n33
decolonization, 9, 50, 67, 68, 81, 88, 101, 193, 204; Islam and Christianity under, 8, 9–10, 216, 227; in Middle Belt, 112–13; political process and leadership during, 91–95, 122; religious identity and, 95–98; Repugnancy Clause and, 162; post–World War II, 7, 62–63
Decree No. 34, 117, 118
Deeper Life Bible Church (Pentecostal), 144, 145, 151, 257n88
De Foucauld, Charles, 83, 84
DeGraft, William, 31
Dellaji, Emir Umoru, 22
democracy: fragility of, 125, 182; transition to, 121–22, 132, 135–38, 182, 183, 186
demography, demographics, 19, 26, 27, 82
Denning, Lord Alfred Thompson, 99
diaspora, 15, 154; identities of, 36–38
Dikwa District, 60
Docasta, Olubi, 188
Donli, Hansen, 132

Eastern Region, 91, 94, 97, 118, 247n7; Eastern Solidarity Group and, 135
Eclectic Movement, 186, 195
economic resources, 15, 31, 156, 197–98
economic transformation, 69, 71, 72, 82, 125, 224
ecumenicalism, ecumenism, 120–21, 129, 130
Edo, 94, 123, 146, 150
education, 4, 67, 88, 110, 156, 186, 195, 264n33; almajiri system of, 192; Christian, 29, 176; elementary, 49, 88; Islamic, 54, 115, 176; mission schools, 54, 84, 87, 94, 156; moral and religious, 120–21; in North, 53–54, 90; post-secondary, 98, 115; of talakawa, 21, 176; vocational, 27,

29, 35; Western, 73; of women, 21, 54, 176, 204, 269n42
Efik, 94, 135
Egbados, 26
Egbas, 24, 26, 27, 30
Egbe, Fred, 184
Egypt, 43–44, 46, 81
Ejoor, Major David, 116
Ekiti, 27, 28, 29, 31
emirates, emirs, 21, 57, 105; Hausa-Fulani, 91, 127; of Kano, 51, 107, 109, 194; in Northern Provinces, 64, 116, 117, 251n24, 251n25; sharia and, 89, 179; social structure and, 74
English common law. *See* law, English common
Enwerem, Iheanyi, 114, 120
Episcopal Church, Episcopalians, 129, 194, 267n92
Eritrea, 44
Essien, E., 165
Ethiopia, 43, 44, 81
ethnic groups and ethno-national identity, 6, 36–38, 63, 94; diversity of, 1, 94; Igbo, 94; religion and, 137, 215–16. *See also names of specific peoples*
evangelicals, evangelism, 1, 25, 36, 84, 145, 149, 152, 199; as missionaries, 3, 236n58; in Southern Nigeria, 13–14, 24, 27–29; student groups, 142–44; *See also* Pentecostal churches and movement; *and* "Christian" entries

Fajuyi, Col. F. Adekunle, 116, 118
Falae, Olu, 210
Falola, Toyin, 73
Fawehinmi, Gani, 197
Federal Executive Council, 118
Federal Military Government (FMG), 117, 118, 121, 128, 132, 137
Federation of Muslim Women's Association of Nigeria (FOMWAN), 205, 206
dan Fodio, Abdullahi, 18, 20, 203; works of, 17, 19–20

dan Fodio, Usman, 45, 91, 92, 113, 115, 203, 269n42; Islamic reformist teaching of, 16, 134; legacy of, 43, 47, 93; Sokoto Jihad and, 16–24, 93; tomb of, 54, 114; works of, 19
Freeman, Thomas Birch, 31, 32
Fulani Muslims, 46, 49, 56, 94; Mahdism and, 43, 47; as reformers, 1–2, 5, 6, 14, 15, 235n14; as rulers, 21, 22, 41, 51–52, 58, 64

Gade, 50, 61–62
Gaffar, Abdul, 177
Gambari, Alhaji Ibrahim Sulu, 172, 202
Gambia, 92, 239n10
gardawa, 125
Gbadamosi, Tajudeen, 196
gender: identity and, 2; in Islam, 152, 169, 204; under sharia, 189, 197. *See also* women
geocultural regions, 5, 6, 13, 27
globalization, 155–56; economic, 148, 193, 257n84; Islam and, 170, 171, 193; media and, 148–150; Pentecostalism and, 154–57; religious movements and, 13, 149
Gobir, 14, 235n14, 235n32; Usman dan Fodio and, 16, 17, 235n32
Goje, Mohammed Danjuma, 222
Gold Coast, 31, 35, 97, 117
Goldie, George Taubman, 25
Gombe, 62–63, 126, 159, 175; sharia in, 221–22
Gordon Memorial College (University of Khartoum), 46, 67
Gowon, Lt. Col. Yakubu, 116, 122, 133, 192, 252n44; death of, 134; Hausa-Fulani Muslim rulers and, 118–19, 251n29, 251n31; reconstruction policy of, 120, 121
Grant, Charles, 24
Great Depression, 66
Great Nigerian Peoples Party, 124
Grier, S. M., 60
Gudu, 17
Guinea, 92, 239n10
Gulf states, 156, 169

Gumi, Sheikh Abubakar, 115, 134, 163, 211–12, 251n29; as reformist, 122, 133–34
Guy, J. C., 56
Gwandu, 20
Gwani, Gideon, 216
Gwari, 14, 50; headmen, 57

Hackett, Rosalind, 147
Hadejia uprising (1906), 40
hadith, 18, 134, 173, 202; Qur'an and, 165, 168, 206, 269n43
Hamsa, Chiroma, 52, 53
Harnischfeger, Johannes, 164, 189, 200, 210, 214–15
Hartford, James, 66
Hashidu, Governor Abubakar Habu, 175, 221–22
Hausa-Fulani Muslim rulers, 21, 49, 50, 54, 88, 105, 108, 122, 127, 159, 176, 205, 214, 235n14, 247n33, 250n23; Boko Haram and, 219; British colonial rulers and, 9–10, 41, 60, 94, 118, 176, 226; centralization and, 40, 52; challenges to, 5, 9, 116–17; Christians and, 82–83, 93–94, 98, 208–11, 250–51n23; conservatism of, 53; consolidate power base, 6, 50, 61, 65–68, 93; decolonization and, 227; Gowon administration and, 251n29, 251n31; identity of, 6, 94, 178, 231; as non/indigenes, 211–12, 215; Islamization and, 124; Izala and, 134; misrule by, 21, 93; non-Muslims marginalized and abused by, 80, 90, 112–13; in North, 7–8, 11, 224; pagan tribes and, 58, 59, 61–62, 67; reforms and, 167; resistance to, 69; settlers and, 152; sharia crisis and, 200, 211–16, 228; Sokoto Jihad and, 225; taxation and tribute and, 56, 57–58, 241n78
Hausas, 2, 5, 8, 14, 15, 21, 49, 50, 93, 94, 184, 235n14, 243n17; city-states of, 1, 38; culture and language of, 6, 20, 86, 95, 108, 110, 134, 234n1; in Northern Protectorate, 6, 13
Hausawa, 14
Haynes, Jeffrey, 84, 85

Hefner, Robert, 5, 18
Heerey, Archbishop Charles (Catholic), 97
Held, David, 155
Hinderer, David, 30, 72, 73
hisba, 19–20, 171, 206, 217–18, 220
Horton, Robin, 3–4, 233n5, 233n7
House of Assembly, 105, 109, 158, 165, 166, 173, 184, 216
Howard, Resident, 63
humanitarianism and human rights, 129, 194, 166–67, 182, 194, 202, 203, 205, 221; Human Rights Watch and, 212–14
Hussaini, Safiya, 205

Ibadan, 27, 34, 78, 176, 178, 237n72; cocoa cultivation in, 72; as new garrison town, 27; CMS bookshop in, 34; conference in, 117–18; conversion to mission Christianity in, 28, 243n12; Christian missions in, 28, 30, 69, 72–74, 146, 243n12; cotton in, 238n97; education in, 30, 73, 98; identities in, 74; Islam and, 74; migration to, 31; news media outlets of, 176, 192; rulers of, 27, 117; transformations in, 72–76; University of, 142, 143, 144; violence in, 178
Ibibios, 32, 94, 135
Ibrahim, Waziri, 124
Ibrahim, Yakubu Yahay, 174
Idahosa, Benson, 146, 150
identity, 2, 23, 34, 36, 154, 155, 211, 235n14; Christian, 10, 187, 211, 215; communal, 7, 60; ethno-religious, 6, 7, 68; ethnonational, 6, 7, 38; Fulani, 22, 63; Hausa-Fulani Muslim, 6, 68, 178, 231; Middle Belt regional, 6, 210, 216; Muslim, 166, 167, 178, 171, 195; religious, 4, 60, 163, 187, 215; self-, 5; sociopolitical, 6, 193; Yoruba and, 7, 34, 36, 226
Idoma, 82, 97
Ife, 27, 28, 34, 38, 150, 152, 233n5, 237n72
Igbos, 26, 32, 94, 116–19, 135, 197, 210, 251n31, 265n51; as Catholics, 86, 129, 130; as Christians, 30, 184, 196, 200,

300 Index

250–51n23; Igboland and, 35; as nonindigenes, 211–12; NPN and, 123
Ijaye, 27, 28, 31
Ijaw, 94, 193
Ijebu, 24, 72–76, 94, 243n12
Ijebu Ode, 28, 30, 69, 34, 72–76
Ijesa, 27
Ikenne, 94
Ikorodu, 28
Ile-Ife, 34, 150; as cradle of Yoruba civilization, 38, 237n72
Ilesanmi, Simeon, 140, 150, 155
Ilorin emirate, 20, 26, 27, 39–40, 172, 202, 214
Imagbo War, 74, 75
immigration, immigrants, 59, 127, 155, 162; from Nigeria, 156, 257n88; of skilled workers, 156; Southern Christian, 31, 75, 95, 157, 188
imperialism, 6, 80, 102, 235n14; anti-, 159; British, 25, 35, 37, 60, 78, 225; Mahdism and, 43; mission Christianity and, 35, 76–78, 83, 236n58, 243n9, 243n12; Sokoto and, 21, 62
independence, 94, 110, 112, 142, 159
India, 24, 30, 47, 99, 106
indigenes, 211, 214–15; in Kaduna State, 184; Northern Christian, 125, 182, 190
indigenous religions, 1–3, 28, 37, 81, 151, 233n4, 233n5; Christianity and, 69, 70, 149, 243n2, 243n5; cosmologies of, 4, 141, 243n17; in Northern Nigeria, 5, 58, 61
indirect rule, 51–64; in Kaduna State, 182; Lugardian system of, 47, 58, 60, 61, 65, 80, 82, 84, 100, 231; in Northern Provinces, 88
Institute of Administration, Zaria, 109, 110
intellectualist paradigm (Horton and Peel), 3, 4
International Monetary Fund, 136
Inusa, Mallum, 105
Iran, 92, 179, 180, 191
Iraq, 92, 180
Ironsi, Major General Johnson Thomas Umunnakwe Aguiyi-, 116–18, 122, 251n23

Islam, 1, 2, 4, 7, 19, 21, 95, 121; aristocracy of, 55; Christianity and, 83, 84, 129, 230–31; colonial rule and, 8, 39–68; conversion from, 84, 129, 132; conversion to, 2–4, 114; Council of Mallams, 114–16, 119; culture of, 176; decolonization and, 216; doctrines of, 42, 96–97, 133, 239n5; egalitarianism in, 93; extremism in, 124, 223; growth of, 49; Hausa and, 15; holy places of, 131; moderate, 45; mosques and, 21, 92, 126, 128, 137, 191, 196; prayer in, 114, 115; radical, 45, 228; reformism in, 1–2, 5, 14, 23; schools and, 54; social justice in, 93; society and, 223–28; women in, 134, 197, 206; as world religion, 7; Yorubas and, 37, 243n11, 243n17. *See also* Allah; Muslims; Prophet Muhammad; Qur'an, Quran; sharia; Sokoto Jihad; world religions
Islamic Development Bank, 133, 164
Islamic law and courts, 19, 21, 99, 152, 168, 195, 251n39, 259n41; alkali courts, 21, 48, 55, 59, 105, 109, 133; Aminu Kano and, 93; common law and, 162–63, 172; Constitution and, 162, 201–2; contending issues in, 99–104; eroded authority of, 49; evolution of, 171–72; fiqh, 167–68; formalization of, 41, 48; history of, 179; under indirect rule, 58; intolerance and, 185; jurisprudence, 168–70; in Kano, 55; military government and, 251n39; lack of confidence in, 53; legal context of, 160–62; military government and, 251n39, 252n40; native administration and, 47–50; neo-Salafi models of, 169; in Northern Nigeria, 99–111; overlapping jurisdictions of, 52–53; political context of, 160–62; provocation in, 104, 107–8; in Qur'an, sunnah, and hadith, 173; reform of, 66–67; rents and taxes in, 53, 56; as specific law, 100; state law and, 159; Usman dan Fodio on, 18, 19; women and, 169, 203–6; written, 165–66. *See also* Penal Code; *and "sharia" entries*

Islamic reformism, 8, 16, 18, 101, 153, 170; Izala and, 133–34, 152, 169; Muhammad al-Maghili and, 15; Pentecostals and, 153–54; resurgence of, 152, 230; by Sokoto Caliphate, 13, 158; Sokoto Jihad as, 16; youth and, 178
Islamic thought, 15, 16, 19, 167–177
Islamization, 92, 119, 179, 183, 187, 193
Ismail, Aishat, 184
Iwo, 179, 237–38n86
Izala (Jama't Izalat al Bid'a Wa Iqamat as Sunna), 133–34, 169, 178, 193

Jakada caliphate, 57, 241n76
Jalo, Barrister Abdullahi, 175
Jamat-Ul-Islamiyya, 196
Jama'atu Nasril Islam (JNI) (Society for the Victory of Islam), 115, 119, 133, 171, 195, 196
Jam'iyyar Mutanen Arewa, 93
jangali, 22
Jatau, Right Reverend Peter, 199
Jigawa State, 159, 207, 212
jihad, jihads 16, 17, 26. *See also* Sokoto Jihad
John Paul II, Pope, 126, 129–30
Jonathan, Goodluck, 221
Jordan, 92
Jos, 99, 103, 120, 134, 143, 218; Catholics in, 86, 120; violence in, 212, 215–16
Judicial Reform Committee, 105–6
Judicial Service Commission, 161
Jukun, 210, 212
Junaidu of Sokoto, 115
justice, 21, 153, 165

Kabara, Nasiru, 96
Kaduna, 103, 106, 132, 134, 199, 201, 212, 218; Christians flee, 179, 197; colonial administrators in, 58, 68; Kaduna State Polytechnic, 192, 264n33; politics in, 49; as regional capital, 66, 115, 251n25; riots in, 131–33, 137, 178–79, 184–85, 195, 209, 213, 264n33; schools in, 115; sharia in, 159, 183, 216, 221; Yoruba diaspora churches in, 31
Kafanchan, 31, 86; religious violence in, 131–32
Kaita, Isa, 108
Kajes, 216
Kalu, Ogbu, 8, 140, 144, 151
Kalu, Governor Orji Uzor, 210
Kanawa, 14
Kanem-Bornu Empire, 17, 21, 40; British and, 9, 225; Sokoto Jihad and, 20, 247n33
Kano, 14, 15, 20, 48, 51–54, 64, 121, 176, 239n11; Catholics in, 120; churches burned in, 126; courts in, 50, 54, 55; emirate and emir of, 51, 52, 54–55, 56, 96, 107, 109, 194; hisba in, 217–19; law school in, 67, 133; missions in, 82; mosques in, 137; as principal city, 125; railroad to, 49; schools and education in, 15, 53–54; sharia in, 159, 207, 220; slavery in, 53; Sufis in, 96; tensions between orders in, 42, 96; violent riots in, 125, 137
Kano, Aminu, 93, 115, 123, 133
Kanuri, 94, 95, 124
Karsar Hausa, 14
Kashim, Shettima, 105
Katafs, 192, 216
Katsina, 14, 82, 97, 127, 191, 218; emirs of, 22, 116; expanded sharia in, 159, 176; Islamic university in, 176; religious riots in, 137–38; sharia in, 159, 173–74, 220
Katsina, Major Hassan, 116, 117, 251n24, 251n25
Katsinawa, 14
Kebbi, 14, 159, 213
Kendhammer, Brandon, 171
Khartoum, 46, 67
Kingdom of Tlemcen, 15
kinship identity, 2, 103
Kofa system, 57
Kolapo, Femi J., 37
Kolo, Right Rev. Jonah G., 186, 190
Korororfa, 14
kufar (unbelievers), 46

Kukah, Reverend Dr. Matthew Hassan, 95, 132, 171, 195
Kumuyi, William Folorunso, 144
Kuta, 57
Kuwait, 92, 115
Kwankwaso, Rabiu Musa, 217, 220
Kwara, 123, 180; as new Middle Belt state, 118, 119, 251n29
Kwara State College of Islamic Studies, 163
Kwoiranga, 63
Kwoiranga II, 64

Ladigbolu, Alaafin Siyanbola, 77
Laffia, 82, 112
Lagos, 27, 29, 76, 79, 95, 123, 145, 176, 178; Afro-Brazilian returnees in, 36; churches in, 146, 151; colonial administrators in, 25, 28, 58, 60, 65, 66, 68, 96, 107; education in, 29–32, 35, 238n86; evangelizing in, 25, 27, 28, 31, 69, 75; middle class and, 35; migration and, 31, 75; military authorities in, 251n25; Muslim influence in, 24; news media in, 34, 176, 182, 186, 191, 192, 194, 203, 212, 238n93; politics in, 91, 123; railroad to, 49; University of, 143, 144; violence in 178, 179; Western Christian schools in, 31, 32, 238n86; as Yoruba state, 123
Lamido, Sule, 172
Lander, John, 39
Lander, Richard, 39
Larémont, Rene, 67
Last, Murray, 200, 215, 218, 235n4; on emirates, 47, 170; on Islamic law, 21, 171, 217
al Latif, Ali Abd, 46
Latosisa, Are, 74
law and courts: customary, 99, 100, 101, 103, 121, 251n39, 252n40; general, 99–100; native, 100; specific, 99, 100. *See also* Islamic law; law, English common; sharia
law, English common, 89, 91, 102, 107, 110, 162–65; Christian roots of, 202; corruption in, 174–75; courts of, 48, 106, 161; doctrines of, 100; forms of, 99; general law and, 99–100; inheritance in, 103; native law and, 99, 107, 109–10, 172; sharia and, 49, 89, 98, 100, 103–4, 160, 162–63, 166, 168, 170, 172, 174, 182, 228; training in, 91, 161
law, sharia. *See* sharia
Lawal, Amina, 205
Lebanon, 92
Lejeune, Father, 32
Lekwot, General Zamani, 186
Letchworth, T. E., 58, 61–62, 67
Lethem, G. J., 42, 43, 44, 45–46, 47, 60
Libya, 92, 105, 180, 188
Lipshutz, Ronnie, 193
Lokoja, 39
London, 94, 105, 257n88; conferences in, 93, 94, 99
Lubeck, Paul, 125, 153–54, 159, 169, 174, 187, 193
Ludwig, Frieder, 188–89, 190, 191
Lugard, Colonel Frederick, 40, 45, 85; indirect rule and, 47, 58, 60, 61, 65, 80, 82, 84, 100, 231
Lutheran mission, 82
Lutz, Father, 32

Mac, Tee, 189–90
Macaulay, Zachary, 24
Maccido, Alhaji Muhammadu, 137, 178
Macpherson, Sir John Stuart, 89, 90, 91–92, 119, 246n27
Macpherson Conference and Constitution (1951), 89–90
al-Maghili, Muhammad, 15
Maghreb, 15, 16, 83, 161
Maguire, Reverend, 86, 87–88
Mahdi (the Direct One) and Mahdism, 21, 42–47, 96
mahdiyya (Sufi order), 42; state of, 43
Maiduguri, 214
Maitatsine, 219
Makaman Bida, 123, 252n48
Makarfi, Ahmed Mohammed, 221

Makerere College Conference (1953), 99
Makurdi, 82, 120, 250n4
Malami, Shehu, 123
Maliki law, 21, 41, 48, 56, 108, 168, 169, 170
Mann, Kristin, 70–71
Maratta, 16
Marshall, Hedley, 106–7, 108, 246n13
Marshall, Ruth, 140, 153
Martin, Anna, 72
Marwa, Mohammed, 219
Masina, 16
masu sarauta, 42, 95, 111, 116, 117, 120, 133, 204; legitimacy of, 113, 122; NPC and, 115, 123
Matthew, Dr. David, 97
Mauritania, 180, 239n10
Mbang, Dr. Sunday, 182
McGarvey, Kathleen, 203
McGrew, Anthony, 155
Mecca, pilgrimages to, 196, 265n45
merchants and trade, 5, 25–26, 27
Methodists, 27, 28, 30, 32, 37, 73, 75, 83, 98, 182
methodology of book, 2, 5, 7
Middle Belt region, 1, 6, 9, 62, 99, 116, 247n36, 251n29; Christian minorities in, 95, 118, 184, 227, 247n36, 250n1, 251n31, 252n44; Christian missionaries in, 84, 85, 87, 97–98, 103, 120; Christian radicals in, 91, 92; ethnic diversity in, 87; migration to, 68, 103; as non-Muslim, 5, 8, 242n98; Pentecostalism in, 187, 230; religious tension in, 50, 112, 124–25, 210–15, 218, 228, 264n33; social transformations in, 10, 215, 224
Mid-West Region, 116, 119, 123
military government, 19, 122, 193, 251n39; coups and, 116, 125, 252n44; Muslim-Christian relations under, 127–34; religion and national politics and, 116–21; transition to democracy, 135–38, 186, 252n50
millenarianism, 43, 46, 96
Miller, Ethel, *The Truth about Mohammed*, 84, 85

Miller, Dr. Walter Samuel, 84
mission Christianity, 5, 6, 8–9, 61, 37, 80, 139, 225, 243n9; colonialism and, 9, 242n98, 243n9; Yoruba ethno-national identity and, 7, 10, 36–37, 38, 243n11, 243n12
missions, missionaries, 35, 50; Catholic, 85–88; colonial administrators and, 46, 97, 98; impact of, 4, 225–27; in Northern Provinces, 67, 234n19; Saro, 28, 29, 33, 36, 76, 244n28; schools of, 54, 86, 94; in Southern Provinces and Middle Belt, 10, 97; Yoruba, 37, 38. *See also* Church Missionary Society
modernization, 28, 70, 71, 72–76, 164, 170; Pentecostalism and, 139, 150
Mohammed, General Murtala, 121, 122, 133, 252n50; assassination of, 208, 252n44
Mohammed, Brigadier General Sagir, 178
monotheism, 3, 102
Morley, J. A. E., 62
Morocco, 92, 128, 180
Mu'azu, Ahmadu Adamu, 220–21
ibn Muhammad, Abdullahi, 44
multireligiosity, 163–65
Muryar Hisba (The Voice of Hisba), 217
Musa, Balarabe, 123, 201
Muslim, Muslims, 92, 95, 121, 152, 169, 250n23; anti-sharia, 176; attack Christians, 131–33, 264n33, 267n94; Catholics and, 129; clash with Christian missionaries, 83, 84; as clerics, 15; "good" and "bad," 40–41; Hausa-Fulani, 5; Mahdism and, 43; marry Christians, 129; modernist reasoning and, 169; Northern, 172, 177–80; on OIC Consultative Committee, 128; reformist movements of, 1, 6, 14, 133, 235n14; relations between Christians and, 127–34, 153; students as radical, 130; tensions among, 96, 126, 133; women as, 129, 184, 205, 206, 269n42, 269n43; Yoruba as, 137, 196, 197. *See also* Fulani Muslims; Islam
Muslim Brotherhood, 180

304 Index

Muslim Court of Appeal, 101–2, 109
Mustapha, Abubakar, 171

Nafate, Yunfa, 17
Nasarawa, 50, 61, 62, 108, 159
Nasir, Jemila, 201
National Council for Religious Affairs (NCRA), 130
National Council of Nigeria Citizens (NCNC), 94–95, 123–24
National Council of State (NCS), 207
National Human Rights Commission, 190
National Institute of Moral and Religious Education, 120–21
National Judiciary Council, 161
National Movement, 122, 124, 252n46
National Party of Nigeria (NPN), 122–23, 124, 125, 135
National Youth Service Corp (NYSC), 143–44, 192
nation-state, postcolonial, 7, 8, 10, 12; military rule and politics in, 116–21
native authorities (NAs), 92, 95, 97, 100, 104, 112
Native Court Law (1956), 101–2
Nazaru tariqa, 45
neo-Mahdists, 223, 228
neoliberalism: consequences of, 139, 152, 223, 227; Pentecostalism and, 10, 140, 146, 148, 154
neopatrimonial political system, 7, 125, 135, 223, 225, 227, 229; globalization and, 10, 155; sharia and, 160–62, 177, 227
newspapers and magazines: *Africa Confidential*, 189; journalists and, 184; *National Concord*, 179, 186, 191, 192; *New Nigerian*, 170, 173, 175; *New York Times*, 195–96; *Tempo*, 194; *Times* (London), 91; *Weekend Concord*, 182; *West Africa*, 252n48; Yoruba, 238n93
Ngban, Moni Odo, 183, 185
Niass, Sheikh Ibrahim, 96, 113, 114–15, 239n11
Niger, 57, 207, 214, 238n97; expanded sharia in, 158, 159, 186, 188, 190

Niger, Republic of, 92, 127, 180 229, 239n10
Nigeria, 1, 12, 98, 253n70; Boko Haram vs., 272n7, 272n8; economic crisis in, 127, 136; Federal Court of Appeal of, 161; Federal Republic of, 124, 158, 161, 188, 191, 250–51n23, 252–53n56, 265n51, 272n7, 272n8; John Paul II visits, 126; modern, 7, 12, 13, 14, 117, 126, 127, 131, 136, 238n90; National Assembly of, 161, 166, 213; Police Force of, 216, 218–19; regions of, 1, 7–8, 89; religious structures in making of, 12, 14; state-society formation in, 7, 13; Supreme Court, 66, 67, 95, 161, 165, 200, 201. *See also under specific names of geographic regions and political divisions*
Nigerian Baptist Convention, 209
Nigerian-Biafra Civil War (1967–70), 10, 115, 118–20, 129, 141, 251n23, 251n31, 252n40. *See also* Biafra, Republic of
Nigerian Inter-Religious Council, 196
Nigerian People's Party (NPP), 124
Nigerian Supreme Council for Islamic Affairs (NSCIA), 121, 130, 131, 176
Niger River, 24, 31, 35, 94, 247n27; confluence of, 5, 39; delta of, 123, 193, 197
Nmehielle, Vincent, 202
non-indigenes, 126, 211, 214–15
North Africa, 96
Northern Civil Service, 110
Northern Elements Peoples Union (NEPU), 92–93, 95, 115, 123, 176, 204
Northern Nigeria: Code of, 166; fragmented society of, 6; Igbo Christians attacked in, 119–20, 250–51n23, 267n94; Islamic law in, 99–111; Islamic reformist movement and, 13, 14; local colonial administration in, 242n94; Muslim unity in, 115; non-Muslim areas of, 70; pagan tribes of, 5; roadbuilding in, 246–47n27; tijaniyya in, 239n10, 239n11. *See also* Northern Nigerian Protectorate; Northern Nigerian Provinces; Northern Region

Northern Nigerian Protectorate, 38, 40, 62, 63, 65; colonial rule in, 8, 9–10, 55, 110; conversion of pagans in, 113; Hausa region in, 6, 14; Islam in, 8, 39–68, 74; non-Muslim Middle Belt in, 8, 69; slavery in, 53; Sokoto Caliphate in, 39–40; Sokoto Jihad in, 1, 21. *See also* Northern Nigeria; Northern Nigerian Provinces; Northern Region

Northern Nigerian Provinces, 10; Catholic Brothers in, 85–88; Christian missions in, 82–85, 234n19, 242n98; education in, 53–54; lieutenant governor of, 55–56; migration of Ogbomosho natives to, 31; native authority system in, 65, 66; non-Muslims in, 88; "pagan" tribes in, 58; tensions among Muslims in, 96. *See also* Northern Nigeria; Northern Nigerian Protectorate; Northern Region

Northern Peoples Congress (NPC), 90, 93, 119, 178, 250n4; Ahmadu Bello and, 113–14, 123; base of, 93; Bornu Youth Movement vs., 247n33; conservatism of, 94; Islamization policy of, 183; in Middle Belt, 112–13, 247n36; NEPU vs., 115, 204; Niass and, 115; opposition to, 95; in Regional Government, 90, 95, 98, 104–5, 113; UMBC and, 112

Northern Region, 90, 95, 118, 120, 246n13; anti-Igbo sentiments in, 118–19, 251n23; Christian minorities in, 92, 117, 121, 181–82, 186, 187, 227, 234n19, 250n1; courts in, 110–11; as Hausa-Fulani Muslim, 5, 11; legislature of, 108–9; opposition parties in, 92–93; premier of, 91, 250n23; sharia and, 8, 11–12, 104–11, 194, 218, 260n61; shortage of English-trained professionals in, 90–91; Sokoto Jihad in, 1; Southern immigrants in, 95, 102–3, 117; structural imbalance and, 8, 89, 110. *See also* Middle Belt; Northern Nigeria; Northern Nigerian Protectorate; Northern Nigerian Provinces

Northern Region Native Court Law (1956), 103

Nsukka, 35
Nunan, Imanus, 106
Nupe, 14, 20, 27, 94
Nwabueze, Professor Ben O., 165, 196, 265n51
Nwakanma, Ben, 200
Nwobi, Simeon Okezuo, 167, 210, 260n56

Oba, Abdulmumini Adebayo, 101, 109, 160, 162, 201
Obadare, Ebenezer, 148–49, 152–53, 208; on proselytizing fervor of Islamic reformism, 152
Obaje, Yusuf Ameh, 196
Obas of Yoruba, 237n72
Obasanjo, Lieutenant General Olusegun, 137, 178, 208; election of, 138, 150; as Egba-Yoruba, 183; imprisoned, 137, 138; regime of, 122, 157, 188, 195, 199, 252n44, 252n50; sharia crisis and, 199–201, 206–7, 220
Obin, Festus, 191
Obinna, Reverend Dr. Anthony, 200
Ochonu, Moses, 6, 14, 21, 234n17, 239n1, 250n1, 250n4; on Fulani Islamic reform jihad, 22, 23; on Hausa-Fulani Muslim hegemony, 49, 62
Odeleke, Bishop Margaret, 208
Oduduwa, 38
Ogbomosho, 28, 31, 237n86
Ogundipe, Brigadier Babafemi, 116
Ogun, 123, 137, 209
Oguntuase, Ben, 185
OIC (Organization of Islamic Conference; later Organization of Islamic Cooperation), 180, 253n67; crisis and controversy over, 10, 130–31, 164, 183, 187, 227; Monsignor Adigwe's pamphlet opposing, 127–28, 253n70
oil production, 1, 125, 156; in Niger Delta region, 193, 197
Ojo, Matthew, 144
Okada taxis, 220
Okogie, Archbishop Anthony Olubunmi, 128, 181–82, 199

Okonkwo, Mike, 142
Ojukwu, Lieutenant Colonel Odumegwu, 116, 119
Oke, Felix, 209
Okogie, Anthony Olubunmi, 199
Old Oyo, 74, 237n69; collapse of, 26, 36, 74
Olubi, Daniel, 30
Olugbode, Baale Oyesile, 73
Olukoya, Dr. D. K., 147
Olupona, Jacob, 139 142, 154, 157
Omoni, Pastor Fedelis, 209
Onagoruwa, Olu, 182, 201
Ondo, 28, 30, 34, 123
Onitsha, 32, 129
Oodua Peoples Congress (OPC), 193
Organization of Islamic Conference. See OIC
Organization of Islamic Cooperation. See OIC
Orihaki, Reverend Isaac, 187, 199
orisa, 28, 237n72
Orombi, Bishop Henry Luke, 193
Oshun, 24, 31
Osinowo, Pastor Kehinde, 207–8
Osoba, Olusegun, 209
Osun, 210
Ouddai regime, 46
Ottoman Empire, 44
Owo, 28, 34, 7
Owu, 26
Oyedepo, 146, 147
Oyeniran, Bishop Abraham (Pentecostal), 184, 200
Oyo, 24, 27, 28, 29, 38, 77, 123, 265n51

Pacific, 80
Paden, John N., 96, 180
pagan communities, "pagans," 5, 22, 50, 52, 60, 80, 84, 242n98; conversion of, 113, 114; in Northern Provinces, 58, 59, 61–62; as other, 6, 28. *See also* indigenous religions
Pakistan, 92, 105
Palmer, Herbert Richmond, 55–56, 65, 66–67, 85
patronage-clientage networks, 14–15
Patterson, Bishop Cecil, 97
Paul IV, Pope, 128, 129, 130
Payne, John Augustus Otunba, 34
Peel, John D. Y., 3–4, 5, 7, 70, 233n5, 243n11
Penal Code, 106, 108–9, 170, 172, 188, 191, 260n61; Christians and, 191; Constitution and, 165; sharia and, 107, 158, 166, 174–75, 188, 191, 260n61
Pentecostal churches and movement, 10, 37, 81, 139–57, 149, 193, 207–8, 230, 257n88; charismatism, 151; cosmopolitan image of, 157; doctrine of, 141, 151; Holiness tradition of, 140, 141–45; immigrant churches of, 157, 257n88; leaders of, 184; Living Faith Worldwide (Winners' Chapel International), 146, 147, 151; mass proselytizing through media by, 149; militarization of, 154; modernism and, 139, 150; Mountain of Fire and Miracles Ministries (MFM), 147–48; politics and, 150–51; popular culture and, 149–50; Prosperity tradition of, 140, 145–48; public sphere of, 148–54; Redeemed Christian Church of God (RCCG), 81, 144–45, 151, 196, 209, 257n88; "reverse missions" and, 157; revolution of, 10–11; secularism and, 141; sharia and, 186–87, 196; social networks in, 156; theological opposition to AICs, 81, 151; women and, 152
Pentecostal Fellowship of Nigeria (PFN), 142, 151
People's Democratic Party (PDP), 138, 186; Obasanjo and, 188, 199, 201, 209, 220, 221
Peoples Redemption Party (PRP), 123, 177, 204
Perham, Margery, 55
pilgrimages, 45, 196, 265n45
Plateau Peace Program, 213
Political Bureau, 135
politics: ethno-religious divisions and, 1; as platform for modern Nigeria, 14; transformation of, 3, 14, 69, 82

Index 307

Port Harcourt, 79, 103
postcolonialism, 10; religion in, 112–38
Presbyterians, 83, 98
publishing industry, 34, 238n93
Progressives, 123–24
Prophet Muhammad, 114, 134, 165 168, 179, 212, 214, 267n94
Protestants, 120–21, 140, 141, 149, 152, 193, 196. *See also* Christianity; Christians; *and names of specific denominations*

qadi, 15, 109
qadiriyya, 41, 42, 91, 93, 96, 114, 133, 134, 204, 239n5
Qur'an, Quran, 18, 37, 125, 133, 134, 152, 165, 192, 269n43

Al Rahman, Abd, 44
Ranger, Terence, 3–4
Rannat, Syed Abu, 105, 107–8
Rano, 14
Rashid, Syed Khalid, 160, 161, 179
rebirth, spiritual, 27–29, 151, 208
Reconquista, 15
religion, religions: diversity of, 1; ethnicity and, 215; freedom of, 166–67, 202; identity and, 187; military rule and national politics and, 116–21; movements of, 13; politicization of, 153–54, 252n56; revivalism and, 81, 139–57; state, 259n30; traditions of, 1, 74, 224; violence and, 117, 122–26, 211–14. *See also* world religions; *and names of specific religions*
Republic, First, 113, 118
Republic, Second, 122–23, 125, 126, 135
Republic, Third, 254n118
Republic, Fourth, 11, 138, 158–80, 178, 181, 193, 227, 255n118
Repugnancy Clause, 48, 54, 100, 102, 109, 162
Reynolds, Jonathan, 41–42
Richardson, S. S., 105, 106, 108
Rida, Rashid, 169
Rimi, Abubakar, 123

Rimi, Dan, 51–52
Roman Catholic Mission (RCM), 32
Ross, Captain William A., 77
Royal Niger Company, 25, 35, 39
Rumfa, Mohammed, 15, 16

Sabon garuruwa (new towns), 211, 220
Sahel, 15, 16, 44, 47
St. Andrews College, 29
Sakkwato, Bello Adamu, 175
Salamone, Frank, 84, 235n14
Sambo, Bashir, 175
Sambo, Namadi, 221
Sani, Ahmed, 137, 175, 177, 190; as governor, 158–59, 186–87, 198; sharia and, 173, 192, 194, 220
Sanneh, Lamin, 29, 140
Sanusi, Alhaji, 107, 108
Sanusi, Muhammad, 96
Sanusi, Sanusi Lamido, 165, 194
sanusiyya (Sufi order), 42, 46
sarauta, 14, 15; emirates, 40; Hausa system of, 17; institutions of, 21
sarki, 14, 16
Saros, 28, 29, 33, 35, 36, 76, 244n28
Satiru uprising (1906), 40, 45
Saudi Arabia, 92, 129, 134, 179, 180, 188
Schon, Reverend Jacob Friederich, 25, 29
Scripture Union (SU), 81, 142, 143, 145
secularism, 141, 163–65, 174, 229
Seku Ahmadu, 16
self-rule, 90, 94
Senegal, 16, 92, 96; tijaniyya in, 180, 239n10, 239n11
al-Shafi'i, Imam, 167
Shagari, Shehu, 125, 133, 207, 208, 252n48; as president, 124, 208, 252n49
Shagaya, John, 128
Shanahan, Bishop, 32
Shankar, Shobana, 82
sharia, 15, 16, 20, 21, 48, 49, 90, 120, 134, 157, 252n40, 266n60; anti-activists, 122, 176, 185, 190, 192, 264n33; colonial law and, 48, 89, 107; as crisis in postcolonial

308 Index

Nigeria, 8, 163, 167, 181–98, 199–202, 207–16, 223, 227–28; 1978 debate on, 10, 121–22, 181–94; democracy and, 121–22, 173; English common law and, 99, 107; expansion of, 133, 136, 158–80, 181–98, 220–22, 265n51; hisba and, 19, 217–19; interest banned under, 188, 197; non-Muslims, 173–74; in Northern Muslim states, 11–12, 122, 181; Penal Code and, 158, 191; Pentecostals and, 186–87; as quest for common good, 173–77; reforms of, 159; secularism vs. 229; violence and, 175, 212; women's rights and, 203–6; as word of Allah, 182

sharia courts, 15, 101, 158, 173, 217, 221; of appeal, 106, 109, 121, 165, 258n29, 259n41, 260n61; Constitution on, 164–65; Federal Sharia Court of Appeal (FSCA), 122, 124, 136; morality and, 188; women in, 203

Sharif, Mohammed, 105
Shar min Qblana, 168
Sharwood-Smith, Bryan, 96, 246n13
Sheikh Sabbah College (Kaduna), 115
Shekarau, Ibrahim, 220
Shekari, Stephen, 179
Shema, Ibrahim, 220
Shinkafi, Mahmud Aliyu, 165, 220
Shonekan, Ernest, 137
Shore, John, Lord Teignmouth, 24
Shura, 19
Sierra Leone, 2, 25, 29, 97; Yoruba returnees and, 27, 28, 34
Skinner, Henry, 106
slavery and slave trade, 5, 27, 53; abolition and anti-, 24, 27, 41, 53, 69, 84
slaves, 26, 37, 45; raiding for, 6, 59, 62, 64, 187
"sliding scale," 100, 101
Social Democratic Party, 137
socialism, 93
social mobility and networks, 14, 70–72, 75, 156

social structure, 1, 14–15; transformation of, 3, 13–14, 29, 82, 69, 73, 153
Society for Mission to Africa and the East, 24. *See also* Church Missionary Society
Society of African Missions (SMA), 86
Sodeke, 28
Sokoto Caliphate, 1–2, 51, 54, 60, 62, 121, 123, 125, 176, 177, 214, 224; aristocracy of, 91, 95; as base of NPC, 93; Bello and, 91, 113; British and, 6, 9, 40, 45, 47–48, 52, 69; effects of, 23, 226, 227; emirates of, 39–40, 236n41; establishment and rise of, 8, 14–16; Fulani Muslim reformism of, 6, 13, 158, 235n14, 235n32; insecurity of, 21; modern embodiment of, 115; Mohammed Bello and, 20; moral authority of, 239n1; Muslim missionaries of, 37; political authority from, 84; region of, 7–8; southern fringe of, 5; sultan of, 108, 136, 137, 178; women and, 269n42
Sokoto Jihad, 8, 16, 59, 60, 74, 102, 133, 134, 192, 235n14, 235n32, 243n17; extension of, 114; ideologies and structure of, 13; impact of, 14; Kanem-Bornu assaulted in, 247n33; in Northern Region and, 1–2; as precolonial state-society, 5; reformism and, 5, 16, 38; sharia and, 172; transformations and, 14, 225; Usman dan Fodio and, 16–24, 114; women and, 203–4, 269n42
Sokoto Province and State, 51, 97, 189, 195; Catholics in, 120, 132; expanded sharia in, 159; missions in, 82; resident of, 54; riots in, 115; taxation in, 56–57
South Africa, 156
southern Africa, 3–4
Southern Nigeria, 102; colonial rule in, 4, 40; migration of Christians from, 68, 90, 113; mission Christianity in, 111, 243n11; Pentecostalism in, 230; social transformations in, 10, 13–14, 70
southwest, 2, 3; as Yoruba Muslim-Christian crossroads, 5, 8, 10; Yoruba in, 1, 7
Soyinka, Wole, 188, 200
state religion, 157, 163–65

Index 309

states' rights, 165
state-society, 2, 5, 6, 7, 231
Stone, Reverend Moses Ladejo, 31
Student Christian Movement (SCM), 142, 143
Sudan, 46, 92, 105, 108, 179, 180; Mahdism in, 43, 45; tijaniyya in, 133, 239n10
Sudan Interior Mission (SIM), 82, 83, 234n19
Sudan United Mission (SUM), 83, 234n19
Sufism, Sufis, 41, 42, 113, 114, 133, 180; tariqa of, 96, 239n5, 239n10
Sulaiman, Ibraheem, 19, 20
Sulaiman, Ibrahim K. R., 175
Suleiman, Ibrahim, 202
Sunniism, tariqa of, 239n5, 239n10
Supreme Being: cult of, 3, 233n7; in world religions, 4
Supreme Council of Islamic Affairs, 128
Suwarian tradition, 15
syncretism, 15, 17, 141, 180, 184; of Aladura, 142, 243n5

Tabkin Kwaith, 17
Tafawa Balewa, 221
talakawa, 15, 18, 93, 206; education of, 21, 176. *See also* commoners
Tangale, 210, 214
Tanganyika, 65
Taraba, 137, 212
Tarok, 214
taxes, taxation, 22, 47, 52, 53, 56–57, 60–61, 62, 79; embezzlement of, 52, 62; Usman dan Fodio on, 19, 21; zakat, 44, 174, 189; *zakka*, 22, 53. *See also* tribute
Tayob, Abdulkader I., 113–14
televangelists, 149
Temple, Resident C. L., 52–53, 64
Thompson, Governor Sir Graeme, as, 65, 85
tijaniyya, 46, 91, 93, 114, 133, 134, 180; in Northern Nigeria, 96, 239n11; reformed version of, 96, 113, 115; as Sufi tariqa, 42, 239n10; women and, 204
Timbuktu, 17

Tiv, 86, 112, 250n4; Jukun and, 137, 212; as Middle Belt ethnic group, 82, 86, 94, 97–98, 210, 214
Toronkawa Fulani clan, 16, 235n14
tribute, 6, 9, 22, 57, 237n69, 241n76; Sokoto Caliphate and, 5, 62
Tubi, Reverend Lajide, 31
Tukulor, 16
Tula, 214
Tunisia, 92
Tunku, Dan, 20

Uda, Tony, 185
Uganda, 47, 99, 193
ummah, 18, 19, 158–80
Ibn Umar, Sheikh Jibril, 17
Umar, Mohammed, 15, 16, 40–41
unification of Northern and Southern Provinces (1914), 8, 40, 45, 48–49, 89, 90, 110, 231
United African Company (UAC), 79
United Arab Emirate, 92
United Global Church Association of Nigeria, 184
United Middle Belt Congress (UMBC), 88, 95, 112, 114, 247n36, 250n1, 250n4
United Nations, 105–6
United States, 98, 149, 156, 212, 267n94
Unity Party of Nigeria, 123
Universal Primary Education (UPE), 205
University of Lagos, 196
Usman, Bala, 123
Usman da Fodio University, 195
Usmaniyya movement, 113–14

Venn, Henry, 24–25, 35, 238n90
Venn, Reverend John, 24

Wajas, 62–64, 214
Wali, Isa, 93, 204
Wallace, Sir William, 65
Wariboko, Nimi, 140, 151
waziri, 19, 51, 54, 115
Webster, Resident G. W., 85–86

Weeks, Erik, 193
West Africa, 3, 5, 96, 239n10
West African Frontier Force, 40
Western literary traditions, 33–34
Western Region, 91, 94, 102, 116, 118, 247n7
Whitaker, C. S., Jr., 93
White Flag League, 46
Wilberforce, William, 24
Williams, Rotimi, 165, 182
Williams, Dr. Rowan, Archbishop of Canterbury, 187
Willink Commission (1957), 104–5, 247n36
Wiwa, Ken Saro, 137
women: education of, 21, 54, 134, 176; as Muslims, 205, 206; as religious, 120, 152; rights of, 93, 184, 194, 203–6; sharia and, 169, 189, 197, 220. *See also* gender
world religions, 4, 7, 28, 83, 129, 163, 223, 265n45; Christianity as, 4, 243n12; conversion and, 3–4, 233n4, 243n12; Islam as, 7; Yoruba and, 69, 70. *See also* Christianity; Islam
World War I, 44, 46, 53
World War II, 68, 96, 143; outbreak of, 54, 62, 66, 75, 82; post, 7, 9, 98, 110
Wright, Canon, 76–80
Wuye, Reverend James, 213

Yadudu, Auwalu, 107
Yaki, Tukur Sarkin, 63–64
Yakowa, Patrick Ibrahim, 221
'Yan tatsine ("those who damn"), 125, 223, 228; riots of, 10, 127, 192, 227
Yar'Adua, Governor Umaru Musa, 174, 220, 221
Yauri, 14
Yelwa, 212
Yemen, 92

Yero, Baba, 63
Yobe, 159, 219, 229
Yola, 97, 126, 127
Yoruba International Network, 209
Yorubaland, 123
Yoruba Muslim-Christian crossroads, 5, 8, 10
Yoruba region, 3, 27, 82, 237–38n86, 243n5, 243n12; Christianity in, 69, 224; Islam in, 37, 74; military conflict in, 25; missionaries in, 7, 10, 25, 31, 237–38n86, 243n9, 243n11; native law in, 102; politics in, 123; religious practices in, 28; returnees transform, 27–29, 34; Southern Baptists in, 31, 237–38n86; in southwest, 1, 3, 5, 8; wars, 26–27
Yorubas, 14, 82, 116–19, 123, 131, 135, 193–94, 237n72; as Christians, 138, 179, 182, 185, 195, 225–26, 252n44; coming of Christianity to, 24–38; diaspora churches of, 31, 36; ethno-national consciousness of, 10, 38, 94; Hausa-Fulani and, 214; indigenous religions of, 243n2, 243n5, 243n17; language of, 33, 238n93; as missionaries, 35, 38; as Muslims, 137, 179, 196, 197; society of, 70–72; traditions of, 69; wars of, 7, 26–38, 72, 73, 75, 226
Yuguda, Isa, 221
Yunguru, 58
Yusuf, Mohammed, 219, 223

Zakzaky, Ibrahim, 137, 194
Zambezi River, 99
Zamfara, 14, 158–80, 184–88, 194, 197–98; Christians in, 190–91, 192; sharia in, 176, 177, 180, 187, 191, 203, 207, 216, 218, 220
Zango Kataf riots, 192, 213
Zaria, 14, 31, 49, 55; Christianity in, 126, 188; Institute of Administration, 109, 110

www.ingramcontent.com/pod-product-compliance
Lightning Source LLC
Chambersburg PA
CBHW070750230426
43665CB00017B/2319